Fodor's

PRAGUE

D0986589

Welcome to Prague

One of Europe's best-preserved cities, Prague has a romantic riverside location enhanced by graceful bridges and a magnificent skyline punctuated with medieval church spires. Its historic Old Town follows a plan laid out 1,000 years ago, with ancient squares and winding cobblestoned streets. Haunting Prague Castle looms large across the Vltava River, rising above the exquisite Charles Bridge. Add extravagant, fairy-tale architecture; memorable classical music; and, these days, good food and drink, and it's easy to see why Prague charms everyone who visits.

TOP REASONS TO GO

★ **Historic architecture:** Gothic, baroque, Renaissance, art nouveau—it's all here.

★ **Prague Castle:** This Gothic fortress and soaring cathedral were Kafka's inspiration.

★ **Jewish heritage:** Historic synagogues and sights reflect an 800-year-old legacy.

★ **Old Town Square:** The city's pulsing heart fans out below the twin-spired Týn church.

★ **Excellent beer:** Czechs brew the best pilsner, and Prague pubs know how to pour it.

★ **Classical music:** Musicians from Dvořák to Mozart made their mark in Prague.

Contents

MAPS

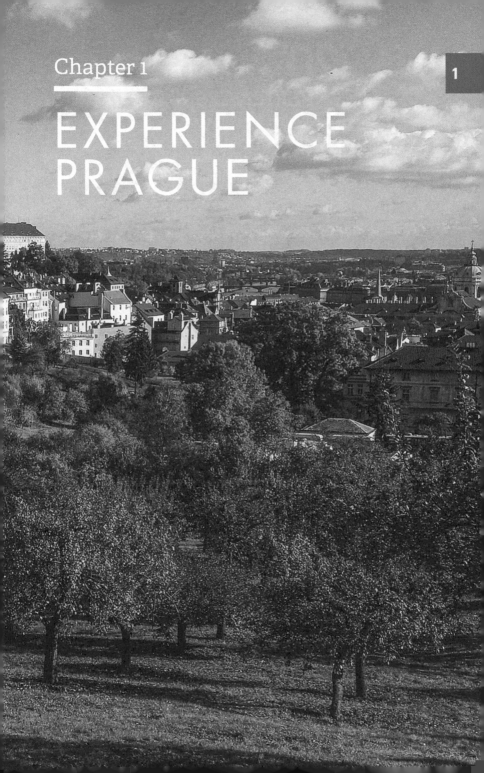

Chapter 1

EXPERIENCE PRAGUE

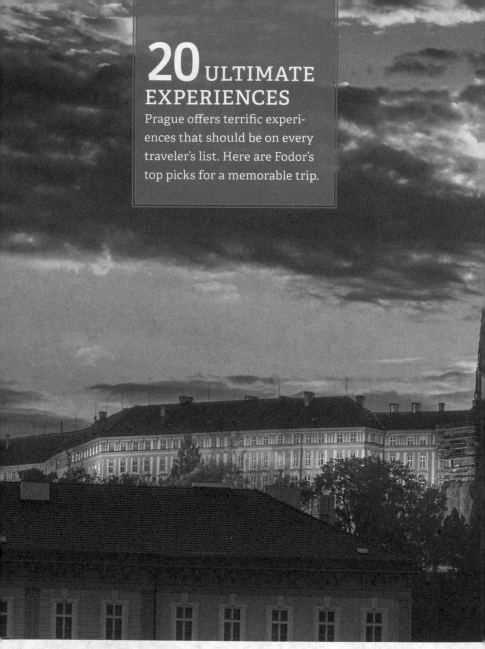

20 ULTIMATE EXPERIENCES

Prague offers terrific experiences that should be on every traveler's list. Here are Fodor's top picks for a memorable trip.

1 Prague Castle

Prague Castle is the largest ancient castle in the world, so don't be surprised if you need a full day to enjoy it. Built on a hill overlooking the city, it's one of the oldest, too—the structure dates back to AD 880. (Ch. 5)

2 Moravian Wine

On the Moravian Wine Trail, you can bike 11 different trails spread over 750 miles, and enjoy stops at wine-making towns on the Austrian border. (Ch. 14)

3 Pancava Falls

Krkonose National Park offers alpine meadows, dramatic granite outcrops speckled with wildflowers, and Pancava Falls, the country's tallest waterfall. (Ch. 14)

4 Czech Dumplings

Dumplings play a starring role in Czech cuisine, and they can come in many forms. Look for fruit-filled *švestkové knedlíky*—made even tastier when topped with melted butter and sprinkled sugar. (Ch. 3)

5 Brno Bar-Hopping

With the Czech Republic's largest student population, Brno has a lively nightlife scene and cool bars that redefine the typical Czech beer-drinking experience. (Ch. 14)

6 Litomyšl

Popular with classical music fans as the home of Bedřich Smetana, a famous Czech composer, this delightful small town has Renaissance arcades, rows of pastel homes, and monastery gardens. (Ch. 11)

7 Prague's Trendy Art District

The edgy-cool twin neighborhoods of Letná and Holešovice (collectively known as Prague 7), are home to the Fine Arts Academy and the Foundation for Contemporary Arts. (Ch. 10)

8 Olomouc

Often called "Little Prague," Southern Moravia's Olomouc has colorful baroque buildings, ornamental fountains, and a thriving arts scene. (Ch. 14)

9 A Vltava River Cruise

One of the best ways to soak up the Vltava's unspoiled beauty is via a scenic boat tour. Options include steamboats and vintage-style canal boats with music and food. (Ch. 3)

10 The Birthplace of Pilsner Beer

Take a tour of the Pilsner Urquell Brewery, where Pilsner Urquell beer was first created in 1842, for an exclusive tasting of unpasteurized pilsner, poured straight from an oak lager cask. (Ch. 13)

11 Find Kafka

Traces of Prague's famous author can be found all over the city, from house No. 22 in Prague Castle, where Kafka lived from 1916 to 1917, to a statue of him in Josefov. (Chs. 3, 5)

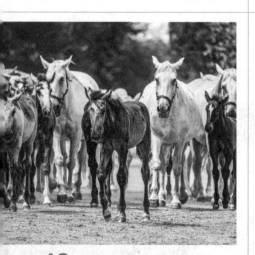

12 Kladruby Horses

A UNESCO World Heritage Site, the royal stables at Kladruby were once used to breed horses for Emperor Rudolf II. Tour the stables and learn about one of the oldest breeds of horses in the world. (Ch. 11)

13 A Night at the Theater

Try for a seat at the opulent Stavovské divadlo, where Mozart premiered his Don Giovanni in 1787, or the ornate Národní divadlo, Prague's main venue for opera, dance, and drama. (Ch. 3)

14 The Clock in Old Town Square

Hundreds of people gather under the clock every hour from 9 am to 11 pm, when statues of the 12 apostles move around the giant clockface and a skeleton rings his bell. (Ch. 3)

15 David Černý's Art

Controversial Czech artist David Černý's work can be found in the most unlikely of places in Prague: one installation features statues of babies crawling up Prague's Žižkov TV Tower. (Ch. 9)

16 Klementium

This former Jesuit university houses a clock tower that was once used by astronomers in the 15th century to observe the skies and a library that hasn't changed since 1727. (Ch. 3)

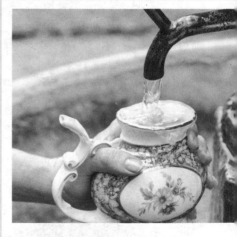

17 Europe's Oldest Synagogue

Though the Jewish Quarter only spans a few city blocks, its history dates to the 10th century. The Staronová synagoga, built in 1270, is the oldest active synagogue in Europe. (Ch. 3)

18 The Healing Waters in Karlovy Vary

Fountains are dotted throughout this historic spa town, and visitors are encouraged to sip the naturally hot mineral-rich water using special porcelain mugs. (Ch. 13)

19 Prague's Most Beautiful Garden

The Valdštejnska zahrada (Wallenstein Palace Gardens), designed by Italian gardeners in 1621, offers reflection ponds, outdoor concerts, and a flock of resident peacocks. (Ch. 4)

20 The Charles Bridge at Sunset

Visit Prague's most congested landmark in the late afternoon, when crowds thin and the setting sun provides a more scenic backdrop. (Ch. 3)

WHAT'S WHERE

1 **Staré Město and Josefov (Old Town and Jewish Quarter).** The area's original Jewish ghetto was largely razed in the 19th century, but the past is still apparent in the restored sites that comprise the Jewish Museum and the active synagogues.

2 **Malá Strana (Lesser Quarter).** This neighborhood is filled with hilly cobblestoned streets edged with baroque buildings.

3 **Prague Castle and Hradčany.** The highlight here is the Prague Castle complex, which shelters a Romanesque basilica and a baroque palace.

4 **Nové Město (New Town).** Prague's so-called New Town was, in fact, laid out in the 14th century.

5 Smíchov and Vyšehrad. Smíchov is one of Prague's best entertainment districts. Vyšehrad contains the remains of Prague's "other castle".

6 Vinohrady and Vršovice. Vinohrady began as a wine-producing region. Neighboring Vršovice is home to arguably Prague's coolest street, Krymská.

7 Žižkov and Karlín. Žižkov is said to have more pubs per square mile than anywhere else in Europe. Meanwhile, the former industrial district of Karlín is now a hipster paradise.

8 Letná, Holešovice, and Troja. Letná is known for its large and historical park. Holešovice's chief attraction is the National Gallery's collection of art. Troja feels like a day-trip destination inside the city.

WHAT'S WHERE

9 Day Trips from Prague. From fairy-tale hilltop castles to human-bone-decorated churches, medieval Gothic cathedrals to chilling Holocaust memorials, there are all manner of fascinating attractions within easy reach of the Czech capital.

10 Southern Bohemia. A landscape lover's paradise, Southern Bohemia is one of the country's favorite hiking, cycling, and kayaking destinations. Dotted among the rolling hills and snaking rivers are several lovely towns and cities, not least the impossibly pretty Český Krumlov.

11 Western Bohemia.
This is a region
dominated by charming
spa towns, from the
pretty, park-filled
Františkovy Lázně
(Franzensbad) to the
perennially popular
Karlovy Vary (Carls-
bad)—famed for its
annual film festival.
Come to take to the
waters or enjoy a
massage, but stay for the
beautiful Empire
architecture.

12 Moravia. It may be less
visited than Bohemia, but
the Czech Republic's
eastern element has
plenty of charms of its
own, including the excel-
lent locally grown wine,
the regular folk music
and dance shows, and the
gorgeous town squares of
Telč and Olomouc. It also
has the country's second
city, Brno.

What's New in Prague

The "City of a Hundred Spires" is as staggeringly beautiful as ever, attracting record numbers of visitors to see its array of historical, architectural, and cultural gems. But over the last decade or so, this much-cherished heritage and tradition has been allied with a more modern, internationalist outlook. The 2011 death of former president Václav Havel—a global icon and hero of the 1989 Velvet Revolution—seemed to jolt Czechs into the realization that nothing stands still, and Prague has since been on a relentless drive to catch up with Western trends and sensibilities. A walk around the city center reveals some of these transformations, from long-term renovations of landmark buildings to an increased choice of international restaurants. But for those who really want to see what modern Prague has to offer, head a little farther afield to neighborhoods like Karlín, Smíchov, and Vršovice, where contemporary art galleries, cool coffee shops, art house cinemas, craft beer bars, and independent boutiques await.

THE RISE OF CRAFT

When it comes to beer, the Czech Republic rules the roost. After all, the world's first lager, Pilsner Urquell, was brewed here, and the country still has the highest beer consumption per capita in the world. However, this grand brewing tradition meant a resistance to change and a glacially slow adoption of the microbrewing craze. Luckily, Prague has now more than caught up, with its expert brewers producing an impressive array of pale ales, porters, and saisons—along with classic pilsner lagers, of course. Taste the revolution for yourself at one of the city's many excellent microbreweries, from the fast-expanding Vinohradský Pivovar to the microbrewery at Strahov Monastery.

As well as beer, Prague's gone all crafty with coffee, too. Since the fall of communism, coffee in the city has slowly evolved from a cup of low-quality grind doused with hot water to Italian imports like Illy and Lavazza and big-name chains like Starbucks and Costa. Today, it's all about aeropresses and vacuum pots. For a taste of the current craft coffee craze, head to the Vietnamese-influenced and vegan-friendly Cafefin in Vinohrady, or the shabby-chic hipster haven Vnitroblock in Holešovice.

STICKING WITH KORUNY

The Czech Republic was admitted into the European Union way back in 2004, but—despite innumerable promises and passed deadlines—the country has yet to adopt the euro. What gives? Well, mostly, the euro crisis of the early 2010s greatly dented the currency's prestige. Since then, there's been no great push to join the common currency. Each new government pushes the target date further and further away.

PACK YOUR APPETITE

Since 2008, when Prague gained the first Michelin star of anywhere in the former Eastern Bloc, the city has built on its success to become the undisputed culinary king of the region. Today, fine-dining restaurants abound, from the 19th-century-inspired Czech fare of La Degustation Bohême Bourgeoise to the Scandinavian-slanted contemporary cooking of Field.

However, it's not all about formal, high-end dining. Fresh food, slow food, locally grown, seasonal, organic…call it what you want, Praguers have fully embraced the notion that food should be local, tasty, and sustainable. Weekend farmers' markets are all over town, bringing fresh, locally sourced fruits, vegetables, meats, and cheeses to the urban masses. Pubs and restaurants have gotten in on the act, too, rewriting menus to embrace domestic ingredients and old-fashioned Czech cooking.

WORK IN PROGRESS

Deep down, Prague must have some kind of inferiority complex. What else could explain the perpetual need to make a beautiful city even more beautiful?

In the last few years, there have been major, multiyear renovations of the Astronomical Clock and tower, Wenceslas Square, the Národní muzeum (National Museum), and both sides of the waterfront. While it's wonderful to see many long-neglected buildings dazzling once more, it does feel as though the grand city project will never end. Be prepared that you may have to crop construction equipment out of your favorite vacation snaps.

The Best Castles in Prague and the Czech Republic

KARLŠTEJN CASTLE

Karlštejn, a large castle close to Prague, was built to house the crown jewels and was once Charles IV's summer palace. It's a steep climb up to see it, mind you, on a path lined with tacky souvenir stalls, but it's worth it for the battlements, turrets, and towers that reward you at the top.

KŘIVOKLÁT

This romantic 12th-century château is a favorite with Czechs because of its appearances in various works of literature. Its monumental tower steals the glory, but the atmospheric chapel, library, and dungeons are worth a visit, too.

VYŠEHRAD CITADEL

Prague's "second castle" is much less visited but it has an awesome history, fascinating buildings, and lovely views over the Vltava River. The tour of the casemates, which house some of the original baroque statues from the Charles Bridge, is not to be missed. Ask for a text in English.

PRAGUE CASTLE

From jousting and defenestrations (literally, chucking one's enemies out of the window—it happened several times in the history of Bohemia) to more modern moments like the arrival of Adolf Hitler in Prague or the inauguration of President Václav Havel, Prague Castle has seen it all, and it remains the official residence of the Czech president. Sightswise, it boasts the dazzling St. Vitus Cathedral, several palaces, medieval treasure, historic courtyards, stunning, hilly gardens, and the bewitching Golden Lane.

KONOPIŠTĚ CASTLE

Konopiště, a château in a huge, beautiful park, traded hands between nobles in the centuries following its construction around the 13th century, but it is best known for its supporting role in a piece of modern history: it was the country residence for the doomed Archduke Franz Ferdinand, whose 1914 assassination sparked World War I. In World War II, it housed some units of the German SS.

LOUČEŇ CASTLE

You can stay overnight at this romantic baroque château in central Bohemia, and we don't just mean inadvertently if you get stuck in one of the many garden mazes. Tours around the castle can be taken with a costumed prince, princess, their valet, or even a forester, and the 11 garden labyrinths in the castle's large English-style park enhance the vibe.

Loučeň Castle

There are three suites in the castle itself for those who really want to take the whole "king for a day" fantasy to the max, and the Maximilian hotel on-site is housed in a building dating from 1834 but boasts modern amenities like a swimming pool in a nearby annex.

ARCHBISHOPS' CHÂTEAU

The entire town in Kroměříž is an attractive stop in Moravia, but the real draw here is the Archbishops' Château, a spectacular residence designed for the powerful archbishops of Olomouc in 1260. The gardens are beautiful and UNESCO listed, too. The château's Assembly Hall is considered to be one of the most jaw-dropping rococo halls in the Czech Republic.

STATE CHÂTEAU HLUBOKÁ

Possibly the most beautiful and romantic castle in the country, located in Southern Bohemia, Hluboká has roots in the 13th century but really came into its own in the hands of a wealthy family in the 19th, who remodeled it based on Britain's Windsor Castle, which gives you an idea of the grandeur on offer here.

LEDNICE-VALTICE CULTURAL LANDSCAPE

Two châteaus for the price of one, with vineyards and a gorgeous park to boot. This absolutely immense complex in southern Moravia was transformed between the 17th and 20th centuries into the striking 200-km (124-mile) landscape visitors find today.

ČESKÝ KRUMLOV CASTLE

There is a reason the entire historic center of this town in Southern Bohemia, including its 13th-century castle, has been a UNESCO World Heritage Site since 1992: it is storybook perfect. You can also go rafting on the river that snakes through the town's center.

Best Beer Experiences in the Czech Republic

BEER SPA

It's a beer lover's dream: bathe in water made from the same ingredients used to make the brew, while drinking ice-cold beer straight from the tap at the Czech Republic's original beer spa in Chodovar.

LOKÁL DLOUHÁÁÁ

Pilsner Urquell as fresh as it comes at this modern take on an old-school Czech pub in Prague's Staré Město draws the crowds all day and all year, so arrive early. The beer itself comes straight from the tanks that you can see at one end of the bar, guaranteeing its taste and purity. The traditional Czech food on offer is as good as the beer, from the fried cheese to the goulash with traditional bread and potato dumplings. Once you've secured your table, settle in for a long session. It's a little more expensive than some of the authentic old venues farther out of town, but it's worth it.

ČESKÉ BUDĚJOVICE

Take a deep dive (not literally) into the beer-making process at the original home of Budvar, České Budějovice, the town housing the famous brewery. The vast Budějovický Budvar complex was founded in 1895, but the 125-year-old, state-owned brewery is showing no signs of slowing down. And as for the beer? Well, it's hard to doubt the quality of a beer made from 984-foot-deep artesian wells in the brewery that pump up water from a lake dating back to the Ice Age. The brewery tours are fantastic and run at 2 daily.

KLÁŠTERNÍ PIVOVAR STRAHOV

At this monastery/brewery, where monks have been brewing beer since the turn of the 14th century, guests can now sample a variety of brews made on-site with traditional methods. Sadly, the monks themselves aren't involved in the brewing anymore, but that doesn't make the atmosphere any less fun, the history any less quirky, or the beers any less good: in particular, the dark St. Norbert has a good reputation, although the seasonal wheat beer is also delicious.

U SLOVANSKÉ LÍPY

Sometimes you don't need all the bells and whistles; this is just a classic Czech pub in Prague's Žižkov district, an area rumored to have more pubs per square kilometer than anywhere else in the world. The beer is good, the atmosphere is fantastic, and there's robust Czech food on offer, too. It claims to be the oldest pub in the neighborhood, too, but that heritage is likely less of a draw than the fantastic and ever-changing range of artisan beers it offers on tap.

BEER GARDENS

For views with your brews, join the rest of Prague in summer at one of the city's lively outdoor drinking spots. Letná Park's river and Staré Město views, the gentle hum of conversation, and dappled shade from the trees above make this the best place to drink in the warmer months, bar none.

České Budějovice

VINOHRADSKÝ PIVOVAR

The craft beer revolution of recent years has seen hyperlocal neighborhood breweries spring up in many of Prague's districts, from Vinohrady to Anděl. Vinohradský pivovar is one of the breakout successes of the trend, and its brews can be found at a number of other bars around town. Its HQ is a modern, chill spot, too, down some steps on a main street at the border of Vinohrady and Vršovice, with classic Czech grub, several varieties of the in-house beer, and portholes to glimpse the beer tanks and pipes.

BEER FESTIVALS

Predictably and wonderfully, there are beer festivals all over the Czech Republic. Pilsner Fest in Plzeň in October, celebrating the first ever brewing of a pilsner-style lager and also featuring bands, is one of the biggest and best. The Řečkovice festival on the grounds of an old brewery in Brno showcases microbreweries, and an annual shindig at Prague Castle—offering around 140 different kinds of beer brewed by small outfits—is another standout. Smaller festivals happen almost weekly throughout the summer.

CUSTOMS

As beer is the Czech Republic's national drink, the customs and traditions surrounding it are enshrined in every Czech's heart. Passing the citizenship exam for immigrants who want to become permanent residents even requires some beer knowledge. Win hearts by saying "Na zdraví" (cheers) before you take your first sip, and find yourself a beer mat quickly to avoid spilling the frothy head onto the table. Those ordering a *malý pivo* (small beer), particularly men, can expect a little ribbing: the phrase is a gentle insult in Czech. One of the best (and riskiest) traditions is still upheld in the more authentic bars and involves bringing more beers as soon as a patron's glass is empty, unless they have signaled that they are finished by placing their beer mat on the glass.

U FLEKŮ

Dating back to 1499, this boisterous, touristy, giant beer hall is still fantastic fun. It's famous for its dark beer, but it recently added a light beer as well. While the service at the venerable U Fleků can be downright rude, that's all part of the atmosphere. Vast, ancient, and a bit kitschy, there are eight separate dining halls and a beer garden in the summer. Beers can also be bought to take away or even be delivered.

What to Buy

BOHEMIA CRYSTAL

For centuries, Czech-made glassware, known as Bohemia crystal or Bohemian glass, has been internationally recognized for its quality and beauty. Czech crystal chandeliers hang, for example, in Milan's La Scala, in Rome's Teatro dell'Opera, in Versailles, and at the Hermitage Museum.

BEER

It's the Czech Republic's most famous export and you can easily take a bottle or two home. Get them direct from the source at the Staropramen Brewery in Anděl or go deliciously niche by hunting down a small Czech brewer with the help of the staff at a beer shop like Pivní Mozaika in Karlín. As well as generally making you feel good, Czech beer can also make you look good. Hop promotes healthy hair growth, reduces scalp irritations, and adds strength and shine, so be sure to look for organic shampoos and shower gels in the beauty aisles. Brands to look for include Manufaktura, Ryor, and Saela.

GARNET JEWELRY

Czech garnets (also known as Prague garnets or Bohemian garnets) are usually deep red but can also be black or clear. Garnets have been mined in the Czech Republic since the early 17th century. In modern-day Prague and the Czech Republic, garnet prices vary according to their quality, quantity, and size. Real Bohemian garnets tend to be small and dark red. Some touristy shops try to palm off inferior imported stones, especially as large centerpieces, so make sure to get a certificate of authenticity upon purchasing. The beautiful deep-red glint of Bohemian garnet is best showcased by Wollem in Old Town and Halada and Granat Turnov, which have several locations in Prague.

COMMUNIST MEMORABILIA

Browse junk shops and flea markets to pick up eerie reminders of Prague's dark past, from signs and posters to badges emblazoned with the red communist star. The standout is Bric a Brac, right by Old Town Square: talk to the owner, who speaks good English, about his fascinating but pricey treasure trove.

CZECH DESIGN

Modern design in the Czech Republic is thriving, and there are lots of studios and ateliers where you can grab something unique and, often, even meet the designer. Try the CzechDesign Shop in New Town or the amazing Vnitroblock in a former factory in hip Holešovice.

MARIONETTES AND WOODEN TOYS

Puppetry has UNESCO-heritage status in Czechia and Slovakia, and the traditional wooden marionettes are wonderful souvenirs. There are figures from folklore as well as more modern characters, from robots to politicians, plus puppetry courses, DIY lessons, and kits. The Centre for Contemporary Puppetry sits right next to a puppet shop on the main route up to the castle on Nerudova Street in Malá Strana.

Marionettes

NATURAL COSMETICS
Botanicus and Manufaktura, among others, have been pioneering natural, organic cosmetics made from local plant-based ingredients, using traditional methods, for years. Look for Bohemian lavender and Czech beer products.

KOH-I-NOOR PENCILS
This historic brand pretty much invented the first pencil in the 1790s and has been making top-end stationery and art supplies ever since. Its shops are iconic in Prague, with a huge gorilla made entirely out of pencils in one of them, and its stationery top-notch; the best buy is one of the pencils that made the company's name.

OPLATKY (SPA WAFERS)
You might wish you could take the restorative spa water of Karlovy Vary home with you, but you can in a way, because the spa wafer treats you nibble on during spa visits are made with it. They are also protected by the European Union as unique geographical products (like Champagne or feta cheese), so stock up! You can find Czech wafers in supermarkets and grocery stores.

KAFKA
There's something special about buying one of 20th-century visionary author Franz Kafka's books in the city where he grew up, after strolling the streets he walked as a boy in the Jewish Quarter or visiting the museum dedicated to his work and memory. Or, even better, from the atmospheric bookshop bearing his name on Široká.

CLASSICAL MUSIC
The Czech Republic has produced many famous classical music composers: Bedřich Smetana, Antonín Dvořák, Leoš Janáček, and Bohuslav Martinů, to name just the most famous ones, so classical music CDs and records are a great souvenir. Music fans should check out Supraphon Musicpoint, from the distinguished Czech music label, located in Nové Město. The store has a classical music section and hosts readings, listening sessions, concerts, and autograph sessions.

Under-the-Radar Prague

PRAGUE'S SECRET GARDENS
The abundance of charming, sanctuary-like gardens hidden around Prague includes the Vrtbovská zahrada (Vrtba Garden), a gorgeous baroque terraced garden that's concealed in the back of the Aria Hotel.

STEFANIK OBSERVATORY
This hilltop working observatory dedicated to Slovak astronomer Milan Rastislav Stefanik has amateur guides to explain what you're seeing through the viewfinder and an exhibit room with sundials, lunar globes, and an octant from the 18th century.

DIVADLO ALFRED VE DVOŘE
Look for imaginative storytelling by independent artists from all over Europe, all for the reasonable price of $10. Even the space is arresting: a pavilion theater with an eye-catching geometric design, built in the courtyard of an old apartment building.

CONTEMPORARY ART
Officially known as Prague 7, the neighboring districts of Letná and Holešovice are home to Vnitroblock, an old factory that's been turned into a multifaceted performance space that also comprises a café, art gallery, vinyl shop, and even a small cinema; The Chemistry Gallery, a cutting-edge gallery focused solely on works by young Czech artists today; and DOX, one of Prague's main contemporary art galleries.

PRAGUE'S COOLEST CINEMA
Bio Oko is a refurbished cinema from the 1950s that wouldn't be out of place in Brooklyn. On the program is a mix of current and classic films, including everything from *Star Wars* to obscure European animated features. Show up early to nab a seat in the vintage 1987 Trabant limousine that's parked in the front row.

A HIDDEN PUB
Skautský institut, run by the Czech scouting movement, has affordable beer and snacks with a view overlooking Old Town Square. It is a favorite haunt of students, though everyone's welcome. It is hidden inside a historical building with a large atrium. There are frequent concerts and events.

A TUNNEL OF BOOKS
Located inside the lobby (no entrance fee required) of the Prague Municipal Library, the Infinite Book Tunnel, by Slovak artist

Klementinum

Matej Kren, is a cylindrical tower of books that mimics the way an inspiring, hard-to-put-down novel can feel; mirrors are inserted, so when you poke your head in the tunnel, it appears to travel upward forever.

THE KLEMENTINUM
Hidden among the *trdelník* stands and souvenir shops on Karlova ulice is an old library that remains unchanged since the 1700s. To reach it, you have to sign up for a guided tour, which costs $12. Ascending the narrow spiral staircase, you're brought to a hushed gallery filled with old-world mechanical globes, ceiling frescoes above, and ancient texts. Continue on the tour to reach the top of the tower, and you'll be rewarded with one of the prettiest views in Prague.

BEER MAKING AT U MEDVÍDKŮ
One of the best ways to tap into one of the city's oldest pubs' history is by signing up for a beer-making class. The nine-hour course walks you through the entire beer-making process, from mashing to cooling. As a reward for your full day's work, the ticket ($326) includes refreshments, lunch, and a tasting in the bar.

CZECH VENICE
Book a Venice-style gondola tour of the Vltava River and the Čertovka Canal and you'll be cruising in an original Venetian gondola built in 1858. The guides provide Italian sparkling wine in summer and mulled wine in winter.

TAKE A UNIQUE STREET TOUR
"Street tour" takes on a whole new meaning with the guys at Pragulic, who employ current or formerly homeless people as tour guides. Part social experiment, part immersive study, the two-hour tours offer a candid look at a side of Prague rarely seen by tourists.

What to Eat and Drink

Trdelník

TRDELNÍK

This crusty, sugar-coated morsel proves that Prague is a paradise for sweets lovers. Despite its Hungarian origin, a *trdelník* is the most ubiquitous Czech treat—a hollow pastry cone cooked over an open flame, rolled in sugar, and often filled with ice cream.

VĚNEČEK

Věneček has been compared to a cruller doughnut, though since this is Eastern Europe, expect more dough and a healthy dollop of cream. It comes sliced in half with a layer of cold custard in the middle, making it a bit like a doughnut sandwich. It's best eaten cold with a strong, hot coffee.

SVÍČKOVÁ

Like a Slavic Thanksgiving on a plate, this entrée consists of larded sirloin beef slathered in a creamy root-vegetable sauce and served with *knedlíky*, or bread dumplings (and sometimes, cranberry sauce). The beef is braised directly with the vegetables and copious amounts of butter, while the dumplings soak up all the meaty goodness.

Svíčková

SCHNITZEL
Meat connoisseurs could spend hours weighing the virtues of traditional Czech schnitzel, which is made with pork, against the Austrian version, which uses veal. For the rest of us, suffice to say, this is a perfectly breaded, delicately fried, and incredibly tasty piece of meat, almost always accompanied by a heaping serving of mashed potatoes.

FRUIT DUMPLINGS
Fruit dumplings, or *ovocné knedlíky*, are an instantly recognizable Czech specialty. And they are just what they say on the box: hot, sweet, jammy fruit-filled steamed dumplings, served with a side of melted butter, poppy seeds, or farmer cheese.

SAUERKRAUT SOUP
Nothing says Czech comfort food like a bowl of hot sauerkraut soup. Traditionally a vegetarian breakfast eaten by forest workers to brace for a long day outside, the recipe was gradually expanded to include smoked sausage. Luckily, you won't have to trek into the woods to find it for yourself.

GOULASH
Flavored with paprika (a nod to its Hungarian heritage), this deceptively simple stew is the cornerstone of any Czech menu. The recipe marries beef, onions, and sometimes sauerkraut, which simmer in a single pot for at least two hours. The spongy, addictive bread dumplings that accompany the stew are something of a delicacy themselves.

PICKLED CHEESE
Pickled cheese is a little like the Charles Bridge: Overhyped? Perhaps. But you're going to remember it. Best enjoyed spread on dark Czech bread.

PILSNER
Known for its light, hoppy flavor, pilsner is not only a necessary refresher during the warmer months—it's also a major point of pride for Czechs across the country. Originating in Plzeň, just 40 miles south of Prague, the most popular version comes from Pilsner Urquell, the largest brewery in the country.

BECHEROVKA
This Czech digestif makes a potent palate cleanser at the end of a heavy meal. Bestowed with an herb-like flavor, the liquor has been produced the same way—in the same town—since 1807.

What to Watch and Read

THE TRIAL AND THE METAMORPHOSIS BY FRANZ KAFKA

Seize this opportunity to read the masterpieces of Prague's most famous literary son, Franz Kafka. Kafka wasn't considered Czech during his life, as a German-speaking Jew in Prague, but he's been reclaimed since, often by tourist touts selling Kafka-themed junk. His books, however, are far more substantial: haunting and visionary, disturbing and dystopian, they remain darkly enjoyable and shouldn't be seen as daunting. Kafka's prose is elegant but accessible, and the stories are short.

PRAGUE SPRING BY SIMON MAWER

This book is a tremendously evocative depiction, told through the eyes of outsiders, of the events of 1968, when Russian troops crushed the flowering of freedom in communist Czechoslovakia. The book is packed full of historical and geographical detail that readers will easily place in modern-day Prague, as well as identifiable characters whose lives and loves keep the story from feeling too dense.

THE UNBEARABLE LIGHTNESS OF BEING BY MILAN KUNDERA

Perhaps the most famous work of Czech literature globally, this postmodern classic is a love story at heart, although don't expect happy endings. Also set at the time of the Prague Spring in 1968, the philosophical work follows Tomáš, a surgeon in Prague who sleeps around, and traces the repercussions of both his actions and the wider societal upheaval at the time.

HAVEL

A 2020 biopic looks at Václav Havel during his years as a dissident and playwright, while the political events unfolding around him force him reluctantly to have to embrace politics. Actor Viktor Dvořák bears a strong physical resemblance to the future Czechoslovak president.

AMADEUS

This 1984 Oscar winner from renowned Czech director Miloš Forman was partly filmed in Prague's historically relevant locations and in other suitably stunning places around the country. It follows the life of Wolfgang Amadeus Mozart, and is epic, ostentatious, over the top, and fun, with (obviously) a fantastic score, and plenty of darkness, too.

I SERVED THE KING OF ENGLAND

Based on the book by Bohumil Hrabal (the writer Bill Clinton asked to have a beer with when he was in town in the 1990s), this critically acclaimed 2006 film directed by Jiří Menzel follows the life of a young Czech man who wants to be a millionaire but who mainly works as a waiter in the Hotel Paris and skips all over the city. The weight comes from the historical setting of the movie, part of the so-called Czech New Wave, which is mainly during the Nazi occupation of Prague.

KOLYA

With a particularly famous scene in the otherwise unremarkable Anděl Metro station, this well-received film from the 1990s about an old bachelor musician taking in an abandoned boy toward the end of the Russian occupation of the Czech Republic comes from a leading Czech father-son duo. Directed by Jan Svěrák, the film also stars his father, Zdeněk Svěrák, who wrote the script from a story by Pavel Taussig.

Chapter 2

TRAVEL SMART

Updated by
Raymond Johnston

★ **CAPITAL:**
Prague

👫 **POPULATION:**
1.3 million

💬 **LANGUAGE:**
Czech

$ **CURRENCY:**
Koruna (crown)

☎ **COUNTRY CODE:**
420

⚠ **EMERGENCIES:**
112

🚗 **DRIVING:**
On the right

⚡ **ELECTRICITY:**
230 c/50 cycle, plugs have
two round pins, or two pins
and a hole.

🕐 **TIME:**
6 hours ahead of New York

🌐 **WEB RESOURCES:**
www.czechtourism.cz;
www.prague.eu;
www.praguecitytourism.cz

✈ **AIRPORT:**
PRG

Know Before You Go

What should you pack? How can you get a good photo of the Charles Bridge? Is English widely spoken? Is it Czechia or the Czech Republic? And *is* beer really cheaper than water? Plus tips on using the ATM, dodging the crowds, tipping, and taxis.

HELLO, MY NAME IS CZECHIA

The country recently changed its name from the Czech Republic to Czechia. Why? Who knows? Certainly not its inhabitants: two-thirds of Czechs polled by a newspaper when the name changed said they didn't like the new moniker, which was suddenly imposed by the government without any real explanation. The official reasoning is that it makes it easier for English speakers to pronounce, and easier for companies and sports teams to use on branding, although critics said it makes foreigners even more likely to confuse it with Chechnya. Fun fact: it's actually just the short name for the country, as France is for the official "The French Republic" (who knew). And as for the Czechs themselves? Most of them couldn't care less what you call their homeland; they call it Česko, anyway.

PSA: IT'S COLD IN WINTER AND HOT IN SUMMER!

It gets cold in winter, with temperatures regularly well below freezing. Make sure you have a serious coat, hat, gloves, and most importantly, boots (the cobbles in the snow or frost are extremely slippery, and nobody wants cold feet while sightseeing). Build time in your schedule to dip into warm pubs or cafés (not really a hardship), and bear in mind that lots of the more outdoorsy sights are closed in winter. At the opposite end of the scale, the height of summer can get very hot; pack sunscreen and cover-up hats, and like all warm-weather destinations, avoid the hottest parts of the day for serious pavement pounding. Luckily, the beer gardens are shady and some hotels and restaurants have air-conditioning. There are also a host of outdoor pools and even lakes and ponds within easy reach of the city for a cooling dip, including at the Podolí complex by the river.

YOU'LL NEED TO DUCK THE CROWDS

Prague is one of the most visited cities in the world, so be prepared for hordes, and rise early to avoid them. Plus, get off the beaten track in Staré Město (especially the main route to the Charles Bridge) and you'll find some surprisingly quiet streets; in particular, the streets around Konvikstka and the lower end of Karoliny Světlé can be quite calm. And if you want to take that perfect picture of the view from the bridge itself, here's a tip: go to the next bridge up in either direction (Mánesův most, or Mánes Bridge, to the north, and Most Legií, or Legion Bridge, to the south), where the crowds are much smaller and your picture of the gorgeous vista beyond will include the famous bridge, too. Alternatively, head out to neighborhoods like Vršovice and Vinohrady to gaze at some of Prague's stately signature architecture (and find some great cafés and bars). Lastly, if you hate bachelor parties (known as "stag parties" in Europe), perhaps try to avoid the biggest bars in Staré Město and Nové Město on a Saturday night.

AVOID STREET TAXIS

Taxis in Prague are notorious rip-offs, so try to avoid flagging one down on the street. This is easy to do these days, as ride-sharing apps like Uber and Bolt are as omnipresent here as they are in most major global cities. One word of warning though: don't rely on them in the middle of the night for a ride to the airport, for example; there just aren't enough drivers working at 3 am in the city to make it guaranteed that there will be a car for you. Instead, there are some reliable taxi services you can call or book online, such as the reasonably priced Modrý Anděl, which has English-speaking operators. If all else fails, city buses go to the airport at all hours.

MOST PEOPLE SPEAK SOME ENGLISH
English is widely spoken, and with astonishing fluency by a lot of the younger generation working in hotels and restaurants, but a bit of Czech (ahoj—pronounced ahoy—for hello, dekuji for thank you) goes down very well.

PART OF THE EU WITHOUT THE EUROS PART
Czech crowns, not euros, are the order of the day, and they are usually in the region of 23–25 koruny (Kč) to the dollar depending on the current exchange rate. Try not to get huge bills from the ATM, as they can be hard to change or spend: while the machine will try to dispense notes in the 1,000 or even 2,000 denomination, try to withdraw multiples of 100 instead so that you can break the note more easily.

TIPPING IS APPRECIATED
The tradition is just to round up to the nearest whole number, but the international 10% standard is fine, too. It's really up to you, but the gesture is appreciated (and the ferocity of the glare that will greet you if you force your server to fumble around with 1 Kč coins is best avoided).

DON'T FALL FOR THE RUSSIAN DOLLS
Don't get taken in by the gaudy Russian stacking dolls sold everywhere, particularly in the Jewish Quarter and around Old Town Square. These souvenirs have nothing to do with Czech culture but are a throwback to the 1990s, when Prague was one of the first former Soviet bloc places that tourists started to visit. If you're looking for traditional Czech gifts, consider beer, wooden puppets, Koh-i-noor pencils, or Bohemian crystal instead.

BEER IS NOT ALWAYS CHEAPER THAN WATER, SORRY
Beer is a way of life in the Czech Republic, where citizens drink more per capita than anywhere else in the world. But the rumors about it being cheaper than water are sadly exaggerated; while it is true that in some pubs it can occasionally be cheaper than bottled water (and it's certainly

cheaper than coffee or soft drinks like Coca-Cola in many locales), it's not quite the unbelievable bargain it used to be. And more importantly, most places now will provide you with tap water entirely gratis, too.

Getting Here and Around

Prague is divided into 10 major administrative districts (with numbers above 10 being used for administrative purposes for some of the larger public housing developments and outlying areas). Most visitors spend their time in "Prague 1," which encompasses Staré Město (Old Town), Malá Strana (Lesser Quarter), part of Nové Město (New Town), and Hradčany (Castle Area). Residents in conversation will often refer to the districts by number to orient themselves geographically ("x is in Prague 1" or "y is in Prague 7"). These district numbers correspond roughly to the city's traditional neighborhoods. The neighborhood of Vinohrady, which lies just to the east of Václavské náměstí (Wenceslas Square), for example, is mostly in Prague 2. Other common neighborhoods and district numbers include Žižkov, Prague 3; Smíchov, Prague 5; and Holešovice, Prague 7. These names—along with the district numbers—appear on street signs.

Air

Prague is served by a growing number of budget carriers, which connect the Czech capital to several cities in the United Kingdom and across the European continent. These airlines are a great and cheap way to travel within Europe—though since the flights are popular, be sure to book well in advance. Budget carriers, however, are usually not much help in cutting costs when traveling from North America. Most of these carriers operate out of secondary airports (for example, Stansted in London instead of Heathrow, where most transatlantic flights land; or Orly in Paris instead of the larger Charles de Gaulle airport). This means travelers must change not only airlines but also airports, which can add frustration and expense. Also, consider limits on both carry-on and checked baggage, which are often more stringent on budget carriers than on large international carriers. For flights within Europe, low-cost airlines are sometimes a viable alternative to bus and train travel.

The nonstop flight from New York to Prague takes about eight hours, but the entire journey will take longer (12–15 hours) if you have to change planes at a European hub. The flight from London to Prague takes about two hours; the flight from Vienna to Prague takes less than an hour.

AIRPORT

Prague's Václav Havel Airport (formerly Ruzyně Airport) is the country's main international airport and lies about 15 km (10 miles) northwest of the city center. The airport has two main terminals— Terminal 1 (T1) and Terminal 2 (T2)—so make sure to read your ticket carefully to see where you are arriving and departing from. There is also a Terminal 3 for private and charter flights. The trip from the airport to the downtown area by car or taxi will take about 30 minutes—add another 20 minutes during rush hour (7–9 am and 4–6 pm).

AIRLINES

Delta Airlines offers nonstop flights from the United States (from New York's JFK airport) to Prague in the summer (daily flights during the busiest season). No carrier offers direct service in the winter. Most major U.S.-based airlines fly to Prague through code-share arrangements with their European counterparts. However, nearly all the major European airlines fly there, so it's usually easy to connect through a major European airport (such as London–Heathrow, Paris, Amsterdam, or Vienna) and continue to Prague; indeed, flights between the United Kingdom and Prague are numerous and frequent, including some on cheap discount airlines, though in London most of these leave from Gatwick or Stansted airports rather than Heathrow, making them less attractive options for Americans. Fares from the United States tend to rise dramatically during the busy summer season, particularly from June through August or September. There are many discounts during the slow winter months.

Bus

The Czech complex of regional bus lines known collectively as ČSAD operates its dense network from the sprawling Florenc station. For information about routes and schedules, consult the confusingly displayed timetables posted at the station or visit the information window in the lower-level lobby, which is open daily from 6 am to 9 pm. The company's website will give you bus and train information in English (click on the British flag).

There are also private bus companies servicing routes between Czech towns and cities. Many of these have newer buses with added services and comfort, as well as competitive prices and seasonal deals.

Most, but not all, buses use the Florenc station. Some buses—primarily those heading to smaller destinations in the south of the country—depart from above Roztyly Metro station (Line C [red]). You won't know beforehand which buses leave from Roztyly or from one of several other hubs, so you will have to ask first at Florenc or check the website. There's no central information center at most other hubs; you simply have to sort out the timetables at the bus stops or ask someone.

Buses offer an easier and quicker alternative to trains for many destinations. The Western Bohemian spa town of Karlovy Vary, for example, is an easy two-hour bus ride away. The same journey by train—because of the circuitous rail route—often takes 3½ hours.

Car

Traveling by car has some obvious advantages: it offers much more flexibility and is often quicker than a bus or train. But these advantages can be outweighed by the costs of the rental and gasoline, as well as the general hassles of driving in the Czech Republic. Most roads in the country are of the two-lane variety and are often jammed with trucks. And then there's parking. It's impossible in Prague and often difficult in the larger cities and towns outside the capital.

A special permit is required to drive on expressways and other four-lane highways. Rental cars should already have a permit affixed to the windshield. Temporary permits—for 10 days (310 Kč) or one month (440 Kč)—are available at border crossings, post offices, and service stations.

PARKING

Finding a parking spot in Prague can be next to impossible. Most of the spaces in the city center, Prague 1, 2, 3, 5, 6,

Getting Here and Around

7, 8, and 10, are reserved for residents, so you'll have to look for public lots with machines that issue temporary permits (look for the big blue P on machines). To use the machines, use a debit card, then place the printed ticket in a visible spot on the dashboard. Violators will find their cars towed away or immobilized by a "boot" on the tire. Some hotels offer parking—and this is a real advantage—though you may have to pay extra. A few streets also have meter parking that sells tickets to put in your window, but finding a spot is a virtual impossibility.

Parking is generally unrestricted in some outer areas of the city, though vacant spots can still be hard to find. There's an underground lot at Náměstí Jana Palacha, near Old Town Square. There are also park-and-ride (p+r) lots at distant suburban Metro stations, including Skalka (Line A), Zličín and Černý Most (Line B), and Nádraží Holešovice and Opatov (Line C). These charge as little as 50 Kč per 24 consecutive hours, substantially cheaper than downtown parking.

RULES OF THE ROAD

The Czech Republic follows the usual continental rules of the road. A right turn on red is permitted *only* when indicated by a green arrow. Signposts with yellow diamonds indicate a main road where drivers have the right of way. The speed limit is 130 kph (78 mph) on four-lane highways, 90 kph (56 mph) on open roads, and 50 kph (30 mph) in built-up areas and villages. Passengers under 12 years of age or less than 5 feet in height must ride in the back seat.

CAR RENTAL

Several major rental agencies have offices at the airport and also in the city. Prices can differ greatly, so be sure to shop around. Major firms like Avis and Hertz offer Western-style cars starting at around $40 per day or $200 per week, which includes insurance, damage waiver, and V.A.T. (value-added tax); cars equipped with automatic transmission and air-conditioning are available but are generally more expensive. Small-size "city cars," like Smart cars or Mini Coopers, are cheaper. It's best to reserve your rental car before you leave home, and it may be less expensive as well. Smaller local companies, on the other hand, can rent Czech cars for significantly less, but the service and insurance coverage may be inferior.

Drivers from the United States need no international driving permit to rent a car in the Czech Republic, only a valid domestic license, along with the vehicle registration. If you intend to drive across a border, ask about restrictions on driving into other countries. The minimum age required for renting is usually 21 or older, and some companies also have maximum ages; be sure to inquire when making your arrangements. The Czech Republic requires that you have held your driver's license for at least a year before you can rent a car.

 # Metro

Prague has an excellent public transit system, which includes a clean and reliable underground subway system—called the Metro—as well as an extensive tram and bus network. Metro stations are marked with an inconspicuous M sign. Refurbished historical trams (Nos. 41 and 42) travel through Staré Město and Malá Strana on summer weekends but cost extra. Beware of pickpockets, who often operate in large groups on crowded trams and Metro cars and all other forms of transportation, including intercity buses. The basic Metro, bus, and tram ticket costs 40 Kč. It permits 90 minutes of travel throughout the Metro, tram, and bus network. Short-term tickets cost 30 Kč and allow 30 minutes' ride on a tram, bus, ferry, or Metro. If you're carrying a big bag, you need to buy an additional 20 Kč ticket. Travel on the funicular on Petřín costs 60 Kč. Most local people have monthly or annual passes, so while it may look like almost everyone is riding for free, they do have tickets. A matter of politeness: Czechs keep to the right side of escalators, leaving the left side free to people who want to walk up or down.

Tickets (*jízdenky*) can be bought at dispensing machines in Metro stations and at some newsstands. If you have a SIM card from a Czech service provider, tickets can also be purchased by texting 902–06–26. If you send an SMS that says DPT24 or DPT32 to the number, you will receive a virtual ticket for 24 Kč or 32 Kč. Trams now also allow people to buy tickets with a contactless payment card from an orange dispenser. English instructions can be selected from a menu by touching the British flag icon.

You can buy a one-day pass allowing unlimited use of the system for 120 Kč or a three-day pass for 330 Kč. Validated one- or three-day passes allow traveling with a child 6–15 years old for free. The passes can be purchased at main Metro stations, from ticket machines, and at some newsstands in the center. A pass is not valid until stamped in the yellow machines in a Metro station or aboard a tram.

The trams and Metro shut down around midnight, but special night trams (Nos. 91–99) and some buses run all night. Night trams run at 20- to 30-minute intervals, and all routes intersect at the corner of Lazarská and Spálená ulice in Nové Město, near the Národní třída Metro station. Schedules and regulations in English are on the transportation department's official website. Travel information centers provide all substantial information about public transport operation, routes, timetables, and so on. They are at major Metro stations and at both terminals at the airport.

Validate your Metro ticket at a yellow stamping machine before descending the escalator. Trains are patrolled often; the fine for riding without a valid ticket is 1,500 Kč, but the fine is reduced to 1,000 Kč if you pay on the spot or within 15 days. Tickets for buses are the same as those used for the Metro, although you validate them at machines inside the bus or tram. Information about tickets, route changes, and fines is on the city transit company website.

Taxi

Taxis are a convenient way of getting around town, particularly in the evening, when the number of trams and Metro trains starts to thin out. But be on the lookout for dishonest drivers, especially if you hail a taxi on the street or from one of the taxi stands at heavily touristed areas like Wenceslas Square. Typical scams include drivers doctoring the meter or failing to turn the meter on and then demanding an exorbitant sum at the end of the ride. In an honest cab, the meter starts at 60 Kč and increases by 36 Kč

Getting Here and Around

per km (½ mile) or 7 Kč per minute at rest. Most rides within town should cost no more than 150 Kč–250 Kč. Separate slightly higher rates have also been set for electric taxis. The best way to avoid getting ripped off is to ask your hotel or restaurant to call a cab for you. If you have to hail a taxi on the street, agree with the driver on a fare before getting in. (If the driver says he can't tell you what the approximate fare will be, that's almost a sure sign he's giving you a line.) If you have access to a phone, a better bet is to call one of the many radio-operated companies, like AAA Taxi. The drivers are honest, and the dispatchers speak English.

Smartphone-based ridesharing services like Uber, Liftago, and Bolt are also available in Prague. They are now legally allowed to operate by using an app instead of a meter.

 Train

Prague is serviced by two international train stations, so always make certain you know which station your train is using. The main station, Hlavní nádraží, is about 500 yards east of Wenceslas Square via Washingtonova ulice. The other international station is Nádraží Holešovice, located about 2 km (1 mile) north of the city center along Metro Line C (red). Nádraží Holešovice is frequently the point of departure for trains heading to Berlin, Vienna, and Budapest. Two other large stations in Prague service mostly local destinations. Smíchovské nádraží—southwest of the city center across the Vltava (on Metro Line B [yellow])—services destinations to the west, including trains to Karlštejn. Masarykovo nádraží,

near Náměstí Republiky in the center of the city, services mostly suburban destinations.

For train times, consult the timetables posted at the stations or online schedules. On timetables, departures (odjezd) appear on a yellow background; arrivals (příjezd) are on white. There are two information desks at the main station, Hlavní nádraží. The main Čedok office downtown can advise on train times and schedules.

On arriving at Hlavní nádraží, the best way to get to the center of town is by Metro. The station lies on Metro Line C (red) and is just one stop from the top of Wenceslas Square (Muzeum station)—travel in the direction of Haje station. You can also walk the 500 yards or so to the square, though the walk is not advisable late at night. A taxi ride from the main station to the center should cost about 100 Kč. To reach the city center from Nádraží Holešovice, take the Metro Line C (red) four stops to Muzeum; a taxi ride should cost roughly 200 Kč–250 Kč.

The state-run rail system is called České dráhy (ČD). On longer runs, it's not really worth taking anything less than an express (rychlík) train, marked in red on the timetable. Tickets are inexpensive: a second-class ticket from Prague to Brno (a distance of 200 km [124 miles]) costs about 230 Kč. A 40 Kč–60 Kč supplement is charged for the excellent international expresses, EuroCity (EC) and InterCity (IC), and for domestic SuperCity (SC) schedules. Seats can be reserved online or over a mobile app for free on domestic journeys, but cost from 35 Kč up to 500 Kč. Seat reservations are mandatory for the high-speed Pendolino train, which goes to Plzeň, Pardubice, Olomouc, and

Ostrava. If you haven't bought a ticket in advance, you can buy one aboard the train but for an extra fee. It's possible to book sleepers (*lůžkový*) or the less-roomy couchettes (*lehátkový*) on most overnight trains. You do not need to validate your train ticket before boarding.

Private firms have been allowed to operate trains. Two companies, Leo Express and RegioJet, have routes from Prague to other major cities and also some international destinations. Tickets are not interchangable between companies.

The Eurail Pass and the Eurail Youthpass are valid for travel within the Czech Republic, and if you're traveling through to neighboring countries like Hungary, Austria, or Poland, it can be an economic way to bounce between the regions. (A pass for four days of second-class travel in one month starts at $253 for adults or $191 for students.) The many Czech rail passes available are useful chiefly by regular travelers. A discount applies to any group of 2–30 people traveling second class (*sleva pro skupiny*). It's always cheaper to buy a return ticket. Foreign visitors will find it easiest to inquire at the international booking offices of major stations for the latest discounts and passes that will apply to them. Rail schedules are available at ⊕ *ldos.cz*.

Essentials

🏃 Activities

Czechs are avid sportsmen and sportswomen. In the summertime, Prague empties out as residents head to their country cottages to hike or bike in clean air. In winter, the action shifts to the mountains, a few hours to the north and east of the city, for decent downhill and cross-country skiing. City districts and private entities operate pop-up skating rinks and ski trails in the winter.

The most popular spectator sport, bar none, is ice hockey. Czechs are world hockey champions, and the Czech gold medal at the Nagano Winter Olympics in 1998 is held up as a national achievement practically on par with the 1989 Velvet Revolution. If you're here in wintertime, witness the fervor by seeking out tickets to an Extraliga game. The main Prague teams are Sparta and Slavia.

Soccer plays a perennial second fiddle to hockey, although the Czech national soccer team ranks among the best in the world. Prague's main professional team, Sparta, plays its home games at Toyota Arena near Letná.

BICYCLING
Much of the Czech Republic is a cyclist's dream of gently sloping tracks for pedalers. The capital, however, can be unkind to bicyclers. Prague's ubiquitous tram tracks and cobblestones make for hazardous conditions—as do the legions of tourist groups clogging the streets. Nevertheless, cycling is increasingly popular, and there are now several adequate yellow-marked cycling trails that crisscross the city. From April to October two bike-rental companies provide decent bikes—as well as locks, helmets, and maps. There are also several bike-sharing programs that can be used via phone apps. Instructions can be found on the bikes.

City Bike
BIKING | City Bike Prague runs guided tours leaving at 10:30, 1:30, and 4:30. Your English-speaking guides offer fun tidbits of history and point out architecture but do not offer a full tour. The ride's pace is comfortable for those who haven't taken a spin in a while.
⚠ **Be warned, Prague is not a bike-friendly city.** ✉ *Králodvorská 5, Prague* ☎ *766–180–284* ⊕ *www.citybike-prague.com* Ⓜ *Line B: Náměstí Republiky.*

Praha Bike
BIKING | One of the multicultural teams from Praha Bike can casually guide you around several routes. The "classic" and "panoramic" are the most popular. There are also beer-garden and pub tours, a ride out of Prague to Karlštejn, and night tours. ✉ *Dlouhá 24, Prague* ☎ *732–388–880* ⊕ *www.prahabike.cz* Ⓜ *Line B: Náměstí Republiky.*

HOCKEY
A feverish national fixation, ice hockey becomes a full-blown obsession during the World Championships (held every year in late spring) and the Winter Olympics.

The Czech national hockey league, Extraliga, is one of the most competitive in the world, and the best players regularly move on to the North American National Hockey League. Slavia Praha and Sparta are the two best teams, both in Prague. Hockey season runs from September to March. Tickets cost 250 Kč–995 Kč and are reasonably easy to get.

HC Slavia Praha
HOCKEY | Although a relative giant in the Czech Republic, HC Slavia Praha usually finds itself chasing the leaders of the pack in international matches. ✉ *Zimní stadion Eden, Vladivostocká 1460/10, Prague* ☎ *267–311–417* ⊕ *www.hc-slavia.cz.*

HC Sparta Praha

HOCKEY | HC Sparta Praha is routinely regarded as the premier team in an excellent local league—until players are lured across the Atlantic. Come to spot the next Jágr or Hašek. ✉ *O2 Arena, Českomoravská 2345/17, Prague* ☎ *266–727–443* ⊕ *www.hcsparta.cz* Ⓜ *Line B: Českomoravská.*

PARKS AND PLAYGROUNDS

Praguers are gluttons for a sunny day in the park. A pleasant weekend afternoon brings out plenty of sun worshippers and Frisbee tossers, with their blankets, books, and dogs. Two of the city's best beer gardens can be found at Letenské sady (Letná Park) and Riegrovy sady (Rieger Park).

Kampa

HIKING & WALKING | Under the noses of the throng on the Charles Bridge, take the steps off the bridge onto Na Kampě and follow the wide cobbled street to the end; Kampa is a diminutive gem hidden in the heart of Malá Strana. It's a location for lazing in the sunshine and resting your eyes from all the busy baroque architecture, with a playground for when the kids grow restless from the endless palaces and churches. ✉ *Malá Strana* Ⓜ *Tram 15 to Malostranské náměstí.*

Letenské sady (*Letná Park*)

HIKING & WALKING | With killer views of the city across the river, this park is eternally busy. It has a huge restaurant and beer garden, for chilling like a local, located around Letenský zámeček, near the intersection of Kostelní and Muzejní. The large grassy northern plateau is also a great place to throw a Frisbee or kick a soccer ball. An excellent playground sits in the center near the tennis courts, just to the west of Letenský zámeček. Long-term construction projects in the area often hinder the tram routes. ✉ *Holešovice* Ⓜ *Tram 12 or 17 to Sparta.*

Riegrovy sady (*Rieger Park*)

HIKING & WALKING | This lush park climbs sharply up the slopes of Vinohrady. On the east side of the park, lovely landscaping surrounds a large beer garden and playground. A smaller and cozier beer stand with rooftop seating is in the center. It offers lavish views of Prague Castle on the distant horizon. It has become popular with exchange students and other English-speaking people. ✉ *Vinohrady* Ⓜ *Line A: Jiřího z Poděbrad.*

Stromovka

HIKING & WALKING | King of all Prague parks, these lands were formerly royal hunting grounds. Today the deer have been usurped by horse riders and dog lovers. Remarkably rustic for a city-based park, it's primarily a place for walking rather than loafing about. Many of the paths and ponds were recently renovated. There are a few places to stop for a beverage or a snack. ✉ *Holešovice* Ⓜ *Tram 6 to Výstaviště.*

SKIING

Czechs are enthusiastic and gifted skiers, and the country's northern border regions with Germany and Poland hold many small ski resorts. Czechs generally acknowledge the Krkonoše Mountains, which straddle the border with Poland, to be the best. Experienced skiers may find the hills here a little small and the facilities not quite up to international standards. (Hard-core Czech skiers usually head to Austria or France.) Nevertheless, if you're here in midwinter and you get a good snowfall, the Czech resorts can make for a fun overnight trip from the capital. All the area ski resorts are regularly served by buses leaving from Florenc.

Černá Hora

SKIING & SNOWBOARDING | Černá Hora is 180 km (112 miles), about a four-hour drive) east of Prague. The resort has a

Essentials

cable car, one chairlift, and a couple of drag lifts. The "Black Mountain" is not the biggest of ski resorts but is often fairly quiet, meaning less waiting and a nice unofficial run, with plenty of forest to explore, directly under the cable car. ⊠ *Cernohorská 265, Janské Lázne* ☎ *840–888–229* ⊕ *www.skiresort.cz/en.*

Harrachov

SKIING & SNOWBOARDING | On weekends, when you want to take in some crisp mountain air and clap on a pair of skis, head for Harrachov. In the west of the Krkonoše, around 120 km (74 miles, a three-hour drive) from the capital, the resort offers red and blue runs served by two chairlifts and 11 rope tows. This small and friendly resort is ideal for beginners and intermediates. ⊠ *Harrachov* ☎ *481–529–600 for town info center* ⊕ *www.harrachov.cz.*

Skiareal Špindlerův Mlýn

SKIING & SNOWBOARDING | The biggest and most popular ski resort in the Czech Republic is Skiareal Špindlerův Mlýn, which is 160 km (99 miles, about a 3½-hour drive) from Prague. The twin slopes, Svatý Petr and Medvedín, gaze at each other over the small village and offer blue, red, and black runs served by four chairlifts and numerous rope tows. Weekends here are mobbed to a point well past frustration. ⊠ *Špindleruv Mlýn* ☎ *499–467–101* ⊕ *www.skiarealspindl.cz.*

SOCCER

Games for the domestic Czech league, the Fortuna liga, run from August to May with a break in December and January. The games and the fans tend to be somewhat lackluster. Tickets are plentiful enough on match days (except for tournaments). International matches are hosted at Sparta's stadium.

AC Sparta Praha

SOCCER | AC Sparta Praha has an enthusiastic fan base, with the stadium roar to match. Although it has seen its fortunes dip a little recently, the team remains a domestic Goliath and a stone-slinging David in European competition. ⊠ *Generali arena, Milady Horákové 98, Letná* ☎ *296–111–400* ⊕ *www.sparta.cz* Ⓜ *Line A: Sparta.*

Bohemians 1905

SOCCER | Bohemians 1905 are back in the top league after a few difficult years. Fans are highly enthusiastic. ⊠ *Doliček stadion, Vršovická 31, Prague* ☎ *245–005–014* ⊕ *www.bohemians.cz* Ⓜ *Tram 22 to Vršovice Nám.*

SK Slavia Praha

SOCCER | Sparta's success is much to the chagrin of its bitter rival, SK Slavia Praha, which now plays in the modern Fortuna Arena, though most fans still refer to it by its old name, Eden. ⊠ *Sinobo Stadium, Vladivostocká 1460/10, Prague* ☎ *272–118–311* ⊕ *www.slavia.cz* Ⓜ *Tram 4, 7, 22, or 24 to Slavia.*

TENNIS

Tennis is one of the favorite local sports, but the national passion remains at a simmer instead of a rolling boil. The best-known Czech players have been Ivan Lendl and, by ethnicity at least, Martina Navratilova. But there is a crop of younger players out there trying to crowd into the top 10. Prague is blessed with several public tennis courts; most are cinder or clay surface.

Český Lawn Tennis Klub

TENNIS | Some of the city's best tennis courts can be found right next door to the tennis stadium, Český Lawn Tennis Klub, which in its time has hosted ATP events. Open to the public for 300 Kč–630 Kč per hour are 10 outdoor courts and six indoor courts, all hard surface or clay, despite the name. ⊠ *Ostrov Štvanice 38, Prague* ☎ *222–316–317* ⊕ *cltk.cz* Ⓜ *Line C: Vltavská.*

SK Hradčany
TENNIS | At SK Hradčany outdoor courts cost 270 Kč–420 Kč per hour. ⊠ *Diskařská 1, Prague* ☎ *603–509–950* ⊕ *tenispraha.cz* Ⓜ *Tram 22 or 25 to Malovanka.*

🍴 Dining

DISCOUNTS AND DEALS
Most pubs and restaurants, especially near office buildings, serve good lunch specials of Czech cuisine standards for a very reasonable price from 11 to 3. Some places still also distinguish between *hotová jídla* (ready meals) and *minutky* (meals that require preparation). Ready meals, heavy on gravy and dumplings, are cheaper.

PAYING
Most restaurants take credit cards, but some smaller places do not. It's worth asking. Servers in the center are starting to expect Western-style tips, but in general 10% is standard, with more only for exceptional service. Outside the city center, rounding the bill up to the closest 10 Kč is still common. Restaurants are required to give printed receipts, and it is a good idea to check them for items that weren't ordered, surprise service charges, or pre-calculated tips. Unless stated on the menu, service charges and tips can't be added automatically.

RESERVATIONS AND DRESS
Reservations are recommended for some of the top upscale restaurants in the center, but most others can accommodate walk-ins. Business casual is fine in most cases for high-end places, while jeans will pass muster in most other venues. Shorts and T-shirts are fine for outdoor dining in the summer. If you have doubts, call the restaurant and ask.

MEALS AND MEALTIMES
Late-night dining hasn't really caught on, and it's difficult to find a good place that serves after 11, though fast food is available around the clock. Some high-end restaurants close between lunch and dinner. Many places have a lunch special until 3. Places outside the center tend to close at 10 or earlier and may be closed Sunday or Monday.

SMOKING
Smoking is banned in all restaurants and bars, with a few exceptions for water pipes and vaping.

WHAT IT COSTS in Koruny			
$	$$	$$$	$$$$
AT DINNER			
under 150 Kč	150 Kč–400 Kč	401 Kč–700 Kč	over 700 Kč

➕ Health

Make sure food has been thoroughly cooked and is served to you fresh and hot. If you have problems, mild cases of traveler's diarrhea may respond to Imodium (known generically as loperamide) or Pepto-Bismol. Be sure to drink plenty of fluids; if you can't keep fluids down, seek medical help immediately.

Infectious diseases can be airborne or passed via mosquitoes and ticks and through direct or indirect physical contact with animals or people. Some, including Norwalk-like viruses that affect your digestive tract, can be passed along

Essentials

through contaminated food. Condoms can help prevent most sexually transmitted diseases, but they aren't absolutely reliable, and their quality varies from country to country. Speak with your physician and/or check the CDC or World Health Organization websites for health alerts, particularly if you're pregnant, traveling with children, or have a chronic illness.

Pharmacies in Prague are well stocked with prescription and nonprescription drugs, though you may have trouble persuading a pharmacist to fill a foreign prescription. Pharmacies are generally open during regular business hours, from 9 to 6, with some offering night and weekend service. A law requires a standard 30 Kč fee per prescription. During off-hours, pharmacies will often post the name and address of the nearest open pharmacy on their doors. Pharmacies not only sell prescription medicines but are the only licensed dealers of typical over-the-counter products like pain relievers and cough medicines. Most standard U.S. over-the-counter products have Czech equivalents. Aspirin is widely available. However, items such as aspirin cannot be found outside pharmacies. The most common non-aspirin pain reliever is Ibalgin (ibuprofen), sold in 200 mg and 400 mg doses.

■TIP➔ **Pharmacists may not speak English or know a drug's non-Czech brand name but will certainly know the drug's generic name ("acetaminophen" for Tylenol, for example). Be sure to call a drug by its generic name when asking for it.**

COVID-19

Most travel restrictions, including vaccination and masking requirements, have been lifted except in healthcare facilities and nursing homes. Some travelers may still wish to wear a mask in confined spaces, including on airplanes, on public transportation, and at large indoor gatherings, but that is increasingly a personal choice. Be aware that some local mandates still exist and should be followed. Since COVID-19-related quarantine requirements and other restrictions still exist in some destinations, it is wise to have travel insurance that will cover you for COVID-19-related cancellations and other expenses.

Lodging

PRICES

Summer is the main season, but spring and fall have been catching up. Significant rate drops are only seen in the winter. Pricing is still very competitive, especially among three- and four-star hotels. Some big hotels outside of the historical area are cheaper and less crowded, but some lack good public transit connections.

RESERVATIONS

Prague is one of Europe's top destinations, so hotels tend to be near capacity. Reservations in the summer are essential if you want to stay in the center for a reasonable rate. New Year's Eve and the time around Christmas can also book up months in advance; otherwise, last-minute bookings can be found in winter.

WHAT IT COSTS in Koruny			
$	$$	$$$	$$$$
FOR TWO PEOPLE			
under 2,500 Kč	2,500 Kč–4,500 Kč	4,501 Kč–8,000 Kč	over 8,000 Kč

Where Should I Stay?

	NEIGHBORHOOD VIBE	PROS	CONS
Staré Město (Old Town)	Most tourist attractions are in Staré Město, which is filled with historical buildings.	Easy access to all the main sights, many lovely places to take photos. Some hotels have wonderful views.	Noisy, crowded, expensive, and few locals, as many flats are now short-term rentals. Parking is almost impossible.
Nové Město (New Town)	"New" means 1348, when Nové Město was established. It's more relaxed than Staré Město, with a mix of modern and historical architecture.	Less crowded than Staré Město but still near the main attractions.	Still on the expensive side and filled with late-night noise.
Vinohrady	The former royal vineyard has art nouveau buildings, upscale eateries, and relaxing parks.	Still close to tourist attractions but with a warm and friendly ambience.	Some smaller pubs and stores have limited English. New restaurants can be hit or miss in quality.
Karlín	Rebuilt after floods in 2003, the former industrial area is now home to modern offices and new nightlife but still has some derelict buildings.	Good public transit makes it just minutes from the center. Some good restaurants that cater to the office crowd.	Parts can get a bit desolate after dark, and some streets are a bit seedy.
Smíchov	The district is a colorful blend of people and places. Modern housing developments are slowly filling in abandoned lots.	Cinema multiplexes, bars, and shopping centers make it a center of nightlife.	Some side streets are still very run-down and best avoided. Rail tracks and busy roads make walking around a bit difficult.
Žižkov	A lively middle-class neighborhood used to be an independent city and still marches to its own beat.	Prague's Brooklyn has old-school pubs and restaurants with very affordable prices.	Groups of people making lots of noise at all hours of the night are common. Some sections are iffy, even in the daytime.
Holešovice	Abandoned factories have been redeveloped into art centers, attracting a new generation to the area.	Lots of international cuisine and quirky cafés plus easy access to two huge parks.	Parts still have an industrial feel and are a bit far from public transit.
Vršovice	The least touristy of the central districts gives a real feel of Czech life.	The area around Krymská ulice has become a hipster paradise with modern architecture landmarks.	Large parts of the area still haven't gotten the memo about becoming trendy. Only a few small hotels.

Essentials

$ Money

The Czech koruna has been maintained at a level to promote foreign trade and tourism, though prices for some items are close to those of Western Europe. Many hotel prices are more realistic thanks to tough competition, and it's easy to find last-minute bargains. Prices at tourist resorts outside the capital are lower and, in the outlying areas and off the beaten track, very low. The story is similar for restaurants, with Prague being comparable to the United States and Western Europe, whereas outlying towns are much more reasonable. The prices for castles, museums, and other sights are rising but still low by outside standards.

ATMs are common in Prague and most towns in the Czech Republic and more often than not are part of the Cirrus and Plus networks, meaning you can get cash easily. Outside of urban areas, machines can be scarce, and you should plan to carry enough cash to meet your needs.

In Czech an ATM is called a *bankomat*, and a PIN is also a PIN, just as in English.

Prices throughout this guide are given for adults. Substantially reduced fees are almost always available for children, students, and senior citizens.

Banks in the United States never have every foreign currency on hand, and it may take as long as a week to order. If you're planning to exchange funds before leaving home, don't wait until the last minute.

TIPPING
Service is not usually included in restaurant bills. In pubs or ordinary places, simply round up the bill to the next multiple of 10 (if the bill comes to 83 Kč, for example, give the waiter 90 Kč in nicer places; 10% is considered appropriate for good food and service). Tip porters who bring bags to your rooms 40 Kč–50 Kč total. For room service, a 20 Kč tip is enough. In taxis, add 10%. Give tour guides and helpful concierges 50 Kč–100 Kč for services rendered.

🛄 Packing

Prague's climate is continental, so in summer plan on relatively warm days and cool nights. Spring tends to be wet and cool; fall is drier but also on the chilly side. In winter, pack plenty of warm clothes and plan to use them. An umbrella is a good idea any time of year. Note that areas in higher elevations tend to stay very cool even in midsummer.

In general, pack for comfort rather than for style. Casual dress is the norm for everyday wear, including at most restaurants. Men will need a sport coat for an evening out at a concert or the opera.

Many areas are best seen on foot, so take a pair of sturdy walking shoes and be prepared to use them. High heels can present considerable problems on the cobblestoned streets of Prague.

Some items that you take for granted at home are occasionally unavailable or of questionable quality in Eastern and Central Europe, though the situation has been steadily improving. Toiletries and personal-hygiene products are relatively easy to find, but it's always a good idea to bring necessities when traveling in outlying areas, especially on weekends.

⊕ Passports

Citizens of the United States need only a valid passport to enter the Czech Republic and can stay for as long as 90 days without a visa. It's a good idea to make sure your passport is valid for at least six months on entry. If you plan on living or working in the Czech Republic, be advised that long-term and work visas must be obtained outside the country. Contact the Czech embassy or consulate in your home country well in advance of your trip. The Czech Republic is part of the Schengen area, meaning that once a visitor enters one of the countries in the zone, which covers most of Europe, he or she will not have to show a passport at each border; a visitor's three-month stay begins upon the first point of entry into the Schengen area. Travelers are still required to have a valid passport, and spot checks still occur.

$ Taxes

Taxes are usually included in the prices of hotel rooms, restaurant meals, and items purchased in shops. The price on the tag is what you'll pay at the register.

The Czech value-added tax (V.A.T.) is called DPH (*daň z přidané hodnoty*), and there are two rates. The higher one (21%) covers nearly everything—gifts, souvenirs, clothing, and food in restaurants. Food in grocery stores and books are taxed 15%. Exported goods are exempt from the tax, which can be refunded. All tourists outside the European Union are entitled to claim the tax back if they spend more than 2,000 Kč in one shop on the same day. Global Blue processes V.A.T. refunds in the Czech Republic and will give you your refund in

cash (U.S. dollars or euros) from a booth at the airport; be aware that the Czech Republic does *not* provide a postage-paid mailer for V.A.T. refund forms, unlike most other European countries.

When making a purchase, ask for a V.A.T. refund form and find out whether the merchant gives refunds—not all stores do, nor are they required to. Have the form stamped like any customs form by customs officials when you leave the country or, if you're visiting several European Union countries, when you leave the EU. After you're through passport control, take the form to a refund-service counter for an on-the-spot refund (which is usually the quickest and easiest option), or mail it to the address on the form (or the envelope with it) after you arrive home. You receive the total refund stated on the form, but the processing time can be long, especially if you request a credit-card adjustment.

Global Blue is a Europe-wide service with 240,000 affiliated stores and more than 700 refund counters at major airports and border crossings. Its refund form, called a Tax Free Check, is the most common across the European continent. The service issues refunds in the form of cash, check, or credit-card adjustment.

Tours

Major U.S. agencies often plan trips covering Prague and the Czech Republic. Abercrombie & Kent, Inc., is one agency that offers package tours to the area. The largest Czech agency, Čedok, also offers package tours.

You can take a 30- to 60-minute boat trip along the Vltava year-round with several boat companies that are based on the quays near the Malá Strana side of the Charles Bridge. It's not really necessary to buy tickets in advance, though you can; boats leave as they fill up. One of the cruise companies stands out, and it's on the Staré Město side of the bridge. Prague-Venice Cruises operates restored, classic canal boats from the late 19th century; the company operates one larger boat that holds 35 passengers and eight smaller boats that hold 12 passengers.

■ TIP→ Take one of the smaller boats—particularly one of the uncovered ones—if you can, for a more intimate narrated cruise of about 45 minutes along the Vltava and nearby canals.

Refreshments are included in all cruises. You actually set sail from beneath the last remaining span of Judith's Bridge (the Roman-built precursor to the Charles Bridge). Look for the touts in sailor suits right before the bridge; they will direct you to the ticket office. Cruises are offered daily 10:30–6 from November through February, until 8 from March through June and September through October, and until 11 in July and August. Cruises cost 440 Kč.

Čedok offers a 3½-hour "Prague Castle in Detail" tour, a combination bus and walking venture that covers the castle and major sights around town in English. The price is about 1,000 Kč. Stop by the main office for information on other tours and tour departure points. You can also arrange a personalized walking tour. Times and itineraries are negotiable; prices start at around 400 Kč per hour.

Very similar tours by other operators also depart daily from Náměstí Republiky, Národní třída near Jungmannovo náměstí, and Wenceslas Square. Prices are generally a couple of hundred crowns less than for Čedok's tours.

Tours of Prague come under the supervision of Prague Information Service, which is reliable and always informative. The partly city-funded company organizes walking tours in Prague's city center and in the outskirts, including excursions from Prague. Many tailor-made tours can be arranged. Nonregistered guides can also be found, but unless they come with a personal recommendation from someone you trust, their services cannot be guaranteed. Due to a loophole in the law, many guides offer so-called free tours but ask for "tips" at the end so they can avoid regulation.

Czech Tourism has a free app for Android and iPhone called Czech Republic Land of Stories, with suggested trips, maps, and other information for Prague and other cities. The app uses GPS to help people stay on track.

One small private company that does an excellent tour of the city is Custom Travel Services, operated by Jaroslav Pesta. The service offers a wide range of touring options. A full-day private walking tour of Prague with a boat ride for two or three people is 4,000 Kč, or 5,000 Kč for five to six people. The firm offers 100 different tours across the country and also will customize a tour according to your interests.

One reason visitors come to the Czech Republic is to connect with their Jewish heritage. Wittmann Tours provides not only coverage of the main sights in Prague but excursions to smaller Czech towns and to Trebíč.

Themed walking tours are popular in Prague. You can choose from tours on medieval architecture, Velvet Revolution walks, visits to communist monuments, and any number of pub crawls. Each year, four or five small operators do these tours, which generally last a couple of hours and cost from 150 Kč to more than 1,000 Kč. Inquire at Prague Information Service or a major ticket agency for the current season's offerings. Most walks start at the clock tower on Old Town Square.

A special guide service is available in the Czech Republic designed to examine and explain the country's Jewish history. The company, Wittmann Tours, offers several different tours within Prague and also outside, including the Terezín concentration camp.

For gourmands, Prague has upped its food game in recent years. Several different food tours can be booked that showcase Czech cuisine, craft beer, and small bistros with wine.

Czech Helpful Phrases

BASICS

Hello	Ahoj	ah-hoy
Yes/No	Ano/ne	ah-no/nay
Please	Prosím	pro-seem
Thank you	Děkuju	dyek-oo-yoo
You're welcome	Není zač!	nah-nee zatch
I'm Sorry (apology)	Omlouvám se	oh-mloo-vam say
Sorry (Excuse me)	Promiňte	pro-min-tye
Good morning	Dobrý ráno	doh-bree rah-no
Good day	Dobrý den	doh-bree den
Good evening	Dobrý večer	doh-bree veh-chair
Goodbye	Na shledanou	nah sklad-en-owe
Mr. (Sir)	Pan	pahn
Mrs.	Paní	pahn-nee
Miss	Slečna	stetch-nah
Pleased to meet you	Těší mě!	teh-shee-mye
How are you?	Jak se máš	yahk say mahsh

NUMBERS

one-half	Půl	puhl
one	Jeden/jedna/jedno	jeh-den/jeh-dnah/jeh-dnoh
two	Dva/dvě	dvah/dvyay
three	Tři	trzhee
four	Čtyři	sht-ear-zhee
five	Pět	pyet
six	Šest	shest
seven	Sedm	sed-uhm
eight	Osm	aw-suhm
nine	Devět	dehv-yet
ten	Deset	deh-set
eleven	Jedenáct	jeh-den-atst
twelve	Dvanáct	dvah-natst
thirteen	Třináct	trzhee-natst
fourteen	Čtrnáct	shter-natst
fifteen	Patnáct	paht-natst
sixteen	Šestnáct	shest-natst
seventeen	Sedmnáct	sed-uhm-natst
eighteen	Osmnáct	aw-suhm-natst
nineteen	Devatenáct	dehv-aht-ay-natst
twenty	Dvacet	dva-test
twenty-one	Dvacet jeden/jedna/jedno	dvah-tset jeh-den/jeh-dnah/jeh-dnoh
thirty	Tricet	trzhee-tset
forty	Čtyřicet	shteer-ee-tset
fifty	Padesát	pah -deh-saht
sixty	Šedesát	sheh-deh-sat
seventy	Sedmdesát	seh-dum-deh-sat
eighty	Osmdesát	aw-suhm-deh-sat
ninety	Devadesát	deh-vah-deh-sat
one hundred	Sto	stow
one thousand	Tisíc	rih-seets
one million	Milión	Mih-lee-yon

COLORS

black	Černý/černá/černé	cher-nee/cher-nah/cher-nay
blue	Modrý/modrá/modrá	moh-dree/moh-drah/moh-dray
brown	Hnědý/hnědá/hnědé	hned-ee/hned-ah/hned-ay
green	Zelený/Zzlená/zelené	zehl-en-ee/zehl-en-ah/zehl-en-ay
orange	Oranžový/oranžoáý/oranžové	ahr-ahn-zho-vee/ahr-ahn-zho-vah/ahr-ahn-zho-vay
red	Červený/červená/červené	cher-veh-nee/cher-veh-nah/cher-veh-nay
white	Bílý/bílá/bílé	bil-ee/bil-ah/bil-ay
yellow	Žlutý/žlutá/žluté	zhlooh-tee/zhlooh-tah/zhlooh-tay

DAYS OF THE WEEK

Sunday	Neděle	neh-dyeh-leh
Monday	Pondělí	pon-dye-lee
Tuesday	Úterý	ooh-teh-ree
Wednesday	Středa	strzeh-dah
Thursday	Čtvrtek	stver-tehk
Friday	Pátek	pah-tek
Saturday	Sobota	soh-boh-ta

MONTHS

January	Leden	leh-dehn
February	Únor	ooh-nor
March	Březen	brzeh-zen
April	duben	dooh-ben
May	Květen	kvyeh-ten
June	Červen	cher-ven
July	Červenec	cher-ven-ets
August	Srpen	sir-pen
September	Záři	zahr-zhee
October	Říjen	rzhee-jen
November	Listopad	lihs-to-pad
December	Prosinec	pro-see-nets

USEFUL WORDS AND PHRASES

Do you speak English?	Mluvíte anglicky?	nluh-viy-tey ang-lits-kee
I don't speak [Language].	Nemluvím česky	nay-mlooh-veem ches-kee
I don't understand.	Nerozumím	neh-rohs-ooh-meem
I don't know.	Nevím	neh-veem
I understand.	Rozumím	rohs-ooh-meem
i'm American.	Jsem Američan/Američanka	sem ahm-er-itch-an/ahm-er-itch-an-ka
I'm British.	Jsem Brit/Britka	Sem vbit/btirt-ka

What's your name.	Jak se jmenujete?	jahk say yum-ehn-ooh-jah-tay
My name is ...	Jmenuji se	yum-ehn-ooh-yee say
What time is it?	Kolik je hodin?	koh-lick yay hoe-deen
How?	Jak	yahk
When?	Kdy	ka-dee
Yesterday	Včera	va-chair-ah
Today	Dnes	da-ness
Tomorrow	Zítra	zee-tra
This morning	Toto ráno	tow-tow rah-no
This afternoon	Toto odpoledne	tow-tow od-poe-led-nay
Tonight	Dnes večer	da-ness veh-chair
What?	Co?	tso
What is it?	Co je to?	tso tow jay
Why?	Proč?	proach
Who?	Kdo?	k-doh
Where is ...	Kde je	k-day yay
... the train station?	vlakové nádraží?	vlock-oh-vay nah-drah-zhee
... the subway station?	stanice metra?	stahn-eet-say met-rah
... the bus stop?	autobusová zastávka?	aut-oh-boos-oh-vah zah-stahv-ka
... the airport?	letiště?	leht-ist-yay
... the post office?	pošta?	poh-stah
... the bank?	banka?	ban-kah
... the hotel?	hotel?	hoh-tel
... the museum?	muzeum?	mooh-zay-uhm
... the hospital?	nemocnice?	nehm-ots-nee-tsa
... the elevator?	výtah?	vee-tahk
Where are the restrooms?	Kde jsou toalety?	k-day soh toh-ah-let-ee
Here/there	Tady/tam	tah-dee.tahm
Left/right	Vlevo/vpravo	v-leh-voh/v-prah-voh
Is it near/far?	Je to blízko/daleko?	yay tow blee-zsko/dah-lehk-oh
I'd like ...	Chtěl bych	k-tel bick
... a room	pokoj	poe-koy
... the key	klíč	kleech
... a newspaper	noviny	noh-vin-ee
... a stamp	známku	znahm-kooh
I'd like to buy ...	Chtěl bych koupit	k-tel bick ko-peet
... a city map	mapu města	mah-pooh myest-ah
... a road map	cestovní mapu	tsest-oh-vahn-ee mah-pooh
... a magaine	časopis	chas-owe-pis
... envelopes	obálky	oh-bahl-kee
... writing paper	papír na psaní	pah-peer nah psahn-ee
... a postcard	pohlednici	pih-ledneets-ee
... a ticket	lístek	lee-steck

How much is it?	Kolik to stojí?	ko-lick to stoy-ee
It's expensive/cheap	Je to drahé/levné	yay tow drah-ay/lev-nay
A little/a lot	Trochu/ hodně	trow-kew.hoed-nay
More/less	Více/méně	vitz-ay/men-ay
Enough/too (much)	Dost /příliš mnoho	doast/przee-leash m-no-hoe
I am ill/sick	Jsem nemocný/ nemocná	sem neh-mots-nee/ neh-mots-nah
Call a doctor	Zavolejte lékaře	zah-vol-ay-te lehk-arz-ay
Help!	Pomoc!	poh-mots
Stop!	Stop!	stop

DINING OUT

A bottle of ...	Láhev	la-hev
A cup of ...	Šálek	sha-lehk
A glass of ...	Sklenice	sklen-ee-tse
Beer	Pivo	pee-voh
Bill/check	Účet	ooh-chet
Bread	Chléb	kh-lehb
Breakfast	Snídaně	snee-dah-nay
Butter	Máslo	mah-slow
Cocktail/aperatif	Koktejl/aperitiv	cock-tail/ ap-er-teev
Coffee	Káva	kah-vah
Dinner	Večeře	vech-erzh-ay
Fixed-price menu	Nabídka s pevnou cenou	nah-mid-kah sa pev-noh sen-oh
Fork	Vidlička	vid-litch-kah
I am a vegetarian/I don't eat meat	Jsem vegetarián(ka)/ nejím maso	sem veg-et-air-ee-an(ka)/nay-jeem mah-so
I cannot eat ...	Nemohu jíst ...	nay-moh-oo jeest
I'd like to order ...	Chtěl bych objed-nat ...	k-tel bick o-byed-not
Is service included?	Je servis v ceně?	yay se-vis va tsen-ay
I'm hungry/thirsty	Mám hlad/žízeň	mom hlad.zee-zen
It's good/bad	Je to dobré/špatné	yay toe doh-brzay/ shpat-nay
It's hot/cold	To je teplá/studená	tow yay tep-lah/ stooh-den-ah
Knife	Nůž	noozh
Lunch	Oběd	oh-byed
Menu	Jídelní lístek	yih-del-nee lee-stek
Napkin	Ubrousek	ooh-bro-seck
Pepper	Pepř	pep-erzh
Plate	Talíř	tah-leerzh
Please give me ...	Prosím, dejte mi	ptoh-seem day-ty
Salt	Sůl	soohl
Spoon	Lžíce	lzh-itz-ay
Tea	Čaj	chay
Water	Voda	voh-dah
Wine	Víno	vee-noh

Great Itineraries

7 Days in Prague

Seven days is barely time to scratch this beautiful city's surface.

DAY 1: ARRIVAL, PRAŽSKÝ HRAD (PRAGUE CASTLE)

Even jet lag can't dampen the allure of Prague Castle, so it is a perfect place to hit on your first day in the city. The castle's 17-acre property contains a slew of attractions conveniently linked by internal courtyards. The showstopper is Katedrála sv. Víta (St. Vitus Cathedral, wherein lie the remains of fabled Czechs like Charles IV and St. Wenceslas). But don't forget to hit the Starý Královský palác (Old Royal Palace) and Lobkovický palác (Lobkowicz Palace), too. Also worth a gander is Zlatá ulička (Golden Lane): a row of crooked cottages, one of which was once occupied by Kafka.

DAY 2: JOSEFOV, STARÉ MĚSTO (OLD TOWN), AND NOVÉ MĚSTO (NEW TOWN)

Begin your day early in the Jewish Quarter. (Because it is best approached with a certain solemnity, arriving ahead of the tour groups is a definite advantage.) Here you will find Europe's oldest active synagogue—the Staronová synagóga (Old-New Synagogue), erected in 1270—as well as the Jewish Museum. Once you've seen the latter's evocative exhibits and paid your respects at the topsy-turvy Starý židovský hřbitov (Old Jewish Cemetery), saunter over to Staré Město to explore its centuries-old—and certifiably touristy—tangle of streets. Prepare to linger around Old Town Square, ideally timing your arrival to coincide with the striking of the newly restored astronomical clock. Later you can retrace the "Royal Way" (so named for the kings who trod it) that links the square with Prašná brána (the Powder Tower). Obecní dům (the Municipal House), an eye-popping

20th-century addition to Nové Město's medieval streetscape, is right beside it.

DAY 3: MALÁ STRANA

You shouldn't be surprised if the neighborhood you visit today looks familiar: after all, it has been featured in numerous movies ranging from *Amadeus* to *Spider-Man: Far from Home*. Filmmakers are drawn to its cobbled streets, beautifully preserved baroque buildings, and gorgeous formal gardens. Since the area seems to have a surprise at every turn, aimless wandering is Malá Strana's main pleasure; however, there is one site that deserves thorough investigation: Kostel sv. Mikuláše (Church of St. Nicholas)—an 18th-century beauty dedicated to Ol' Saint Nick. If you choose to climb the 215 steep steps of the church bell tower, you can reward your aching feet afterward by resting in Vrtbovská zahrada (Vrtba Garden) or taking an extended break in leafy Kampa Island Park before returning to Staré Město via the Charles Bridge.

DAY 4: VYŠEHRAD

The "Higher Castle" can be reached by the C line Metro to the Vyšehrad station, just two stops from Muzeum station. Nonetheless, it is off the radar for most people, and much less crowded, offering a bit of a breather from the hectic pace of the center. The origins of the complex go back over 1,000 years. The massive neo-Gothic-style Bazilika sv. Petra a Pavla (Basilika of Sts. Peter and Paul), with an art nouveau interior, has a shoulder bone from St. Valentine among its collection of valuable religious items. Behind the church is a stone column that legend claims was placed there by a devil. A cemetery adjacent to the church has graves of several notable people, including composer Antonín Dvořák. In the park, four large statues depict characters from early Czech history. The tunnels in the fortified walls, accessible to the public, contain some of the original statues from the Charles Bridge. A walk on top of the walls offers a stunning view of the Vltava River and Prague Castle.

DAY 5: HRADČANY AND STRAHOV

Hradčanské náměstí, the square in front of Prague Castle, is filled with palaces. Three are operated by the National Gallery. The Archbishop's Palace, still used by the Catholic Church, and Martinic Palace, in private hands, can be appreciated from the outside. Up the street, Loretánské náměstí has the imposing Černín Palace, now the Ministry of Foreign Affairs, and an attached public garden. Across from it is the Loreta, a baroque pilgrimage cloister with a rich collection of religious artifacts. Across the street from the nearby tram stop at Pohořelec, you can enter Strahov, a monastery complex with a beautifully preserved baroque library, a church where Mozart played the organ, and a microbrewery. On the way out, you can walk down through Petřín Park and stop at Petřín Tower, also called the Little Eiffel Tower.

DAY 6: TROJA, PRAGUE ZOO, AND THE PRAGUE BOTANICAL GARDENS

In the northern part of the city, a vast red-and-white château called Troja, named after the ancient city, has a grand ballroom with an opulent ceiling mural, sculpted staircases, and a large art collection. The baroque garden, with fountains and statues, is accessible without a ticket. Next to the château is Prague Zoo, considered one of the world's finest. New, modern pavilions and a restaurant have been built since the 2003 floods. The zoo actively works to preserve several endangered species. Up the hill from the zoo are the Prague Botanical Gardens, with their Fata Morgana tropical greenhouse, St. Claire's vineyard, and Japanese meditation garden.

DAY 7: DAY TRIP TO KUTNÁ HORA

If you are ready for a break from the city, Kutná Hora—44 miles east of Prague—is a memorable destination. Rich deposits of silver put this town on the map in the 12th century, and the premier local attractions are still tied to them. Chances are you will start your visit at Chrám sv. Barbory (St. Barbara's Cathedral), a divine Gothic sanctuary that was built with miners' donations. Afterward you can get the lowdown on mineralogy at the Czech Museum of Silver, then tour portions of an original silver mine and restored mint. (For a real heavy-metal experience, try coming in late June, when the town relives its glory days during the annual Royal Silvering Festival.) When in the area, it is also worth making a detour to suburban Sedlec to see the spooky Kostnice Ossuary, a bizarre church decorated with human bones. Photography inside is no longer permitted due to selfie-related damage.

Depending on what time you get back to Prague, you might explore a new neighborhood or just rest up for a big night on the town. One tempting alternative is to indulge in some last-minute shopping, whether opting for upscale items on Pařížská ulice or folksy mementos from the shops in the center. (Admit it: you're *dying* to have one of those omnipresent Mozart marionettes!) Before bedding down, revisit the Charles Bridge for a final floodlit look at Golden Prague. Although you'll be hard-pressed to take your eyes off the illuminated castle in the background, do take a moment to search among the many statues that decorate the span for the one depicting St. John Nepomuk. It's the eighth on the right, and—according to legend—travelers who rub it are bound to return.

A Walk through Old Town's Greatest Hits

There's a reason the Old Town is congested with people practically every day of the week—it's stuffed with A-list attractions, surrounded with looping cobblestoned streets, and bordered with eye-candy architecture from subtle *sgraffito* to bold baroque.

THE "ROYAL WAY"

Start on the perimeter of the Old Town. From the bottom of Wenceslas Square, turning right onto **Na příkopě**. A short detour down the first street on your left, Havířská, takes you to the 18th-century **Stavovské divadlo** (Estates Theater).

Return to Na příkopě, turn left, and continue to the street's end, **N áměstí Republiky** (Republic Square). Two stunning buildings, constructed hundreds of years apart, anchor the area. Centuries of grime have not diminished the majesty of the Gothic **Prašná brána** (Powder Tower), with its stately spires looming above the square. Adjacent to this tower, the rapturous art nouveau **Obecní dům** (Municipal Hall) looks like a brightly decorated confection.

Walk through the archway of the Powder Tower and down the formal **Celetná** street, the first leg of the "Royal Way." The cubist building at Celetná No. 34 is the **Dům U černé Matky boží** (House of the Black Madonna); look for the miniature Madonna placed on the corner of the building.

THE HEART OF OLD TOWN

After a few blocks, Celetná opens onto the justly famous **Staroměstské náměstí** (Old Town Square), the beating heart of the Old Town with dazzling architecture on all sides. On the east side of the square, the double-spire church **Kostel Panny Marie před Týnem** (Týn Church) rises from behind a row of patrician houses. To the immediate left of this, at No. 13, is **Dům U Kamenného zvonu** (Stone Bell

A Walk through Old Town's Greatest Hits

WHERE TO START:
The northern end of Wenceslas Square.

TIME/LENGTH:
Three to four hours.

WHERE TO STOP:
The Klementinum complex.

BEST TIME TO GO:
For fewer crowds, time your visit for early morning on the weekends. Hit the Astronomical Clock 10 minutes before the hour.

WORST TIME TO GO:
Saturday afternoon when crowds are at their peak. Evenings are also surprisingly busy.

HIGHLIGHTS:
Stavovské divadlo, Obecní dům, Staroměstské náměstí, Staroměstská radnice, Klementinum.

WHERE TO REFUEL:
Au Gourmand, just outside Old Town Square on Dlouhá street, offers a tranquil garden where you can enjoy pastries or a sandwich. Around the corner from Obecní dům, you'll also find the Hotel Paříž: its café serves up hearty omelets.

House), a baroque town house that has been stripped down to its original Gothic elements. Next door, at No. 12, stands the gorgeous pink-and-ocher **Palác Kinských** (Kinsky Palace), considered the most prominent example of late baroque–rococo in the area. At this end of the square, you can't help noticing the gigantic expressive **Jan Hus monument.**

Beyond this is the Gothic **Staroměstská radnice** (Old Town Hall) with its impressive 200-foot tower that gives the square gravitas. As the hour approaches, join the people milling below the tower's 15th-century astronomical clock for a brief but curiously compelling spectacle. The square's second church is the baroque **Kostel svatého Mikuláše** (St. Nicholas Church).

TOWARD THE KLEMENTINUM
Turn left and continue along U Radnice proper a few yards until you come to **Malé náměstí,** a mini-square with arcades

on one side. Look for tiny Karlova street, which begins in the southwest corner of the square, and take another quick right to stay on it. This cobbled medieval street draws the attention with its quaint souvenir shops, restaurants, and theaters, but keep an eye on where you're going (it has a habit of confounding visitors). While strolling, you may find yourself lured away by the exotic **Clam-Gallas palác** at Husova 20.

A block north, the street opens onto Mariánské náměstí, where you'll discover the entrance to the **Klementinum,** a grouping of historic buildings once used as a Jesuit stronghold.

Contacts

Air

AIRPORT Václav Havel Airport. (*PRG*). ☎ 220–111–888 ⊕ www.prg.aero.

Bus

ČSAD. ✉ Florenc station, Křižíkova 4, Karlín ☎ 221–895–111 ⊕ www.idos.cz Ⓜ Lines B and C: Florenc. **Flixbus.** ✉ Florenc station, Křižíkova 4, Karlín ⊕ www.flixbus.cz Ⓜ Lines B and C: Florenc. **RegioJet.** ✉ Prague ☎ 222–222–221 ⊕ www.regiojet.cz.

Car

CAR RENTAL AGENCIES Avis. ✉ Prague ☎ 810–777–810 in Czech Republic, 800/230–4898 in U.S. ⊕ www.avis.com. **Budget.** ✉ Prague ☎ 800/472–3325 in U.S. ⊕ www.budget.com. **Europcar.** ✉ Prague ☎ 235–364–531 for reservations at Václav Havel Airport in Prague ⊕ www.europcar.com.

Ⓜ Metro

METRO Dopravní Podnik. ✉ Prague ⊕ www.dpp.cz.

TRANSIT INFORMATION CENTERS Muzeum. ☎ 296–191–817. **Nádraží Veleslavín.** ✉ Prague ☎ 296–191–817.

Václav Havel Airport. ✉ Prague ☎ 296–191–817.

Taxi

AAA Radiotaxi. ✉ Prague ☎ 222–333–222 ⊕ www.aaa-taxi.cz. **City Taxi.** ✉ Prague ☎ 257–257–257 ⊕ www.citytaxi.cz. **Tick Tack.** ✉ Prague ☎ 721–300–300 ⊕ www.ticktack.cz.

⊕ Train

Čedok. ✉ Na příkopě 18, Prague ☎ 800/112–112 toll-free, 221–447–256 for incoming tourists ⊕ www.cedok.cz. **Czech Railways.** ✉ Prague ⊕ www.cd.cz. **Eurail.** ✉ Prague ⊕ www.eurail.com. **Leo Express.** ✉ Prague ☎ 220–311–700 ⊕ www.le.cz. **RegioJet.** ✉ Prague ☎ 222–222–221 ⊕ www.regiojet.cz.

⚠ Emergencies

Autoklub Bohemia Assistance. ✉ Prague ☎ 1240 ⊕ www.aba.cz. **Ambulance.** ✉ Prague ☎ 155. **Na Homolce Hospital.** ✉ Roentgenova 2, Prague ☎ 257–271–111 ⊕ www.homolka.cz. **Prague City Police.** ✉ Prague ☎ 156. **State Police.** ✉ Prague ☎ 158 ⊕ www.policie.cz. **ÚAMK Emergency Roadside**

Assistance. ✉ Prague ☎ 261–104–333 ⊕ www.uamk.cz.

DOCTORS AND DENTISTS Dental Office H33. ✉ Hvězdova 33, Prague ☎ 733–737–337 ⊕ www.dental-office.cz/en/. **Lékárna U sv. Ludmily.** ✉ Belgická 37, Nové Mesto ☎ 222–519–731.

🇺🇸 U.S. Embassy/Consulate

U.S. Embassy. ✉ Tržiště 15, Prague ☎ 257–022–000 ⊕ www.usembassy.cz.

🛏 Lodging

APARTMENT AND HOUSE RENTALS Airbnb. ✉ Prague ⊕ www.airbnb.com. **Flipkey.** ✉ Prague ⊕ www.flipkey.com. **Interhome.** ✉ Prague ☎ 800/882–6864 ⊕ www.interhome.us.

◉ Visitor Information

CONTACTS Czech Tourist Authority. ✉ Prague ⊕ www.czechtourism.com. **Prague City Tourism.** ✉ Staroměstska radnice (Old Town Hall), Staroměstské nám., Staré Mesto ☎ 221–714–714 ⊕ www.prague.eu.

Chapter 3

STARÉ MĚSTO (OLD TOWN) AND JOSEFOV

Updated by
Jennifer Rigby

● Sights	🍴 Restaurants	🛏 Hotels	● Shopping	▼ Nightlife
★★★★★	★★★★★	★★★★★	★★★☆☆	★★★★☆

NEIGHBORHOOD SNAPSHOT

TOP EXPERIENCES

- **Old Town Square:** It's not described as one of the most beautiful squares in Europe for nothing. Get here early in the morning to beat the crowds.

- **Lokál Dlouháááá:** Clink foaming mugs of fresh beer and enjoy modern takes on classic Czech cooking.

- **Shopping:** Look for botanical cosmetics made from beer, cool designer clothing, and antique treasure troves.

- **Barokní knihovní sál:** One of the most beautiful concert halls in all of Prague is also home to one of its best classical music ensembles.

- **Bokovka:** Go back in time to a gorgeous twilight crumbling courtyard for delicious local and international wines.

GETTING HERE

- Josefov, the Jewish Quarter, is one of the most heavily visited areas in Prague, especially in peak tourist seasons, when its tiny streets are jammed to bursting. The best way to visit is on foot—it's a short hop over from Staroměstské náměstí (Old Town Square).

GETTING HERE

There's little public transit in Staré Město, so walking is really the most practical way to get around. It takes about 15 minutes to walk from the Prašná brána (Powder Tower, one of the original city gates) across to the Staré Město end of the Charles Bridge, which leads you into Malá Strana (Lesser Quarter). If you're coming to Staré Město from another part of Prague, three metro stops circumscribe the area: Staroměstská on the west, Náměstí Republiky on the east, and Můstek on the south, at the point where Staré Město and Václavské náměstí (Wenceslas Square) meet.

PLANNING YOUR TIME

Remember to be in Old Town Square just before the hour if you want to see the astronomical clock in action, and prepare for crowds. The best (read: less crowded) time to visit Josefov is early morning, when the museums and cemetery first open. The area itself is very compact, and a fairly thorough tour should take only half a day. Don't go on the Sabbath (Saturday), when all the museums are closed.

Staré Město is usually, rightly, the first stop for any visitor to Prague. Old Town Square, its gorgeous houses and churches, and the astronomical clock are blockbuster attractions, and the winding streets around the square are worth visiting in their own right, with shops, restaurants, and historic buildings galore, from Kafka's former apartment to the theater where Mozart premiered *Don Giovanni.*

For centuries Prague had an active, vital Jewish community that was an exuberant part of the city's culture. Much of that activity was concentrated in Josefov, the former Jewish ghetto, just a short walk north of Old Town Square and entirely enclosed by the rest of Staré Město. This area first became a Jewish settlement around the 12th century, but it didn't actually take on the physical aspects of a ghetto—walled off from the rest of the city—until much later.

Staré Město (Old Town)

Founded in 1231 and dense with stellar examples of Gothic architecture, as well as many other styles, history still feels alive on the cobbled streets of Staré Město—that is, if you can ignore the sometimes intrusive crowds, brightly lit shop fronts, and assorted tourist paraphernalia. Approaching the district from the north of Wenceslas Square—its base, the opposite end from the statue and

the museum—is a good place to begin a tour of the area, as this T-intersection marks the border between the old and new worlds in Prague. A quick glance around reveals the often jarring juxtaposition: centuries-old buildings sit side by side with modern retail chains such as Starbucks, but in the main, there are still, astonishingly, authentic places to eat, drink, and be merry, as well as some of the capital's hippest shops. Staying here puts you right in the heart of the action but comes with the caveat that it can be noisy. To drown it out, the classical concerts in some of the city's most beautiful concert halls and churches are a hauntingly beautiful experience, or if jazz is more your style, a handful of atmospheric cellar bars have you covered.

 Sights

Betlémská kaple (*Bethlehem Chapel*)
CHURCH | The original church was built at the end of the 14th century, and the Czech religious reformer Jan Hus was

Sights ▼

1 Betlémská kaple C7
2 Celetná ulice F5
3 Dům U černé
  Matky boží G5
4 Jan Hus monument. E5
5 Klášter sv. Anežky
  České -
  National Gallery F2
6 Klementium B5
7 Kostel Matky
  Boží před Týnem E5
8 Kostel sv. Jiljí D6
9 Kostel sv.
  Martina ve zdi D8
10 Kostel sv.
  Mikuláše D5
11 Palác Kinských E4
12 Prašná brána H5
13 Staroměstská radnice... E5
14 Staroměstské
  náměstí E5

Restaurants ▼

1 Banh-mi-ba G3
2 Cotto Crudo B5
3 Dhaba Beas F4
4 Divinis F4
5 Krčma D4
6 La Degustation
  Bohême Bourgeoise F3
7 La Finestra in Cucina C5
8 Lokál Dlouhááá G3
9 Maitrea E4
10 Marina B4
11 Naše Maso G3
12 V Kolkovně E3
13 Yami G2
14 Zdenek's Oyster Bar F4

Quick Bites ▼

1 Au Gourmand E4
2 Background C7
3 Bakeshop Praha E3
4 Burrito Loco F4
5 Havelská Koruna E6
6 Mansson's Bakery D3
7 Piknik Dhlouhá G3

Hotels ▼

1 Buddha-Bar Hotel G4
2 Design Hotel Jewel
  Prague E7
3 Four Seasons Hotel
  Prague B5
4 Grand Hotel
  Bohemia G5
5 Grand Hotel Praha E5
6 Hotel Residence
  Agnes G2
7 Hotel U Zlatého
  Jelena F5
8 Iron Gate Hotel
  and Suites D6
9 Josef G3
10 The Mozart Prague B7
11 Unitas Hotel C8
12 Ventana Hotel
  Prague F5

KEY

- ❶ Sights
- ❶ Restaurants
- ❶ Quick Bites
- ❶ Hotels
- Ⓜ Metro Station
- 🛈 Tourist
  Information

a regular preacher here from 1402 until his exile in 1412. Here he gave the mass in "vulgar" Czech—not in Latin as the church in Rome demanded. After the Thirty Years' War in the 17th century, the chapel fell into the hands of the Jesuits and was demolished in 1786. Excavations carried out after World War I uncovered the original portal and three windows; the entire church was reconstructed during the 1950s. Although little remains of the first church, some remnants of Hus's teachings can still be read on the inside walls. ⊠ *Betlémské nám. 3, Staré Město* ☎ *234–678–790* ⊕ *bethlehemchapel.eu* 🎟 *60 Kč* Ⓜ *Line A: Staroměstská.*

Celetná ulice
STREET | This is the main thoroughfare connecting Old Town Square and Náměstí Republiky; it's packed day and (most of the) night. Many of the street's façades are styled in the classic 17th- or 18th-century manner, but appearances are deceiving: nearly all of the houses in fact have foundations that, astonishingly, date back to the 12th century. Be sure to look above the street-level storefronts to see the fine examples of baroque detail. ⊠ *Staré Město* Ⓜ *Lines A and B: Můstek.*

Dům U černé Matky boží (*House at the Black Madonna*)
NOTABLE BUILDING | This building, designed by Josef Gočár, is a shining example of (relatively) modern Czech architecture amid Staré Město's historical splendor. In the second decade of the 20th century, young Czech architects boldly applied cubism's radical reworking of visual space to architecture and design, with the characteristic geometric lines and sharp angles of the building's exterior the result. Once a department store, there's now a permanent Czech cubism exhibition inside and a café. Its name— House at the Black Madonna—comes from the 17th-century sculpture that still sits on the building's northeast corner. ⊠ *Ovocný trh 19, Staré Město* ☎ *776–623–016* ⊕ *www.czkubismus.cz/en/*

the-house-at-the-black-madonna 🎟 *150 Kč* ⊘ *Closed Mon.* Ⓜ *Line B: Náměstí Republiky.*

Jan Hus Monument
PUBLIC ART | Few memorials in Prague have consistently elicited as much controversy as this one, dedicated in July 1915, exactly 500 years after Hus was burned at the stake in Constance, Germany. Some maintain that the monument's secessionist style (the inscription seems to come right from turn-of-the-20th-century Vienna) clashes with the Gothic and baroque style of the square. Others dispute the romantic depiction of Hus, who appears here as tall and bearded in flowing garb, whereas the real Hus, as historians maintain, was short and had a baby face. Either way, the fiery preacher's influence is not in dispute. His ability to transform doctrinal disagreements, both literally and metaphorically, into the language of the common man made him into a religious and national symbol for the Czechs. ⊠ *Staroměstské nám., Staré Město* Ⓜ *Line A: Staroměstská.*

Klášter sv. Anežky České - National Gallery (*St. Agnes's Convent*)
ART GALLERY | Near the river between Pařížská and Revoluční ulice, in the northeastern corner of Staré Město, this peaceful complex has Prague's first buildings in the Gothic style. Built between the 1230s and the 1280s, St. Agnes's Convent provides a fitting home for the National Gallery's marvelous collection of Czech and Central European Gothic art, including altarpieces, portraits, and statues from the 13th to the 16th century. There is an interesting collection of contemporary Czech sculpture in the gardens, too, which are free to enter and open year-round. ⊠ *U Milosrdných 17, Staré Město* ☎ *224–301–122* ⊕ *ngprague.cz* 🎟 *220 Kč* ⊘ *Closed Mon.* Ⓜ *Line A: Staroměstská.*

The Klementium's Baroque Library houses more than 20,000 volumes of mostly foreign theological literature from the beginning of the 17th century until recent times.

★ Klementinum

LIBRARY | It's advertised as the most beautiful library in the world and delivers on the hype. The origins of this massive, ancient complex date back to the 12th and 13th centuries, but it's best known as the stronghold of the Jesuits, who occupied it for more than 200 years beginning in the early 1600s. Though many buildings are closed to the public, the resplendent Baroque Library is a hidden gem featuring fabulous ceiling murals that portray the three levels of knowledge, with the "Dome of Wisdom" as a centerpiece. Next door, the Mirror Chapel is a symphony of surfaces, with acoustics to match. Mozart played here, and the space still hosts chamber music concerts, as does the library itself if you're lucky. The Astronomical Tower in the middle of the complex offers stunning 360-degree views of Staré Město and was once used by game-changing astronomer Johannes Kepler and afterward functioned as the "Prague Meridian," where the time was set each day. Nowadays, you can visit the complex and glimpse the beauty, as well as some historic astronomical instruments, only on guided tours, which run every half hour. ■ **TIP→ There is no elevator to the Astronomical Tower rooftop and the steps are steep, so you may want to avoid this section if you have walking difficulties.** ✉ *Mariánské nám. 5, Staré Město* ☎ *222–220–879* ⊕ *klementinum.com* ✉ *300 Kč (incl. tour)* Ⓜ *Line A: Staroměstská.*

Kostel Matky Boží před Týnem (*Church of Our Lady before Týn, or Týn Church*)
CHURCH | The twin-spired Týn Church is an Old Town Square landmark and one of the city's best examples of Gothic architecture, looming over the former school building below. The church's exterior was in part the work of Peter Parler, the architect responsible for the Charles Bridge and Katedrála sv. Víta (St. Vitus Cathedral). Construction of the twin black-spire towers began a little later, in 1461, by King Jiří of Poděbrady, during the heyday of the Hussites. Jiří had a gilded chalice, the symbol of the Hussites, proudly displayed on the front gable between

the two towers. Following the defeat of the Czech Protestants by the Catholic Habsburgs in the 17th century, the chalice was melted down and made into the Madonna's glimmering halo (you can still see it resting between the spires). Much of the interior, including the tall nave, was rebuilt in the baroque style in the 17th century. Some Gothic pieces remain, however: look to the left of the main altar for a beautifully preserved set of early carvings. The main altar itself was painted by Karel Škréta, a luminary of the Czech baroque. The church also houses the tomb of renowned Danish (and Prague court) astronomer Tycho Brahe, who died in 1601. The church's full name—Church of Our Lady before Týn—comes from the name of the courtyard behind it. ⊠ *Staroměstské nám. between Celetná and Týnská, Staré Město* ☎ *222–318–186* ⊕ *tyn.cz* ✉ *Free* ☾ *Closed Mon.* Ⓜ *Line A: Staroměstská.*

Kostel sv. Jiljí (*Church of St. Giles*)
CHURCH | Replete with buttresses and a characteristic portal, this church's exterior is a powerful and beautiful example of Gothic architecture—famed Czech director Miloš Forman certainly thought so, shooting some of his hit film *Amadeus* inside. An important outpost of Czech Protestantism in the 16th century, the church reflects baroque style inside, with a design by Johann Bernhard Fischer von Erlach and sweeping frescoes by Václav Reiner. The interior can be viewed during the day from the vestibule or at the evening concerts held several times a week. ⊠ *Husova 8, Staré Město* ☎ *607–855–215* ⊕ *praha.op.cz* ✉ *Free* Ⓜ *Line A: Staroměstská.*

Kostel sv. Martina ve zdi (*Church of St. Martin-in-the-Wall*)
CHURCH | It was here, in this humble-looking corner church, that Holy Communion was first given to the Bohemian laity in the form of both bread and wine, way back in 1414. (The Catholic custom of the time dictated only bread would

be offered to the masses, with wine reserved for priests and clergy.) From then on, the chalice came to symbolize the Hussite movement. The church's interior doesn't rival other grander religious buildings in Staré Město, but neverthless it is open to the public for a quick peek every afternoon. German- and Czech-language services are held, too, and evening concerts. ⊠ *Martinská 8, Staré Město* ☎ *734–767–335* ⊕ *martinvezdi.eu* ✉ *Free* ☾ *Closed Sun. and until 3 pm and after 5 pm daily (excl. services)* Ⓜ *Lines A and B: Můstek.*

Kostel sv. Mikuláše (*Church of St. Nicholas*)
CHURCH | While there has been a site of worship at this location since the 13th century, the church still standing was designed in the 18th century by Prague's own master of late baroque, Kilian Ignaz Dientzenhofer. Overall, it's probably less successful in capturing the style's lyric exuberance than its name-twin across town, the Kostel sv. Mikulase (Church of St. Nicholas) in Mala Strana; but Dientzenhofer utilized the limited space to create a well-balanced structure, and it

can offer a moment of peace from Staré Město crowds. The interior is compact, with a beautiful chandelier and an enormous black organ that overwhelms the rear of the church. Afternoon and evening concerts for visitors are held almost continuously—walk past and you're sure to get leafleted for one. ✉ Staroměstské nám., Staré Město ☎ 606-064-769 ⊕ svmikulas.cz ✉ Free, fee for concerts Ⓜ Line A: Staroměstská.

Palác Kinských (Kinský Palace)
NOTABLE BUILDING | This exuberant building, built in 1765 from Kilian Ignaz Dientzenhofer's design, is considered one of Prague's finest rococo, late baroque structures. With its exaggerated pink overlay and numerous statues, it looks extravagant when contrasted with the marginally more somber baroque elements of other nearby buildings. (The interior, alas, was "modernized" under communism.) The palace once contained a German school—where Franz Kafka studied for nine misery-laden years—and now houses revolving temporary exhibitions and a shop. Communist leader Klement Gottwald, alongside comrade Vladimír Clementis, first addressed the crowds from this building after seizing power in February 1948—an event recounted in the first chapter of Milan Kundera's novel The Book of Laughter and Forgetting. ✉ Staroměstské nám. 12, Staré Město ☎ 224-301-122 ⊕ ngprague.cz ✉ 220 Kč ☾ Closed Mon. Ⓜ Line A: Staroměstská.

Prašná brána (Powder Tower or Powder Gate)
VIEWPOINT | Once used as storage space for gunpowder, this dark, imposing tower, covered in a web of carvings, offers a striking view of Staré Město and Prague Castle from the top. King Vladislav II of Jagiello began construction—it replaced one of the city's 13 original gates—in 1475. At the time, the kings of Bohemia maintained their royal residence next door, on the site now occupied by the

Sgraffiti Is Not a Crime ⊙

Sgraffiti, the plural of sgraffito, is a process where two contrasting shades of plaster are used on the façade of a building. Often the sgraffiti serve to highlight the original architecture; other times they can produce an optical illusion, painting brickwork and balconies from thin air. Walls can also be covered with lively classical pictures, which make houses resemble enormous Grecian vases. One of the best examples of sgraffiti is on Kafka's former residence, U Minuty, just next to the clock tower on Old Town Square.

Obecní dům (Municipal House). The tower was intended to be the grandest gate of all. Vladislav, however, was Polish and somewhat disliked by the rebellious Czech citizens of Prague. Nine years after he assumed power, fearing for his life, he moved the royal court across the river to Prague Castle. Work on the tower was abandoned, and the half-finished structure remained a depository for gunpowder until the end of the 17th century. The golden spires were not added until the end of the 19th century. The ticket office is on the first floor after you go up the dizzyingly narrow stairwell. ✉ Nám. Republiky 5/1090, Staré Město ☎ 775-400-052 ⊕ prague.eu/prasnabrana ✉ 150 Kč Ⓜ Line B: Náměstí Republiky.

★ **Staroměstská radnice** (Old Town Hall)
NOTABLE BUILDING | The hall draws hundreds of visitors on every hour to hear and watch the mechanical figures of the famous astronomical clock (although it's worth a look, don't be disappointed by the lack of drama. Focus on its astonishing age instead: it was first installed on the tower in 1410). Look to the upper

The most significant square of historical Prague, Old Town Square was founded in the 12th century and has been witness to many historical events.

part of the clock, where a skeleton tolls a death knell and turns an hourglass upside down. The 12 apostles promenade by, and then a cockerel flaps its wings and screeches as the hour strikes. This 15th-century marvel indicates the time by the season, the zodiac sign, and the positions of the sun and moon; the calendar under the clock dates from the mid-19th century, although it's a replica. The building was Staré Město's administrative center beginning in 1338; the impressive 200-foot Town Hall Tower was first built in the 14th century. For a rare view of Staré Město's maze of crooked streets, climb the ramp or ride the elevator to the top of the tower. Tours of the interiors depart from the main desk inside. ✉ Staroměstské nám., Staré Město ⊕ staromestskaradnicepraha.cz 🎫 Tours 250 Kč ⊗ Closed Mon. Ⓜ Line A: Staroměstská.

★ **Staroměstské náměstí** (*Old Town Square*)

PLAZA/SQUARE | The hype about Old Town Square is completely justified.

Picture a perimeter of colorful baroque houses contrasting with the sweeping old-Gothic style of the Týn Church in the background. The unexpectedly large size gives it a majestic presence as it opens up from feeder alleyways. As the heart of Staré Město, the square grew to its present proportions when Prague's original marketplace moved away from the river in the 12th century. Its shape and appearance have changed little since that time (the monument to religious reformer Jan Hus, at the center of the square, was erected in the early 20th century). During the day the square pulses with activity, as musicians vie for the attention of visitors milling about. In summer, the square's south end is dominated by sprawling (pricey!) outdoor restaurants. During the Easter and Christmas seasons it fills with wooden booths of vendors selling everything from simple wooden toys to fine glassware and mulled wine. At night, the brightly lit towers of the Týn Church rise gloriously over the glowing baroque façades. But the square's history is not all wine and music: during the 15th century the square was the focal point of conflict between Czech Hussites and the mainly Catholic Austrians and Germans. In 1422 the radical Hussite preacher Jan Želivský was executed here for his part in storming the Nové Město (New Town) town hall three years earlier. In the 1419 uprising a judge, a mayor, and seven city council members were thrown out a window—the first of Prague's many famous defenestrations. Within a few years the Hussites had taken over the town, expelled many of the Catholics, and set up their own administration. Embedded in the square's paving stones, at the base of Old Town Hall, are 27 white crosses marking the spot where 27 Bohemian noblemen were killed by the Austrian Habsburgs in 1621 during the dark days following the defeat of the Czechs at the Battle of White Mountain. The grotesque spectacle, designed to quash any further national or religious opposition, took about five hours to complete, as the men were put to the sword or hanged one by one. ⊠ *Staré Město* Ⓜ *Line A: Staroměstská.*

🍴 Restaurants

Staré Město is where visitors spend most of their time and where most of the best (and worst) restaurants are found. Ironically, perhaps the worst place to have a meal is directly on Old Town Square. Sadly, pretty much all places here are tourist traps. Instead, try exploring the area around Dlouhá to the northeast of the square, which boasts lots of fine dining, wine bars, and new high-end Czech eateries. As for the other parts of Staré Město, things have improved a lot in recent years, but it's probably still a good area to stick closely to the recommendations in this book. If there's someone hustling for patrons outside or offering "traditional Czech food" via a blackboard with no sign of prices (worst case scenario: with pictures), go elsewhere.

Banh-mi-ba
$$ | VIETNAMESE | Enjoy fresh, zingy Vietnamese food at this small, trendy spot on Rybná, from the eponymous baguettes to rolls, salads, and pho. There are good Vietnamese joints all over Prague thanks to ties between formerly communist Czechoslovakia and Hanoi, but until recently Staré Město was lacking its own standout. **Known for:** tasty Vietnamese baguettes; no glutamate additions; cool Czech couples grabbing a bite. Ⓢ *Average main: Kč150* ⊠ *Rybná 26, Staré Město* ☏ *734–487–324* ⊕ *banhmiba.cz* Ⓜ *Line B: Náměstí Republiky.*

Cotto Crudo
$$$$ | ITALIAN | Having settled into its role as a leading light on Prague's culinary scene, the kitchen here dwells on crafting definitive Italian fare, overseen by chef Marco Veneruso. The comfortable Four Seasons restaurant and terrace (which has fantastic river views) graciously serves some of the finest Mediterranean cuisine in Prague. **Known for:** quality Italian food; faultless service; special-occasion feel. Ⓢ *Average main: Kč800* ⊠ *Four Seasons Prague, Veleslavinova 21, Staré Město* ☏ *221–426–880* ⊕ *facebook.com/cottocrudo* Ⓜ *Line A: Staroměstská.*

Dhaba Beas
$ | VEGETARIAN | Right behind the soaring spires of Staré Město's Týn Church, Beas offers inexpensive, Indian-style vegetarian and vegan food just a short walk from Old Town Square. Don't expect upscale service—you're going to bus your own table—but these dishes are worth the extra work. **Known for:** tasty curries; bringing vegetables to Old Town Square's meat-heavy dining roster; relaxed DIY service. Ⓢ *Average main: Kč80* ⊠ *Týnská 19, Staré Město* ☏ *608–035–727* ⊕ *beas-dhaba.cz* ▭ *No credit cards* Ⓜ *Line B: Náměstí Republiky.*

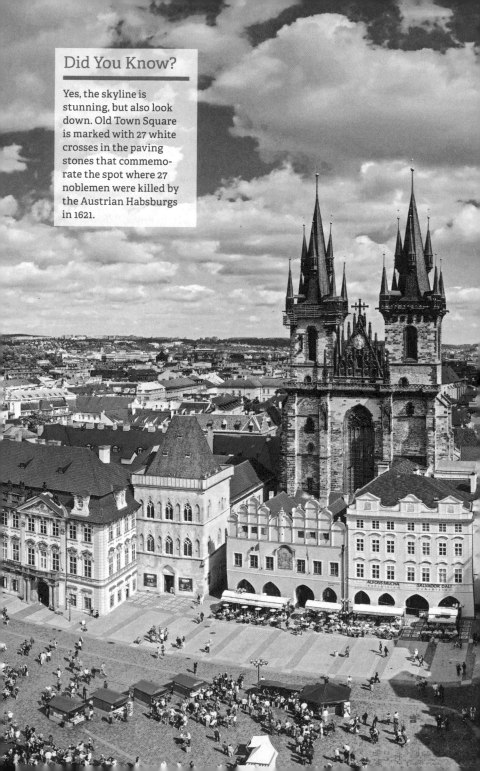

Did You Know?

Yes, the skyline is stunning, but also look down. Old Town Square is marked with 27 white crosses in the paving stones that commemorate the spot where 27 noblemen were killed by the Austrian Habsburgs in 1621.

Hunting for Dumplings

The quality of Bohemian cooking declined precipitously during the communist period, and bad habits were hard to shake in the aftermath of the 1989 revolution. Consequently, Czech cuisine has gotten an undeserved bad rap. Thankfully, some restaurateurs have taken up the baton to right past wrongs, and if you know where to go, it's now pretty easy to find excellent traditional cooking outside the home. And as for the famed dumplings? Well, both the bread and potato versions are a must-try. Note: they can be quite dense (perhaps to fuel locals through the notorious Czech winters).

The Ambiente group, in particular, sees it as a priority to revive historic recipes and cooking techniques. This chain's flagship **La Degustation Bohême Bourgeoise** (✉ Haštalská ☎ 18222–311–234) offers a multicourse tasting menu using recipes from the 19th century. It's a bit pricey but it's stand-out modern Czech cookery. The chain also runs the far cheaper **Lokál Dlouháááá** (✉ Dlouhá ☎ 33222–316–265), and for much less money you can taste excellent renditions of pub staples like guláš and fried pork cutlets in an old-school pub atmosphere.

Brewpubs are another alternative for finding well-done domestic cooking. Good examples are the Pilsner Urquell chain, which runs **V Kolkovně** (✉ V Kolkovně ☎ 8224–819–701) in Josefov, as well as other similar establishments at a few other locations around town, including **Kulat'ák** (✉ Vítězné nám. ☎ 12773–973–037) in Dejvice. Here you'll find high standards for traditional Czech cuisine in a sleek environment with good service and fresh beers.

Divinis
$$$ | ITALIAN | The simple decor—white walls and plank floors—at this wine-centric Italian restaurant on a quiet street near the Týn Church belies the quality and complexity of its food. Whether you stick to a simpler beef carpaccio or try something more complex like goat cheese and truffle mousse, the dishes are skillfully prepared and attractively presented. **Known for:** complex Italian cooking; great wine; celeb chef Zdeněk Pohlreich. Ⓢ *Average main: Kč500* ✉ *Týnská 21, Staré Město* ☎ *220–510–951* ⊕ *divinis.cz* ⊘ *Closed Sun.* Ⓜ *Line A: Staroměstská.*

Krčma
$$ | CZECH | There are lots of pub-restaurants in Staré Město like Krčma—all beer, hearty Czech classics. and brick-lined cellar—but this is the best of the bunch. Staff are friendly, prices are reasonable, it's not usually mobbed, and it retains a whiff of authenticity. **Known for:** traditional Czech food; authentic feel; fresh brews. Ⓢ *Average main: Kč250* ✉ *Kostečná 4, Staré Město* ☎ *725–157–262* ⊕ *krcma.cz* Ⓜ *Line B: Staroměstská.*

★ La Degustation Bohême Bourgeoise
$$$$ | ECLECTIC | One of Prague's two Michelin star holders is this elegant tasting room, where diners are taken on a superlative culinary adventure via a Czech-inspired tasting menu over an extended evening. The menu roves around Czech and European cuisine playfully and stylishly, including classic local specialties with a twist, like pork belly, cabbage, and mustard or a dessert of cream, blueberry, and basil. **Known for:** probably Prague's best food and service; playful and inventive takes on

classic dishes; wine-paired tasting menu. $ Average main: Kč2450 ✉ Haštalská 18, Staré Město ☎ 222–311–234 ⊕ ladegustation.cz Ⓜ Line A: Staroměstská.

★ La Finestra in Cucina

$$$ | **ITALIAN** | One of Prague's hottest tables, La Finestra is the meaty counterpart to its sister restaurant, Aromi, right down to the wooden tables and brick walls. Catering to local gourmands and boldface names, this restaurant lives up to the hype. **Known for:** organic dry-aged meats, foccacia and fried chickpeas to nibble on, and expert al dente pastas like spaghetti with sea urchin; extensive Italian wine selection; cooking classes. $ Average main: Kč500 ✉ Platnéřská 13, Staré Město ☎ 222–325–325 ⊕ lafinestra.lacollezione.cz Ⓜ Line A: Staroměstská.

★ Lokál Dlouháááá

$$ | **CZECH** | Sleek and relatively sophisticated, Lokál Dlouháááá takes the Czech pub concept to a new level with fresh local ingredients, perfectly poured beers, and friendly, efficient service. It makes for an idealized version of a corner restaurant out of another era, right down to the stark white walls, waiters in vests, and bathrooms wallpapered with old pinups and airplane posters. **Known for:** high-quality Czech food; fast and friendly service; always being busy (and noisy). $ Average main: Kč175 ✉ Dlouhá 33, Staré Město ☎ 734–283–874 ⊕ lokal-dlouha.ambi.cz Ⓜ Line B: Náměstí Republiky.

Maitrea

$$ | **VEGETARIAN** | Vegetarians, you're in luck: the Czech Republic's best vegetarian restaurant just happens to be a five-minute walk from Old Town Square. Here, veg food is not viewed as a radical departure from other cuisines; indeed, most of the dishes, a mish-mash of global favorites, look and taste close to the originals, only without the meat. **Known for:** veggie versions of Czech classics like ; Buddhist-inspired vibes; long waits for a table. $ Average main: Kč300 ✉ Týnská

ulička 6, Staré Město ☎ 221–711–631 ⊕ restaurace-maitrea.cz Ⓜ Line A: Staroměstská.

Marina

$$ | **ITALIAN** | You don't have to splurge at expensive places like Kampa Park for regal dining vistas over the Charles Bridge or Prague Castle. For the price of a pizza or pasta, you can sit on the deck of this marina, anchored off the Vltava River. **Known for:** unbeatable views to the castle; reasonable prices for well-executed Italian staples; dining on the water. $ Average main: Kč280 ✉ Alšovo nábř. 1, Staré Město ☎ 605–454–020 ⊕ marinaristorante.cz Ⓜ Line A: Staroměstská.

Naše Maso

$$ | **CZECH** | Butcher shops are serious business in the Czech Republic and many have barely changed for generations, at least in terms of offerings. This newly updated version, with friendlier service and a handy lunch counter, stocks dozens of sausage varieties, classic smoked meats, and delicate fillets of pork and beef. **Known for:** meat galore; standing room only; a glorious. $ Average main: Kč180 ✉ Dlouhá 39, Staré Město ☎ 222–311–378 ⊕ nasemaso.cz ▤ No credit cards ☾ No dinner Thurs.–Sun. Ⓜ Náměstí Republiky.

V Kolkovně

$$ | **CZECH** | For Czechs, this traditional bar–restaurant remains one of the most popular spots to take visitors for a taste of local cuisine without the stress of tourist rip-offs. And it's a solid choice. **Known for:** traditional Czech cuisine done well, like svíčková, roast duck, and fried pork cutlets; warm and welcoming interiors; fresh Pilsner Urquell beer. $ Average main: Kč250 ✉ V Kolkovně 8, Staré Město ☎ 224–819–700 ⊕ vkolkovne.cz Ⓜ Line A: Staroměstská.

Yami

$$ | **JAPANESE** | Yami is sushi without the pretension that often accompanies a sushi place in Prague, and while the prices have crept up in recent years, the sushi sets and rolls are still cheaper than much of the competition (without any compromise in quality). The soups and appetizers are excellent, too. **Known for:** the "Ruby Roll," with tuna, butterfish, avocado, cucumber, and ponzu sauce; good sharing sushi sets; potential crammed feel. $ Average main: Kč350 ✉ Masná 3, Staré Město ☎ 222–312–756 ⊕ yami.cz Ⓜ Line A: Staroměstská.

Zdenek's Oyster Bar

$$$$ | SEAFOOD | Since opening in 2011, Zdenek's Oyster Bar has established itself as the city's best seafood bar. Aside from oysters (more than a dozen different varieties), head chef David Vlášek has developed creative entrées around mussels, shrimp, crab, lobster, and various types of fish. **Known for:** superb seafood alongside seasonal, locally foraged ingredients; extensive Champagne list; fancy vibe but friendly staff. $ Average main: Kč1000 ✉ Malá Štupartská 5, Staré Město ☎ 725–946–250 ⊕ oysterbar.cz Ⓜ Line B: Náměstí Republiky.

🍴 Coffee and Quick Bites

Au Gourmand

$$ | BAKERY | This sweet little café with tiled mosaic floors, globe lights, and mint-green decor provides an inviting spot for a light lunch. It's similar to the nearby Bakeshop Praha, but with a certain Gallic flair. **Known for:** fresh breads; homemade ice cream; refined café feel. $ Average main: Kč150 ✉ Dlouhá 10, Staré Město ☎ 602–305–181 ⊕ augourmand.cz Ⓜ Line A: Staroměstská.

Background

$ | CAFÉ | Great coffee and cool vibes in this cavernous, slightly rough-around-the-edges café in an interesting, historic building, which also doubles as an art and community space. **Known for:** student-y feel; responsible business, welcoming and training refugees; delicious cakes alongside your caffeine hit. $ Average main: Kč90 ✉ Bartolomějská 13, Staré Město ☎ 778–427–047 ⊕ mamacoffee.cz Ⓜ Lines A and B: Můstek.

Bakeshop Praha

$ | BAKERY | A pleasantly airy American-style bakery and café counter, Bakeshop Praha sells familiar U.S. favorites, from avocado BLTs to entire pumpkin pies. Though it gets crowded during peak lunch hours, there is indoor seating, and the space, with penny-tiled floors and ceiling moldings, has a retro charm. **Known for:** proper New York–style cheesecake; homemade breads, including great sourdough; daily cream cheese spread mixes. $ Average main: Kč140 ✉ Kozi 1, Staré Město ☎ 222–316–823 ⊕ bakeshop.cz Ⓜ Line A: Staroměstská.

Burrito Loco

$$ | MEXICAN | While Prague isn't famous for its Mexican food, Burrito Loco is a notable exception: fresh, spicy takeout burritos and nachos, at affordable prices, right by Old Town Square. There are a few branches around the city. **Known for:** tasty tortilla chips on the side; burritos as sloppy and large as they should be; late-night opening. $ Average main: Kč160 ✉ Masná 620/2, Staré Město ⊕ burritoloco.cz Ⓜ Tram 6 to Dlouhá Třída.

Havelská Koruna

$ | CZECH | This old-school canteen dishes up classic Czech grub very cheaply, and aims to do so within five minutes of getting the order, so unsurprisingly it can get very busy at lunchtime. The soups in particular are a bargain and very traditional. **Known for:** fruit dumplings—a classic dessert; svíčková ; all-Czech ingredients. $ Average main: Kč120 ✉ Havelská Koruna 21, Staré Město ⊕ havelska-koruna.com Ⓜ Line A and B: Můstek.

Mansson's Bakery

$ | BAKERY | This little bakery was set up by a Danish chef in 1999, which means predictably good Danish pastries and brilliant breads, including the house special, rye bread with sunflower seeds. **Known** for: delicious Danish pastry, particularly with apricot jam; lots of marzipan; quiet and cute feel. ⑤ *Average main: Kč70* ⊠ *Bílkova 8, Staré Město* ⊕ *mansson-bakery.com* ◔ *Closed Sun.* Ⓜ *Tram 17 to Právnická fakulta.*

Piknik Dlouhá
$ | BAKERY | With its hip signage and location, you could be forgiven for assuming that Piknik is style over substance. But the lines to the counter would quickly set you right, as customers line up for delicious pastries, cakes, sandwiches, breakfasts, and coffee. **Known for:** flaky, fruity pastries; long lines at breakfast; takeaway treats. ⑤ *Average main: Kč90* ⊠ *Dlouhá 52, Staré Město* ☎ *605–052–331* ⊕ *facebook.com/Piknik.Dlouha* Ⓜ *Line B: Náměstí Republiky.*

Hotels

Staré Město, Prague's Old Town, is a highly desirable neighborhood in which to stay. The mix of baroque and Gothic buildings provides a storybook feeling, and all of the city's major sights are within reach via a pleasant cobblestoned stroll. Hotels here are mainly of the old-made-new variety. Don't be surprised to be standing in a hotel lobby that was originally built in the 17th century—or earlier—but looks and smells like a fresh coat of plaster and paint was added a month ago. Trendy restaurants, cute cafés, superior clubs, and the city's best clothing boutiques are all in this area, too.

Buddha-Bar Hotel
$$$ | HOTEL | The concept here is "chinoiserie meets art nouveau," as best as we can tell, meshing the hotel's original 100-year-old structure with Asian script and Buddhas throughout. **Pros:** stylish design, if not particularly "Czech"; mecca for club-going hipsters; great in-house bar. **Cons:** room rates can go up fast if booked late; rooms seem dark; small spa. ⑤ *Rooms from: Kč6000* ⊠ *Jakubská*

8, Staré Město ☎ *221–776–300* ⊕ *buddhabarhotelprague.com* ⬦ *38 rooms* ⓘⓞⓘ *No Meals* Ⓜ *Line C: Náměstí Republiky.*

Design Hotel Jewel Prague
$$ | HOTEL | A friendly jewel-theme hotel that's close to all the Staré Město action, the staff here go the extra mile, from the little afternoon tea cakes brought to your room to the bedtime-story cards distributed in the evening. **Pros:** cute touches; bright, individual rooms; well priced. **Cons:** buffet breakfast could be fresher; some street noise; rooms can feel cramped. ⑤ *Rooms from: Kč3200* ⊠ *Rytířská 3, Staré Město* ☎ *224–211–699* ⊕ *hoteljewelprague.com* ⬦ *10 rooms* ⓘⓞⓘ *No Meals* Ⓜ *Lines A and B: Můstek.*

Four Seasons Hotel Prague
$$$$ | HOTEL | Though it has plenty of competition at the top end of the market, the Prague outpost of the Four Seasons luxury chain keeps up, not least because it simply has one of the best locations in the city: right on the river, close to the Charles Bridge, giving guests beautiful views from many of the rooms and a general fairy-tale feel. **Pros:** sumptuous beds; incredible outlook, some rooms with floor-to-ceiling windows; perfect service. **Cons:** pricey breakfast; conservative styling; some tram noise from one side of the hotel (but this is Prague). ⑤ *Rooms from: Kč10500* ⊠ *Veleslavinova 2A, Staré Město* ☎ *221–427–000* ⊕ *fourseasons.com/prague* ⬦ *157 rooms* ⓘⓞⓘ *No Meals* Ⓜ *Line A: Staroměstská.*

Grand Hotel Bohemia
$$ | HOTEL | This stately old art nouveau *palais* dominates a picturesque corner near the Powder Tower and Náměstí Republiky. **Pros:** city-center location; fascinating history, with a glittering ballroom surprise in the basement; cozy rooms, comfortable beds. **Cons:** a few nickel-and-dime charges (breakfast costs extra in cheaper rooms); pricier than comparable hotels in the area; old-fashioned lobby

and bar, cozy in winter but less appealing in summer. $ Rooms from: Kč4500 ✉ Králodvorská 4, Staré Město ☎ 234–608–111 ⊕ www.grandhotelbohemia.cz ⟿ 78 rooms ⎮❍⎮ Free Breakfast Ⓜ Line B: Náměstí Republiky.

Grand Hotel Praha
$$ | HOTEL | The main selling point here is the amazing location (practically on top of one of Prague's most famous sights, the astronomical clock), but this has its downside: with the wonderful views comes a big tourist scrum from the moment you venture outside. **Pros:** can't get closer to the astronomical clock unless you sleep in its tower; good price, with breakfast included, for the location; baroque Cafe Mozart is a nice place for afternoon tea or cocktails. **Cons:** obviously rooms with the best views of the clock are considerably pricier; Mitteleuropa-style decor is a little tired; can feel a bit hectic. $ Rooms from: Kč3200 ✉ Staroměstské nám. 481/22, Staré Město ☎ 221–632–556 ⊕ grandhotelpraha.cz ▭ No credit cards ⟿ 38 rooms ⎮❍⎮ Free Breakfast Ⓜ Line A: Staroměstská.

★ Hotel Residence Agnes
$$ | HOTEL | This gorgeous hotel, with a chic courtyard and atrium, is tucked away on a quiet alley in Staré Město and is a comfortable haven from the hustle and bustle of Prague. **Pros:** fantastic staff—nothing is too much trouble; homey feel, with welcome wine; tasty breakfast included. **Cons:** rooms sell out quickly; decor perhaps a little simple, although stylish; lacking extras: no spa or restaurant. $ Rooms from: Kč4500 ✉ Haštalská 19, Staré Město ☎ 222–312–417 ⊕ residenceagnes.com ⟿ 22 rooms ⎮❍⎮ Free Breakfast Ⓜ Line B: Náměstí Republiky.

Hotel U Zlatého Jelena
$ | HOTEL | Authentically austere, what U Zlatého Jelena—the Golden Deer—lacks in personality and amenities it makes up for with a killer location off Old Town Square and a sense of history: the building dates from 1366. **Pros:** prime city-center location; large rooms with some typically Czech touches, like parquet floors; good breakfast buffet. **Cons:** no a/c; street noise in noncourtyard rooms; lacking in coziness. $ Rooms from: Kč2000 ✉ Celetná 11, Staré Město ☎ 257–531–925 ⊕ goldendeer.cz ⟿ 19 rooms ⎮❍⎮ Free Breakfast Ⓜ Line B: Náměstí Republiky.

Iron Gate Hotel and Suites
$$ | HOTEL | If you're looking for history, the Iron Gate has it in spades—the original building dates to the 14th century, and the architectural details are fascinating (ask to see a room with painted ceiling beams). **Pros:** real historical pedigree; each room is unique; located on a gorgeous cobblestoned street. **Cons:** hard beds; old building means architectural quirks—stairs, low ceilings—make access challenging; shower/baths don't appeal to everyone. $ Rooms from: Kč3500 ✉ Michalská 19, Staré Město ☎ 225–777–777 ⊕ irongatehotel.com ⟿ 43 rooms ⎮❍⎮ Free Breakfast Ⓜ Line A: Staroměstská.

Josef
$$$ | HOTEL | Cool, clean, white lines dominate the decor of this ultra-hip modern boutique hotel designed by London-based Czech architect Eva Jiricna. **Pros:** large patio for breakfast in the courtyard; some rooms have amazing views of Staré Město—try 801 for the best; great on-site bakery. **Cons:** the minimalist design might not be for everyone; glass dividers in some bathrooms give no privacy; rooms are not large. $ Rooms from: Kč4900 ✉ Rybná 20, Staré Město ☎ 221–700–901 ⊕ hoteljosef.com ⟿ 109 rooms ⎮❍⎮ Free Breakfast Ⓜ Line B: Náměstí Republiky.

★ The Mozart Prague
$$$ | HOTEL | Situated in a beautiful baroque palace right by the river and Charles Bridge, the pleasingly fancy

Lodging Alternatives

Prague's hotel offerings are pretty comprehensive, but it can get pricey, particularly in Staré Město. One option for a more authentic stay, often at lower rates and in really central neighborhoods, is to try an apartment rental. Boris' Apartments (☎ 777–826–826 ⊕ borisapartments. cz), for example, offers gorgeous escapes, including some city-center properties with roof terraces, often for less than half of the price of a hotel room nearby. While you'll miss out on your hotel buffet breakfast and turn-down service, instead you'll get bar and dinner recommendations from the group of friends who started the company, as well as a list of local events updated weekly.

Mozart can't be matched for authenticity. **Pros:** friendly service; giant rooms with decadent details, like springy beds and chandeliers; fascinating centuries-long history including Mozart being locked in a room here until he wrote six sonatas for the owner. **Cons:** some street noise, very busy as soon as you step out of hotel; staff can be disorganized at times; breakfast a touch underwhelming. $ *Rooms from: Kč6500* ⊠ *Karoliny Světlé 34, Staré Město* ☎ *234–705–111* ⊕ *themozart.com* ⌁ *48 rooms* ⦿ *Free Breakfast* Ⓜ *Line A: Staroměstská.*

Unitas Hotel
$$ | HOTEL | The rooms in this former convent once served as interrogation cells for the communist secret police, and the late president Václav Havel was once even a "guest" here—though, fortunately, the lobby and rooms betray nothing of this gloomy past. **Pros:** clean, airy, large, and modern rooms; great location on a quiet street; historical wow factor can't be beat. **Cons:** few amenities; not exactly a bargain; no on-site restaurant. $ *Rooms from: Kč4500* ⊠ *Bartolomějská 9, Staré Město* ☎ *224–230–533* ⊕ *unitas. cz* ⌁ *22 rooms* ⦿ *Free Breakfast* Ⓜ *Line B: Národní třída.*

Ventana Hotel Prague
$$ | HOTEL | Surprisingly quiet considering its location just steps from Old Town Square, the Ventana delivers old-school style and charm in spades. **Pros:** calm and cozy retreat; good location with a swanky bar; staff have old-school charm. **Cons:** can be pricey; rooms vary in terms of individuality and view quality, so check them out carefully; some access issues, for example, beds on mezzanine layers in loft rooms. $ *Rooms from: Kč4500* ⊠ *Celetná 7, Staré Město* ☎ *777–492–492* ⊕ *ventana-hotel.net* ⌁ *29 rooms* ⦿ *Free Breakfast* Ⓜ *Lines A and B: Můstek.*

ⓨ Nightlife

Prague's historical heart is also the heart of its nightlife. It's packed with jazz bars, old pubs, and high-end cocktail bars. Be warned though: on the weekend this area can get a bit party-heavy, and at some of the fancier bars it is a good idea to book a table.

BARS AND PUBS
Bar and Books
BARS | Just off Old Town Square, but worlds away from the raucous touristy venues nearby in terms of atmosphere, sophistication, and quiet, Bar and Books is a grown-up, reliable place for a cocktail that is open late. Try the martini, made as you like it; it's predictably good. ⊠ *Týnská 19, Staré Město* ☎ *224–815–122* ⊕ *barandbooks.cz* ⏱ *Closed Sun.* Ⓜ *Lines A and B: Můstek.*

AghaRTA Jazz club opened the day after jazz legend Miles Davis died in 1991, and is named for his 1970s album.

★ Bokovka

WINE BARS | Pretty much a fairy-tale dream of a European wine bar, established by a group of artsy Praguers: located in a crumbling courtyard and cellar-style cozy archway (check), serving up personally recommended wines to your taste (check), which you sup by candlelight on barrel tables either inside or outside, wrapped in blankets in the winter if you like (check). It's a little hidden: keep an eye out for the wine droplet sign, leading you into the courtyard, and it's on the right. ⊠ *Dlouhá 37, Staré Město* ☎ *731–492–046* ⊕ *bokovka. com* ⊗ *Closed Sun.* Ⓜ *Line B: Náměstí Republiky.*

Champagneria

PIANO BARS | If you like your Champagne bars relaxed, located in ancient buildings with shutters and crumbling exterior walls that are covered with graffiti, this little joint is for you. A cool and welcoming spot, with candles scattered around as the sun sets, Champagneria offers a range of drinks from the fizz of its title to Matuška, a craft brew that many Prague hipsters consider the Champagne of beers anyway. Great acoustics for cheerful conversation, proper Champagne glasses, a tasty snack menu, a piano in the corner, art on the walls and regular musical performances only add to the promise. ⊠ *Průchodní 4, Staré Město* ☎ *735–025–482* ⊕ *champagneria. cz* Ⓜ *Line B: Národní třída.*

Hemingway Bar

COCKTAIL LOUNGES | Absinthe is all over Prague, and if you want to dabble in the green fairy's magic, there are worse places than the sophisticated cocktail bar Hemingway, which is named after the man himself. You won't find any flaming absinthe here, but you will find a range of interesting cocktails, alongside Champagne and 200 varieties of rum— the famous writer's drinks of choice. It's worth reserving a table on weekends. ⊠ *Karolíny Světlé 26, Staré Město* ☎ *773–974–764* ⊕ *hemingwaybar.cz/bar-prague* Ⓜ *Lines A and B: Můstek.*

Monarch
WINE BARS | A classy wine bar and restaurant, with high ceilings, soft lighting, and a vast selection of vintages, including some particularly fine wines from the Czech Republic. Great steak here, too. ⊠ *Na Perštýně 15, Staré Město* ☎ *703–182–801* ⊕ *monarch.cz* ☉ *Closed Sun.* Ⓜ *Line B: Národní třída.*

★ **U Medvídků**
PUBS | A former brewery dating as far back as the 15th century, U Medvídků now serves draft Budvar shipped directly from České Budějovice, as well as its own super-strong X Beer 33, which is brewed on-site. It's perhaps the most authentic of the city-center Czech pubs, which also means that it's often pretty busy and service can be correspondingly slow. However, it's also big enough that you've got a good chance of finding a seat. The interior, including the taps, has a turn-of-the-20th-century feel. Occasionally, the bar offers exclusive Budvar brews available only at this location. There's a hotel on-site, and a beer spa, too, and some tours are available. ⊠ *Na Perštýně 7, Staré Město* ☎ *224–211–900* ⊕ *umedvidku.cz* Ⓜ *Line B: Národní třída.*

★ **U Zlatého tygra**
PUBS | The last of the old, smoky, surly pubs in Staré Město, the "Golden Tiger" is famous for being one of the best Prague pubs for Pilsner Urquell. It's also renowned as a former hangout of one of the country's best-known and beloved writers, Bohumil Hrabal, who died in 1997, as well as Velvet Revolution hero and then president Václav Havel. Reservations are not accepted; one option is to show up when the pub opens at 3 pm, with the rest of the early birds, and settle in for the rest of the night. You won't be disappointed. ⊠ *Husova 17, Staré Město* ☎ *222–221–111* ⊕ *uzlatehotygra.cz* Ⓜ *Line A: Staroměstská.*

JAZZ CLUBS
Ungelt
LIVE MUSIC | Hidden in the side streets behind Old Town Square, this basement has been around since the 15th century and has been a cozy club with good music since 2000. The house bands are decent and play jazz, blues, or fusion, depending on the night. Its central location means there's mainly an international crowd, but you can still see some classic Czech sights—a sleeping dachshund perched on a barstool, unaware of and unimpressed by the stage acts, for example. ⊠ *Týn 2, Staré Město* ☎ *736–441–324* ⊕ *jazzungelt.cz* Ⓜ *Line A: Staroměstská.*

LGBTQ
Friends
DANCE CLUBS | This (appropriately named) friendly bar in Staré Město serves reasonably priced beer—and Western-priced mixed drinks—in a roomy cellar space. There's plenty of seating most weeknights, but it does get busy on weekends. It opens at 7 pm (and stays open until 6 am!), videos play every night, happy hour starts at 9, and a DJ spins after 10 on weekends, luring people onto a small dance floor—try karaoke on Tuesday. There's no cover. ⊠ *Bartolomějská 11, Staré Město* ☎ *226–211–920* ⊕ *friendsprague.cz* Ⓜ *Lines A and B: Můstek.*

LIVE MUSIC CLUBS
Roxy
LIVE MUSIC | Part nightclub, part performance space, the Roxy doubles as a residence for DJs and as a popular venue for electronica and touring cult bands. The large former theater has a comfortable, lived-in feel that borders on warehouse chic. All exits from the club are final, and patrons are encouraged not to hang around the area. Upstairs, the NoD space has all manner of bizarre acts. ⊠ *Dlouhá 33, Staré Město* ☎ *608–060–745 (SMS is best)* ⊕ *roxy.cz* Ⓜ *Line B: Náměstí Republiky.*

⊕ Performing Arts

Prague is a fantastically cultured city: from classical music to theater, there are options for visitors right at the top end of the scale (internationally renowned orchestra performances) down to more experimental, try-anything theater. We've listed some of the best classical music ensembles to watch out for below, with a whistle-stop tour of the most impressive venues (and what kinds of things they offer) to follow.

CLASSICAL MUSIC

Česká filharmonie (*Czech Philharmonic*)
MUSIC | The big daddy in town: Antonín Dvořák conducted the orchestra's first performance back in 1896, and guest conductors have included Gustav Mahler and Leonard Bernstein. Performances are of a consistently high quality, and most programs include some works by Czech composers. They also offer public dress rehearsals for a mere 160 Kč (book early though, because they are an understandably popular bargain). ⊠ *Rudolfinum, Nám. Jana Palacha, Staré Město* ☎ *227–059–227* ⊕ *ceskafilharmonie.cz* Ⓜ *Line A: Staroměstská.*

★ **Prague Symphony Orchestra** (*FOK*)
MUSIC | The group's nickname, FOK, stands for Film-Opera-Koncert. They started in 1934, but it wasn't until 1952 that they became the official city orchestra. In the 1930s they did music for many Czech films, although they don't do much opera and film anymore. The ensemble tours extensively and has a large back catalog of recordings. Programs tend to be quite diverse, from Beethoven to Bruckner. ⊠ *Obecní dům, Nám. Republiky 5, Staré Město* ☎ *222–002–336* ⊕ *fok.cz* Ⓜ *Line B: Náměstí Republiky.*

CHURCH CONCERTS

Bazilika sv. Jakuba (*Basilica of St. James*)
CONCERTS | This is an excellent venue for organ concerts thanks to the church's organ itself, which was finished in 1709 and restored in the early 1980s to its original tone structure. All those years later, it's still one of the best in town. ⊠ *Malá Štupartská 6, Staré Město* ☎ *604–208–490* ⊕ *auditeorganum.cz* Ⓜ *Line A: Staroměstská.*

VENUES

★ **Rudolfinum**
ARTS CENTERS | Austrian Crown Prince Rudolf lent his name to this neo-Renaissance concert space and exhibition gallery built in 1884; it's only been open to the public since 1992. The impressive building has an interesting history: after 1918 it was converted into the parliament of the newly independent Czechoslovakia, until German invaders reinstated it as a space for music in 1939. The large concert hall, named for Antonín Dvořák, who conducted here, hosts concerts with the Czech Philharmonic. The smaller Josef Suk Hall, on the opposite side of the building, is used for chamber concerts. Rival theaters may have richer interiors, but the acoustics here are excellent (and the exterior is also pretty fancy, with some of the cleanest, brightest stonework in the city). Tours are available, but hearing live music here is what it is all about. ⊠ *Alšovo nábř. 12, Staré Město* ☎ *227–059–227* ⊕ *rudolfinum.cz* 🎫 *Concert prices vary; tours are 150 Kč* ☉ *Closed Mon.* Ⓜ *Line A: Staroměstská.*

★ **Stavovské divadlo** (*Estates Theater*)
THEATER | Built in the 1780s in the classical style, this opulent, green *palais* hosted the world premiere of Mozart's opera *Don Giovanni* in October 1787 with the composer himself conducting. Savvy Prague audiences were quick to acknowledge Mozart's genius: the opera was an instant hit here, though it flopped nearly everywhere else in Europe. Mozart wrote some of the opera's second act in Prague at the Villa Bertramka (in Smíchov), where he was a frequent guest. The program these days is mixed, incorporating demanding Czech drama alongside opera, ballet, and musical performances. You must attend a performance to see

inside, although the interior, the history, and the quality of the shows here combined make it absolutely worth it; buy tickets via the National Theater. ✉ *Ovocný trh 1, Staré Město* ☎ *224–901–448 box office* ⊕ *narodni-divadlo.cz* Ⓜ *Lines A and B: Můstek.*

PUPPET SHOWS AND BLACK-LIGHT THEATER

Divadlo Ta Fantastika

SOUND/LIGHT SHOW | Black-light theater—shows using black backgrounds, UV-light and fluorescent paints to create visual spectacles via the acrobatic arts of the performers—has found something of a home in Prague, although its simplistic style isn't for everyone. If it appeals, this venue is probably the best place to see some, namely in a show called *Aspects of Alice,* based loosely on *Alice in Wonderland,* that has run here almost daily for more than 2,000 performances. The theater was established in Florida in 1981, and moved to Prague after the Velvet Revolution. It's been running at its current address, a minor baroque palace, since 1993.

If you are more interested in the world-leading multimedia theater pioneered by Laterna Magika back in 1958, which does include some black-light elements, check out the National Theater's New Stage instead. ✉ *Karlova 8, Staré Město* ☎ *222–221–366* ⊕ *tafantastika.cz* Ⓜ *Line A: Staroměstská.*

⊖ Shopping

A jumble of funky boutiques, bookshops, antiques stores, jewelry dens, and souvenir shops converge in what is arguably Prague's prettiest district.

ANTIQUES

Antik Mucha

ANTIQUES & COLLECTIBLES | This charming antiques shop has so many wares, and such friendly owners, that it has more of the feel of a museum than a store. It focuses on objects from the beginning of

the 20th century and, as such, has some lovely art nouveau pieces, from inkstands to lamps. It also has a "mascot," bulldog Adamek. ✉ *Liliová 12, Staré Město* ☎ *602–316–285* ⊕ *pokus-112.webnode.cz* Ⓜ *Line B: Můstek.*

★ Bric a Brac

ANTIQUES & COLLECTIBLES | If you like the sensation of unearthing your treasure, this wonderfully cluttered antiques store is the ticket. About the size of a closet, this shop uses every nook to display a mix of communist-era badges, tin Pilsner Urquell signs, charming old typewriters, and more. Memorable gifts can be found among the clutter, although some prices are high—that colorful Czech tobacco tin could make a great jewelry box, though. Ask the friendly English-speaking shopkeeper for tips, and pop round the corner to find his slightly larger cave of riches. ✉ *Týnská 7, Staré Město* ☎ *224–815–763* ⊕ *prague-antique-shop.com* Ⓜ *Line A: Staroměstská.*

Starožitnosti Ungelt

ANTIQUES & COLLECTIBLES | Tucked away beneath an archway behind Týn Church, this elegant shop features a selection of art nouveau and art deco items. Beautiful and unusual glass vases from Czech designers sit alongside furniture, glittering brooches, and delicate porcelain butterflies. ✉ *Týn 1, Staré Město* ☎ *224–895–454* ⊕ *antiqueungelt.cz* Ⓜ *Line A: Staroměstská.*

ART GALLERIES

AD Galerie

ART GALLERIES | A bright, interesting room packed with everything from puppets to paintings, jewelry to wire sculptures, this family-run gallery showcasing modern Czech creativity is worth a look for an interesting and unique souvenir. ✉ *Uhelný trh 11, Staré Město* ☎ *732–160–647* ⊕ *adgalerie.cz* Ⓜ *Lines A and B: Můstek.*

Galerie NoD

ART GALLERIES | Above the Roxy music club on Dlouhá ulice, this gallery space is filled with youthful energy. Exhibits feature edgy work by up-and-coming artists focusing on anything from puppets to photography. The gallery also hosts experimental theater, music, and comedy nights and touts an adjacent bar and café sprinkled with twentysomethings on laptops. ⊠ *Dlouhá 33, Staré Město* ☎ *733–307–600* ⊕ *nod.roxy.cz* Ⓜ *Line B: Náměstí Republiky.*

Galerie U Betlémské kaple

ART GALLERIES | Specializing in postwar surrealism, this airy gallery features work from many of the leading Czech artists present and past, including globally significant painter Josef Šíma. If artwork prices are too many koruny for your comfort, a good alternative is picking up a book on the artist's exhibition, also for sale here. ⊠ *Betlémské nám. 8, Staré Město* ☎ *222–220–689* ⊕ *galerieubetlemskekaple.cz* Ⓜ *Line B: Národní třída.*

BEAUTY

Botanicus

COSMETICS | Organic body and bath products here, like "lettuce and olive oil" soap, are crafted from fresh fruits, vegetables, and herbs on a rural Czech farm. Inside the spacious and fragrant store there are myriad other all-natural products that make charming gifts for those back home, including tempting chutneys and condiments. ⊠ *Týnsky Dvůr 3, Staré Město* ☎ *702–207–096* ⊕ *botanicus.cz* Ⓜ *Line B: Náměstí Republiky.*

Havlik Apotek

COSMETICS | The beautiful smell of the organic Czech cosmetics sold by this little store will lure you in, and the cheerful staff, who speak English, will find out exactly what you need in true "apothecary" style. Their "3-minute morning mask" is their most popular; there are also moisturizers for kids too. ⊠ *Jilská 1, Staré Město* ☎ *228–810–111* ⊕ *havlikovaapoteka.cz* Ⓜ *Lines A and B: Můstek.*

Perfumed Prague

PERFUME | It looks like a magician's workshop, accessed through a curved door into a rustic tunnel-style interior, full of potions and bottles, and the truth is not that far off: a perfume studio where customers can conjure up (with the expert help of staff) their own personalized fragrances, in the first outfit of its kind in Prague. There are also off-the-shelf perfumes and candles, and all products are eco-friendly. ⊠ *Karolíny Světlé 20, Staré Město* ☎ *607–800–307* ⊕ *perfumedprague.cz* ⊙ *Closed Sun. and Mon.* Ⓜ *Line B: Národní třída.*

BOOKS AND PRINTS

Galerie Antikvariat Ztichlá klika

BOOKS | Rare books, old books, new books, art—this place is cavernous, but it has something for everyone. It's partly underground too, which only adds to the appeal. Be warned: you might lose hours browsing the shelves and shelves of books and walls of photographs and paintings, all of which are for sale. Be sure to take a moment to appreciate the quirky signage as well—the shop is also known as the "blue tiger," for reasons that will become obvious. It's only open Tuesday–Friday 1–7 pm. ⊠ *Betlémská 10–14, Staré Město* ☎ *222–222–079* ⊕ *ztichlaklika.cz* ⊙ *Closed Sat.–Mon.* Ⓜ *Line B: Národní třída.*

Kavka Book

BOOKS | This attractive store on a quiet Staré Město corner is pretty much a temple dedicated to art books. It's a pleasant place to browse, and while many of the books are in the Czech language, there's a foreign section and art available to buy, too. Some of the photography books are fantastic: Jan Jinda's *Charles Bridge*, which captures the people on the famous structure rather than the bridge itself, is a highlight. ⊠ *Krocínova 5, Staré Město* ☎ *606–030–202* ⊕ *kavkaartbooks.com* ⊙ *Closed weekends* Ⓜ *Line B: Národní třída.*

CLOTHING

Boutique Tatiana

WOMEN'S CLOTHING | There is a nice sense of high drama here, with black and white clothes (mainly) making dramatic silhouettes in this chic shop. A good option for something a little bit more high-end, but still authentically Czech. ⊠ *Dušní 1, Staré Město* ☎ *605–257–191* ⊕ *tatiana.cz* Ⓜ *Line A: Staroměstská.*

Denim Heads

MIXED CLOTHING | Half of the world's population wears jeans every day, reasoned the bloke-y team behind this hip denim shop, so surely there is a gap in the market for a cool, quality denim brand in Prague's Staré Město. They weren't wrong, and it doesn't hurt that their shop—and the team behind it—is fun; they're often found sipping a beer on the street underneath the horse's head mounted by the shop entrance at 6 pm, as the evening shoppers approach. ⊠ *Konviktská 30, Staré Město* ☎ *224–283–974* ⊕ *denimheads.cz* ☉ *Closed Sun.* Ⓜ *Line B: Národní třída.*

DNB

WOMEN'S CLOTHING | In her chic studio close to the river, Czech designer Denisa Nova shows off carelessly sexy clothing that is both wearable and luxurious. Slouchy dresses, velour trousers, and an occasional pop of color (think a bright pink shirt dress) seal the effortless deal. You can get a personal consultation with the designer if you book ahead. ⊠ *Naprstkova 4, Staré Město* ☎ *222–221–342* ⊕ *denisanova.cz* ☉ *Closed weekends* Ⓜ *Line B: Národní třída.*

Klára Nademlýnská

WOMEN'S CLOTHING | This funky boutique just off Old Town Square caters to mon-eyed hipsters. The eponymous Czech designer excels in the little details—unusual draping, old-fashioned flowered dresses amid leather, an unexpected giraffe print—that make each item unique and original. ⊠ *Dlouhá 3, Staré Město* ☎ *224–818–769* ⊕ *klaranademlynska.cz*

Pop-up Prague

The fad for "pop-up" shops has not passed Prague by—so make sure to explore if you see a promising-looking, hastily scrawled sign in Staré Město. Half the fun is getting lost down the alleyways and making your own discoveries anyway.

☉ *Closed weekends* Ⓜ *Line B: Náměstí Republiky.*

★ Leeda

WOMEN'S CLOTHING | This artistic-minded shop is chic, original, and just a little bit mad. Stocked with genuine and original Czech designs, items range from painted dresses to billowing silk skirts. The designer collaborates with graphic designers, photographers, and musicians, which makes the little store feel all the more like a great embodiment of Czech style. ⊠ *Bartolomějská 1, Staré Město* ☎ *775–601–185* ⊕ *leeda.cz* ☉ *Closed Sun.* Ⓜ *Line B: Národní třída.*

Parazit Fashion Store

WOMEN'S CLOTHING | A cool, graffiti-chic space that champions Czech and Slovak fashion students and young designers making limited-edition clothes, accessories, and gifts. The owners take their fashion seriously, adopting their motto from Nicholas Cage's character in the David Lynch film *Wild at Heart*: "This snakeskin jacket represents a symbol of my individuality and a belief in personal freedom." ⊠ *Karlova 25, Staré Město* ☎ *603–561–776* ⊕ *parazit.cz* ☉ *Closed Sun.* Ⓜ *Line A: Staroměstská.*

Šatna

SECOND-HAND | This cool little shop specializes in vintage and secondhand finds. If you can face a bit of rummaging, think extremely promising attic (the name means "cloakroom"), with cut-price pieces for men and women from designers like Ralph Lauren, as well as more random bits and pieces. The store also stocks interesting jewelry, including earrings made of headphones and scissors. ⊠ *Konviktská 13, Staré Město* ⊕ *prevlikarna.cz* Ⓜ *Line A: Staroměstská.*

FOOD AND WINE
Absintherie
WINE/SPIRITS | Absinthe is everywhere in Prague. It's a bit of a tourist cliché, but even if you aren't a fan of the "green fairy," it can be a fun gift for folks back home. This shop is the real deal for the fiery spirit—try a wee nip at the bar while you're there if you're brave enough! There's also an on-site museum with old advertisement posters, bottles, and absinthe spoons. ⊠ *Jilská 7, Staré Město* ☎ *774–229–172* ⊕ *absintherie.cz* Ⓜ *Line A: Staroměstská.*

Merlot d'Or
WINE/SPIRITS | A fantastically atmospheric wine shop and bar, with tapas. Bottles line the walls—it's a good spot for a recommendation—and there's an eye-catching winding iron stairway towards the back, as well as stools helping staff reach the more obscure choices. There are tastings too. ⊠ *Dušní 1, Staré Město* ☎ *731–457–621* ⊕ *merlot.cz* Ⓜ *Line A: Staroměstská.*

GLASS
Material
GLASSWARE | The light dancing on the incredibly eye-catching glassware in this elegant boutique makes it almost impossible to walk on by. But the unusual jewelry, stunning brightly colored chandeliers, and an array of beads and Bohemia crystal will make you want to stay and shop. The prices are not for the fainthearted, but the pieces are worth it if you want to bring home something truly original. ⊠ *Týn 1 (courtyard Ungelt), Staré Město* ☎ *608–664–766* ⊕ *i-material.com* Ⓜ *Line A: Staroměstská.*

Preciosa
GLASSWARE | A genuine Czech glass success story, Preciosa has its headquarters just outside Prague and is now a global manufacturer, melting 40 tons of glass every day. In this sparkling shop in Staré Město, you can buy the chandeliers, glass sculptures, and jewelry the company is famous for. ⊠ *Rytířská 29, Staré Město* ☎ *488–118–106* ⊕ *preciosa.com* Ⓜ *Line A and B: Můstek.*

HOME AND DESIGN
Deelive Design Store
SOUVENIRS | Located inside the SmetanaQ building, a gallery-cum-café-cum–design space right on the river, this fashion and interior design shop showcases the best of Czech design. Some of the artists work in the building's Bottega project on the second floor, and others are located elsewhere, but if you're looking for the most up-to-the-minute Czech design work out there—anything from chic handbags to modernist posters and unusual earrings—get it right from the source here. There's a great assortment of ubercool vases, in particular: much better than an "I love Prague" sweater. ⊠ *SmetanaQ, Smetanovo nábř. 4, Staré Město* ☎ *222–263–526* ⊕ *deelive.cz* Ⓜ *Line B: Národní třída.*

★ Kubista
ART GALLERIES | Located in the stunning House at the Black Madonna, this gorgeous museum shop brings original and replica cubist and art deco pieces into the real world. Marvel at angular black-and-white vases by Vlastislav Hofman, and let your eyes linger on the lines of a 1930s tubular armchair. Maps of Prague's art deco, cubist, and modern architecture are also sold here. ⊠ *Ovocný trh 19, Staré Město* ☎ *224–236–378* ⊕ *kubista.cz* Ⓜ *Line B: Náměstí Republiky.*

★ Qubus Design
HOUSEWARES | Tucked away on a narrow stretch of Rámová, this great homewares shop is made even better by its friendly staff, who might just offer you a cup of

coffee. The lure of what's for sale is really the draw here though—mainly funky home accessories from nonconformist Czech designers, such as a cake-shaped candle holder and a plant made out of glass. ⊠ *Rámová 3, Staré Město* ☎ *775–708–090* ⊕ *qubus.cz* ☉ *Closed Fri.* Ⓜ *Line B: Náměstí Republiky.*

JEWELRY

★ Granát Turnov

JEWELRY & WATCHES | You will see signs all over Staré Město advertising authentic Czech garnet, but this is the real deal, complete with certificates of authenticity. This store is part of the Granát Co-op, the world's most prolific producer of Bohemian garnet jewelry. The elegant Dlouhá branch has two separate rooms. · Gold and silver jewelry, including an especially nice selection of brooches, is to the right. Pricier diamond-clad pieces are to the left. ⊠ *Dlouhá 28, Staré Město* ☎ *222–315–612* ⊕ *granat.cz* Ⓜ *Line B: Náměstí Republiky.*

Swarovksi Bohemia

JEWELRY & WATCHES | There's no avoiding the allure of the crystal on offer from this brand, founded by a Bohemian jeweler living in Austria in 1895. This store, right by Old Town Square, is an attractive outpost, complete with some spectacular crystal pillars. Pick up a playful key-ring charm or glittering bauble at relatively affordable prices. It's worth spending some time reveling in the window-filled space, as shoppers outside point excitedly at the displays. ⊠ *Celetná 7, Staré Město* ☎ *222–315–585* ⊕ *swarovski.com* Ⓜ *Lines A and B: Můstek.*

Wollem

JEWELRY & WATCHES | If you are really looking to make a statement, the red garnets here are authentic, the designs delicate and attractive (set in rose gold), and the shopping experience very approachable, despite the suitably high price tags. ⊠ *Štupartská 11, Staré Město* ☎ *773–521–774* ⊕ *wollem.com* Ⓜ *Lines A and B: Můstek.*

MARKETS

Havelská

MARKET | Havelská is a charming open-air market, centrally located in Staré Město, featuring touristy kitsch, seasonal trinkets, and handmade jewelry alongside fresh fruits and vegetables. The market is open daily. ⊠ *Havelská, Staré Město* Ⓜ *Lines A and B: Můstek.*

MUSIC

Maximum Underground

MUSIC | A grimy, slightly hidden-away music shop that offers the same sense of retro within as its wares—records and CDs—will when you get them home. Friendly staff can help you find what you are looking for among the wall-to-wall music. ⊠ *Jilská 22, 1st fl., Staré Město* ☎ *724–307–198* ⊕ *maximum.cz* ☉ *Closed Sun.* Ⓜ *Lines A and B: Můstek.*

SHOES

★ Botas 66

SHOES | A revival of an old Czech brand once so iconic that it was not only worn by Czechoslovak Olympians but actually became the word for any sports shoe (*botasky*), these cool sneakers still look the part. Originally restarted as a school project in 2008, the graphic-design pedigree of the team behind the brand is obvious, from the clean lines of the shoes themselves to the bright yellow of the shop. As well as trying on the shoes, you can also look into the brand's history while you're in the store. ⊠ *Skořepka 4, Staré Město* ☎ *608–099–278* ⊕ *bteam.cz* Ⓜ *Line B: Národní třída.*

SOUVENIRS

Ecospace Prague

SOUVENIRS | This is a very cute eco and zero-waste shop tucked onto this winding, typically Old Town street. The rolltop bags made of ocean plastic, children's puzzles, vegan ice creams, and candles shaped like cakes are some of the highlights. ⊠ *Jilská 20, Staré Město* ☎ *777–167–087* ⊕ *ecospaceprague.com* Ⓜ *Lines A and B: Můstek.*

Lípa

SOUVENIRS | Forget the overpriced junk available on every corner, and bag yourself some quality souvenirs here, from Czech designers and producers, in a chic minimalist store. There's an impressive variety of products available, too, from jam and soap to soft toys and wooden bowls. ⊠ *Železná 12, Staré Město* ☎ *603–524–782* ⊕ *lipastore.cz* Ⓜ *Lines A and B: Můstek.*

SPORTING GOODS

Hudy Sport

SPORTING GOODS | Czechs love getting out into nature, so if you are planning to join them or just want to feel like a local, head here, where the two floors overflow with hiking, camping, and rock-climbing equipment from top outdoor brands. This store is also a good place to pick up a backpack, laptop bag, or water bottle. Look for end-of-season sale bins. ⊠ *Na Perštýně 14, Staré Město* ☎ *224–218–600* ⊕ *hudy.cz* Ⓜ *Line B: Náměstí Republiky.*

TOYS

★ Pohádka

TOYS | **FAMILY** | You'll be drawn in by the amazing window display, which features anything and everything from puppets climbing trees to wooden airplanes. However, you'll stay to be a part of the sheer joy that bursts out of this two-floor toy shop. Packed with attractive wooden toys, stuffed animals, puzzles, and games, it harks back to a more innocent age. There's also a good selection of marionettes if you have your heart set on taking one of these traditional Czech items home. ⊠ *Celetná 32, Staré Město* ☎ *224–239–469* ⊕ *czechtoys.cz* Ⓜ *Line B: Náměstí Republiky.*

Josefov

The history of Prague's Jews, like those of much of Europe, is mostly a sad one. There were horrible pogroms in the late Middle Ages, followed by a period of relative prosperity under Rudolf II in the late 16th century, though the freedoms of Jews were still tightly restricted. It was Austrian emperor Josef II—the ghetto's namesake—who did the most to improve the conditions of the city's Jews. His "Edict of Tolerance" in 1781 removed dress codes for Jews and paved the way for them to finally live in other parts of the city.

The prosperity of the 19th century lifted the Jews out of poverty, and many of them chose to leave the ghetto. By the end of the century the number of poor Gentiles, drunks, and prostitutes in the ghetto was growing, and the number of actual Jews was declining. At this time, city officials decided to clear the slum and raze the buildings. In their place they built many of the gorgeous turn-of-the-20th-century and art nouveau town houses you see today. Only a handful of the synagogues, the town hall, and the cemetery were preserved.

World War II and the Nazi occupation brought profound tragedy to the city's Jews. A staggering percentage were deported—many to Terezín concentration camp, north of Prague, and then later to German Nazi death camps in Poland. Of the 40,000 Jews living in Prague before World War II, only about 1,200 returned after the war, and merely a handful live in the ghetto today.

The Nazi occupation contains a historic irony. Many of the treasures stored away in the Židovské muzeum v Praze (Prague Jewish Museum) were brought here from across Central Europe on Hitler's orders. His idea was to form a museum dedicated to the soon-to-be extinct Jewish race.

Today, even with the crowds, the former ghetto is a must-see. The Starý židovský hřbitov (Old Jewish Cemetery) alone, with its incredibly forlorn overlay of headstone upon headstone going back

Thousands of graves, some dating to the 15th century, are layered on top of each other in the Old Jewish Cemetery.

centuries, merits the steep admission price the Jewish Museum charges to see its treasures. Don't feel compelled to linger long right at the heart of the ghetto after visiting, though—much of it is tourist-trap territory, filled with overpriced T-shirt, trinket, and toy shops, the same lousy souvenirs found everywhere in Prague. However, the streets around and on the edge of the quarter offer some of the city's best—and weirdly, considering the crush nearby, quietest—bars, shops, and restaurants. Plus, fans of Prague's most famous literary son, Franz Kafka, should spend some time wandering in this area as the writer himself did back in the day. A Czech Jew, he was born in Josefov in 1883, and there are traces of him all over the area, from the houses he lived in to kitschy cafés bearing his name.

■ TIP→ **The Kafka museum in Malá Strana (260 Kč, Cihelná 2B, 257–535–373, kafkamuseum.cz) is worth a visit, too.**

A ticket to the Prague Jewish Museum includes admission to the Old Jewish Cemetery and collections installed in four surviving synagogues and the Obřadní síň (Ceremony Hall). The Staronová synagóga (Old-New Synagogue), a functioning house of worship, does not technically belong to the museum and requires a separate admission ticket. Alternatively, you can buy a slightly pricier combined ticket, which includes all of the Jewish Museum attractions, plus the Old-New Synagogue. It's called the Pražské Židovské město (Prague Jewish Town) ticket.

Sights

Franz Kafka Monument
PUBLIC ART | It is fitting that the monument to Franz Kafka in Prague, located close to his birthplace, has a suitably surreal, Kafkaesque feel, depicting a small Kafka-like figure riding on the shoulders of a giant, empty suit. It was inspired by one of his short stories and created by sculptor Jaroslav Róna in 2003, and it now stands proudly on the corner of Dušní. Check out the base for the tiny tribute to arguably his most

Josefov (Jewish Quarter)

KEY

1 Sights
1 Restaurants
1 Hotels
M Metro Station

Sights ▶

1 Franz Kafka Monument.................**F2**
2 Klausová synagóga.....**D2**
3 Maiselova synagóga......**E3**
4 Pinkasova synagóga **D2**
5 Španělská synagóga **F2**
6 Staronová synagóga **E2**
7 Starý židovský hřbitov....**D2**
8 Uměleckoprůmyslové museum v Praze.........**C2**
9 Židovská radnice..........**E2**

Restaurants ▶

1 Dinitz.......................**F1**
2 Field..........................**F1**
3 Food Lab...................**G2**
4 La Veranda.................**E2**
5 Les Moules.................**D1**
6 Mistral.......................**C3**
7 Pepenero Pizza & Pasta.........**E1**

Hotels ▶

1 Emblem Hotel Prague....**D3**
2 Golden Prague Rooms ...**E2**
3 Hotel Hastal Prague Old Town...............**H1**
4 Maximilian..................**G1**

0   100 yards
0   100 m

famous work, *The Metamorphosis.* There are other highlights for Kafka fans in Josefov, too—for example, his birthplace, on the corner of Maiselova and Kaprova, is marked with a bust. ✉ *Dušní, Josefov* Ⓜ *Line A: Staroměstská.*

Klausová synagóga (*Klausen Synagogue*)
SYNAGOGUE | This baroque synagogue, right by the entrance to the Old Jewish Cemetery, displays objects from Czech Jewish traditions, with an emphasis on celebrations and daily life. The synagogue was built at the end of the 17th century in place of three small buildings (a synagogue, a school, and a ritual bath) that were destroyed in a fire that devastated the ghetto in 1689. In the more recent **Ceremony Hall** that adjoins the Klausen Synagogue, the focus is more staid. You'll find a variety of Jewish funeral paraphernalia, including old gravestones, and medical instruments. Special attention is paid to the activities of the Jewish Burial Society through many fine objects and paintings. ✉ *U starého hřbitova 3A, Josefov* ☎ *222–749–211* ⊕ *jewishmuseum.cz* 🎫 *Jewish Museum combination ticket 350 Kč (excl. Old-New Synagogue) or 500 Kč (incl. Old-New Synagogue)* ☾ *Closed Sat. and Jewish holidays* Ⓜ *Line A: Staroměstská.*

Maiselova synagóga (*Maisel Synagogue*)
SYNAGOGUE | The history of Czech Jews from the 10th to the 18th century is illustrated, accompanied by some of the Prague Jewish Museum's most precious objects. The collection includes silver Torah shields and pointers, spice boxes, and candelabras; historic tombstones; and fine ceremonial textiles—some donated by Mordechai Maisel to the very synagogue he founded. The glitziest items come from the late 16th and early 17th centuries, a prosperous era for Prague's Jews. ✉ *Maiselova 10, Josefov* ☎ *222–749–211* ⊕ *jewishmuseum.cz* 🎫 *Jewish Museum combination ticket 350 Kč (excl. Old-New Synagogue) or 500 Kč (incl. Old-New Synagogue)* ☾ *Closed*

Sat. and Jewish holidays Ⓜ *Line A: Staroměstská.*

Pinkasova synagóga (*Pinkas Synagogue*)
SYNAGOGUE | Here you'll find two moving testimonies to the appalling crimes perpetrated against the Jews during World War II. One astounds by sheer numbers: the walls are covered with nearly 80,000 names of Bohemian and Moravian Jews murdered by the Nazis. Among them are the names of the paternal grandparents of former U.S. secretary of state Madeleine Albright. The second is an exhibition of drawings made by children at the Nazi concentration camp Terezín, north of Prague. The Nazis used the camp for propaganda purposes to demonstrate their "humanity" toward Jews, and for a time the prisoners were given relative freedom to lead "normal" lives. However, transports to death camps in Poland began in earnest in 1944, and many thousands of Terezín prisoners, including most of these children, eventually perished. The entrance to the Old Jewish Cemetery is through this synagogue. ✉ *Široká 3, Josefov* ☎ *222–749–211* ⊕ *jewishmuseum.cz* 🎫 *Jewish Museum combination ticket 350 Kč (excl. Old-New Synagogue) or 500 Kč (incl. Old-New Synagogue)* ☾ *Closed Sat. and Jewish holidays* Ⓜ *Line A: Staroměstská.*

Španělská synagóga (*Spanish Synagogue*)
SYNAGOGUE | This domed, Moorish-style synagogue was built in 1868 on the site of an older synagogue, the Altschul. Here the historical exposition that begins in the Maisel Synagogue continues through to the post–World War II period. The attached Robert Guttmann Gallery has historic and well-curated art exhibitions. The building's painstakingly restored interior is also worth experiencing. ✉ *Vězeňská 1, Josefov* ☎ *222–749–211* ⊕ *jewishmuseum.cz* 🎫 *Jewish Museum combination ticket 350 Kč (excl. Old-New Synagogue) or 500 Kč (incl. Old-New Synagogue)* ☾ *Closed Sat. and Jewish holidays* Ⓜ *Line A: Staroměstská.*

Staronová synagóga (*Old-New Synagogue, or Altneuschul*)
SYNAGOGUE | Dating to the mid-13th century, this is the oldest functioning synagogue in Europe and one of the most important works of early Gothic architecture in Prague. The name refers to the legend that the synagogue was built on the site of an ancient Jewish temple, and the temple's stones were used to build the present structure. Amazingly, the synagogue has survived fires, the razing of the ghetto, and the Nazi occupation intact; it's still in use. The entrance, with its vault supported by two pillars, is the oldest part of the synagogue. Note that men are required to cover their heads inside, and during services men and women sit apart. ⊠ *Červená 2, Josefov* ☎ *222–749–211* ⊕ *jewishmuseum.cz* 🔖 *From 200 Kč* ⊘ *Closed Sat. and Jewish holidays* Ⓜ *Line A: Staroměstská.*

★ **Starý židovský hřbitov** (*Old Jewish Cemetery*)
CEMETERY | An unforgettable sight, this cemetery is where all Jews living in Prague from the 15th century to 1787 were laid to rest. The lack of any space in the tiny ghetto forced graves to be piled on top of one another. Tilted at crazy angles, the 12,000 visible tombstones are but a fraction of thousands more buried below. Walk the path amid the gravestones; the relief symbols you see represent the names and professions of the deceased. The oldest marked grave belongs to the poet Avigdor Kara, who died in 1439; the original tombstone can be seen in the Maisel Synagogue. The best-known marker belongs to Jehuda ben Bezalel, the famed Rabbi Loew (died 1609), a chief rabbi of Prague and a profound scholar, credited with creating the mythical golem. Even today, small scraps of paper bearing wishes are stuffed into the cracks of the rabbi's tomb with the hope that he will grant them. ⊠ *Široká 3, Josefov* ✛ *Entrance through Pinkas Synagogue* ☎ *222–749–211* ⊕ *jewishmuseum.cz* 🔖 *Jewish Museum combination*

ticket *350 Kč* (*excl. Old-New Synagogue*) or *500 Kč* (*incl. Old-New Synagogue*) ⊘ *Closed Sat. and Jewish holidays* Ⓜ *Line A: Staroměstská.*

Uměleckoprůmyslové museum v Praze (*Museum of Decorative Arts, or U(P)M*)
HISTORY MUSEUM | In a custom-built art nouveau building dating to 1897, this wonderfully laid-out museum of exquisite local prints, books, ceramics, textiles, clocks, and furniture will please anyone from the biggest decorative arts expert to those who just appreciate a little *Antiques Roadshow* on the weekend. There are superb rotating exhibits, too, and a fantastic design-led gift shop. ⊠ *17. listopadu 2, Josefov* ☎ *778–543–900* ⊕ *upm.cz* 🔖 *300 Kč* ⊘ *Closed Mon.* Ⓜ *Line A: Staroměstská.*

Židovská radnice (*Jewish Town Hall*)
NOTABLE BUILDING | You can't just wander into this building as a member of the public, but while you're in the area, it's worth paying attention to the outside. The hall was the creation of Mordechai Maisel, an influential Jewish leader at the end of the 16th century. Restored in the 18th century, it was given a clock and bell tower at that time. A second clock, with Hebrew numbers, keeps time counterclockwise. Now a Jewish Community Center, the building also houses Shalom, a kosher restaurant. The restaurant is open to the public for walk-ins during the week, and for Shabbat lunch or dinner if you book, but there are probably better options for dining in this quarter if you don't keep kosher. ⊠ *Maiselova 18, Josefov* ☎ *224–800–812* ⊕ *kehilaprag.cz* Ⓜ *Line A: Staroměstská.*

🍴 Restaurants

Josefov occupies a quiet corner of Staré Město and it can get almost eerie at night. But there are a few good restaurants scattered in and around the neighborhood, and the setting can be magnificent.

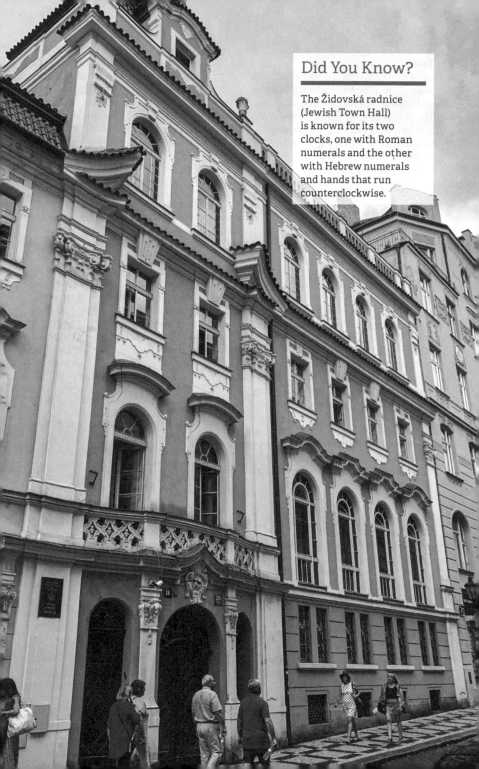

Did You Know?

The Židovská radnice (Jewish Town Hall) is known for its two clocks, one with Roman numerals and the other with Hebrew numerals and hands that run counterclockwise.

Dinitz

$$ | **MIDDLE EASTERN** | As you would expect, Josefov has some solid kosher options for Jewish travelers. Of these, Dinitz is probably the most welcoming to both Jews and non-Jews and is a relaxed, often buzzing spot for Middle Eastern–inspired food and good grilled meat. **Known for:** reasonably priced kosher food; large portions; tasty hummus and schnitzel sandwiches. $ Average main: Kč300 ✉ Bílkova 12, Josefov ☎ 222–244–000 ⊕ dinitz.cz ☯ No dinner Fri. No lunch Sat. Ⓜ Line A: Staroměstská.

Field

$$$$ | **SCANDINAVIAN** | A relative newcomer to Prague's fine-dining scene, Field has made a splash quickly, grabbing a Michelin star for its locally sourced, Scandi-style food. While its tasting menu is astronomically expensive, there are cheats: the shorter weekday lunch tasting menu is much more reasonable, at 950 Kč. **Known for:** sensational seasonal food; tasting menus with simple-sounding but astonishing options like beef and cauliflower or chocolate and yuzu; stripped-back decor with an eye-catching ceiling. $ Average main: Kč950 ✉ U Milosrdných 12, Josefov ☎ 725–170–583 ⊕ fieldrestaurant.cz Ⓜ Line A: Staroměstská.

Food Lab

$$ | **ECLECTIC** | At last! A huge, hip, all-day dining space on the edge of Staré Město's Jewish quarter. **Known for:** one of Prague's best brunches; well-priced; beautiful, plant-filled interior. $ Average main: Kč200 ✉ Haštalská 4, Josefov ☎ 257–310–713 ⊕ food-lab.cz Ⓜ Line A: Haštalská.

★ La Veranda

$$$ | **EUROPEAN** | Despite the quality of the cooking, La Veranda remains somewhat overlooked by visitors (though popular with locals), making a visit to this stylish, softly lighted room feel like you've been let in on a wonderful secret. The food is top-notch, with seasonal specials and a not outrageously priced six-course tasting menu showcasing the restaurant's greatest hits, like an incredibly rich beef tartare with egg yolk and black truffle. **Known for:** delicious, seasonal food; non-touristy vibe; not crazily priced six-course tasting menu. $ Average main: Kč600 ✉ Elišky Krásnohorské 2, Josefov ☎ 224–814–733 ⊕ laveranda.cz ☯ Closed Sun. Ⓜ Line A: Staroměstská.

Les Moules

$$ | **BELGIAN** | Staré Město can sometimes feel relentlessly "olde-worlde" Czech, and Belgian-styled bistro Les Moules represents part of the appeal of dining in Josefov instead, with a more international, modern vibe. There's a nice open terrace and a fine selection of mussels, as you'd expect from the name. **Known for:** mussels prepared 12 different ways; huge Belgian beer selection; brisk, bistro-like feel, overlooking Pařižská. $ Average main: Kč200 ✉ Pařižská 19, Josefov ☎ 222–315–022 ⊕ lesmoules.cz Ⓜ Line A: Staroměstská.

Mistral

$$ | **EUROPEAN** | For travelers sick of heavy dumplings, rich fare, and dimly lit cellar pubs, Mistral is an oasis: light, bright, and modern, with a short international menu featuring fresh salads, soups, and pastas, with some Czech specials thrown in. Service is always friendly and somehow the place never seems to be too busy, despite its central location. **Known for:** a gentle hum of conversation in many different languages; fresh cakes; an unusual (in this part of town) focus on vegetables—particularly salads. $ Average main: Kč200 ✉ Valentinská 11, Josefov ☎ 222–317–737 ⊕ facebook.com/cafemistral Ⓜ Line A: Staroměstská.

Pepenero Pizza & Pasta

$$ | **ITALIAN** | Whether Pepenero serves some of the best pizza in Prague is the source of constant debate among locals, but one thing is for sure: it has the city's best mozzarella. Tangy and creamy, the cheese is as authentic as can be. **Known**

for: quick and easy food and service; delicious margherita pizza; lively spot. ⑤ *Average main: Kč230* ✉ *Bílkova 4, Josefov* ☎ *222–315–543* ⊕ *pepenero.cz* Ⓜ *Line A: Staroměstská.*

Hotels

★ Emblem Hotel Prague

$$$ | HOTEL | Rivaling the best design hotels in capital cities around the world, this unique retreat goes toe to toe with many of the city's grande dame hotels; it's smart, fresh, and funky, with a modern art deco theme created by a host of top-notch designers. **Pros:** major design chops; good restaurant; unique focus on modern art. **Cons:** rooms are a little small; rooftop Jacuzzi is an extra charge; underground hotel bar could have more atmosphere. ⑤ *Rooms from: Kč5800* ✉ *Platnéřská 19, Josefov* ☎ *226–202–500* ⊕ *emblemprague.com* ⟿ *59 rooms* ⑩ *No Meals* Ⓜ *Line A: Staroměstská.*

Golden Prague Rooms

$$ | HOTEL | A quiet, affordable boutique hotel right in the heart of the Jewish Quarter, the entrance is so subtle you could almost walk past it. **Pros:** chic, cubist-style decor; good location; great value. **Cons:** no elevator; some rooms are small; no air-conditioning. ⑤ *Rooms from: Kč2500* ✉ *Elišky Krásnohorské 11/4, Josefov* ☎ *703–147–073* ⊕ *golden-prague-rooms.com* ⟿ *38 rooms* ⑩ *No Meals* Ⓜ *Line A: Staroměstská.*

★ Hotel Hastal Prague Old Town

$$ | HOTEL | A well-priced, charming, family-run hotel located in a quiet spot just a few minutes from Old Town Square, with welcoming touches including complimentary all-day coffee in the lobby or courtyard—oh, and a golem statue out front. **Pros:** great location on a quiet street; pleasant rooms with a/c, some with views over the square; lovely welcome from family who have run the hotel for six generations. **Cons:** breakfast room can get busy; folksy feel might not

appeal to everyone; rooms vary in size. ⑤ *Rooms from: Kč2500* ✉ *Haštalská 16, Josefov* ☎ *222–314–335* ⊕ *hastal.com* ⟿ *31 rooms* ⑩ *Free Breakfast* Ⓜ *Line A: Staroměstská.*

Maximilian

$$$ | HOTEL | This design hotel in the heart of Staré Město is a tasteful fusion of light, airy modernism, a look that works perfectly in the lobby, with chrome lamps and square armchairs, but is less successful in the blue rooms, which can be a bit gloomy. **Pros:** unique vibe: guests can even borrow a goldfish to keep them company; cozy library and honesty bar; relaxing on-site Planet Zen spa. **Cons:** upper-floor rooms could use more light; can be some street noise; breakfast is not extensive. ⑤ *Rooms from: Kč4900* ✉ *Haštalská 14, Josefov* ☎ *225–303–111* ⊕ *maximilianhotel.com* ⟿ *71 rooms* ⑩ *Free Breakfast* Ⓜ *Line A: Staroměstská.*

Nightlife

Josefov specializes in the stylish cocktail crowd, plus it's the place to catch the boat for most of the evening cruises. One big advantage to this end of Staré Město is fewer stag and hen parties to contend with.

BARS AND PUBS

L'Fleur

COCKTAIL LOUNGES | One of a gaggle of swanky cocktail bars that have recently taken Prague by storm, L'Fleur mixes it with the best of them, blending old-school elegance—although arguably the decoration feels a little generic—and classic cocktails with local flavors (try the Parfum for a hit of traditional Czech spirit Becherovka). The menu contains some unusual ingredients—so much so that it can be a bit incomprehensible—but friendly staff are happy to explain. ✉ *V Kolkovně 920/5, Josefov* ☎ *734–255–665* ⊕ *facebook.com/LFleurBar* Ⓜ *Line A: Staroměstská.*

Public Interest Bar

COCKTAIL LOUNGES | With a cooler, more modern and stripped-back cocktail bar vibe than some of the others in this quarter, Public Interest has one of those drinks lists where everything is tempting, although Heroes is our current favorite (gin, grapefruit, lemongrass, and Prosecco—what's not to like?). It also serves good coffee if you are looking for a slightly less decadent after-dinner drink. ☒ *U Milosrdných 12, Josefov* ☎ *725–821–878* ⊕ *publicinterest.cz* ◷ *Closed Sun.* Ⓜ *Line A: Staroměstská.*

Tretter's

COCKTAIL LOUNGES | The lost elegance of the 1930s, with clean lines on dark wood, is re-created in a bar that serves Manhattans, martinis, and other classic cocktails, sometimes with live jazz in the background. This was a trendsetter in Prague when it first opened for classic cocktails, and it remains a great joint for a sophisticated tipple, although it can feel a bit sleazy depending on the crowd. Make sure to book in advance on weekends. ☒ *V Kolkovně 3, Josefov* ☎ *224–811–165* ⊕ *tretters.cz* Ⓜ *Line A: Staroměstská.*

U Rudolfina

BREWPUBS | Some people claim that the way the beer is tapped here makes it the best in town, which probably explains the constant crowds. This was one of the first places in the world to offer unpasteurized beer from tanks, rather than kegs. And the place still retains its old-fashioned charm, making it one of the best authentic Czech pubs in a heavily touristed area. Groups should make reservations—a free table is rare. ☒ *Křížovnická 10, Josefov* ☎ *222–328–758* ⊕ *urudolfina.cz* Ⓜ *Line A: Staroměstská.*

EVENING BOAT TRIPS

Dinner Cruise with Music

BOATING | This "dinner cruise" can become a sing-along once the drinks kick in, so be prepared for boisterous merriment. The boat is heated, and this cruise runs in both winter and summer. The relatively early departure hour (7 pm) means you can catch the sunset in the summertime, and then dine by candlelight, which is lovely. The entry price includes a buffet dinner and welcome drink, but no additional beverages. ☒ *Dvořákovo nábř., under Čechův most, Josefov* ☎ *742–202–505* ⊕ *evd.cz/en/dinner-on-board* 🎫 *1,200 Kč* Ⓜ *Line A: Staroměstská.*

Jazzboat

BOATING | Jazz, food, drinks, floating down the Vltava, and spectacular views of Prague—if you're a jazz fan (or a fan of river cruises), it doesn't get much better than this. The Jazzboat sails throughout the year; blankets are provided if it gets chilly for those sitting outside. The fee includes a welcome drink, but your food bill is separate and there's an extra 100 Kč fee for peak nights, and for window seats.

■ TIP→ **Be punctual, as the boat sails at 8:30 pm on the dot.** ☒ *Josefov* ✛ *Usually takes off from Pier 2, under Čechův most* ☎ *731–183–180* ⊕ *jazzboat.cz* 🎫 *690 Kč* Ⓜ *Line A: Staroměstská.*

Performing Arts

CHURCH CONCERTS

Kostel sv. Šimona a Judy (Church of Sts. Simon and Jude)

CONCERTS | This decommissioned church with a restored organ and frescoes is used by the Prague Symphony Orchestra for chamber concerts and recitals, and it's also a popular venue for music festivals. The baroque altar is actually an elaborate painting on the wall. ☒ *Dušní ul., Josefov* ☎ *222–002–336* ⊕ *fok.cz/cs/kostel-sv-simona-judy* Ⓜ *Line A: Staroměstská.*

🛍 Shopping

Shopping in Josefov is a tale of two cities. Firstly, and most dramatically, it is bisected by Pařížská, Prague's swankiest shopping street. A long, straight boulevard from Old Town Square down to the river, Pařížská boasts all of the world's fanciest labels and parking spaces housing Bugattis and Bentleys, but not much in the way of a unique Czech feel. It's a nice enough tree-lined stroll, though, if only to see how the other half lives. More interesting, however, are the side streets that wind around this ancient quarter, housing fantastic and unique boutiques of all hues, as well as bookshops and even an old-fashioned general store.

ACCESSORIES
★ BackYard Boutique
MIXED CLOTHING | A large, extremely hip space that is more than just a shop; it's also a design collective where you can meet jewelers and fashion designers, see their work, hear lectures, or just have a coffee or a glass of wine. The neon sign glimpsed from across the street is enticing, and the light-filled interior does not disappoint: from Nastassia Aleinikava's rose-gold strawberry necklaces and out-there specs to unique jackets made from recycled jeans from Restore by Acarin, these are some of the coolest modern design pieces in the city. ⊠ U Obecního dvora 2, Josefov ☎ 605–894–096 ⊕ www.back-yard.cz Ⓜ Line A: Staroměstská.

BEAUTY
Ingredients
COSMETICS | An extremely swanky beauty boutique run by two Czechs, with Sisley Boudoir, the on-site aromatherapy and treatment center. Rare perfumes, skin-care products, and candles are displayed amid contemporary Czech art in such a crisp display that it borders on clinical. ⊠ Maiselova 41/21, Josefov ☎ 211–150–159 ⊕ ingredients-store.cz Ⓜ Line A: Staroměstská.

CLOTHING
La Sartoria
MEN'S CLOTHING | Big, luxurious rugs, Frank Sinatra playing in the background,

a set of whiskey glasses in the window, and the dartboard. Oh, right: there are clothes, too, such as beautifully made Neapolitan-style men's suits and jackets perfect for a weekend in the country. There's a tailoring service as well. ⊠ Haštalska 9, Josefov ☎ 606–788–878 ⊕ lasartoria.cz Ⓜ Line A: Staroměstská.

Space Praga
MEN'S CLOTHING | One of the coolest shops in Prague, Space is usually teeming with funky young Czechs on the lookout for something new and different. The garments, from a mixture of local and global, and new and established, fashion houses, are beautiful, from the distressed jackets to the bright shirts; browsing the racks makes you feel like you're looking through somebody's wonderful closet. This is the menswear branch; the women's shop, which collaborates with leading Czech leather and fur specialist Ivana Mentlova, is a few streets over at Rámová 1. ⊠ Vězeňská 6, Josefov ☎ 725–100–317 ⊕ spacepraga.com Ⓜ Line A: Staroměstská.

Tina Hollas
WOMEN'S CLOTHING | This hidden-away little studio and shop offers organic clothing and accessories, following the designer Martina Hollasová's belief that the materials we have close to our bodies can have a real impact on our lives. The pieces are elegant, expensive, and simple, but never boring, from beige swing coats to loose cream dresses. Custom consultations are available. ⊠ U Obecního dvora 4, Josefov ☎ 602–325–125 ⊕ tinahollas.com Ⓜ Line A: Staroměstská.

★ Vidda
WOMEN'S CLOTHING | Do not waste your time with the typical multinational brands stationed on Pařížská. Instead, pop round the corner to this lovely, minimalist clothing and lifestyle store, check out its roster of stylish Czech and Slovak fashion, and buy yourself a cup of coffee while you chat with the friendly owner, perched on one of the small tables by

the entrance. A lovely place to while away half an hour or more, while also picking up some unique items to take home. ⊠ *Elišky Krásnohorské 9, Josefov* ☎ *739–333–444* ⊕ *lagallery.cz* ⊘ *Closed Sun.* Ⓜ *Line A: Staroměstská.*

FOOD AND DRINK

★ Masna na Kozím plácku

FOOD | This food shop on a quiet stretch of Kozí is like walking into a bygone era before supermarkets took over the high street. Think the best bread, meat, and cheese shop from the 18th century that you can possibly imagine, and you've just described this place. Shelves groan with fresh produce, the air is full of delicious smells, and friendly staff are ready to help tease your taste buds.

■ **TIP→ You can get freshly cooked meaty meals here, too—a worthy alternative to the extremely popular, and busy, Naše maso butcher's shop on Dlouhá. Dobrou chuť!** (That's Czech for "Bon appétit!") ⊠ *Kozí 9, Josefov* ☎ *255–795–404* ⊕ *masnakozi.cz* ⊘ *Closed weekends* Ⓜ *Line A: Staroměstská.*

HOME AND DESIGN

Glassimo

JEWELRY & WATCHES | Josefov's answer to Staré Město's glass stores certainly holds its own. A bright space filled with amazing Czech glass sculptures, as well as porcelain pieces and contemporary art, Glassimo is a good option if you just have to take home some Bohemian glassware. The light fittings made by Kateřina Smolíková and Italy bowls and vases by Jiří Pačínek are unique to the store. ⊠ *Elišky Krásnohorské 3, Josefov* ☎ *702–181–804* ⊕ *glassimo.eu* Ⓜ *Line A: Staroměstská.*

JEWELRY

Antiques Cinolter

ANTIQUES & COLLECTIBLES | This traditional antiques store, with its wares displayed in cases and on dark wood tables, specializes in jewelry and gems but also has a great line in silverware of various kinds. There are some really unusual rings and brooches, as well as pieces like a porcelain Japanese cat and a red hyalite glass vase. Established in 1991 by gemologist Martin Cinolter, the store also makes bespoke pieces, including a miniature version of the Czech crown jewels for the Dalai Lama when he visited Prague. ⊠ *Maiselova 9, Josefov* ☎ *222–319–816* ⊕ *antiquesprague.cz* Ⓜ *Line A: Staroměstská.*

Halada

JEWELRY & WATCHES | This classy Czech-German jewelry company, set up by a couple in the 1970s, supplies trinkets by carefully chosen brands and produces its own pieces and is among the only home-grown brand on swanky Pařížská. It holds its own against the international big hitters, offering stunning pearls in different shades, as well as gold, silver, and platinum items. This branch offers the most varied selection, while the serene shop on Na příkopě focuses on pearls. ⊠ *Pařížská 7, Josefov* ☎ *724–986–111* ⊕ *halada.cz* Ⓜ *Line A: Staroměstská.*

Zlatnictví Miloslav Ráž

JEWELRY & WATCHES | The real treat at this old-school jewelry store is getting a glimpse of the jeweler at work—he may even give you a wave if you're lucky. The store has a variety of items including rings and other jewels, some of which are displayed in the window, but you can also create your own unique piece with a designer. It can be expensive, but you're getting handcrafted items with real gems, after all. ⊠ *V Kolkovně 8, Josefov* ☎ *603–440–874* ⊕ *zlatnictviraz.cz* ⊘ *Closed weekends* Ⓜ *Line A: Staroměstská.*

Chapter 4

MALÁ STRANA

4

Updated by
Jennifer Rigby

👁 **Sights**
★★★☆☆

🍴 **Restaurants**
★★★★☆

🛏 **Hotels**
★★★★☆

🛍 **Shopping**
★★★☆☆

🍸 **Nightlife**
★★☆☆☆

CHARLES BRIDGE

This is Prague's signature attraction. The view from the foot of the bridge on the Staré Město side, encompassing the towers and domes of Malá Strana and the soaring spires of Katedrála sv. Víta (St. Vitus Cathedral), is nothing short of breathtaking.

This heavenly vista subtly changes in perspective as you walk across the bridge, attended by a host of baroque saints that decorate the bridge's peaceful Gothic stones. At night its drama is spellbinding: St. Vitus Cathedral lit in a ghostly green, the castle in monumental yellow, and the Church of St. Nicholas in a voluptuous pink, all viewed through the menacing silhouettes of the bowed statues and the Gothic towers. Night is the best time to visit the bridge, which is choked with visitors and vendors by day. The later the hour, the thinner the crowds—though the bridge is never truly empty, even at daybreak.

The bridge is open all day, every day, and entry is free. The easiest way to find the bridge from Staroměstské náměstí (Old Town Square) is to follow the narrow, winding Karlova lane, which begins on the western end of Malé náměstí, just next to Old Town Square, and takes you, twisting and turning, to the foot of the bridge. From the Malá Strana side, start from central Lesser Quarter Square and follow the street Mostecká directly to the bridge (you can't miss it).

A BRIEF HISTORY OF THE BRIDGE

When the Přemyslid princes set up residence in Prague during the 10th century, there was a ford across the Vltava here—a vital link along one of Europe's major trading routes. After several wooden bridges and the first stone bridge washed away in floods, Charles IV appointed the 27-year-old German Peter Parler, the architect of St. Vitus Cathedral, to build a new structure in 1357. It became one of the wonders of the world in the Middle Ages.

After 1620, following the disastrous defeat of Czech Protestants by Catholic Habsburgs at the Battle of White Mountain, the bridge became a symbol of the Counter-Reformation's vigorous re-Catholicization efforts.

The religious conflict is less obvious nowadays, leaving behind only an artistic tension between baroque and Gothic that gives the bridge its allure.

ABOUT THE TOWER

Staroměstská mostecká věž (Old Town Bridge Tower), at the bridge entrance on the Staré Město side, is where Peter Parler, the architect of the Charles Bridge, began his bridge building. The carved façades he designed for the sides of the tower were destroyed by Swedish soldiers in 1648, at the end of the Thirty Years' War. The sculptures facing Staré Město, however, are still intact (although some are recent copies). They depict an old and gout-ridden Charles IV with his son, who became Wenceslas IV. Above them are two of Bohemia's patron saints, Adalbert of Prague and Sigismund. The top of the tower offers a spectacular view of the city for 150 Kč; it's open daily from 10 to 9 in the summer, closing earlier in the winter.

TOURING THE BRIDGE, STATUE BY STATUE

Take a closer look at some of the statues while walking toward Malá Strana. The third one on the right, a bronze crucifix from the mid-17th century, is the oldest of all. The fifth on the left, which shows St. Francis Xavier carrying four pagan princes (an Indian, Moor, Chinese, and Tartar) ready for conversion, represents an outstanding piece of baroque sculpture. Eighth on the right is the statue of St. John of Nepomuk, who according to legend was wrapped in chains and thrown to his death from this bridge. Touching the statue is supposed to bring good luck or, according to some versions of the story, a return visit to Prague.

NEIGHBORHOOD SNAPSHOT

TOP EXPERIENCES

- **Charles Bridge:** Walk over very early in the morning to avoid the crowds and take in breathtaking views.

- **Baráčnická rychta:** Pretend you're a local, supping beers with the authentic crowd at this joint.

- **Shopping:** Browse intriguing stores for souvenirs and Czech design at Artisème, or the best Czech puppets in town at Marionety.

- **Terasa U Zlaté studně:** Break the bank—it's worth it—here, with a swanky lunch accompanied by a drop-dead-gorgeous view.

- **Kampa:** Soak up the riverside calm (don't miss the weird baby sculptures or the graffiti at the nearby John Lennon wall), or head up peaceful Petřín.

- **Kostel sv. Mikuláše (Church of St. Nicholas):** One of the most beautiful examples of baroque church architecture in Prague (and that's really saying something).

VIEWFINDER

- There's no better way to arrive at Malá Strana than via a scenic downhill walk from the castle or a lovely stroll from Staré Město (Old Town) across the Charles Bridge or (for less crowds and a view of the bridge itself) across the much quieter Mánesův bridge, just north of the main event.

GETTING HERE

Metro Line A leads you to Malá Strana (Lesser Quarter), with Malostranská station the most central stop (from here, you can either walk or take Tram 12, 20, or 26 one stop to Malostranské náměstí, or Lesser Quarter Square). Trams also come into the main square from all over town, including Trams 15, 22, and 23.

PLANNING YOUR TIME

Note that in summer, the heat builds up during the day in this area—as do the crowds—so it's best visited before noon or in the early evening, and allow at least a couple of hours to tick off the main sights. On pretty much every block there are plenty of cafés in which to stop, sip coffee or tea, and people-watch and a wealth of gardens and parks ideal for resting in the cool shade.

Established in 1257, this is Prague's most perfectly formed neighborhood. Translated as the "Lesser Quarter" and also known as "Little Town," it was originally home to the merchants and craftsmen who served the royal court, itself housed in the famous castle that sits just above this district. Don't let the diminutive moniker fool you, though; Malá Strana is small, but its charm more than stands up to the rest of the city center, and it can be less crowded, particularly off the main drag.

Though it is not nearly as confusing as the labyrinth that is Staré Město, the streets here can baffle, but they also bewitch, with hidden alleyways, uneven, ancient stone steps, and baroque gems on every corner. Originally a cluster of noble homes and palaces, today the area holds embassies, Czech government offices, historical attractions, and galleries, mixed in with the usual glut of pubs, restaurants, and souvenir shops. The neighborhood also boasts some pretty squares, gorgeous gardens, and the green spaces of Kampa and Petřín, giving it a sense of calm that's a welcome bonus, particularly after tackling the crowds that rightfully pack themselves onto Charles Bridge for some of the most arresting urban vistas in the world.

Other than the bridge, Malá Strana isn't as studded with "must-sees" as Staré Město, but take time to explore the architecture and the history of its streets. The shopping is an interesting mix, with some cool Czech design interspersed with more traditional tourist fare. Malá Strana also has an interesting culinary scene, including down-to-earth Czech joints as well as some of the city center's fanciest restaurants. The area is quiet at night, which can make for enchanting lamplit walks and a good option for those who prefer quieter accommodations, often featuring the historical quirks that make this centuries-old, architecturally rich neighborhood such a magical place to explore.

 Sights

★ **Charles Bridge** (*Karlův most*)
BRIDGE | This is Prague's signature monument, and quite rightly so. The view from the foot of the bridge on the Staré Město

Sights ▼

1 Charles Bridge **H4**
2 Franz Kafka Museum... **H3**
3 Kampa **G5**
4 Kostel Panny
   Marie vítězné............ **E4**
5 Kostel sv.
   Mikuláše **E3**
6 Malostranské
   náměstí **E3**
7 Museum Kampa **G5**
8 Na Kampě **G4**
9 Nerudova ulice......... **D2**
10 Palácové zahrady
   pod Pražským
   hradem.................... **F1**
11 Petřínské sady **C5**
12 Schönbornský palác ... **D3**
13 Valdštejnska
   zahrada **G1**
14 Velkopřevorské
   náměstí **F4**
15 Vojanovy sady.......... **G2**
16 Vrtbovská zahrada...... **D4**

Restaurants ▼

1 Atelier Red&Wine **E8**
2 Café de Paris............ **F4**
3 Ichnusa Botega &
   Bistro..................... **F7**
4 Kampa Park **G5**
5 Loki Burgers.............. **F7**
6 Luka Lu................... **E5**
7 NOI **E6**
8 Pastař.................... **G7**
9 The Sushi Bar **F7**
10 Terasa U Zlaté
   studně................... **E1**
11 Tlustá myš **F6**
12 U Modré kachničky...... **F5**

Quick Bites ▼

1 Angelato **E6**
2 Bread Gap **E3**
3 Café Savoy **F7**
4 Cukrkávalimonáda....... **F4**
5 Kafíčko................... **F4**
6 Roesel.................... **F3**

Hotels ▼

1 Alchymist Grand
   Hotel and Spa **D3**
2 Appia Hotel
   Residences.............. **B3**
3 Aria Hotel **D3**
4 Augustine, a Luxury
   Collection Hotel,
   Prague **F2**
5 Boutique Hotel
   Constans................. **C3**
6 Dům u velké boty/House
   at the Big Boot........... **C3**
7 Golden Well Hotel **E1**
8 Hotel Bishop's House ... **F3**
9 Hotel Neruda............ **B2**
10 Mandarin Oriental
   Prague **F4**
11 Pod Věží.................. **F3**
12 Sax Vintage
   Design Hotel.............. **C3**
13 U Tří Pštrosů.............. **F3**

KEY

1 *Sights*
1 *Restaurants*
1 *Quick Bites*
1 *Hotels*
M *Metro Station*

side, encompassing the towers and domes of Malá Strana and the soaring spires of St. Vitus Cathedral, is nothing short of breathtaking. This heavenly vista subtly changes in perspective as you walk across the bridge, attended by a host of baroque saints that decorate the bridge's peaceful Gothic stones. At night its drama is spellbinding: St. Vitus Cathedral lit in a ghostly green, Prague Castle in monumental yellow, and the Church of St. Nicholas in a voluptuous pink, all viewed through the menacing silhouettes of the bowed statues and the Gothic towers. Night is the best time to visit the bridge, which is choked with visitors, vendors, and beggars by day. The later the hour, the thinner the crowds—though the bridge is never truly empty, even at daybreak. Tourists with flash cameras are there all hours of the night, and as dawn is breaking, revelers from the dance clubs at the east end of the bridge weave their way homeward, singing loudly and debating where to go for breakfast. When the Přemyslid princes set up residence in Prague during the 10th century, there was a ford across the Vltava here—a vital link along one of Europe's major trading routes. After several wooden bridges and the first stone bridge washed away in floods, Charles IV appointed the 27-year-old German Peter Parler, the architect of St. Vitus Cathedral, to build a new structure in 1357. It became one of the wonders of the world in the Middle Ages. After 1620, following the disastrous defeat of Czech Protestants by Catholic Habsburgs at the Battle of White Mountain, the bridge became a symbol of the Counter-Reformation's vigorous re-Catholicization efforts. The many baroque statues that appeared in the late 17th century, commissioned by Catholics, came to symbolize the totality of the Austrian (hence Catholic) triumph. The Czech writer Milan Kundera sees the statues from this perspective: "The thousands of saints looking out from all sides, threatening you, following you,

hypnotizing you, are the raging hordes of occupiers who invaded Bohemia 350 years ago to tear the people's faith and language from their hearts." The religious conflict is less obvious nowadays, leaving behind an artistic tension between baroque and Gothic that gives the bridge its allure. Staroměstská mostecká věž (Old Town Bridge Tower), at the bridge entrance on the Staré Město side, is where Peter Parler, the architect of the Charles Bridge, began his bridge building. The carved façades he designed for the sides of the tower were destroyed by Swedish soldiers in 1648, at the end of the Thirty Years' War. The sculptures facing Staré Město, however, are still intact (although some are recent copies). They depict an old and gout-ridden Charles IV with his son, who became Wenceslas IV. Above them are two of Bohemia's patron saints, Adalbert of Prague and Sigismund. The top of the tower offers a spectacular view of the city for 100 Kč; it's open daily year-round from 10 am to between 6 and 10 pm. Take a closer look at some of the statues while walking toward Malá Strana. The third one on the right, a bronze crucifix from the mid-17th century, is the oldest of all. It's mounted on the location of a wooden cross destroyed in a battle with the Swedes (the golden Hebrew inscription was reputedly financed by a Jew accused of defiling the cross). The fifth on the left, which shows St. Francis Xavier carrying four pagan princes (an Indian, Moor, Chinese, and Tartar) ready for conversion, represents an outstanding piece of baroque sculpture. Eighth on the right is the statue of St. John of Nepomuk, who according to legend was wrapped in chains and thrown to his death from this bridge. Touching the statue is supposed to bring good luck or, according to some versions of the story, a return visit to Prague. On the left-hand side, sticking out from the bridge between the 9th and 10th statues (the latter has a wonderfully expressive vanquished Satan), stands a Roland

(Bruncvík) statue. This knightly figure, bearing the coat of arms of Staré Město, was once a reminder that this part of the bridge belonged to Staré Město before Prague became a unified city in 1784. For many art historians the most valuable statue is the 12th on the left, near the Malá Strana end. Mathias Braun's statue of St. Luitgarde depicts the blind saint kissing Christ's wounds. The most compelling grouping, however, is the second from the end on the left, a work of Ferdinand Maxmilian Brokoff (son of Johann) from 1714. Here the saints are incidental; the main attraction is the Turk, his face expressing extreme boredom at guarding the Christians imprisoned in the cage at his side. When the statue was erected, just 31 years after the second Turkish siege of Vienna, it scandalized the Prague public, who smeared it with mud. During communist rule, Prague suffered from bad air pollution, which damaged some of the baroque statues. In more recent years, the increasing number of visitors on the bridge has added a new threat. To preserve the value of the statues, most of the originals were removed from the bridge and replaced with detailed copies. Several of the originals can be viewed in the Lapidárium museum. A few more can be found within the casemates at the Vyšehrad citadel. ⊠ *Malá Strana* Ⓜ *Line A: Staroměstská.*

Franz Kafka Museum
OTHER MUSEUM | The great early-20th-century Jewish author Franz Kafka wasn't considered Czech and he wrote in German, but he lived in Prague nearly his entire short, anguished life, so it's fitting that his shrine is here too. Because the museum's designers believed in channeling Kafka's darkly paranoid and paradoxical work, they created exhibits true to this spirit. And even if the results are often goofy, they get an A for effort. Facsimiles of manuscripts, documents, first editions, photographs, and newspaper obits are displayed in glass vitrines, which in turn are situated in "Kafkaesque" settings: huge open filing cabinets, stone gardens, piles of coal. The basement level of the museum gets even freakier, with expressionistic representations of Kafka's work itself, including a model of the horrible torture machine from the "In the Penal Colony" story—not a place for young children, or even lovers on a first date, but fascinating to anyone familiar with Kafka's work. Other Kafka sites in Prague include his home on Zlatá ulička (Golden Lane), his Staré Město birthplace at Náměstí Franze Kafky 3, and Jaroslav Rona's trippy bronze sculpture of the writer on Dušní street in Staré Město. (Speaking of sculptures, take a gander at the animatronic *Piss* statue in the Kafka Museum's courtyard. This rendition of a couple urinating into a fountain shaped like the Czech Republic was made by local enfant terrible sculptor David Černý, who also did the babies crawling up the Žižkovská televizní věž [Žižkov TV Tower].) ⊠ *Cihelná 2B, Malá Strana* ☎ *257–535–507* ⊕ *kafkamuseum. cz* ⊠ *240 Kč* Ⓜ *Line A: Malostranská.*

Kampa
CITY PARK | FAMILY | Prague's largest island is circled by the narrow Čertovka streamlet and filled with beautiful, historic buildings. The name Čertovka, or "Devil's Stream," reputedly refers to a cranky old lady who once lived on Maltézské náměstí. During the historic 2002 floods, the well-kept lawns of the Kampa Gardens, which occupy much of the island, were underwater, as was much of the lower portion of Malá Strana. Evidence of flood damage occasionally marks the landscape, along with a sign indicating where the waters crested. These days, the green space is a lovely, calm place to avoid crowds, even on the hottest days. Don't miss another of leading Czech public artist David Černý's works in the middle of the island, too: giant crawling babies with what look like barcodes in place of their faces. ⊠ *Malá Strana* Ⓜ *Line A: Malostranská.*

4

Malá Strana

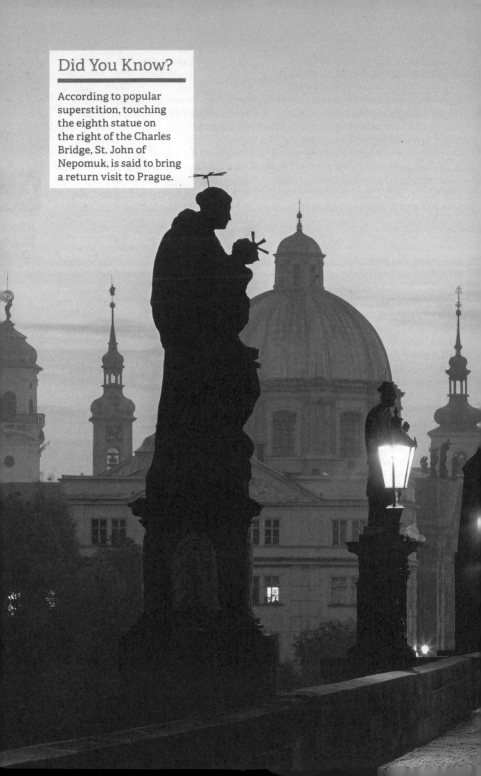

Did You Know?

According to popular superstition, touching the eighth statue on the right of the Charles Bridge, St. John of Nepomuk, is said to bring a return visit to Prague.

Kostel Panny Marie vítězné (*Church of Our Lady Victorious*)

CHURCH | This beautiful church is home to Prague's most famous religious artifact, the Pražské Jezulátko (Infant Jesus of Prague). Originally brought to Prague from Spain in the 16th century, the wax doll holds a reputation for bestowing miracles on many who have prayed for its help. A measure of its widespread attraction is reflected in the prayer books on the kneelers in front of the statue, which have prayers of intercession in 20 different languages. The Bambino, as he's known locally, has an enormous and incredibly ornate wardrobe, some of which is on display in a museum upstairs. Nuns from a nearby convent change the outfit on the statue regularly. Don't miss the souvenir shop (accessible via a doorway to the right of the main altar), where the Bambino's custodians flex their marketing skills. ⊠ *Karmelitská 9A, Malá Strana* ☎ *257–533–646* ⊕ *pragjesu.cz* ⊿ *Free* Ⓜ *Line A: Malostranská plus Tram 12, 20, or 22.*

Kostel sv. Mikuláše (*Church of St. Nicholas*)

CHURCH | With its dynamic curves, this church is arguably the purest and most ambitious example of high baroque in Prague. The celebrated architect Christoph Dientzenhofer began the Jesuit church in 1704 on the site of one of the more active Hussite churches of 15th-century Prague. Work on the building was taken over by his son Kilian Ignaz Dientzenhofer, who built the dome and presbytery. Anselmo Lurago completed the whole thing in 1755 by adding the bell tower. The juxtaposition of the broad, full-bodied dome with the slender bell tower is one of the many striking architectural contrasts that mark the Prague skyline. Inside, the vast pink-and-green space is impossible to take in with a single glance. Every corner bristles with life, guiding the eye first to the dramatic statues, then to the hectic frescoes, and on to the shining faux-marble pillars. Many of the statues are the work of Ignaz Platzer and constitute his last blaze of success. Platzer's workshop was forced to declare bankruptcy when the centralizing and secularizing reforms of Joseph II toward the end of the 18th century brought an end to the flamboyant baroque era. The tower, with an entrance on the side of the church, is open in summer. The church also hosts chamber music concerts in summer, which complement this eye-popping setting but do not reflect the true caliber of classical music in Prague. For that, check the schedule posted across the street at **Líchtenštejnský palác** (Liechtenstein Palace), where the faculty of HAMU, the city's premier music academy, sometimes also gives performances. ⊠ *Malostranské nám., Malá Strana* ☎ *257–534–215* ⊕ *stnicholas.cz* ⊿ *100 Kč, concerts 490 Kč* Ⓜ *Line A: Malostranská plus Tram 12, 20, or 22 to Malostranské náměstí.*

Malostranské náměstí (*Lesser Quarter Square*)

PLAZA/SQUARE | This charming square is flanked on the east and south sides by arcaded houses dating from the 16th and 17th centuries. The Czech government resides partly in the gaudy yellow-and-green palace on the square's north side, partly in several buildings behind the square and towards the river. The huge bulk of the Church of St. Nicholas divides the lower, busier section—buzzing with restaurants, street vendors, clubs, and shops, including an unfortunately prominent Starbucks—from the quieter upper part. There are weekend markets, too. ⊠ *Malá Strana* Ⓜ *Line A: Malostranská.*

Museum Kampa

ART GALLERY | Kampa Island's gem is a remodeled flour mill that displays the private collection of Jan and Meda Mládek, leading Czech exiles during the communist period who supported the then Czechoslovak nonconformist artists. There's a large collection of paintings by

Czech artist František Kupka, considered one of the founders of modern abstract painting, and first-rate temporary exhibitions by both Czech and other Central European visual wizards. The aim of the museum is to showcase the work and the difficult circumstances under which it was created. The museum itself has had some tough times: it was hit hard by flooding in 2002 and 2013 but rebounded relatively quickly on both occasions. The outdoor terrace offers a splendid view of the river and historic buildings on the opposite bank. ⊠ *U Sovových mlýnů 2, Malá Strana* ☎ *257–286–144* ⊕ *museumkampa.cz* ✉ *350 Kč* Ⓜ *Line A: Malostranská plus Tram 12, 20, or 22.*

Na Kampě

PLAZA/SQUARE | Take the stairs on the left of the Charles Bridge as you approach Malá Strana (making sure to peek at the lucky soul who has a balcony overlooking the bridge), and you will come upon one of the most picturesque little squares in Prague. This understated square has a few spots for a beer, a couple of hotels, a regular market, and a wonderfully chill, almost local feel considering how central it is. If you double back on yourself and go under the bridge, that vibe continues with a kid's playground with a stunning view directly onto the Charles Bridge. ⊠ *Malá Strana* Ⓜ *Line A: Malostranská plus Tram 12, 20, or 22.*

Nerudova ulice

STREET | This steep street used to be the last leg of the "Royal Way," the king's procession before his coronation (naturally, he rode a horse rather than climbing). It was named for 19th-century Czech journalist and poet Jan Neruda and has a historical quirk: until 18th-century reforms, house numbering was unknown in Prague. Before this, each house bore a name, depicted pictorially on the façade. Check out No. 6 here, U červeného orla (At the Red Eagle), and No. 12, U tří housliček (At the Three Fiddles), where the Edlinger violin-making family once

lived. Two palaces designed by baroque architect Giovanni Santini (who lived at No. 14), are worth pausing at: the Morzin Palace, on the left at No. 5, has an allegorical "night and day" façade created in 1713 by Ferdinand Brokoff, of Charles Bridge statue fame. Across the street at No. 20 is the Thun-Hohenstein Palace, with its eagle gateway designed by the other great bridge statue sculptor, Mathias Braun. Keep an eye out for the winding passageway under the arch of No. 13, a typical feature of this quarter; note No. 33, the Bretfeld Palace, where Mozart and Casanova stayed when *Don Giovanni* had its world premiere in 1787. ⊠ *Malá Strana* Ⓜ *Tram 12,15, and 20 to Malostranské náměstí.*

Palácové zahrady pod Pražským hradem (*Gardens below Prague Castle*)

GARDEN | A break in the houses along Valdštejnská ulice opens to a gate that leads to five beautifully manicured and terraced baroque gardens, which in season are open to the public. A combined-entry ticket allows you to wander at will, climbing up and down the steps and trying to find the little entryways that lead from one garden to the next. Each of the gardens bears the name of a noble family and includes the Kolovratská zahrada (Kolowrat Garden), Ledeburská zahrada (Ledeburg Garden), Malá a Velká Pálffyovská zahrada (Small and Large Palffy Gardens), and Furstenberská zahrada (Furstenberg Garden). ⊠ *Valdštejnská 12–14, Malá Strana* ☎ *257–214–817* ⊕ *palacove-zahrady.cz* ✉ *130 Kč* Ⓜ *Line A: Malostranská.*

Petřínské sady (*Petřín Park or Petřín Gardens*)

CITY PARK | FAMILY | For a superb view of the city—from a slightly more solitary perch than by the castle—the park on top of Petřín Hill includes a charming playground for children and adults alike, with a miniature (but still pretty big) Eiffel Tower. You'll also find a *bludiště* (mirror maze), as well as a working observatory and the seemingly abandoned Sv. Vavřinec (St. Lawrence) church, which does still hold Sunday Mass. To get here from Malá Strana, simply hike up Petřín Hill (from Karmelitská ulice or Újezd) or ride the funicular railway (which departs near the Újezd tram stop). Regular public-transportation tickets are valid on the funicular.

From Hradčany, you can also stroll over from Strahov klášter (Strahov Monastery), following a wide path that crosses above some fruit orchards and offers breathtaking views over the city below. ⊠ Petřín Hill, Malá Strana ◪ Observatory 90 Kč, tower 150 Kč, maze 100 Kč Ⓜ Line A: Malostranská plus Tram 12, 20, or 22 to Újezd (plus funicular).

Schönbornský palác (Schönborn Palace) **NOTABLE BUILDING** | Franz Kafka had an apartment in this massive baroque building at the top of Tržiště ulice in mid-1917, after moving from Golden Lane. The U.S. Embassy and consular office now occupy this prime location. Although security has been stepped down compared with a few years ago, the many police, guards, and Jersey barriers don't offer much of an invitation to linger. ⊠ Tržiště 15, at Vlašská, Malá Strana Ⓜ Line A: Malostranská plus Tram 12, 20, or 22.

★ **Valdštejnska zahrada** (Wallenstein Palace Gardens) **GARDEN** | With its high-walled gardens and vaulted Renaissance sala terrena (room opening onto a garden), this palace displays superbly elegant grounds. Walking around the formal paths, you come across numerous fountains and statues depicting figures from classical mythology or warriors dispatching a variety of beasts. However, nothing beats the trippy "Grotto," a huge dripstone wall packed with imaginative rock formations, like little faces and animals hidden in the charcoal-color landscape, and what's billed as "illusory hints of secret corridors." Here, truly, staring at the wall is a form of entertainment. Albrecht von

Wallenstein, the one-time owner of the house and gardens, began a meteoric military career in 1622 when the Austrian emperor Ferdinand II retained him to save the empire from the Swedes and Protestants during the Thirty Years' War. Wallenstein, wealthy by marriage, offered to raise an army of 20,000 men at his own cost and lead them personally. Ferdinand II accepted and showered Wallenstein with confiscated land and titles. Wallenstein's first acquisition was this enormous area. After knocking down 23 houses, a brick factory, and three gardens, in 1623 he began to build his magnificent palace. Most of the palace itself now serves the Czech Senate as meeting chamber and offices. The palace's cavernous former Jízdárna, or riding school, now hosts art exhibitions. ⊠ Letenská 10, Malá Strana ☎ 257–075–707 ⊕ senat. cz ◪ Free ◷ Closed Nov.–Mar. Ⓜ Line A: Malostranská.

Velkopřevorské náměstí (Grand Priory Square) **PLAZA/SQUARE** | Located south and slightly west of the Charles Bridge, this square is fronted by the Grand Prior's Palace—considered one of the finest baroque buildings in the area. Though now part of the Embassy of the Sovereign Military Order of Malta—the contemporary (and very real) descendants of the Knights of Malta. Alas, it's closed to the public. Opposite you'll find the flamboyant orange-and-white stucco façade of the Buquoy Palace, built in 1719 by Giovanni Santini and now the French Embassy. The nearby John Lennon Peace Wall was once a monument to youthful rebellion, emblazoned with political slogans and the large painted head of the former Beatle during the communist era in Prague. Back then, it was regularly painted over by the authorities; nowadays, Lennon's visage is seldom seen because it is usually covered instead with political and music-related graffiti. For now, you can still take a pen and add your own, but there's talk of regulations to prevent obscene daubings by inebriated tourists. ✉ *Malá Strana* Ⓜ *Line A: Malostranská plus Tram 12, 20, or 22.*

Vojanovy sady (*Vojan Park*)
CITY PARK | FAMILY | Once the gardens of the Monastery of the Discalced Carmelites, later taken over by the Order of the English Virgins, this walled garden now provides a peaceful haven in summer, with weeping willows, fruit trees, and benches. Exhibitions of modern sculpture are occasionally held here, contrasting sharply with the two baroque chapels and the graceful Ignaz Platzer statue of John of Nepomuk standing on a fish at the entrance. At the other end of the park you can find a terrace with a formal rose garden and a pair of peacocks that like to aggressively preen for visitors under the trellises. The park is surrounded by the high walls of the old monastery and new Ministry of Finance buildings, with only an occasional glimpse of a tower or spire to remind you of the world beyond. ✉ *U lužického semináře 17, Malá Strana* ✛ *Between Letenská ul. and Míšeňská ul.* ☎ *221–097–411* Ⓜ *Line A: Malostranská.*

Vrtbovská zahrada (*Vrtba Garden*)
GARDEN | An unobtrusive door on noisy Karmelitská hides the entranceway to a fascinating sanctuary with one of the best views of Malá Strana. The street door opens onto the intimate courtyard of the Vrtbovský palác (Vrtba Palace). Two Renaissance wings flank the courtyard; the left one was built in 1575, the right one in 1591. The original owner of the latter house was one of the 27 Bohemian nobles executed by the Habsburgs in 1621. The house was given as confiscated property to Count Sezima of Vrtba, who bought the neighboring property and turned the buildings into a late-Renaissance palace. The Vrtba Garden was created a century later. Built in five levels rising behind the courtyard in a wave of statuary-bedecked staircases and formal terraces reaching toward a seashell-decorated pavilion at the top, it's

a popular spot for weddings, receptions, and occasional concerts. (The fenced-off garden immediately behind and above belongs to the U.S. Embassy—hence the U.S. flag that often flies there.) The powerful stone figure of Atlas that caps the entranceway in the courtyard and most of the other statues of mythological figures are from the workshop of Mathias Braun, perhaps the best of the Czech baroque sculptors. ✉ *Karmelitská 25, Malá Strana* ☎ *272–088–350* ⊕ *vrtbovska. cz* ⊠ *120 Kč* ⊘ *Closed Nov.–Mar.* Ⓜ *Line A: Malostranská plus Tram 12, 20, or 22 to Hellichova.*

🍴 Restaurants

Malá Strana has come into its own as a dining destination of late. In the past it was either tourist central or high-end, with little in between, but today there is a wider spread of options to suit every palate and budget. One highlight is places with lovely views, of the river or the rooftops below; Terasa U Zlaté studně is the standout choice.

Atelier Red&Wine
$$$ | CONTEMPORARY | Don't let the slightly weird name and offbeat location fool you: this is a gem. Great seafood, service, and wine at this hidden-away restaurant on the edge of the Mala Strana district, serving choice meals from all over the world. **Known for:** great daily lunch menu; interesting art on the walls; excellent fish dishes. ⑤ *Average main: Kč500* ✉ *Rošických 4, Malá Strana* ☎ *775–932–345* ⊕ *atelier-restaurant.cz* Ⓜ *Line A: Malostranská.*

Café de Paris
$$$ | FRENCH | The twin stars of the show at this Gallic import are beef entrecote and French fries. Café de Paris even makes its own "special sauce" (béarnaise with a hint of mustard). **Known for:** warm and welcoming atmosphere; house specials; waiters serving the steak frites at the table from laden trays.

The John Lennon Peace Wall on the Kampa island continues to be marked with free-spirited, antiwar graffiti years after his death.

⑤ *Average main: Kč500* ✉ *Velkopřevorské nám. 4, Malá Strana* ☎ *603–160–718* ⊕ *www.cafedeparis.cz* ▭ *No credit cards* Ⓜ *Line A: Malostranská.*

Ichnusa Botega & Bistro
$$ | ITALIAN | Tucked into a side street between Malá Strana and Smíchov, the Ichnusa Botega & Bistro evokes the island of Sardinia, with Mediterranean-blue accents, rustic wall decor, and plenty of seafood and wines from Italy's southern reaches. The owners are Sardinian, so the experience is authentic overall. **Known for:** the grilled fish—it can't be beat; fresh and flavorful Italian specialties; sharing cheese and meat platters. ⑤ *Average main: Kč350* ✉ *Plaská 5, Malá Strana* ☎ *605–375–012* ⊕ *ichnusa. business.site* ⊗ *Closed Sun. No lunch Sat.* Ⓜ *Line A: Malostranská plus Tram 12, 20, or 22 to Újezd.*

Kampa Park
$$$$ | EUROPEAN | The zenith of riverside dining is offered at this legendary restaurant just off the Charles Bridge, known almost as much for its chic decor and celebrity guests as it is for its elegant continental cuisine and great wines— it's the kind of place where European royals and heads of state mingle with their head-of-studio counterparts from Hollywood. But the real star power arrives on the plate, with dishes like olive-oil-poached halibut with truffle pearls or tuna tartare with caviar butter. **Known for:** romantic riverside setting; some of Prague's finest food; incredibly attentive staff. ⑤ *Average main: Kč950* ✉ *Na Kampě 8B, Malá Strana* ☎ *296–826–112* ⊕ *kampapark.com* Ⓜ *Line A: Malostranská.*

Loki Burgers
$$ | BURGER | Sometimes, only a beer and a burger will do, and until recently, that would have been a difficult ask in this historic part of town. Enter Loki Burgers, with quality patties and a relaxed atmosphere, at the Petřín park end of town rather than up the hill by the castle. **Known for:** beer and cider on tap, plus a fun cocktail menu; generous portions; the stink burger topped with

mature cheddar, limetta mayonnaise, and caramelized onion. ⑤ *Average main: Kč270* ✉ *Vítězná 15, Malá Strana* ☎ *608–348–065* ⊕ *lokiburgers.cz* Ⓜ *Line A: Malostranská.*

Luka Lu

$$ | MEDITERRANEAN | The decor is bright and eccentric—think cats in fake windows, Picasso-esque murals, and bells hanging from the ceiling—but the ambience is friendly at this pan-Balkan restaurant on a busy stretch of the Malá Strana. Taking cues from Bosnian, Serbian, and Macedonian cuisine, the menu branches out to cover the best of the coasts and hill country plus hearty regional wines from family-run vineyards. **Known for:** authentic specialties like ; Balkan wines; garden at the foot of Petřín. ⑤ *Average main: Kč300* ✉ *Újezd 33, Malá Strana* ☎ *257–212–388* ⊕ *lukalu.cz* Ⓜ *Line A: Malostranská.*

NOI

$$ | THAI | A loungy spot on a well-trafficked stretch of Újezd, NOI delivers on the promise of its Zen interior by cooking excellent Thai classics. Lithe staff are quick to accommodate their hip clientele at low tables surrounded by Buddha statues. **Known for:** fried shrimp cakes; pleasant patio for summer dining; curt but efficient service. ⑤ *Average main: Kč250* ✉ *Újezd 19, Malá Strana* ☎ *608–322–035* ⊕ *noirestaurant.cz* Ⓜ *Line A: Malostranská plus Tram 12, 20, or 22 to Újezd.*

Pastař

$$ | ITALIAN | The clue is in the name here (although beware of the pronunciation: the diactric above the 'r' here makes it sound more like a 'rzz'). Great pasta and other Italian classics at this family-style Italian restaurant, just over the river from the National Theater, making it a good option for a comfortable pre-show bite. **Known for:** some Czech classics (tartare) among the pasta; focus on quality; pleasingly short menu. ⑤ *Average main: Kč350* ✉ *Malostranské nábř. 1, Malá Strana*

Scenic Spots

Prague's best rooftop views probably belong to the fantastic restaurant at the Golden Well Hotel, **Terasa U Zlaté studně,** (✉ *U Zlaté studně* 4 ☎ 257–011–213), although **Ginger & Fred,** on top of Frank Gehry's Tančící dům (Dancing House) across the river (✉ *Rašínovo nábř. 80* ☎ 221–984–160), also makes a reasonable claim. If you're visiting in the summer months, sit on the terrace. If the Charles Bridge is your ideal vista, try the outdoor seating at **Hergetova Cihelna** (✉ *Cihelná 2B* ☎ 296–826–103). The restaurant keeps blankets and heat lamps for when the nights get nippy.

4

Malá Strana

☎ *777–009–108* ⊕ *pastar.cz* Ⓜ *Line A: Malostranská.*

The Sushi Bar

$$$ | SUSHI | This narrow little room across the river from the Narodní divadlo (National Theater) is home to some of the city's best sushi. It was the first sushi place to open in Prague, back in 1999, and the selection remains first-rate by Central European standards. **Known for:** great soft-shell crab maki and seaweed salad; creative menu; melt-in-the-mouth fish. ⑤ *Average main: Kč450* ✉ *Zborovská 49, Malá Strana* ☎ *603–244–882* ⊕ *sushi.cz* Ⓜ *Line A: Malostranská.*

★ Terasa U Zlaté studně

$$$$ | INTERNATIONAL | On top of the boutique Golden Well Hotel, lunch or dinner, either inside or on the terrace of this Michelin-rated restaurant overlooking the city's rooftops, is a delicious experience that more than lives up to the views and prices. The menu runs the gamut from the full degustation (3,400 Kč) to more reasonably priced à **Known for:** exceptional cooking of an inventive international menu; among the best views in Prague;

Cafe Savoy is known for its long lines but the spectacular art nouveau interior is worth the wait.

feeling of exclusivity. $ *Average main: Kč1000* ✉ *Golden Well Hotel, U Zlaté studně 4, Malá Strana* ☎ *257–533–322* ⊕ *terasauzlatestudne.cz* Ⓜ *Line A: Malostranská.*

Tlustá myš

$$ | CZECH | With no-frills, well-priced, hearty Czech cooking in an atmospheric cellar, this is the kind of restaurant where tourists and locals happily intermingle. The menu boasts the big hitters of Czech cuisine at non-rip-off prices and hosts many happy patrons chowing down— with large mugs of pilsner, of course. **Known for:** satisfying goulash, schnitzel, and fried cheese; friendly staff; delicious garlic soup that's perfect on cold days. $ *Average main: Kč150* ✉ *Všehrdova 19, Malá Strana* ☎ *257–320–409* ⊕ *tlustamys.cz* Ⓜ *Line A: Malostranská.*

★ U Modré kachničky

$$$ | CZECH | This old-fashioned tavern puts on airs, but if you're looking for the perfect Czech venue for a special occasion, it's hard to beat the "Blue Duckling." Dusty portraits hanging on the walls and lavish curtains and table settings impart a certain slightly frilly 19th-century look. The menu, filled with succulent duck and game choices, brings things down to earth a notch. **Known for:** gloriously gamey menu; beautiful old-world interior; friendly service staff. $ *Average main: Kč520* ✉ *Nebovidská 6, Malá Strana* ☎ *257–320–308* ⊕ *umodrekachnicky.cz* Ⓜ *Line A: Malostranská plus Tram 12, 20, or 22 to Hellichova.*

☕ Coffee and Quick Bites

Angelato

$ | ICE CREAM | Across from the Újezd tram stop, this gelato gem offers delicious, homemade ice cream and gelato almost all year. **Known for:** options from the adventurous (olive) to the classic (salted caramel); vegan options; monthly changing flavors. $ *Average main: Kč65* ✉ *Újezd 24, Malá Strana* ⊕ *angelato.cz.*

Bread Gap

$ | CAFÉ | For a quick lunch on the go, walk smugly past the greasy international chains and come here for tasty fresh sandwiches, salads, and barista-brewed coffees. **Known for:** friendly owner and welcoming staff; tramezzini (Italian finger sandwiches); fantastic chocolate hazelnut and strawberry apricot pastries. ⑤ *Average main: Kč90* ✉ *Tržiště 3, Malá Strana* ☎ *773–097–003* ⊕ *breadgap.cz* Ⓜ *Tram 12, 15, 20 to Malostranské náměstí.*

★ **Café Savoy**

$$ | CZECH | One of the best of Prague's traditional turn-of-the-century-style grand cafés, the Savoy is popular day and night for its brunches, coffees, Czech classics, and pastries. In particular, try the *větrník*, a Czech classic made of choux pastry with cream and caramel. **Known for:** lavish interior; warm and efficient staff; long lines. ⑤ *Average main: Kč150* ✉ *Vítězná 5, Malá Strana* ☎ *731–136–144* ⊕ *cafesavoy.ambi.cz* Ⓜ *Tram 1, 9, 20, 22, 23, 25, 97, 98, or 99 to Újezd.*

★ **Cukrkávalimonáda**

$$ | CAFÉ | An excellent pit stop while exploring Malá Strana, this warm, inviting café and bakery serves freshly made soups, salads, sandwiches, and pasta dishes, making it a convenient oasis for lunch. Or just rest your feet with a coffee and a slice of pie or cake. **Known for:** unique heritage-hipster interior; delicious Viennese-style confections; great value for its location. ⑤ *Average main: Kč190* ✉ *Lázeňská 7, Malá Strana* ☎ *257–225–396* ⊕ *cukrkavalimonada.com* ▭ *No credit cards* Ⓜ *Line A: Malostranská plus Tram 12, 20, or 22 to Hellichova.*

Kafíčko

$ | CAFÉ | The "Little Coffee" grinds freshly roasted beans from Brazil, Kenya, Colombia, and other renowned growing regions. Superlative strudel and small snacks in a peaceful setting make this a pleasant stop for refueling. **Known for:** great location between Charles Bridge and the John Lennon Wall; occasional live music performances; cute latte art drawn in the foam by baristas. ⑤ *Average main: Kč50* ✉ *Maltézské nám. 15, Malá*

Strana ☎ *724–151–795* ⊕ *facebook.com/cafekaficko* ▭ *No credit cards* Ⓜ *Line A: Malostranská.*

Roesel

$ | CAFÉ | Craft beer and cake is a great refueling combination in this cute, family-run café in a historic building (check out the mini-exhibition on the way in). **Known for:** great bottle selection, including a mango IPA and unusual local brews; streets ahead of touristy haunts nearby; lovely courtyard. ⑤ *Average main: Kč100* ✉ *Mostecká 20, Malá Strana* ⊕ *roesel-beer-cake.business.site* Ⓜ *Tram 12, 15, 20 to Malostranské náměstí.*

 Hotels

With a bewitching storybook suite of baroque palaces and Renaissance façades, Malá Strana—at the other end of the Charles Bridge from Staré Město—is the darling of Prague. Mostly a quiet area, removed from the bustle across the river, it also has some good traditional restaurants and pubs. Malá Strana provides an excellent location for visiting Prague Castle just up the hill but may not be the best choice for people with mobility problems. Other cons: car access on the narrow cobblestoned streets is restricted, parking is difficult, and you'll spend a lot of your time walking on the Charles Bridge to get to Staré Město.

★ **Alchymist Grand Hotel and Spa**

$$$ | HOTEL | A baroque fever dream of Prague masterminded by an Italian developer, the Alchymist doesn't go the understated route. **Pros:** astonishing renovation of a 16th-century building; afternoon wine tastings; central yet tucked away. **Cons:** steep uphill walk from the tram; loud a/c; some rooms and suites in need of a refresh. ⑤ *Rooms from: Kč5500* ✉ *Tržiště 19, Malá Strana* ☎ *257–286–011* ⊕ *alchymisthotel.com* ⮥ *46 rooms* ❯❮ *Free Breakfast* Ⓜ *Line A:*

4

Malá Strana

Malostranská plus Tram 12, 20, or 22 to Malostranské náměstí.

Appia Hotel Residences

$$ | HOTEL | A stylish hotel comprising rooms and apartments, in a slightly off-the-beaten-track location in Malá Strana. **Pros:** lovely courtyard and 12th-century hall; quiet and stylish; location allows for exploration of undervisited parts of Malá Strana. **Cons:** too quiet for some; staff professional but not warm; some may find the beds a little firm. ⑤ *Rooms from: Kč4000* ✉ *Šporkova 3/322, Malá Strana* ☎ *257–215–819* ⊕ *www.appiaresidencesprague.cz* ⌁ *21 rooms* ⍩ *Free Breakfast* Ⓜ *Line A: Malostranská.*

Aria Hotel

$$$ | HOTEL | This charming music-themed property kicked off Prague's luxury hotel boom in the early 2000s and still holds up well against the competition. **Pros:** set in gorgeous gardens; excellent restaurant and breakfast; iPads in all the rooms, along with killer sound systems. **Cons:** proximity to the embassy can lead to tiresome security checks; some of the suites are small and might be better labeled as standard rooms; slightly standard-issue furniture in otherwise personality-filled hotel. ⑤ *Rooms from: Kč6700* ✉ *Tržiště 9, Malá Strana* ☎ *225–334–111* ⊕ *www.ariahotel.net* ⌁ *51 rooms* ⍩ *Free Breakfast* Ⓜ *Line A: Malostranská.*

★ Augustine, a Luxury Collection Hotel, Prague

$$$$ | HOTEL | There's plenty of competition in Prague's high-end hotel market, but the Augustine—now part of Marriott's Luxury Collection—continues to come out on top. **Pros:** impeccable service and tranquil feel; clever design, with hidden garden spaces; impressive spa and restaurant. **Cons:** breakfast not always included; sometimes noisy wood floors; no swimming pool. ⑤ *Rooms from: Kč10000* ✉ *Letenská 12, Malá Strana* ☎ *266–112–234* ⊕ *marriott.com*

⌁ *101 rooms* ⍩ *No Meals* Ⓜ *Line A: Malostranská.*

Boutique Hotel Constans

$$ | HOTEL | This pretty little hotel has a luxurious—if retro—feel, which comes in at a reasonable price. **Pros:** offers parking, a rarity in hotels here; some rooms with balconies; many repeat guests are a sign of the hotel's charm. **Cons:** car park only suitable for small vehicles and costs extra; somewhat eclectic breakfast options; some areas can feel cramped because of age of the building. ⑤ *Rooms from: Kč3500* ✉ *Bretislavova 14, Malá Strana* ☎ *234–091–818* ⊕ *hotelconstans.com* ⌁ *32 rooms* ⍩ *Free Breakfast* Ⓜ *Line A: Malostranská.*

★ Dům u velké boty

$$ | B&B/INN | This sweet bed-and-breakfast just below Prague Castle offers something a little different in a district that has its fair share of grande dame hotels. **Pros:** friendly family in charge; central but quiet; big beds. **Cons:** not suitable for guests with disabilities due to age of the house; up a hill; fewer amenities than bigger hotels. ⑤ *Rooms from: Kč3000* ✉ *Vlašská 30, Malá Strana* ☎ *257–532–088* ⊕ *www.dumuvelkeboty.cz* ⌁ *15 rooms* ⍩ *Free Breakfast* Ⓜ *Line A: Malostranská.* House at the Big Boot

★ Golden Well Hotel

$$$ | HOTEL | Consistently rated one of Prague's best boutique hotels, the Golden Well Hotel is hidden away at the top of a narrow side street in Malá Strana. **Pros:** fabulous restaurant; always gracious service; spacious, attractive rooms. **Cons:** outlet shortage due to building age; a little far from the Metro and tram stops, up a hill; wooden floors can be noisy. ⑤ *Rooms from: Kč6600* ✉ *U Zlaté studně 4, Malá Strana* ☎ *257–011–213* ⊕ *goldenwell.cz* ⌁ *19 rooms* ⍩ *No Meals* Ⓜ *Line A: Malostranská.*

Hotel Bishop's House

$$ | HOTEL | An ancient building just a few strides away from the world-famous

Charles Bridge, the rooms in this little design-style hotel remain chic and comfortable. **Pros:** historic building but rooms have all modern amenities; option to stay in the "bishop's tower"; bright rooms, some with frescoed ceilings. **Cons:** room sizes vary; some may find the interior a little plain; staff reception can be mixed. ⑤ *Rooms from: Kč3500 ⊠ Dražického náměstí 6, Malá Strana ☎ 257–532–320 ⊕ hotelbishopshouse.cz* ❮⊙❯ *Free Breakfast* Ⓜ *Line A: Malostranská.*

Hotel Neruda
$$ | HOTEL | Built in 1348, this landmark—now a flashy boutique hotel with major design chops—is where the author Jan Neruda and his mother lived in 1860. **Pros:** designer rooms have lots of character, including bathubs enclosed in glass and splashes of color; buffet breakfast included with local touches; comfortable beds and pillows. **Cons:** design can impinge on the livability of the hotel; no nearby Metro and an uphill walk from the nearest tram stop; rooms can get hot. ⑤ *Rooms from: Kč3000 ⊠ Nerudova 44, Malá Strana ☎ 257–535–557 ⊕ designhotelneruda.com* ❮⊙❯ *42 rooms* ❮⊙❯ *Free Breakfast* Ⓜ *Line A: Malostranská.*

★ Mandarin Oriental Prague
$$$$ | HOTEL | Architects retained many of this Dominican monastery's original flourishes when it was reincarnated as a hotel, creating a peaceful, inspired backdrop for the Mandarin Oriental's luxurious offerings. **Pros:** wonderful, attentive staff offers personalized service; lovely peaceful setting; superb breakfast buffet. **Cons:** some rooms are small; a/c seriously underpowered; lack of outlets in bathrooms. ⑤ *Rooms from: Kč10500 ⊠ Nebovidská 1, Malá Strana ☎ 233–088–888 ⊕ www.mandarinoriental.com/prague* ❮⊙❯ *99 rooms* ❮⊙❯ *No Meals* Ⓜ *Line A: Malostranská.*

Pod Věží
$$ | HOTEL | The family-friendly Pod Věží is perched on the end of the famous Charles Bridge, so close you

even get a free ticket to the tower if you stay here. **Pros:** nice touches like daily gifts for guests; couldn't be closer to one of Prague's main attractions; large rooms. **Cons:** can be loud; hectic location with constant stream of tourists outside the door; some of the beautiful beam rooms are accessible only by staircase. ⑤ *Rooms from: Kč3000 ⊠ Mostecká 58/2, Malá Strana ☎ 257–532–041 ⊕ www.podvezi.com* ❮⊙❯ *28 rooms* ❮⊙❯ *Free Breakfast* Ⓜ *Line A: Malostranská.*

Sax Vintage Design Hotel
$ | HOTEL | This bold, bright, and affordable hotel was favored by former secretary of state Madeleine Albright (there's a framed letter of thanks on the wall). **Pros:** daily happy hour with free wine, beer, and homemade pastries; located on a quiet street; unique and lively decor. **Cons:** design might be too much for those with more conservative tastes; not convenient to Prague nightlife; some noise in rooms near communal areas. ⑤ *Rooms from: Kč2000 ⊠ Jánský vršek 3, Malá Strana ☎ 775–859–694 ⊕ hotelsax.cz* ❮⊙❯ *22 rooms* ❮⊙❯ *Free Breakfast* Ⓜ *Line A: Malostranská.*

U Tří Pštrosů (At the Three Ostriches)
$$ | HOTEL | This historic inn has taken a couple of licks—first it was flooded, then burned to the ground, then rebuilt, only to be taken by the communists, and finally restituted to the family owners. **Pros:** location, location, location; sense of grandeur; huge buffet breakfasts. **Cons:** small rooms up top; no elevator; too in the thick of it for some. ⑤ *Rooms from: Kč2600 ⊠ Dražického nám. 12, Malá Strana ☎ 257–288–888 ⊕ utripstrosu.cz* ❮⊙❯ *18 rooms* ❮⊙❯ *Free Breakfast* Ⓜ *Line A: Malostranská.*

🌙 Nightlife

A mix of tourist traps, café-bars, and authentic late-night haunts, Malá Strana is a beguiling place to drink, in the

Mozart once played the pipe organ at the Church of St. Nicholas. Check the church's website for a program of classical music concerts.

shadow of Prague Castle—although it's nowhere near as buzzy or varied as Staré Město, just across the river.

BARS AND PUBS
Bluelight Bar
WINE BARS | Despite its location just off the main drag up from the Charles Bridge, the Bluelight Bar manages to remain a laid-back, grungy haunt for some dedicated late-night drinking. The rock walls of the cavelike space are covered in graffiti, and the clientele is a mixed bag, but somehow it works. This is the perfect destination for a nightcap—just don't blame us if you're still ensconced hours later. ⊠ *Josefská 42/1, Malá Strana* ☎ *257–533–126* ⊕ *bluelight-bar.cz* Ⓜ *Line A: Malostranská.*

Café Club Míšeňská
CAFÉS | From morning until it closes at midnight, this relaxed, hip café-bar serves up decent drinks and cakes, but what it really trades on is its creative and cultural atmosphere. Open mic nights and an archway entrance, plus chill courtyard seating when the weather allows,

complete the picture. ⊠ *Míšeňská 3, Malá Strana* ☎ *722–659–139* ⊕ *facebook. com/misenskafe* Ⓜ *Line A: Malostranská.*

Kampa Naplavka
BEER GARDENS | It is about time that this side of the river got in on the riverside drinking action. With deck chairs laid out on the lawn by a hut, this is a remarkably relaxed place to sup wine, beer, or even a cocktail while the Vltava rolls by. ⊠ *Malostranské nábř., Malá Strana* ⊕ *facebook. com/kampa.naplavka* ⊘ *Closed in Winter.* Ⓜ *Line A: Malostranská.*

Kellyxír
COCKTAIL LOUNGES | An atmospheric haunt that calls itself an "alchemical pub" (probably thanks to its location in the same building as the Museum of Alchemists), this bar likely hasn't worked out how to turn base metals into gold or discovered the elixir of life yet, but it's a pretty fun gimmick nonetheless. Try the cocktails (complete with dry ice) and enjoy the drinks in flasks, pipes on the ceilings (allegedly full of said elixir), and drawings and diagrams on the

walls. ⊠ *Jánský vršek 8, Malá Strana* ☎ *733–402–824* ⊕ *kellyxir.cz* Ⓜ *Line A: Malostranská.*

Na břehu Rhôny
WINE BARS | Every branch of this mini-chain of wine bars in the Czech capital has its own charm, but the Malá Strana location is among the best, not least because it has a distinct lack of competition in the immediate area. It's easily the best place in this district for a crisp glass of white in the courtyard in summer, or a reviving red in the cozy interior in the colder months. ⊠ *Maltézské nám., Malá Strana* ☎ *733–785–577* ⊕ *nabrehurhony. cz* ☻ *Closed Sun. and Mon.* Ⓜ *Line A: Malostranská.*

★ Olympia
BREWPUBS | A hot spot from the 1930s returned to its former glory provides a somewhat romanticized but enjoyable take on a Czech pub. Part of the Kolkovna chain that has locations around the city, Olympia appeals to visitors and locals alike who like the special unpasteurized Pilsner Urquell. There's also a great menu of Czech classics to help soak up all that delicious beer. Try the schnitzel or the steak tartare. ⊠ *Vitežná 7, Malá Strana* ☎ *251–511–080* ⊕ *kolkovna.cz* Ⓜ *Line A: Malostranská.*

JAZZ CLUBS
U Malého Glena
LIVE MUSIC | Commonly known as "Little Glen," patrons are willing to cram in to hear solid house jazz and blues bands, as well as a few visiting acts. Get there early to stake out a seat near the stage; the tunnel-shape vault can be crowded but that only adds to the atmosphere. Upstairs they serve food until midnight. ⊠ *Karmelitská 23, Malá Strana* ☎ *257–531–717* ⊕ *malyglen.cz* Ⓜ *Line A: Malostranská.*

LIVE MUSIC CLUBS
Malostranská Beseda
LIVE MUSIC | Once the town hall, then a mecca for writers and artists, it's now a three-story music and theater club. Every level of this attractive building has something different going on—there's an art gallery under the roof, a "video café," a live music bar, a restaurant, a café, and a basement beer pub.

■**TIP**➜ **The live acts are mostly popular Czech bands.** ⊠ *Malostranské nám. 21, Malá Strana* ☎ *257–409–112* ⊕ *malostranska-beseda.cz* Ⓜ *Line A: Malostranská.*

❀ Performing Arts

There are a couple of pleasant venues where visitors can catch some classical music in Malá Strana, although it isn't as stuffed with options as nearby Staré Město.

VENUES
Lichtenštejnský palác (*Liechtenstein Palace*)
CONCERTS | Home to the Czech music academy (HAMU), this baroque palace from the 1790s has the large Martinů Hall for professional concerts and a smaller gallery occasionally used for student recitals. The pleasant courtyard sometimes has music in the summer months. ⊠ *Malostranské nám. 13, Malá Strana* ☎ *234–244–111* ⊕ *hamu.cz* Ⓜ *Line A: Malostranská.*

❂ Shopping

There are plenty of souvenir shops just off the Charles Bridge, one or two of which are worth your koruny, but explore the other streets for more unusual options.

BOOKS AND PRINTS
Shakespeare & Sons
BOOKS | The cozy Malá Strana store boasts two floors of books, mostly in English, and displays work by local and international artists. Bookworms will be intoxicated by the sheer choice and reverent attitude to the tomes; this is a real old-school bookshop. Everyone else can soak up the expat atmosphere

and pretend that they, too, never have to leave the Golden City. ✉ *U Lužického semináře 10, Malá Strana* ☎ *257–531–894* ⊕ *shakes.cz* Ⓜ *Line A: Malostranská.*

HOME AND DESIGN

★ Artěl

GLASSWARE | This American company, led by designer and long-time Praguer Karen Feldman, merges modern style with traditional Czech techniques. Artists use mouth-blown molten crystal and showcase hand-painted glassware, for instance. Items are so painstakingly crafted that they're bound to become family heirlooms, but all are far from prim. The company also makes handbags to order. ✉ *U Lužického semináře 82/7, Malá Strana* ☎ *770–152–112* ⊕ *artelglass.com* ◔ *Closed Tues.* Ⓜ *Line A: Malostranská.*

MARIONETTES

Marionety

CRAFTS | A fresh wooded scent greets visitors to this pleasant puppet shop on steep Nerudova ulice, which is next door to Prague's Center of Contemporary Puppetry. Discover an array of linden-wood marionettes, including classic characters like Tinkerbell and Charlie Chaplin, eerily reptilian wizards, and princesses in pink—plus some modern politicians. Artist biographies are found alongside a few displays, and plaster puppets—cheaper but not quite as charming—are also on offer, as well as custom-made ones for those who have really signed on to this Czech tradition. ✉ *Nerudova 51, Malá Strana* ☎ *604–230–945* ⊕ *loutky.cz* Ⓜ *Line A: Malostranská.*

Truhlář Marionety

CRAFTS | Among Prague's many marionette peddlers, this shop below the Charles Bridge stands out for its selection of unadorned linden-wood marionettes handmade by local and regional artisans. There's also a quirky stock of decorative wooden toys, such as rocking horses and giant mermaids, fit for a lucky child's bedroom. ✉ *U Lužického semináře 5, Malá Strana* ☎ *602–689–918* ⊕ *marionety.com* Ⓜ *Line A: Malostranská.*

SOUVENIRS

Amadea

SOUVENIRS | A slightly kitschy but still lovely woodwork shop, where you can start small, with hand-carved Christmas decorations, and work your way up to beautifully crafted tables and chairs. ✉ *Zlatá ulička 20, Malá Strana* ☎ *737–193–738* ⊕ *amadea.cz* Ⓜ *Line A: Staroměstská.*

★ Artisème

HOUSEWARES | Right by the John Lennon Wall, and in some ways effectively the graffitied attraction's gift shop, Artisème is also so much more than that. It boasts a beautiful selection of vases and other gorgeous design products, including jewelry and dinnerware, and the peaceful garden location is a nice spot. ✉ *Velkopřevorské nám. 4A, Malá Strana* ☎ *776–493–169* ⊕ *artiseme.com* Ⓜ *Line A: Malostranská.*

Malostranské náměstí Market

MARKET | Regular markets, including a mix of fresh vegetables, souvenirs, and craft beer, are a pleasingly Czech take on open-air shopping. Check the website to see what is on, and when, during your stay. ✉ *Malostranské nám., Malá Strana* ☎ *602–763–238* ⊕ *facebook.com/MalostranskeTrhy* Ⓜ *Line A: Malostranská.*

Smaltum

SOUVENIRS | **FAMILY** | These cute enamelware products are a proper homegrown success story, from a sister-and-brother team who started off selling them on Charles Bridge. The look has now taken off, but these are the original and best, with their bright mugs, decorated with animals, now gracing a million homes worldwide, the team estimate. ✉ *Nerudova 31, Malá Strana* ☎ *283–870–070* ⊕ *smaltum.eu* Ⓜ *Line A: Malostranská.*

PRAGUE CASTLE AND HRADČANY

Updated by
Joseph Reaney

Sights
★★★★★

Restaurants
★★★★☆

Hotels
★★★★☆

Shopping
★★☆☆☆

Nightlife
★★☆☆☆

NEIGHBORHOOD SNAPSHOT

TOP EXPERIENCES

■ **Last Judgment Mosaic:** Head to the south-facing side of Katedrála sv. Víta (St. Vitus Cathedral) to see this extraordinary triptych mosaic, which dates back to 1371.

■ **Holiday Shopping:** Visiting in December? Browse for gifts at the castle's festive market or pick up a retro wooden toy from the Rocking Horse Toy Shop.

■ **City Views:** Enjoy one of the finest panoramas in— and *of*—Prague from the Strahov Garden Viewpoint, just beneath Strahov Monastery.

■ **Golden Lane:** Poke your head into the cute, colorful cottages that line charming Zlatá ulička (Golden Lane) to read about the people that once lived in them.

■ **Classical Music:** Tune into one of the excellent classical concerts regularly held in Prague Castle's Romanesque Bazilika sv. Jiří (St. George's Basilica).

PLANNING YOUR TIME

The castle is at its best in early morning and late evening, when it holds an air of mystery and intrigue. The cathedral deserves an hour—but bear in mind that, as the number of visitors allowed inside is limited, the lines can be long. Another hour should be spent in the Starý Královský palác (Old Royal Palace). And you can spend several more hours taking in the museums, the views of the city, and the hidden nooks of the castle. Add in the many restaurants and shops of surrounding Hradčany (Castle Area), and you should budget a day for the whole experience.

GETTING HERE

■ There are two Metro Line A stations fairly close to Hradčany: Malostranská and Hradčanská. The former sits at the bottom of the neighborhood, with easy access to the Old Castle Stairs that lead up through the castle complex. The latter is a 15-minute (relatively flat) walk to the main castle entrance near St. Vitus Cathedral. Prefer not to walk? Tram 22 to Pražský hrad drops you just outside the main castle entrance. Taxis work, too, of course, but they can be expensive. The castle is compact and easily navigated, but it also teems with huge crowds practically year-round.

Despite its monolithic presence, Prague Castle is not a single structure but a collection of structures dating from the 10th to the 20th centuries, all linked by internal courtyards. The most important buildings within the castle complex are the St. Vitus Cathedral, a grand Gothic house of worship clearly visible soaring above the castle walls, and the Old Royal Palace, the official residence of kings and presidents and still the center of political power in the Czech Republic.

To the west of Prague Castle is the residential Hradčany, a town that emerged from a collection of monasteries and churches in the early 14th century. The concentration of history packed into Prague Castle and Hradčany challenges those not versed in the ups and downs of Bohemian kings, religious uprisings, wars, and oppression—but there's no shame in taking it all in on a purely aesthetic level.

 Sights

Bazilika sv. Jiří (*St. George's Basilica*)
CHURCH | Inside, this church looks more or less as it did in the 12th century; it's the best-preserved Romanesque relic in the country. The effect is at once barnlike and peaceful, as the warm golden yellow of the stone walls and the small arched windows exude a sense of enduring harmony. Prince Vratislav I originally built it in the 10th century, though only the

foundations remain from that time. The father of Prince Wenceslas (of Christmas carol fame) dedicated it to St. George (of dragon fame), a figure supposedly more agreeable to the still largely pagan people. The outside was remodeled during early baroque times, although the striking rusty-red color is in keeping with the look of the Romanesque edifice. The painted, house-shape tomb at the front of the church holds Vratislav's remains. Up the steps, in a chapel to the right, is the tomb Peter Parler designed for St. Ludmila, grandmother of St. Wenceslas. ✉ *Nám. U sv. Jiří, Pražský Hrad* ☎ *224–371–111* ⊕ *www.hrad.cz* 🎫 *Included in 2-day castle ticket (from 250 Kč)* Ⓜ *Line A: Malostranská plus Tram 22 to Pražský Hrad.*

Druhé nádvoří (*Second Courtyard*)
PLAZA/SQUARE | Cross the tree-lined ravine known as **Jelení příkop** (Stag Moat) and you'll enter the castle through the northern entrance, emerging into the Second

Prague Castle and Hradčany

KEY

- ① Sights
- ① Restaurants
- ① Quick Bites
- ① Hotels
- Ⓜ Metro Station

Sights

- 1 Bazilika sv. Jiří **F1**
- 2 Druhé nádvoří **D2**
- 3 Hradčanské náměstí **D2**
- 4 Katedrála sv. Víta **E2**
- 5 Královská zahrada **E1**
- 6 Lobkovický palác **G1**
- 7 Loreta **B2**
- 8 Nový Svět **B1**
- 9 První nádvoří **D2**
- 10 Schwarzenberský a Šternberský palác **D2**
- 11 Starý královský palác **E2**
- 12 Strahovský klášter **A3**
- 13 Třetí nádvoří **E2**
- 14 Zlatá ulička **F1**

Restaurants

- 1 Kuchyň **D2**
- 2 Malý Buddha **B3**

Quick Bites

- 1 Kavárna Nový Svět **B1**
- 2 Lobkowicz Palace Café **G1**

Hotels

- 1 Hotel U raka **A1**

St. George's Basilica is the oldest church building within the Prague Castle complex.

Courtyard. It was built in the late 16th and early 17th centuries under Rudolf II, who amassed an impressive collection of fine and decorative art, scientific instruments, and other treasures. The bulk of this was either looted by the Swedes during the Thirty Years' War, removed to Vienna after Rudolf's death, or auctioned off during the 18th century, but artworks that survived are displayed here. The **Obrazárna** (Picture Gallery) is currently closed for renovation, so a selection of highlights can be found in the nearby **Císařská konírna** (Imperial Stable).

Except for the view of the spires of St. Vitus Cathedral, the courtyard offers little for the eye to feast on. Empress Maria Theresa's court architect, Nicolò Pacassi, remade the Second Courtyard in the 1760s, and his attempts to impart classical grandeur meant a loss of earlier Gothic and Renaissance styles. This main sight here today is the **Kohlova kašna** (Kohl's Fountain), which was created in 1686 and restored in 2020. Look for the Eagle of the Holy Roman Empire at the

top. ✉ *Pražský Hrad* ☎ *224–372–423* ⊕ *www.hrad.cz* 🎫 *Free* Ⓜ *Line A: Malostranská plus Tram 22 to Pražský Hrad.*

Hradčanské náměstí (*Hradčany Square*)
PLAZA/SQUARE | With its fabulous mixture of baroque and Renaissance houses, topped by Prague Castle itself, this square had a prominent role in the film *Amadeus* (as a substitute for Vienna). Czech director Miloš Forman used the house at No. 7 for Mozart's residence, where the composer was haunted by the masked figure he thought was his father. The flamboyant rococo **Arcibiskupský palác**, on the left as you face the castle, was the Viennese archbishop's palace. For a brief time after World War II, No. 11 was home to a little girl named Marie Jana Korbelová, better known as former U.S. secretary of state Madeleine Albright. ✉ *Hradčany* Ⓜ *Line A: Malostranská plus Tram No. 22 to Pražský Hrad.*

★ **Katedrála sv. Víta** (*St. Vitus Cathedral*) **CHURCH** | With its graceful, soaring towers, this Gothic cathedral—among the most beautiful in Europe—is the spiritual heart of Prague Castle and of the Czech Republic itself. The cathedral has a long and complicated history, beginning in the 10th century and continuing to its completion in 1929. Inside, the six stained-glass windows to your left and right and the large rose window behind are modern masterpieces; see if you can spot the contributions of art nouveau master Alfons Mucha. Other highlights include the Svatováclavská kaple (Chapel of St. Wenceslas); the Kralovské oratorium (Royal Oratory), a perfect example of late Gothic architecture; the ornate silver sarcophagus of St. John of Nepomuk; and the eight chapels around the back of the cathedral. Don't miss the Last Judgment mosaic on the south side of the cathedral's exterior, constructed from a million glass and stone tesserae and dating from the 1370s. It's possible to enter the cathedral for free to take in the splendor from the back, but for the full experience, buy a ticket and walk around. Cathedral entry is included in the combined ticket to see the main castle sights; an audio guide is highly recommended. ⊠ *Hrad III. nádvoří 2, Pražský Hrad* ☎ *224–372–434* ⊕ *www.katedralasvatehovita.cz* 🎫 *Included in 2-day castle ticket (from 250 Kč)* Ⓜ *Line A: Malostranská plus Tram 22 to Pražský Hrad.*

Královská zahrada (*Royal Garden*) **CITY PARK** | This peaceful swath of greenery affords lovely views of St. Vitus Cathedral and the castle's walls and bastions. Originally laid out in the 16th century, it endured devastation in war, neglect in times of peace, and many redesigns, reaching its present parklike form in the early 20th century. Luckily, its Renaissance treasures survived. One of these is the long, narrow **Míčovna** (Ball Game Hall), built by Bonifaz Wohlmut in 1568, its garden front completely covered by a dense tangle of allegorical *sgraffiti*.

The **Královský letohrádek** (Royal Summer Palace, aka Queen Anne's Summer Palace or Belvedere) at the garden's eastern end deserves its reputation as one of the most beautiful Renaissance structures north of the Alps. Designed by Italian architects in the mid-1500s, it has a copper roof that looks like an upturned boat's keel riding above the graceful arcades of the ground floor. During the 18th and 19th centuries, military engineers tested artillery in the interior, which had already lost its rich furnishings to Swedish soldiers during their 1648 siege of Prague. The Renaissance-style *giardinetto* (little garden) adjoining the summer palace centers on another masterwork: the Italian-designed, Czech-produced Singing Fountain, which resonates from the sound of falling water. ⊠ *Between U Prašného mostu ul. and Mariánské hradby ul., Pražský Hrad* ☎ *224–372–435* ⊕ *www.hrad.cz* Ⓜ *Line A: Malostranská plus Tram 22 to Pražský Hrad.*

Lobkovický palác (*Lobkowicz Palace*) **CASTLE/PALACE** | Greatly benefiting from a recent renovation, this palace is a showcase for baroque and rococo styling. Exhibits here trace the ancestry of the Lobkowicz family, who were great patrons of the arts in their heyday (Beethoven was just one of the artists who received their funding). The audio tour adds a personal touch: it's narrated by William Lobkowicz, the family scion who spearheaded the property's restitution and rehabilitation, and includes quite a few anecdotes about the family through the years. Art highlights here include Pieter Bruegel's *Haymaking*, a stunning oil painting of a hay harvest, and Canaletto's two enormous London city landscapes. Although inside the Prague Castle complex, this museum has a separate admission fee. ⊠ *Jiřská 3, Hradčany* ☎ *233–312–925* ⊕ *www.lobkowicz.cz* 🎫 *290 Kč* Ⓜ *Line A: Malostranská.*

Queen Anne's Summer Palace was commissioned by Ferdinand I in 1538 for his loving wife, but she never stepped foot in it as she passed away while delivering her 15th child.

★ Loreta

CHURCH | Sitting outside the castle complex, the sometimes-overlooked Loreta is home to one of Prague's greatest architectural treasures: a replica of the original Santa Casa, said to be the house in Nazareth where the Archangel Gabriel first appeared to the Virgin Mary. Constructed in the early 1620s and a place of pilgrimage for 400 years, the building is covered in spectacular stucco figures of Old Testament prophets and scenes from the life of the Virgin Mary. The cloisters surrounding the casa are also home to treasures of their own, including beautiful frescoes, sculpted fountains, and soaring bell towers. Look out for the Prague Sun monstrance, an incredibly valuable golden vessel encrusted with thousands of diamonds. ⊠ *Loretánské nám. 7, Prague* ☎ *220–516–740* ⊕ *www.loreta.cz/* ✉ *180 Kč* Ⓜ *Line A: Malostranská plus Tram 22 to Pohořelec.*

★ Nový Svět (*New World*)

STREET | This picturesque street may only be a short walk from Hradčanské náměstí, but it feels like a whole world away. Nový Svět was developed in the 1300s as a residential district for the castle's workers, and later became home to famous names including 16th-century court astronomer Tycho Brahe. Today, visitors can take a stroll along the (relatively) quiet cobbled street and admire its colorful 17th-century cottages; look out for house signs depicting everything from a golden pear to a human foot. There are a handful of restaurants and cafés along the way, as well as a small children's play park, if you want to extend your visit. ⊠ *Nový Svět, Hradčany* Ⓜ *Line A: Malostranská plus Tram 22 to Brusnice.*

První nádvoří (*First Courtyard*)

PLAZA/SQUARE | The main entrance to Prague Castle from Hradčanské náměstí is certain to impress any first-time visitor. Going through the wrought-iron gate, guarded at ground level by uniformed

Czech soldiers and from above by the ferocious *Battling Titans* (a copy of Ignaz Platzer's original 18th-century work), you enter this courtyard, built on the site of old moats and gates that once separated the castle from the surrounding buildings and thus protected the vulnerable western flank. The courtyard is one of the more recent additions to the castle, designed by Maria Theresa's court architect, Nicolò Pacassi, in the 1760s. Today it forms part of the presidential office complex. Pacassi's reconstruction was intended to unify the eclectic collection of buildings that made up the castle, but the effect of his work is somewhat flat.

At its eastern end of the courtyard is **Matyášova brána** (Matthias Gate). Built in 1614, this stone gate once stood alone in front of the moats and bridges that surrounded the castle. Under the Habsburgs, the gate survived by being grafted as a relief onto the palace building. As you go through it, notice the ceremonial white-marble entrance halls on either side that lead up to the Czech president's reception rooms (which are only rarely open to the public).

■ TIP➜ **Try to arrive on the hour to witness the changing of the guard; the fanfare peaks at noon with a special flag ceremony in the First Courtyard.** ⊠ *Pražský Hrad* ☎ *224-372-434* ⊕ *www.hrad.cz* Ⓜ *Line A: Malostranská plus Tram 22 to Pražský Hrad.*

Schwarzenberský a Šternberský paláce (*Schwarzenberg and Sternberg Palaces*) ART MUSEUM | These two beautiful historical buildings, which stand on opposite sides of Hradčanské náměstí, are home to the National Gallery's collection of antiquities and paintings by European masters from the 16th to the 18th centuries. Holdings include impressive works by El Greco, Hans Holbein, Rubens, Rembrandt, and van Dyck. The exterior of the Schwarzenberg Palace is particularly striking, with its black-and-white

sgraffito, though the interior is less impressive. Pick up a combined ticket for 500 Kč—free if you're 26 or under—and you'll get entry not only to these two exhibitions but to all of the National Gallery's buildings throughout Prague for 10 days. ⊠ *Schwarzenberský palác, Hradčanské nám. 2, Hradčany* ☎ *233-081-730* ⊕ *www.ngprague.cz* 🖾 *500 Kč* ⊘ *Closed Mon.* Ⓜ *Line A: Malostranská plus Tram 22 to Pražský Hrad.*

Starý královský palác (*Old Royal Palace*) CASTLE/PALACE | A jumble of styles and add-ons from different eras are gathered in this palace. The best way to grasp its size is from within the **Vladislavský sál** (Vladislav Hall), the largest secular Gothic interior space in Central Europe. Completed in 1493 by Benedikt Ried, the room imparts a sense of space and light, softened by the sensuous lines of the vaulted ceilings and brought to a dignified close by the simple oblong form of the early Renaissance windows. In its heyday, the hall held jousting tournaments, festive markets, banquets, and coronations. In more recent times, it has been used to inaugurate presidents, from the communist leader Klement Gottwald (in 1948) to modern-day leaders like Václav Havel.

From the front of the hall, turn right into the rooms of the **Česká kancelář** (Bohemian Chancellery). This wing was built by Benedikt Ried only 10 years after the hall was completed, but it shows a much stronger Renaissance influence. Pass through the portal into the last chamber of the chancellery. In 1618 this room was the site of the second defenestration of Prague, an event that marked the beginning of the Bohemian rebellion and, ultimately, the Thirty Years' War throughout Europe. The square window used in this protest is on the left as you enter the room.

At the back of Vladislav Hall a staircase leads up to a gallery of the **Kaple všech**

svatých (All Saints' Chapel). Little remains of Peter Parler's original work, but the church contains some fine works of art. The large room to the left of the staircase is the **Stará sněmovna** (Council Chamber), where the Bohemian nobles met with the king in a prototype parliament of sorts. The descent from Vladislav Hall toward what remains of the **Romanský palác** (Romanesque Palace) is by way of a wide, shallow set of steps. This **Jezdecké schody** (Riders' Staircase) was the entranceway for knights who came for the jousting tournaments. ✉ *Hrad III. nádvoří, Hradčany* ☎ *224–372–434* ⊕ *www.hrad.cz* ✑ *Included in 2-day castle ticket (from 250 Kč)* Ⓜ *Line A: Malostranská plus Tram 22 to Pražský Hrad.*

★ **Strahovský klášter** (*Strahov Monastery*) **RELIGIOUS BUILDING** | Founded by the Premonstratensian order in 1140, the monastery remained theirs until 1952, when the communists suppressed all religious orders and turned the entire complex into the **Památník národního písemnictví** (Museum of National Literature). The major building of interest is the **Strahov Library**, with its collection of early Czech manuscripts, the 10th-century Strahov New Testament, and the collected works of famed Danish astronomer Tycho Brahe. Also of note is the late-18th-century **Philosophical Hall**. Its ceilings are engulfed in a startling sky-blue fresco that depicts an unusual cast of characters, including Socrates' nagging wife Xanthippe; Greek astronomer Thales, with his trusty telescope; and a collection of Greek philosophers mingling with Descartes, Diderot, and Voltaire. ✉ *Strahovské nádvoří 1, Pražský Hrad* ☎ *233–107–704* ⊕ *www.strahovskyklaster.cz* ✑ *150 Kč library* Ⓜ *Line A: Malostranská plus Tram 22 to Pohořelec.*

Třetí nádvoří (*Third Courtyard*) **PLAZA/SQUARE** | The contrast between the cool, dark interior of St. Vitus Cathedral and the pastel-shaded Pacassi façades of the Third Courtyard is startling. Noted Slovenian architect Josip Plečnik created the courtyard's clean lines in the 1930s, but the modern look is a deception. Plečnik's paving was intended to cover an underground world of house foundations, streets, and walls from the 9th through 12th centuries and was rediscovered when the cathedral was completed; you can see a few archways through a grating in a wall of the cathedral. Plečnik added a few features to catch the eye, including a granite obelisk to commemorate the fallen of World War I, a black-marble pedestal for the Gothic statue of St. George (a copy of the National Gallery's original statue), and a tucked-away entrance to his Bull Staircase leading down to the south garden. This courtyard also provides the best view of St. Vitus Cathedral's Last Judgment mosaic, as well as access to its South Tower viewpoint. ✉ *Pražský Hrad* ☎ *224–372–434* ⊕ *www.hrad.cz* Ⓜ *Line A: Malostranská plus Tram 22 to Pražský Hrad.*

★ **Zlatá ulička** (*Golden Lane*) **STREET** | A jumbled collection of tiny, ancient, brightly colored houses crouched under the fortification wall looks remarkably like a set for *Snow White and the Seven Dwarfs*. Purportedly, these were the lodgings for an international group of alchemists whom Rudolf II brought to the court to produce gold. But the truth is a little less romantic: the houses were built during the 16th century for the castle guards. By the early 20th century, Golden Lane had become the home of poor artists and writers. Franz Kafka, who lived at No. 22 in 1916 and 1917, described the house on first sight as "so small, so dirty, impossible to live in, and lacking everything necessary." But he soon came to love the place. As he wrote to his fiancée, "Life here is something special, to close out the world not just by shutting the door to a room or apartment but to the whole house, to step out into the snow of the silent lane." The lane now houses tiny

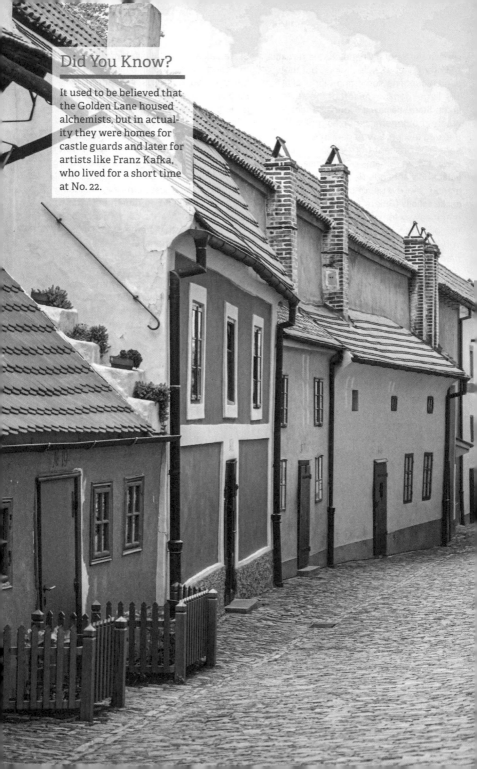

stores selling books, music, and crafts, as well as including some exhibitions on former residents and their professions (including some tucked away to the left of the entrance). The houses are cute, but crowds can be uncomfortable, and the fact remains that you are paying money for the privilege of walking down a narrow street. Within the walls above Golden Lane, a timber-roof corridor (enter between No. 23 and No. 24) is lined with replica suits of armor and weapons (some of them for sale), mock torture chambers, and a shooting gallery.

As you exit Golden Lane, you will also have an opportunity to visit **Daliborka** on the same ticket. This round cannon tower dates back to 1496 and gained notoriety through the centuries for its use as a brutal prison. Some of the instruments of torture used on its inmates, including the knight Dalibor of Kozojedy (for whom the tower is named), are now on display. ✉ *Pražský Hrad* ☎ *224–372–423* ✇ *www. hrad.cz* ✍ *Included in 2-day castle ticket (from 250 Kč)* Ⓜ *Line A: Malostranská.*

🍴 Restaurants

The streets surrounding main square Hradčanské náměstí have several restaurants and cafés open for lunch, as does the area around Strahov Monastery. But for dinner, with Prague Castle having closed down for the day and tourists having dissipated, you'll find the best dining options in the farther reaches of Hradčany.

★ Kuchyň
$$ | CZECH | It may no longer be the novel, menu-less restaurant of old—the COVID pandemic put an end to the concept of people choosing their meals from communal pots—but this castle-side restaurant still serves up great, traditional Czech cuisine. Take a seat and order from a small menu of dishes ranging from fresh cow's cheese with pickled

vegetables to duck leg with rustic bread dumplings and red cabbage. **Known for:** soft sourdough bread to dip in soups; wonderful location by the castle; drinks including unfiltered dark beer. ⑤ *Average main: Kč245* ✉ *Hradčanské nám. 1, Prague* ☎ *736–152–891* ✇ *kuchyn.ambi. cz* Ⓜ *Line A: Malostranská plus Tram 22 to Pražský Hrad.*

Malý Buddha
$$ | ASIAN | Bamboo, wood, paper, and incense are all part of the decor at this earthy hilltop hideaway near Prague Castle. It's as much about the atmosphere as the food here, which isn't complex but is cooked with heart; expect spring rolls, vegetable stir-fries, and various fish and chicken dishes, all in generous portions. **Known for:** lovely candlelit setting; extensive tea menu; service can be brusque. ⑤ *Average main: Kč200* ✉ *Úvoz 46, Prague* ☎ *220–513–894* ✇ *www.malybuddha.cz* ▭ *No credit cards* ☾ *Closed Mon.* Ⓜ *Line A: Malostranská plus Tram 22 to Pohořelec.*

☕ Coffee and Quick Bites

Kavárna Nový Svět
$ | CAFÉ | This cozy little café, which is tucked away on one of the city's prettiest backstreets, is a great stop for coffee and cake. It's only open from mid-morning to early evening (and not at all on Mondays), so you'll need to time it right. **Known for:** vegan options; location on the charming New World street in Hradčany; board games galore. ⑤ *Average main: Kč125* ✉ *Nový Svět 2, Prague* ☎ *242–430–700* ✇ *kavarna.novysvet.net* ☾ *Closed Mon.* Ⓜ *Tram 22 to Brusnice.*

Lobkowicz Palace Café
$$ | CAFÉ | If you're visiting Lobkowicz Palace (or even if you aren't), save time for a coffee, pastry, or even lunch at this lovely little café. The menu is full of tasty treats, from Czech classics like goulash and schnitzel to simple fare like soups,

salads, and grilled cheese sandwiches. **Known for:** wonderful city panoramas; simple snacks; Czech classics. $ *Average main: Kč360* ✉ *Lobkovický palác, Jiřská 3, Prague* ☎ *731-192-281* ⊕ *www. lobkowicz.cz* Ⓜ *Line A: Malostranská.*

Hotels

For some, Prague Castle and Hradčany are the romantic heart of this city. Though it is a hectic spot during the day with a lot of foot traffic, it completely empties in the evening, so staying in this area can feel like having Prague all to yourself.

★ Hotel U raka

$$ | **HOTEL** | With the quaint look of a woodsman's cottage from a bedtime story, this private guesthouse is saturated with romance. **Pros:** near Prague Castle but feels secluded; in-room fireplaces in some rooms; has a peaceful garden. **Cons:** tiny size makes rooms hard to come by; private parking costs extra; no Metro station nearby. $ *Rooms from: Kč4400* ✉ *Černínská 10, Prague* ☎ *220-511-100* ⊕ *www.hoteluraka.cz* ⇌ *6 rooms* ⏍ *Free Breakfast* Ⓜ *Line A: Malostranská plus Tram 22 to Brusnice.*

ⓨ Nightlife

There are a few good bars dotted around Prague Castle and Hradčany. Head up the castle hill to quaff beers that were brewed in a 13th-century monastery.

BARS AND PUBS

★ Klášterní pivovar Strahov

BREWPUBS | The first references to this gorgeous hilltop brewery inside a monastery are from the turn of the 14th century. And the tasty Pivo Sv. Norbert continues to be brewed on this spot, although it's no longer made by monks. There's a decent food menu and outdoor seating too. ✉ *Strahovské nádvoří 10, Prague* ☎ *233-353-155* ⊕ *www.klasterni-pivovar. cz* Ⓜ *Line A: Malostranská plus Tram 22 to Pohořelec.*

Performing Arts

CHURCH CONCERTS

Bazilika sv. Jiří (*St. George's Basilica*) **CONCERTS** | Listen to small ensembles playing well-known Vivaldi and other classical "greatest hits" in this spectacular Romanesque setting, dating back to the 11th century. ✉ *Nám. U sv. Jiří, Prague* ☎ *224-371-111* ⊕ *www.kulturanahrade. cz* Ⓜ *Line A: Malostranská.*

⬤ Shopping

Hradčany is more about history and views than shopping, but there are a few traditional craft shops dotted around the neighborhood.

Rocking Horse Toy Shop

SOUVENIRS | **FAMILY** | Take a trip back in time to when toys were made from wood and model cars were cherished. Everything about this store will make you smile, from the friendly owner's greeting to the stock of cheerful wind-up music boxes and animal figurines. Look closely at those wood-carved rocking horses and three-headed dragons; many items are handmade by Czech craftsmen. The shop even sells kits with colored pencils and pastels for budding young artists. It's only open in the afternoons, but easily combined with a visit to the Loreta. ✉ *Loretánské nám. 3, Hradčany* ☎ *603-515-745* Ⓜ *Line A: Malostranská plus Tram 22 to Pohořelec.*

Chapter 6

NOVÉ MĚSTO

Updated by
Jennifer Rigby

● Sights   🍴 Restaurants   🛏 Hotels   🛍 Shopping   🍸 Nightlife

★★★☆☆   ★★★★☆   ★★★★☆   ★★★★★   ★★★☆☆

NEIGHBORHOOD SNAPSHOT

TOP EXPERIENCES

■ **Wencelas Square:** Stand here and feel the weight of history: this is where Czechs overthrew communism via the massive protests of the Velvet Revolution in 1989.

■ **Kantýna:** The Czechs know their meat, and that's particularly evident at recently opened Kantýna, a butcher-cum-restaurant with top-quality cuts and a convivial atmosphere in a former bank.

■ **Lucerna:** Whether you're looking for a grand hall, an underground music bar, a historic former palace, some cheeky modern art, a café, a cinema, or even a rooftop bar, this wonderful building has it all (and is a good example of the *pasáže*, or arcades, in this area).

■ **Náplavka:** All of Nové Město (New Town) has good shopping, but to really feel like a local, hit up Náplavka's farmers' market by the river on a Saturday.

■ **Café Culture:** Make like a turn-of-the-century intellectual at one of Prague's grand cafés; the best are at the Obecní dům (Municipal House) and Café Slavia.

■ **National Theater:** Book in advance for great prices for opera and ballet performances in a grand setting.

QUICK BITES

■ **Cukrárna Myšák.** Visitors with a sweet tooth should not miss this historic pastry shop in Nové Město, where Czech desserts, cakes, sweets, and treats are showcased over two floors. Opened in 1911 by František Myšák, the First Republic feel has been faithfully reconstructed. ✉ *Vodičkova 31, Nové Město* ⊕ *mysak. ambi.cz* Ⓜ *Můstek*

GETTING HERE

The best Metro stops for this area are those at Karlovo náměstí (Line B), Muzeum (Lines A and C), and Můstek (Lines A and B). Various trams run around the neighborhood, too, particularly along Vodičkova and Národní.

PLANNING YOUR TIME

Václavské náměstí (Wenceslas Square) is well connected by public transport, and a short walk from most of the city center hotels. From here, leave at least an hour to cover the surrounding area, and then head up to Karlovo náměstí (Charles Square) or down the main pedestrianized shopping street, Na příkopě, to Náměstí Republiky. Leave an hour or two for the museums, churches, or parks at either end of Nové Město

Though Nové Město translates as "New Town," its origins go all the way back to the 14th century and Emperor Charles IV. As Prague outgrew its Staré Město (Old Town) parameters, Charles IV extended the city's fortifications. A high wall surrounded the newly developed 2½-square-km (1½-square-mile) area south and east of Staré Město, tripling the walled territory on the Vltava's right bank. The wall extended south to link with the fortifications of the citadel called Vyšehrad.

But don't come here looking for Staré Město charm; although there are still some beautiful spots and fantastic period architecture, the magical alleyway vibe of that part of the city is completely absent. This part of Prague was instead thoroughly rebuilt in the mid-19th century in the neoclassical and neo-Renaissance styles and today forms the modern heart of the capital, particularly around the two main squares: Wenceslas Square and Charles Square. The area is great for hotels and restaurants, but the number of traditional sights is relatively small, with just a handful of important museums and churches. It does feel more like a "proper" city here, though, and it gets less clogged with tourists, so it can be a good base for practical travelers.

◉ Sights

Františkánská zahrada (*Franciscan Garden*)
GARDEN | A peaceful green space in the heart of the city, the Franciscan Garden was established by monks from the nearby Carmelite Monastery to grow herbs and spices back in the 14th century, around the same time as Nové Město itself was founded. It remains a small oasis, with benches shaded by rose bushes, low hedges, a playground, and fruit trees and herb gardens that refer back to its original function. There's also a very cute café in the corner, Truhlárna, which does excellent cakes. ✉ *Jungmannovo nám., Nové Město* ☎ *221–097–231* ✆ *Free* Ⓜ *Lines A and B: Můstek.*

Sights ▼

1 Františkánská zahrada ... **E4**
2 Karlovo náměstí. ... **D6**
3 Klášter Emauzy. ... **D7**
4 Kostel Panny Marie Sněžné ... **E4**
5 Mucha Museum ... **F3**
6 Muzeum Antonína Dvořáka ... **F6**
7 Muzeum komunismu ... **F2**
8 Národní divadlo ... **C4**
9 Národní muzeum ... **F5**
10 Národní památník hrdinů heydrichiády ... **C6**
11 Novoměstská radnice ... **D5**
12 Obecní dům ... **F2**
13 Palác Lucerna ... **E4**
14 Statue of St. Wenceslas. ... **F5**
15 Tančící dům ... **C6**
16 Václavské náměstí. ... **F4**

Restaurants ▼

1 Ginger & Fred ... **C6**
2 Jáma ... **E4**
3 Kantýna ... **F3**
4 Le Grill ... **F2**
5 Lemon Leaf ... **C5**
6 Levitate ... **E5**
7 Palo Verde Bistro ... **F5**
8 Pho Bar ... **H1**
9 Pizza Nuova ... **F1**
10 Potrefená Husa Hybernská ... **G2**
11 Sansho ... **G1**

Quick Bites ▼

1 Cacao ... **F2**
2 Café Slavia ... **C4**
3 Crème de la Crème ... **D4**
4 Globe Bookstore & Café ... **C5**
5 Kavárna Obecní dům ... **F2**
6 Lahůdky Zlatý kříž ... **E4**
7 Mamacoffee ... **E5**

Hotels ▼

1 Art Deco Imperial Hotel ... **G1**
2 Art Nouveau Palace Hotel. ... **F3**
3 Dancing House Hotel ... **C6**
4 The Grand Mark ... **F2**
5 Hotel Boho Prague ... **F2**
6 Hotel Cosmopolitan ... **G1**
7 Hotel Élite Prague ... **D4**
8 Hotel Grandium Prague ... **F4**
9 Hotel Meteor Plaza Prague ... **F2**
10 Hotel Salvator ... **F1**
11 Ibis Praha Old Town Hotel ... **F1**
12 Ibis Praha Wenceslas Square Hotel ... **F6**
13 The ICON ... **E4**
14 Jalta Boutique Hotel ... **F4**
15 Michelangelo Grand Hotel. ... **D4**
16 NH Collection Prague Carlo IV ... **G2**

KEY

1 Sights
1 Restaurants
1 Quick Bites
1 Hotels
M Metro Station
i Tourist Information

Karlovo náměstí (*Charles Square*)
PLAZA/SQUARE | This square began life as
a cattle market, a function chosen by
Charles IV when he established Nové
Město in 1348. The horse market (now
Wenceslas Square) quickly overtook it as
a livestock-trading center, and an untidy
collection of shacks accumulated here
until the mid-1800s, when it became a
green park named for its patron. Glassy,
modern buildings clash with surrounding
older architecture, but it's quite representative of Prague's past and present
united in one spot. ⊠ *Nové Město*
⚜ *Bounded by Řeznická on the north, U
Nemocnice on the south, Karlovo nám.
on the west, and Vodičkova on the east*
Ⓜ *Line B: Karlovo náměstí.*

Klášter Emauzy (*Emmaus Monastery*)
CHURCH | Another of Charles IV's gifts
to the city, the Benedictine monastery
sits south of Charles Square. It's often
called Na Slovanech (literally, "At the
Slavs"), which refers to its purpose when
established in 1347. The emperor invited
Croatian monks here to celebrate mass
in Old Slavonic and thus cultivate religion
among the Slavs in a city largely controlled by Germans. A faded but substantially complete cycle of biblical scenes
by Charles's court artists lines the four
cloister walls. The frescoes, and especially the abbey church, suffered heavy
damage from a raid by Allied bombers
on February 14, 1945; it's believed they
may have mistaken Prague for Dresden,
121 km (75 miles) away. The church lost
its spires, and the interior remained a
blackened shell until a renovation was
begun in 1998; the church reopened to
the public in 2003. ⊠ *Vyšehradská 49,
Nové Město* ⚜ *Cloister entrance on left
at rear of church* ⊕ *emauzy.cz* 🎟 *60 Kč*
☽ *Open for worship only on Sun.* Ⓜ *Line
B: Karlovo náměstí.*

Kostel Panny Marie Sněžné (*Church of Our
Lady of the Snows*)
CHURCH | This beautiful church with its
poetic name (Church of Our Lady of the

Snows—one of the titles used for the
Virgin Mary in Catholicism) was intended
to rival Katedrála sv. Víta (St. Vitus Cathedral), in the castle complex, for grandeur
when Charles IV started building it in the
14th century. Alas, it was never finished,
and still has a slightly odd shape as a
result of that today, taller than it is long.
It has the highest vaults and column altar
in the city. ⊠ *Jungmannovo nám. 753/18,
Nové Město* 🕾 *222-246-243* ⊕ *pms.ofm.
cz* 🎟 *Free* Ⓜ *Lines A and B: Můstek.*

Mucha Museum
OTHER MUSEUM | For decades it was
almost impossible to find an Alfons
Mucha original in his homeland, but in
1998 this private museum opened with
nearly 100 works from this justly famous
Czech artist's long career. Everything you
expect to see from the man famed for
his art nouveau style is here—the theater
posters of actress Sarah Bernhardt, the
eye-popping advertising posters, and the
sinuous, intricate designs. Also exhibit-
ed are paintings, photographs taken in
Mucha's studio (one shows Paul Gauguin
playing the piano in his underwear), and
even Czechoslovak banknotes designed
by Mucha. ⊠ *Panská 7, Nové Město* ⚜ *1
block off Václavské nám., across from
Palace Hotel* 🕾 *224-216-415* ⊕ *mucha.cz*
🎟 *280 Kč* Ⓜ *Lines A and B: Můstek.*

Muzeum Antonína Dvořáka (*Antonín
Dvořák Museum*)
OTHER MUSEUM | The stately red-and-yel-
low baroque villa housing this museum
displays the 19th-century Czech composer's scores, photographs, viola, piano,
and other memorabilia. The statues
in the garden date to about 1735; the
house is from 1720. Check the schedule
for classical performances, as recitals
are often held in the first floor of the
two-story villa. ⊠ *Ke Karlovu 20, Nové
Město* 🕾 *224-923-363* ⊕ *antonin-dvorak.
cz/muzea* 🎟 *50 Kč* ☽ *Closed Mon.* Ⓜ *Line
C: I. P. Pavlova.*

Muzeum komunismu (*Museum of Communism*)

HISTORY MUSEUM | Formerly and perhaps ironically located in the Savarin Palace next to the twin capitalist symbols of the yellow arches of a McDonald's and a casino, the Museum of Communism has relocated into a brightly lit and larger new space in V Celnici, albeit still next to a supermarket. The expanded museum offers a vivid look at life in Prague and then-Czechoslovakia under the totalitarian regime that held power from the coup in February 1948 through the Velvet Revolution in November 1989. Find works of social realist art, original texts and photos from the archives of the Security Services, film, and dozens of exhibits that explore the days of the ČSSR through sport, education, art, propaganda, and censorship. Exhibits tread the line between menacing and enlightening, showing aspects of daily life as well as the terrifying repercussions of noncompliance. ⊠ *V Celnici 4, Nové Město* ☎ *224–212–966* ⊕ *muzeumkomunismu.cz* 🖾 *380 Kč* Ⓜ *Line B: Náměstí Republiky.*

Národní divadlo (*National Theater*)

THEATER | Statues representing Drama and Opera rise above the riverfront side entrances to this theater, and two gigantic chariots flank figures of Apollo and the nine Muses above the main façade. The performance space lacks restraint as well: it's filled with gilding, voluptuous plaster figures, and plush upholstery. The idea for a Czech national theater began during the revolutionary decade of the 1840s. In a telling display of national pride, donations to fund the plan poured in from all over the country, from people of every socioeconomic stratum. The cornerstone was laid in 1868, and the "National Theater generation" who built the neo-Renaissance structure became the architectural and artistic establishment for decades to come. Its designer, Josef Zítek, was the leading neo-Renaissance architect in Bohemia. The nearly

Prague by Pedalo

There is no better way to see the beautiful riverside buildings of Staré Město and Nové Město on one side, and the magnificent vista of the castle on the other, than by boat. Specifically, a *pedalo*. Rent one from Slovanka boat rental on the island by the National Theater (⊠ Slovanský ostrov, Nové Město ☎ 777–870–511 ⊕ slovanka. net). And because this is beer-loving Prague, there's a pedal-up bar on the same island where you can get a drink to fuel your journey.

finished interior was gutted by a fire in 1881, and Zítek's onetime student Josef Schulz saw the reconstruction through to completion two years later. Today, it's still the country's leading dramatic stage.

■ **TIP→ Guided tours in English (for groups only) can be arranged by phone or email in advance.** ⊠ *Národní 2, Nové Město* ☎ *224–901–448 for box office* ⊕ *narodni-divadlo.cz* 🖾 *Tours 200 Kč* Ⓜ *Line B: Národní třída.*

★ **Národní muzeum** (*National Museum*)

HISTORY MUSEUM | Housed in a grandiose neo-Renaissance structure that dominates the top of Wenceslas Square, the National Museum was built between 1885 and 1890 as a symbol of the Czech national revival. Indeed, the building's exterior is so impressive that invading Soviet soldiers in 1968 mistook it for parliament. The holdings are a cross between natural history and ethnography and include dinosaur bones, minerals, textiles, coins, and many, many other things. There are rotating exhibitions too, and the building itself remains a pretty spectacular draw in its own right. The gift shop has lots of treasures, too, including

Lovers of art nouveau can take in Obecní dům's architecture by day on a tour or by night at a concert.

brooches made of the museum's original parquet flooring. ✉ *Václavské nám. 68, Nové Město* ☎ *224–497–111* ⊕ *nm.cz* 🎫 *250 Kč* Ⓜ *Lines A and C: Muzeum.*

★ **Národní památník hrdinů heydrichiády** (*National Monument to the Heroes of Heydrich*)
CHURCH | This incredibly moving monument to the seven Czech and Slovak parachutists who assassinated the Nazi "Butcher of Prague," Reinhard Heydrich, in 1942, tells their astonishing story—the movie *Anthropoid* is based on what took place—and takes visitors into the crypt where they made their last, doomed stand against the occupying authorities, underneath the Church of Sts. Cyril and Methodius. ✉ *Resslova 9A, Nové Město* ☎ *222–540–718* ⊕ *vhu.cz* 🎫 *Free* ☉ *Closed Mon.* Ⓜ *Line B: Karlovo náměstí.*

Novoměstská radnice (*New Town Hall*)
VIEWPOINT | At the northern edge of Charles Square, the New Town Hall has a late-Gothic tower similar to that of Staroměstská radnice (Old Town Hall),

plus three tall Renaissance gables. The first defenestration in Prague occurred here on July 30, 1419, when a mob of townspeople, followers of the martyred religious reformer Jan Hus, hurled Catholic town councilors out the windows. Historical exhibitions and contemporary art shows are held regularly in the gallery, and you can climb the tower for a view of Nové Město. As in Staré Město, this town hall is a popular venue for weddings. ✉ *Karlovo nám. 23, at Vodičkova, Nové Město* ☎ *224–948–225* ⊕ *nrpraha. cz* 🎫 *Tower and exhibits on tower premises 60 Kč, gallery shows vary, combination ticket 350 Kč (incl. Old Town Hall)* ☉ *Closed Mon. and 30 min. between noon and 1 daily* Ⓜ *Tram 2,3,6, and 14 to Novoměstská radnice.*

Obecní dům (*Municipal House*)
NOTABLE BUILDING | The city's art nouveau showpiece still fills the role it had when it was completed in 1911 as a center for concerts, rotating art exhibits, and café society. The mature art nouveau style echoes the lengths the Czech middle

class went to at the turn of the 20th century to imitate Paris. Much of the interior bears the work of Alfons Mucha, Max Švabinský, and other leading Czech artists. Mucha decorated the Hall of the Lord Mayor upstairs with impressive, magical frescoes depicting Czech history; unfortunately, these are visible only as part of a guided tour. The beautiful Smetanova síň (Smetana Hall), which hosts concerts by the Prague Symphony Orchestra as well as international players, is on the second floor. The ground-floor restaurants are overcrowded with tourists but still impressive, with glimmering chandeliers and exquisite woodwork. There's also a beer hall in the cellar, with decent food and ceramic murals on the walls. Tours are normally held at two-hour intervals in the afternoons; check the website for details. ✉ *Nám. Republiky 5, Staré Mesto* ☎ *222–002–101* ⊕ *obecnidum.cz* ⬛ *Guided tours 290 Kč* Ⓜ *Line B: Náměstí Republiky.*

★ **Palác Lucerna** (*Lucerna Palace*)
NOTABLE BUILDING | This art nouveau palace houses one of the city's many elegant pasáže, in this case a hallway studded with shops, restaurants, a beautiful grand hall, and a music club. It is also home to a gorgeous cinema and a cheeky David Černý sculpture referencing the statue of St. Wenceslas in the square outside (to give you a hint, it's often described as the hanging horse). Even better, in summer you can go onto the roof of the palace, which is a treat for two reasons: one, the makeshift bar at the top, with great views and a good vibe, and two, the chance to ride in an old-school, slightly terrifying paternoster lift to get up there. ✉ *Štěpánská 61, Nové Město* ☎ *224–225–440* ⊕ *lucerna.cz* Ⓜ *Lines A and B: Můstek.*

Statue of St. Wenceslas
PUBLIC ART | "Let's meet at the horse" is the local expression referring to the traditional meeting place that is Josef Václav Myslbek's impressive equestrian

representation of St. Wenceslas surrounded by other Czech patron saints. In 1939, Czechs gathered here to oppose Hitler's annexation of Bohemia and Moravia. In 1969, student Jan Palach set himself on fire near here to protest the Soviet-led invasion of the country a year earlier (there's a moving monument to him in the cobbles). And in 1989, many thousands successfully gathered here and all along the square to demand the end of the communist government. ✉ *Václavské nám., Nové Město* Ⓜ *Lines A and C: Muzeum.*

★ **Tančící dům** (*Dancing House*)
NOTABLE BUILDING | This whimsical building, one of Prague's most popular modern structures, came to life in 1996 as a team effort from architect Frank Gehry (of Guggenheim Bilbao fame) and his Croatian-Czech collaborator Vlado Milunic. A wasp-waisted glass-and-steel tower sways into the main columned structure as though they were a couple on the dance floor—the "Fred and Ginger" effect gave the building its nickname, the Dancing Building. It's notable for a Gehry piece, as it's more grounded in the surrounding area than his larger projects. It now houses a hotel and top-floor restaurant, but even if you aren't staying or eating there, it's worth marveling at the building itself, either from the near side of the river or the far. ✉ *Rašínovo nábř. 80, Nové Město* Ⓜ *Line B: Karlovo náměstí.*

Václavské náměstí (*Wenceslas Square*)
PLAZA/SQUARE | This "square"—more of a very long, very thin rectangle—was first laid out by Charles IV in 1348, and began its existence as a horse market at the center of Nové Město. Today, it functions as the commercial heart of the city center and is far brasher and more modern than Staroměstské náměstí (Old Town Square). Throughout much of Czech history, Wenceslas Square has served as the focal point for public demonstrations and celebrations. It was here in the

heady days of November 1989 that some 500,000 people gathered to protest the policies of the then-communist regime. After a week of demonstrations, the government capitulated without a shot fired or the loss of a single life. After that, the first democratic government in 40 years (under playwright-president Václav Havel) was swept into office. This peaceful transfer of power is referred to as the Velvet Revolution. (The subsequent "Velvet Divorce," when Czechoslovakia was peacefully divided into the Czech Republic and the Slovak Republic, took effect in 1993.)

■TIP➜ Look up when you glimpse the Marks & Spencer shop sign—during the Velvet Revolution in 1989, Václav Havel addressed the crowds from this building's balcony. ⊠ Nové Město Ⓜ Lines A and C: Muzeum or Lines A and B: Můstek.

🍴 Restaurants

The sprawling area of Nové Město, which surrounds Staré Město in a huge arc running from Charles Square in the south, through the Můstek area, and then on to Náměstí Republiky, holds hundreds of pubs and restaurants. There are clusters of good places to eat near all the quarter's main commercial centers— some traditional, some international, some very fancy—including Charles Square, the strip along Národní třída, Na příkopě, and Wenceslas Square. Important Metro stations include Náměstí Republiky and Karlovo náměstí on Line B, Můstek on Lines A and B, Muzeum on Lines A and C, and Florenc on Line C.

Ginger & Fred
$$$ | FRENCH | Serving possibly Prague's most scenic meal, Ginger & Fred occupies the top floor of Frank Gehry's iconic Dancing House along the Vltava River, and the modern French-style food and service live up to the quality of the castle views. Of course, diners pay a premium for the view, and the wine list, though extensive, suffers from extreme markup. **Known for:** modern use of local ingredients; light-filled dining space; indulgent menu. ⑤ Average main: Kč600 ⊠ Rašínovo nábř. 80, Nové Město ☎ 601–158–828 ⊕ gfrest.cz Ⓜ Line B: Karlovo náměstí.

Jáma
$$ | ECLECTIC | American expatriates, Czech politicians, international consultants, and a constant crowd of students make this Czech–American hybrid pub feel like a place where everyone is welcome—especially when there's a big soccer game. **Known for:** relaxed international vibes; good pub food; inexpensive three-course lunch menus. ⑤ Average main: Kč180 ⊠ V Jámě 7, Nové Město ☎ 733–605–408 ⊕ jamapub.cz ☉ Closed Sun. Ⓜ Lines A and B: Můstek.

★ Kantýna
$ | STEAKHOUSE | With a grand setting in a gorgeous former bank, you can bank on this cool butcher-shop-meets-meat-market-and-bar being packed when you arrive. There's a butcher's counter at the front where you can select the exact meat you want. **Known for:** the best burgers in town; excellent Czech meats, to either eat on-site or take away; cool vibes in a historic building. ⑤ Average main: Kč100 ⊠ Politických vězňů 5, Nové Město ☎ 605–593–328 ⊕ kantyna.ambi.cz Ⓜ Lines A and C: Muzeum.

Le Grill
$$$ | EUROPEAN | The main restaurant of the Grand Mark Hotel has established itself as one of the best restaurants in the country. Don't expect lots of innovation here, but dishes are skillfully prepared and presented, and the focus is on seasonal ingredients, with a monthly changing menu. **Known for:** good for business dinners; elevated versions of classics like chicken supreme; the "Grand Mark" cake, unique to the hotel. ⑤ Average main: Kč600 ⊠ Grand Mark Hotel, Hybernská 12, Nové Město ☎ 226–226–126 ⊕ grandmark.cz Ⓜ Line B: Náměstí Republiky.

The Dancing House, or Fred and Ginger house, was controversial when first built because the nontraditional design stands out among the baroque, Gothic, and art nouveau buildings for which Prague is famous.

Lemon Leaf

$$ | THAI | Lemon Leaf serves a long list of Thai classics to an appreciative, dedicated clientele. Airy and luminous, with big pots of plants, tall windows, and funky lamps, this spot provides a solid alternative to European cuisine for lunch or dinner. **Known for:** crunchy spring rolls and traditional Thai soups; spicy curries; good for groups. ⑤ *Average main: Kč250* ✉ *Myslíkova 14, Nové Město* ☎ *224–919–056* ⊕ *lemon.cz* Ⓜ *Line B: Karlovo náměstí.*

Levitate

$$$$ | SCANDINAVIAN | The global trend for Nordic cuisine hasn't bypassed Prague, as evidenced by this hip basement restaurant with living plant walls, sounds of nature, and inventive, seasonal cooking delivered via tasting menus that are a blend of Scandinavian and Asian influences. There are only 22 seats, so it's best to book. **Known for:** surprising tasting menus; zero-waste approach; daily changing drinks. ⑤ *Average main: Kč1000* ✉ *Štěpánská 611/14, Nové Město* ☎ *724–516–996* ⊕ *levitate.cz* ⊗ *Closed Sun. and Mon. No lunch* Ⓜ *Lines A and B: Můstek.*

Palo Verde Bistro

$$ | VEGETARIAN | Among the nicest of a little clutch of vegan restaurants that have opened in recent years in this fairly businesslike part of New Town, Palo Verde has a gentle feel, with hanging plants and fairy lights providing the backdrop to fresh plant-based food, including salads and burgers, as well as good coffee and lemonades. There's a vegan hotel, Salvator Verde, next door. **Known for:** bright spot on an uninspiring strip; delicious breakfast and brunch choices; fresh, crunchy salads. ⑤ *Average main: Kč220* ✉ *Žitná 45, Nové Město* ☎ *775–285–430* ⊕ *paloverdebistro.cz* Ⓜ *Lines A and B: Můstek.*

Phở Bar

$$ | VIETNAMESE | Prague has long had reliable Vietnamese food (thanks in part to a program between the "brother" communist nations in the 1980s, which brought thousands of Vietnamese people

Prague's Plaques

The famous, the forgotten, and the victims. Throughout the center of town a large number of plaques and even busts are attached to the sides of buildings marking the famous and sometimes not-so-famous people who lived or worked there. Composer Frederic Chopin can be found across from the Municipal House on the side of the Czech National Bank. Scientists like Albert Einstein—who was friends with author Franz Kafka, according to a marker on Old Town Square— also turn up. Some Czech figures like composer Bedřich Smetana or painter Josef Manés might be recognizable, while many plaques commemorate totally obscure teachers, civic organizers, or members of the 19th-century national awakening.

One set of plaques stands out from the rest—those marking the victims of the Prague Uprising that took place May 5–8, 1945. These mark where Prague citizens who tried to battle the German army at the end of World War II were killed. Many plaques depict a hand with two upraised fingers and the phrase *věrni zůstaneme*, meaning "remain faithful." Foil-covered wreaths are still regularly hung underneath them.

The area around Wenceslas Square has several, including one on the side of the main post office on Jindřišská ulice. Two plaques can even be found on the back of the plinth of the Jan Hus statue on Old Town Square.

Some of the more touching ones have black-and-white photographs of the victims, such as a marker for 23-year-old Viktorie Krupková, who was killed on Újezd near Říční ulice, just across from Petřín.

The area around Czech Radio headquarters on Vinohradská ulice in Vinohrady has many, as well as some plaques for victims of the 1968 Soviet-led invasion. Fighting for control of the radio station was fierce during the invasion.

to then-Czechoslovakia for training or study). But this newish joint is not a bad option in the city center, particularly for the eponymous dish. **Known for:** bustling feel and a hum of conversation; generous portions; more Asian fusion than traditional Vietnamese. $ *Average main: Kč150* ✉ *Národní 18, Nové Město* ☎ *776–236–286* ⊕ *phobar.cz* Ⓜ *Line B: Národní třída.*

Pizza Nuova
$$ | PIZZA | FAMILY | Turning out tasty pies in true Neapolitan style, Pizza Nuova serves chewy pizzas that tend to get a bit soggy in the center—they're 100% authentic, if not the easiest to eat. The huge bilevel space, decked out in light and dark wood, also boasts a small outdoor eating area on Náměstí Republiky. **Known for:** good burrata cheese; crisp, thin pizzas; buzzing vibe and views over Náměstí Republiky. $ *Average main: Kč270* ✉ *Revoluční 1, Nové Město* ☎ *731–141–847* ⊕ *pizzanuova.cz* Ⓜ *Line B: Náměstí Republiky.*

Potrefená Husa Hybernská
$$ | CZECH | The "Wounded Goose" is a casual restaurant and sports bar, serving up bar staples such as chicken wings as well as Czech classics, soups, pastas, and salads. If you like meat-heavy dishes and big portions, this is a solid bet for dinner. **Known for:** affordable classics, especially the daily menu; lively atmosphere for big sports games; full selection of beers. $ *Average*

Haute Czech

Czech cuisine isn't limited to the simpler dishes you'll find at pubs; it can also go upscale and experimental. Aside from **La Degustation Bohême Bourgeoise** (✉ Haštalská 18 222–311–234) in Staré Město, an excellent high-end Czech meal can be had at **U Modré kachničky** (✉ Nebovidská 6 ☎257–320–308) in Malá Strana (Lesser Quarter). The specialty here, a restaurant whose name translates as the "Blue Duckling," is duck, naturally, and it's expertly prepared. But don't be limited to restaurants that focus on Czech food; many high-end "continental" restaurants will spotlight a local dish or local ingredients, too. Among the best of these is the aerie atop the Frank Gehry building known as Dancing House, **Ginger & Fred** (✉ Jiráskovo nám. 6 ☎221–984–160). The focus is French, but the restaurant works almost exclusively with local suppliers and there is a delicious take on veal tartare.

main: Kč220 ✉ Dlážděná 7, Nové Město ☎ 224–243–631 ⊕ potrefena-husa.eu Ⓜ Line B: Karlovo náměstí.

★ Sansho

$$$$ | ASIAN | When Sansho opened just over a decade ago, it radically redefined the local dining scene. Head chef Paul Day introduced many novel concepts to Prague's foodies, like pairing a simple, unadorned interior with highly intricate Asian-fusion cuisine, leaving the full focus on the plate. **Known for:** a nose-to-tail philosophy; impeccable unstuffy service; best quality-to-value ratio in Prague. ⑤ Average main: Kč1500 ✉ Petrská 25, Nové Město ☎ 739–592–336 ⊕ sansho. cz Ⓜ Lines B and C: Florenc.

☕ Coffee and Quick Bites

Cacao

$$ | CAFÉ | Tasty, fresh superfoods, smoothies, and bowls sit alongside rather more indulgent desserts at this pleasant café just off Náměstí Republiky. They offer vegan options, and there are plenty of tables as it is housed in a pretty and spacious historic building. **Known for:** friendly, calm feel; breakfasts ranging from a healthy mango bowl to pancakes; homemade ice cream. ⑤ Average main:

Kč150 ✉ V Celnici 1031/4, Nové Město ⊕ cacaoprague.cz Ⓜ Line B: Náměstí Republiky.

★ Café Slavia

$$ | EUROPEAN | Overlooking the river and next to the National Theater, this old-school continental European-style café is one of a clutch in Prague where you can imagine playwright-turned-independence hero Václav Havel holding court or composer Bedřich Smetana winding down after a performance. Actually, you're not just imagining it: all sorts of Czech artistic luminaries have supped here, including the above, and Havel liked it so much he even lobbied for it to reopen when it closed for reconstruction in the 1990s. **Known for:** historical setting; affordable daily menu; Czech-style café culture. ⑤ Average main: Kč250 ✉ Smetanovo nábř. 2, Nové Město ☎ 777–709–145 ⊕ cafeslavia.cz Ⓜ Line B: Národní třída.

Crème de la Crème

$ | ICE CREAM | With queues outside on even mild days, this gelato shop is considered to serve the best scoops in the city. It's a great option for refreshment while you are sightseeing, particularly as it is conveniently located on the main drag that marks the border between

Old and New Town. **Known for:** traditional and intriguing flavours, from walnut to sea buckthorn; generously sized scoops; vegan gelato options. $ *Average main: Kč90* ✉ *Národní 23, Nové Město* ☎ *725–556–706* ⊕ *cremedelacreme.cz* Ⓜ *Line B: Národní třída.*

Globe Bookstore & Café

$$ | CAFÉ | Prague's first English-language bookstore with a café continues to draw both foreigners and Czechs for its large selection of novels, regional nonfiction, popular brunches, and memories of the go-go '90s. The recently upgraded menu includes an excellent burger, good salads, and various American classics. **Known for:** U.S.-style portion sizes; English-language quiz night; decadent desserts including New York cheesecake. $ *Average main: Kč240* ✉ *Pštrossova 6, Nové Město* ☎ *224–934–203* ⊕ *globebookstore.cz* Ⓜ *Line B: Karlovo náměstí.*

Kavárna Obecní dům

$$ | CAFÉ | This ground-floor café is every bit as opulent as the magnificent art nouveau Municipal House it sits in. Step through the doors and into another era—the first decade of the 20th century to be specific—when the practice of coffee drinking was given white-glove treatment. **Known for:** gorgeous interior; sweet treats; historical appeal. $ *Average main: Kč200* ✉ *Obecní dům, Nám. Republiky 5, Nové Město* ☎ *222–002–763* ⊕ *kavarnaod.cz* Ⓜ *Line B: Náměstí Republiky.*

Lahůdky Zlatý kříž

$ | CZECH | Choose from more than 50 varieties of *chlebíček* (Czech traditional open sandwich) at this old-school lunch stop. **Known for:** delicious fruit pies; occasionally long lines; doing traditional favorites right. $ *Average main: Kč100* ✉ *Jungmannova 34, Nové Město* ⊕ *lahudkyzlatykriz.cz* Ⓜ *Lines A and B: Můstek.* Golden Cross Deli

Mamacoffee

$ | CAFÉ | Top-quality coffee (the founders were inspired to start their business after

a trip to Ethiopia) and good grub, too, at this large, light coffee shop and roastery. **Known for:** vegan and veggie meals; one of the best places to get a coffee hit in the city; plant-filled interior. $ *Average main: Kč100* ✉ *Vodičkova 6, Nové Město* ⊕ *mamacoffee.cz* Ⓜ *Tram 3. 5,6, and 9 to Lazarská.*

Hotels

Not exactly "new," this district dates back to the 14th century and includes bustling Wenceslas Square. Nové Město isn't as clean and architecturally fragile as Staré Město, but what it loses in baroque curls it makes up for in good location at slightly cheaper prices.

Art Deco Imperial Hotel

$$ | HOTEL | The real sell here is the hotel's Café Imperial, one of Prague's grand cafés, with its astonishing mosaic ceiling and ceramic wall tiles, formerly frequented by writer Franz Kafka, among others, and now run by celebrity chef Zdeněk Pohlreich; but the renovated hotel rooms don't let the side down either. **Pros:** perhaps one of the most attractive hotel breakfast rooms in Prague; recently renovated rooms with modern comforts and art deco charm; mosaic-walled fitness and wellness center with sauna and steam bath. **Cons:** Café Imperial is very popular, so can be hard to secure a reservation; some street noise; some rooms have no real view. $ *Rooms from: Kč3500* ✉ *Na Poříčí 15, Nové Město* ☎ *246–011–663* ⊕ *hotel-imperial.cz* ⤳ *126 rooms* ⦿ *No Meals* Ⓜ *Line B: Náměstí Republiky.*

Art Nouveau Palace Hotel

$$ | HOTEL | This stately but reasonably priced pistachio-green art nouveau building trumpets its Victorian origins. **Pros:** good deals available; great location, one block from Wenceslas Square and adjacent to the shopping bonanza of Na příkopě; a certain faded-grandeur charm. **Cons:** a little old-fashioned; gilded style not for everyone; some street noise. ⓢ *Rooms from: Kč3200* ✉ *Panská 12, Nové Město* ☎ *224–093–181* ⊕ *palace-hotel.cz* ⤵ *124 rooms* ⫶◎⫶ *Free Breakfast* Ⓜ *Line A: Můstek.*

Dancing House Hotel

$$ | HOTEL | The owners of this stylish riverside hotel have sensibly encompassed its biggest selling point in its name: the chance to sleep in arguably Prague's most iconic piece of modern architecture, the Frank Gehry–designed Dancing House. **Pros:** stylish rooms; stone bathrooms feel luxurious; fantastic views from the rooftop bar. **Cons:** rooftop attracts crowds and can delay elevators; small reception area; staff could be friendlier. ⓢ *Rooms from: Kč3850* ✉ *Jiráskovo nám. 1981/6, Nové Město* ☎ *720–983–172* ⊕ *dancinghousehotel. com* ⤵ *21 rooms* ⫶◎⫶ *Free Breakfast* Ⓜ *Line B: Karlovo náměstí.*

The Grand Mark

$$$ | HOTEL | Set in a 15th-century palace just steps from Náměstí Republiky, this stunning hotel and spa brings a high level of service and attention to detail to a still-scruffy part of the center. **Pros:** big, beautiful garden; caring and attentive staff; gorgeous bathrooms with mosaic tiling and soft lighting. **Cons:** only a small gym; the street is not especially attractive; functions held at the hotel can be noisy or restrict access to some areas. ⓢ *Rooms from: Kč6800* ✉ *Hybernská 12, Nové Město* ☎ *226–226–111* ⊕ *grand-mark.cz* ⤵ *75 rooms* ⫶◎⫶ *No Meals* Ⓜ *Line B: Náměstí Republiky.*

Hotel Boho Prague

$$$ | HOTEL | This isn't the flowing hippie boho vibe that the name implies: Hotel Boho is chic, sleek, cool, and located on a fairly uninspiring but quiet street not far from bustling Náměstí Republiky. **Pros:** trendy mid-20th-century-style bar; gorgeous gold-tiled spa and softly lit small pool; comfortable modern rooms in neutral tones with some stylish retro furnishing. **Cons:** a little impersonal

decor-wise, although little extra touches from staff help; located on an uninspiring street; mirrored glass doors in bathrooms can feel a bit much. ⓢ *Rooms from: Kč6000* ✉ *Senovázná 1254/4, Nové Město* ☎ *234–622–600* ⊕ *hotelbohoprague. com* ⤵ *57 rooms* ⫶◎⫶ *No Meals* Ⓜ *Line B: Náměstí Republiky.*

Hotel Cosmopolitan

$$ | HOTEL | This art nouveau property—sister hotel of the Imperial, almost next door—shares the same sophisticated vibe and even the same big-draw celebrity chef in its restaurant (Zdeněk Pohlreich), but it has a more intimate, low-key feel. **Pros:** classy feel throughout, with great service; contemporary-elegant rooms; top-notch restaurant. **Cons:** only a small fitness studio and sauna, but guests can use the Imperial's wellness facilities; no bar; can get expensive in high season. ⓢ *Rooms from: Kč4200* ✉ *Zlatnická 3, Nové Město* ☎ *295–563–000* ⊕ *hotel-cosmopolitan.cz* ⤵ *106 rooms* ⫶◎⫶ *No Meals* Ⓜ *Line B: Náměstí Republiky.*

Hotel Élite Prague

$ | HOTEL | A 14th-century Gothic façade and many poetic architectural details have been preserved in this affordable hotel, thanks to an extensive renovation. **Pros:** historic feel with modern comforts; close to the National Theater; good amenities. **Cons:** the neighborhood can get overrun with partygoers at night; smoking is allowed in the courtyard; some rooms can be noisy. ⓢ *Rooms from: Kč2100* ✉ *Ostrovní 32, Nové Město* ☎ *211–159–858* ⊕ *hotel-elite.cz* ⤵ *78 rooms* ⫶◎⫶ *Free Breakfast* Ⓜ *Line B: Karlovo náměstí.*

Hotel Grandium Prague

$$ | HOTEL | A sprightly presence on an imperious street (think communist-era blocks), the Hotel Grandium offers modern design at good prices. **Pros:** close to Wenceslas Square; good breakfast spread; free access to sauna and gym. **Cons:** bland rooms; slow, overworked

elevator; rooms are not huge. ⑤ *Rooms from: Kč3000* ✉ *Politických vězňů 12, Nové Město* ☎ *234–100–100* ⊕ *hotel-grandium.cz* ➹ *196 rooms* ¶⊙¶ *Free Breakfast* Ⓜ *Lines A and B: Můstek.*

Hotel Meteor Plaza Prague

$$ | **HOTEL** | This hotel may occupy a baroque town palace, but the owners have gone for modern chain-hotel convenience, especially in the serviceable room furnishings. **Pros:** just a few steps from the Municipal House and five minutes on foot from Staré Město; some historical details such as 14th-century wine cellar; quiet, leafy patio. **Cons:** interior not very inspiring; breakfast room can fill up quickly; tiny elevator. ⑤ *Rooms from: Kč2500* ✉ *Hybernská 6, Nové Město* ☎ *224–192–111* ⊕ *hotel-meteor.cz* ➹ *88 rooms* ¶⊙¶ *Free Breakfast* Ⓜ *Line B: Náměstí Republiky.*

Hotel Salvator

$ | **HOTEL** | This efficiently run establishment just outside Staré Město offers more comforts than most in its class, as well as a pretty setting arranged around a central courtyard and plant-filled balconies. **Pros:** lovely Spanish-themed restaurant and courtyard; in-house tourist office; good value. **Cons:** courtyard-facing rooms can be noisy at mealtimes; bland room decor; not all rooms have a/c. ⑤ *Rooms from: Kč1500* ✉ *Truhlářská 10, Nové Město* ☎ *222–312–234* ⊕ *salvator. cz* ➹ *39 rooms* ¶⊙¶ *Free Breakfast* Ⓜ *Line B: Náměstí Republiky.*

Ibis Praha Old Town Hotel

$ | **HOTEL** | Reliable quality and low prices, and a location pretty much across the street from the Municipal House, win the day for this chain hotel. **Pros:** within easy walking distance of Old Town Square; good value for money; reliable. **Cons:** expensive buffet breakfast; rooms are small and can be dark; no restaurant. ⑤ *Rooms from: Kč2200* ✉ *Na Poříčí 5, Nové Město* ☎ *266–000–999* ⊕ *accorhotels.com* ➹ *271 rooms* ¶⊙¶ *Free Breakfast* Ⓜ *Line B: Náměstí Republiky.*

Ibis Praha Wenceslas Square Hotel

$ | **HOTEL** | Despite its name, this hotel isn't actually on the square itself, but a few minutes' walk away; regardless of this dodgy geography, it is still probably the cheapest modern air-conditioned place you can find this close to the city center. **Pros:** comfortable and clean; quality beds; guests can use wellness center at Novotel next door (for a fee). **Cons:** very little nightlife in the area; except for corner locations, rooms are rather small; bland decor. ⑤ *Rooms from: Kč2500* ✉ *Kateřinská 36, Nové Město* ☎ *222–865–777* ⊕ *accorhotels.com* ➹ *181 rooms* ¶⊙¶ *Free Breakfast* Ⓜ *Line C: I. P. Pavlova.*

★ The ICON

$$ | **HOTEL** | From the fashionable staff to its plush, all-natural bedding, this hotel is dressed to impress. **Pros:** youthful, exuberant staff; all-day breakfast spread; good Metro and tram connections. **Cons:** small spa; street-facing rooms are loud; busy urban locale won't appeal to all. ⑤ *Rooms from: Kč2500* ✉ *V Jámě 6, Nové Město* ☎ *221–634–100* ⊕ *iconhotel.eu* ➹ *31 rooms* ¶⊙¶ *Free Breakfast* Ⓜ *Lines A and B: Můstek.*

Jalta Boutique Hotel

$$ | **HOTEL** | The Jalta is arguably the smartest, most interesting hotel on central Wenceslas Square, with a historically protected façade that dates to the 1950s in the socialist realist style first developed in the Soviet Union. **Pros:** underground nuclear shelter and museum; sleek, modern rooms; some rooms have balconies facing the square and National Museum. **Cons:** may be too close to the action for some; the cheaper rooms are small; some street noise although windows are good at blocking it. ⑤ *Rooms from: Kč3500* ✉ *Václavské nám. 45, Nové Město* ☎ *222–822–111* ⊕ *hoteljalta.com* ➹ *94 rooms* ¶⊙¶ *Free Breakfast* Ⓜ *Lines A and C: Muzeum.*

Michelangelo Grand Hotel

$$ | **HOTEL** | Large, airy, and located inside an attractive, 19th-century building that used to be a municipal meeting hall, this serviceable but still stylish hotel (lots of purple tones) is based in an interesting part of Nové Město that manages to be both quiet and close to a lot of nightlife. **Pros:** high-end toiletries; good deals in off-season; on-site beer spa. **Cons:** less touristy location may not appeal to everyone; service can be mixed; rooms are spacious but not particularly individual. $ *Rooms from: Kč4000* ✉ *Vladislavova 1477/20, Nové Město* ☎ *222–500–177* ⊕ *michelangelograndhotel.com* ⇨ *134 rooms* ❘◯❘ *Free Breakfast* Ⓜ *Line B: Národní třída.*

NH Collection Prague Carlo IV

$$$ | **HOTEL** | Dripping with glamour, this mammoth 19th-century neoclassical palace is now part of the NH Collection. **Pros:** luxurious and historic vibe; beautiful spa; cool bar in a former bank vault. **Cons:** sometimes rude staff; views are not great; room sizes vary. $ *Rooms from: Kč6000* ✉ *Senovážné nám. 13, Nové Město* ☎ *224–593–111* ⊕ *marriott.com* ⇨ *152 rooms* ❘◯❘ *No Meals* Ⓜ *Line B: Náměstí Republiky.*

☿ Nightlife

Some areas of the neighborhood, particularly around Wenceslas Square, are still dealing with the aftereffects of the stag-party craze, but others have embraced funky, alternative evening offerings. It's still best to steer clear of most of the nightlife right on or immediately around the square if you want to keep away from the tackier places, which can still get packed with groups of inebriated men. But there are plenty of other choices if you know where to look, frequented by locals and visitors alike.

BARS AND PUBS

Gin and Tonic Club

COCKTAIL LOUNGES | With 6,400 combinations, this stylish gin palace offers everything from a perfect traditional tipple with ice and a slice to a G&T with sun-dried tomatoes or even bacon. Small plates complement the gin-heavy menu, and there's a gorgeous little candlelit garden for mild nights. ✉ *Navrátilova 11, Nové Město* ☎ *777–669–557* ⊕ *gintonicclub.com* Ⓜ *Lines A and B: Můstek.*

★ Náplavka

GATHERING PLACES | One of the coolest places to drink and hang in Prague just got cooler (and considerably more appealing during the chilly winter months than it previously was). This riverside promenade near the Dancing House began with little more than pop-up pubs on benches and boats, but newly reclaimed former storage pods inside the waterfront walls offer cafés, galleries, and even a branch of the municipal library. Don't worry, sunset beers are still central to the vibe, with plenty of pop-up pubs and tethered boat/bars still present. ✉ *Náplavka, Nové Město* ⊕ *prazskenaplavky.cz* Ⓜ *Line B: Karlovo náměstí.*

Parlour

COCKTAIL LOUNGES | They call themselves cocktail artists and, although it is slightly cringe, it's hard not to agree. The team here make drinks based on your tastes rather than from a menu, and they are invariably great. There is no sign: look for the door with the little white horse. This haven is still astonishingly close to the bustle of Wenceslas Square. ✉ *Krakovská 15, Nové Město* ☎ *777–200–015* ⊕ *parlour.cz* Ⓜ *Lines A and B: Můstek.*

Pilsnerka Národní

BREWPUBS | An authentic shopfront with a modern brewery-style look behind, Pilsnerka has a very alluring vibe. It's worth the drop-in, too; good, fresh Pilsner Urquell from the tanks—one of several spots around town affiliated with

Náplavka is home to a popular weekly farmers' market but is at peak popularity in summer when its bargebars are the place to be.

the brewery, and serving the freshest version of probably the most famous Czech export out there—and affordable, tasty takes on Czech classics in a part of town that has not previously excelled in this kind of bar/restaurant. ⊠ *Národní 22, Nové Město* ☎ *266–710–418* ⊕ *pilsner-urquell.cz/pilsnerka/narodni* Ⓜ *Line B: Národní třída.*

★ Pivovarský dům

BREWPUBS | This brewpub may be short on history, but it makes up for that with outstanding beer. The dark, light, and seasonal microbrew beers are stellar. (Fermenting beer can be viewed through a window.) The food is good but a slight letdown when compared with the drinks, which include sour-cherry beer and even a Champagne beer for the more adventurous. Take heed: there is often a line to get in. ⊠ *Lípová 15, Nové Město* ☎ *296–216–666* ⊕ *pivo-dum.cz* Ⓜ *Lines A and B: Můstek.*

U Fleků

BREWPUBS | The oldest brewpub in Europe—open since 1499—makes a tasty, if overpriced, dark beer and serves around 2,000 pints of it every day. But the steady stream of tours means it can be hard to find a seat (in the evenings, at least), even though the place is cavernous, spread over eight halls and a garden. There's also a brewery museum and cabaret shows.

⚠ **Beware of waiters putting unordered shots of liquor on your table.**

If you don't insist they remove them right away, they'll be on your bill, and service can be indifferent to rude. But the raucous, beer-swilling, mug-clinking bonhomie makes up for that. ⊠ *Křemencova 11, Nové Město* ☎ *224–934–019* ⊕ *ufleku.cz* Ⓜ *Line B: Karlovo náměstí.*

Vinárna U Sudu

WINE BARS | Although Prague is beer territory, this bar is all about wine. A mazelike, multilevel cellar forms the large wine bar in a baroque building, and there's a garden too. Make note of where your traveling companions are or you might never find them again—the interior is that labyrinthine. But this also makes for a cozy drinking hole in the cold winter months, and it's open extremely late.

■ TIP→ This is usually one of the first places during the year to crack open burčák, tasty new wine served shortly after harvest. ⊠ Vodičkova 10, Nové Město ☎ 222-232-207 ⊕ usudu.cz Ⓜ Line B: Karlovo náměstí.

★ Výtopna

BARS | FAMILY | Located on the very touristy Wenceslas Square, the drinks here are delivered by miniature train on 900 meters of track (including five drawbridges). It's gimmicky but great fun when the drinks pull up to the table. ⊠ Václavské nám. 56, Nové Město ☎ 777-444-554 ⊕ vytopna.cz Ⓜ Line C: Muzeum.

Vzorkovna

LIVE MUSIC | Currently the holder of the unofficial title of Prague's most alternative city-center pub and music venue, Vzorkovna operates a confusing chip system for payment (you get the change back at the end of the night, but don't lose the chip or they'll charge you). It's an acquired taste, with a rough pop-up feel of bars in metropolises like London or New York, plus that uniquely Prague junkyard vibe, with dusty floors, and often a giant dog wandering around. The beers on tap are from the award-winning Únětický Pivovar brewery, and reasonably priced for such a centrally located bar. ⊠ Národní 339/11, Nové Město ☎ No phone ⊕ vzorkovna.biz Ⓜ Line B: Národní třída.

CLUBS

Duplex

DANCE CLUBS | While Duplex is effectively an all-nighter, strobe-heavy superclub in the center of Prague, it also boasts a gorgeous roof terrace right on Wenceslas Square and a restaurant. Prices can be

high and it is obviously touristy, but the location makes up for it, and if you do feel like hitting the dance floor afterward, this is where the biggest global dance music names perform. ⊠ Václavské nám. 21, Nové Město ☎ 732-221-111 ⊕ duplex.cz Ⓜ Lines A and B: Můstek.

LGBTQ

Q Café

CAFÉS | This friendly and pretty hip LGBTQ café-bar opens at 3 every day and dishes up small bites, decent coffee, and reasonable beer and cocktails over two floors. This is one of the places in Prague to embrace Kofola—Czech communist-era Coca-Cola—which is worth a try. There's a library, too. ⊠ Opatovická 166/12, Nové Město ☎ 776-856-361 ⊕ q-cafe.cz Ⓜ Line B: Národní třída.

LIVE MUSIC CLUBS

★ Lucerna Music Bar

LIVE MUSIC | Rock bands on the comeback trail, touring bluesmen, and other solid performers across many different musical genres, including some Czech acts, make up the live schedule of this basement music venue in the historic pasáž. The crowds are always friendly and up for it, and the acoustics are good, making it a great place to see live music in the city center. Book tickets in advance for the bigger acts. Another big draw are the nights—usually Saturday—of 1980s or '90s music videos. The nostalgia-fest will have you dancing your socks off until the wee hours, alongside what feels like half of Prague and much of the rest of Europe as well. ⊠ Vodičkova 36, Nové Město ☎ 224-215-957 ⊕ musicbar.cz Ⓜ Lines A and B: Můstek.

★ Reduta

LIVE MUSIC | This jazz club is where President Bill Clinton jammed with Czech president Václav Havel in 1994, and lots of pictures of that night are still hanging around the joint. Reduta was one of the bigger clubs in the 1960s and '70s, and it still feels a little like a dated museum of those glory days (or like a funky retro tribute to that era, depending on your persuasion). The coat-check person can be pretty aggressive, which is another throwback to the pre-1989 era, but the jazz is worth any aggravation.

■ TIP→ **If you go on a quiet weeknight, staff might upgrade you to the VIP seats, where Bill and Václav sat back in the day.** ⊠ *Národní 20, Nové Město* ☎ *737–773–343* ⊕ *redutajazzclub.cz* Ⓜ *Line B: Národní třída.*

⭐ Performing Arts

VENUES

★ **Národní divadlo** (*National Theater*)
ARTS CENTERS | This is the main stage in the Czech Republic for drama, dance, and opera. The interior, with its ornate and etched ceilings, is worth the visit alone. Most of the theater performances are in Czech, but some operas have English supertitles, and ballet is an international language—right? Book the opera online ahead of time for fantastic discounts; you'll get to see top-quality performances in sumptuous surroundings at a snip of the price you could pay in other European capitals. The New Stage, next door, as well as the Estates Theater and Prague State Opera are all part of the National Theater system. ⊠ *Národní 2, Nové Město* ☎ *224–901–448* ⊕ *narodni-divadlo. cz* Ⓜ *Line B: Národní třída.*

Obecní dům (*Municipal House*)
ARTS CENTERS | The main concert hall, a true art nouveau gem named after composer Bedřich Smetana, is home to the Prague Symphony Orchestra and many music festivals. A few smaller halls, all named for famous figures, host chamber concerts. Tours of the building are also offered. It's well worth a visit, even if you only pop your head in. ⊠ *Nám. Republiky 5, Nové Město* ☎ *222–002–101* ⊕ *obecnidum.cz* Ⓜ *Line B: Náměstí Republiky.*

A Night at the Opera

Opera has a long and strong tradition in the Czech Republic, and fans are rewarded with quality productions almost every night of the week for very reasonable prices. The imposing National Theater and the Stavovské divadlo (Estates Theater) in Staré Město are the best venues to see opera, as well as, of course, the beautiful Statní opera Praha (Prague State Opera), which reopened in 2020 after several years of renovations. Branch out from the usual composers with a Czech composer like Janáček, Dvořák, or Smetana.

Statní opera Praha (*Prague State Opera*)
OPERA | With the most ornate interior of any venue in Prague, this theater has more than a touch of *Phantom of the Opera*. Marble sculptures support the loges, and a fresco adorns the ceiling. The building started life as the German Theater in 1887 and has undergone several name changes since, and recently reemerged, like a butterfly from its chrysalis, from several years of renovations. It's a spectacular place to see quality opera, despite its slightly unfortunate position overlooking one of Prague's busiest roads. ⊠ *Wilsonova 4, Nové Město* ☎ *224–901–448* ⊕ *narodni-divadlo.cz/en/ state-opera* Ⓜ *Lines A and C: Muzeum.*

Velký sál, Lucerna (*Great Hall, Lucerna*)
ARTS CENTERS | Part of the fascinating Lucerna complex, the Great Hall is a beautiful art nouveau ballroom with a big main floor and some loges. It hosts everything from swing dances to graduation balls, Czech and international rock and pop stars to Christmas concerts, and even the occasional boxing match, in wonderful historic surroundings.

Everyone from Ray Charles to Maurice Chevalier has played here, so soak up the history as you sway to the beat. ✉ *Štěpánská 61, Nové Město* ☎ *603–502–156* ⊕ *lucpra.com* Ⓜ *Lines A and B: Můstek.*

PUPPET SHOWS AND BLACK-LIGHT THEATER

★ **Nová Scéná** (*The New Stage*)
PUPPET SHOWS | The cool glass-block façade of the New Stage, which opened in 1983, stands out among the ornate 19th-century buildings in the area. Black-light theater company Laterna Magika (which takes its name from the original black-light presentation at Expo '58) performs here, and the rest of the program schedule is handled through the National Theater. Contemporary dance pieces and other language-free performances dominate the calendar. ✉ *Národní 4, Nové Město* ☎ *224–901–448* ⊕ *novascena.cz* Ⓜ *Line B: Národní třída.*

🛍 Shopping

Prague's Nové Město is home to all the big department stores and international brands, which are located in two main shopping areas—Wenceslas Square and Na příkopě. But don't miss the various covered arcades, or "passages," around the city, because they are home to a few interesting boutiques as well as nail bars and wine shops.

ANTIQUES

JHB Starožitnosti

ANTIQUES & COLLECTIBLES | This attractive shop's specialty is timepieces of all kinds, from a wide array of luxury wristwatches to clocks from the 18th and 19th centuries hailing from Austria, the Czech Republic, France, and Germany. Antique pocket watches featured in the window displays also draw longing stares from knowing collectors and passing tourists alike. ✉ *Panská 1, Nové Město* ☎ *222–245–836* ⊕ *jhbvykup.cz* Ⓜ *Lines A and B: Můstek.*

BOOKS AND PRINTS

Antikvariát Karel Křenek

ANTIQUES & COLLECTIBLES | Despite the extensive collection of antique maps, prints, and engravings dating from the 16th century, this shop is refreshingly bright. Among the shop's treasures: beautiful Japanese woodblocks and a well-known map depicting Asia as the winged horse Pegasus. The shop also mounts and frames works on request. ✉ *Národní 20, Nové Město* ☎ *222–314–734* ⊕ *karelkrenek.com* Ⓜ *Line B: Národní třída.*

Globe Bookstore & Café

BOOKS | A fine place to peruse the shelves of English-language titles, this friendly store leads to a café and bar down the hall, where lattes, laptops, and expats are de rigueur. If you're hoping to attend English-language literary, film, or arts events while in Prague, check out the wall of flyers near the front desk. ✉ *Pštrossova 6, Nové Město* ☎ *224–934–203* ⊕ *globebookstore.cz* Ⓜ *Line B: Národní třída.*

Knihy na hory

BOOKS | With more than 10,000 items in stock (including those featured on the online store), you'll find English-language travel guides, useful local maps, books about travel, and even a few globes scattered around the premises, now in the Traveler's Club restaurant—but in keeping with the adventurous spirit, you might need to hunt them down a bit (the name means "books on the mountains"). ✉ *Masarykovo nábř. 22, Nové Město* ☎ *739–016–881* ⊕ *knihynahory.cz* ⊘ *Closed weekends* Ⓜ *Line B: Národní třída.*

★ Koh-i-noor

ART SUPPLIES | This iconic Czech stationery and art supplies brand has two outposts in Nové Město—one on Na příkopě and the other here on Vodičkova—and both are pleasant, airy places to nab a bit of history. The brand, established in 1790, was the first to patent modern pencil lead and pioneered colored pencils, too, and it now sells all of the art kits you would expect as well as cute kids' drawing equipment, along with an unexpected gorilla made of drawing pencils. ⊠ *Vodičkova 710/31, Nové Město* ☎ *734–799–551* ⊕ *koh-i-noor.cz* Ⓜ *Line B: Národní třída.*

Luxor

BOOKS | With its four floors, music section, and coffee shop, this bookstore is the biggest in the Czech Republic, reminiscent of major American chains and known as "the palace." Only a small area in the basement is set aside for English-language books, but the store is an excellent source for maps of the Czech Republic and other European cities and countries and has some travel guidebooks in English. It also hosts various literary events. ⊠ *Václavské nám. 41, Nové Město* ☎ *296–110–372* ⊕ *luxor. cz* Ⓜ *Line A and C: Muzeum.*

Mucha Museum Shop

SOUVENIRS | The perfect place for your art nouveau or Alfons Mucha fix (the world-famous Czech artist who made his name painting Sarah Bernhardt in fin de siècle Paris), this charming shop is located in a museum dedicated to the artist. You'll find posters, postcards, calendars, glass, jewelry, scarves, books, lamps, and more, all with the signature Mucha motifs. ⊠ *Mucha Museum, Panská 7, Nové Město* ☎ *224–216–415* ⊕ *mucha.cz* Ⓜ *Lines A and B: Můstek.*

Terry's Posters

OTHER SPECIALTY STORE | A must-see for movie buffs, this cool little shop has everything from the films themselves on DVD, to clothes, to a carefully curated section of vintage Czechoslovak movie posters. The cinema housing the shop has a rotating exhibition of some of its best stock. ⊠ *Vodičkova 4, Nové Město* ✛ *Inside the Svetozor cinema* ☎ *224–946–829* ⊕ *terryhoponozky.cz* Ⓜ *Lines A and B: Můstek.*

CLOTHING

Cvrk

MIXED CLOTHING | A hodgepodge of jewelry, clothing, and bags gives this design-led Czech store a slight jumble-sale feel, and it's none the worse for that. Finding the unexpected, like robot faces on a skirt, is all part of the fun. There are a few branches around the capital. ⊠ *U Stýblů passage, Václavské nám. 28, Nové Město* ☎ *777–999–788* ⊕ *cvrk.cz* ⊙ *Closed Sun.* Ⓜ *Lines A and B: Můstek.*

Ivana Follová

WOMEN'S CLOTHING | Ivana Follová's little boutique and atelier at the top of Wenceslas Square showcases her wares in a chic, green space in central Prague. The designer specializes in silk, which she dyes in bold colors, patterns, and shapes into gauzy garments, from wedding dresses to coats. She also stocks distinctive accessories like chunky costume jewelry by other Czech designers. ⊠ *Mezibranská 9, Nové Město* ☎ *222–211–357* ⊕ *ivanafollova.cz* ⊙ *Closed weekends* Ⓜ *Lines A and C: Muzeum.*

Navarila

WOMEN'S CLOTHING | Czech designer Martina Nevarilova offers a great line of relaxed and cozy knitwear, often in bold colors or stripes. The shops are worth a look if you're feeling the chill of the Prague winter or if you're on the hunt for a classy and unique cover-up for other occasions. ⊠ *Vodičkova 677/10, Nové Město* ☎ *732–654–311* ⊕ *navarila.cz* Ⓜ *Line B: Národní třída.*

The Room

MEN'S CLOTHING | The Room stocks creative European brands for fashion-conscious men, from cool Chinese-French Three Animals to Alex Monhart's swanky Czech-made black backpacks. ⊠ *Školská 7, Nové Město* ☎ *222–967–770* ⊕ *basmatee.cz* ⊙ *Closed Sun.* Ⓜ *Lines A and B: Můstek.*

Studio Cielo

MIXED CLOTHING | Boasting various urbane brands and occupying several residences on a posh street, Studio Cielo is great fun to browse in for both men and women. From Luisa Cerano's soft knits and chic coats to Richard J Brown's luxury denim, always with that extra decorative detail, there are plenty of options to tempt you to part with your koruny. ✉ *Obecní dům, Nám. Republiky 5, Nové Město* ☎ *606–607–698* ⊕ *onvi.cz* Ⓜ *Line B: Náměstí Republiky.*

FOOD AND WINE

Cellarius

WINE/SPIRITS | Try out acclaimed Moravian wines, or pick up a select imported bottle at the lovely, historic Lucerna passage store and bar, which also offers tastings. ✉ *Lucerna passage, Štěpánská 61, Nové Město* ☎ *224–210–979* ⊕ *cellarius.cz* Ⓜ *Lines A and B: Můstek.*

★ Les Houbeles

FOOD | A quintessentially Czech shop right in the center: you've got to love it. How many other capital cities in the world would have a store dedicated to all things mushroom and mushroom-picking (a slightly risky national pastime—don't do it yourself without an expert present), a street or two away from the retail prime time? Les Houbeles sells mushroom-growing supplies, kitschy clothes, and, of course, the fungi themselves. ✉ *Růžová 7, Nové Město* ☎ *604–288–601* ⊕ *leshoubeles.cz* Ⓜ *Line A/B: Můstek.*

Oxalis

FOOD | Located in the beautiful U Nováku building, a former department store, with its art nouveau entrance and decorated façade, this Czech tea and coffee company offers tastings, gift sets, teapots, and lots of different teas and blends in a high-ceilinged, airy store. ✉ *Vodičkova 30, Nové Město* ☎ *733–182–413* ⊕ *oxalis.cz* Ⓜ *Lines A and B: Můstek.*

GLASS

Moser

GLASSWARE | Elegant glass stemware and decorative bowls and candlesticks are hand-blown or-cut and gorgeous enough to outfit the dining tables of Europe's aristocratic elite. This historic Czech company, established in Karlovy Vary in 1857, maintains two Prague locations—here and on Old Town Square. Both stores are breathtaking (although this location is a bit less hectic), boasting chandeliers, tea sets, and porcelain figurines on multiple floors, in addition to all that graceful glass. ✉ *Na příkopě 12, Nové Město* ☎ *224–211–293* ⊕ *moser-glass.com* Ⓜ *Line B: Náměstí Republiky.*

HOME

Le Patio

FURNITURE | This properly chic Czech lifestyle and furniture boutique gives a glimpse of how the most stylish Prague locals live. From the fact that their pieces are often rented out to filmmakers, to the fact that the shop itself is in the Mozarteum Palace, designed in 1913 by Czech architect Jan Kotěra, it's worth a visit; plus, they ship globally. ✉ *Jungmannova 748/30, Nové Město* ☎ *224–934–402* ⊕ *lepatio.cz* Ⓜ *Lines A and B: Můstek.*

★ Modernista

HOUSEWARES | Innovation is revered at this store inside the Municipal House, a magnet for fans of cubist and modernist furniture and decor. Originals, reproductions, and work by new Czech designers are available, making it nearly impossible to leave without something distinctive—a streamlined steel liquor cabinet or a cool cubist vase, perhaps. There are other branches in Vinohrady and in the Museum of Decorative Arts; this store focuses on ceramics and porcelain. ✉ *Obecní dům, Nám. Republiky 5, Nové Město* ☎ *222–002–102* ⊕ *modernista.cz* Ⓜ *Line B: Náměstí Republiky.*

MARKETS
★ Náplavka
MARKET | Every Saturday (in the warmer months) sees the hipster riverside hangout of Náplavka transformed into a farmers' market selling staples like potatoes and apples as well as more artisanal products like traditional Czech dumplings and honey wine, smoked meats, and tortellini. ⊠ *Náplavka, Nové Město* ⊕ *farmarsketrziste.cz* ⊗ *Closed Jan.* Ⓜ *Line B: Karlovo náměstí.*

SHOES
Baťa
SHOES | Shoes, glorious shoes! Five floors of them, to be exact, are housed in this shoe giant that has locations around the world but got its start right here in the Czech Republic.

■**TIP**➔ **There's a clearance section on the top floor for bargain hunters.** ⊠ *Václavské nám. 6, Nové Město* ☎ *731–618–781* ⊕ *bata.cz* Ⓜ *Lines A and B: Můstek.*

Queens
SHOES | Global brands here are paired with Czech-designed accessories at this flagship store for one of the country's largest sneaker and streetwear shops. Just off Wenceslas Square, the bright, light space is a trendy place to pick up a new pair of sneakers or an own-brand sweater. ⊠ *Jindřišská 16, Nové Město* ☎ *222–210–988* ⊕ *queens.global* ⊗ *Closed Sun.* Ⓜ *Lines A and B: Můstek.*

SHOPPING MALLS AND DEPARTMENT STORES
Kotva
DEPARTMENT STORE | A warren-like hexagonal layout makes this Czech department store feel more adventurous than most. Across the tram tracks from the massive Palladium, it houses the standard clothing and household goods shops as well as electronics, beauty products, and luggage, and even a small minigolf course. There's a great roof bar, too. ⊠ *Nám. Republiky 8, Nové Město* ☎ *224–801–691* ⊕ *od-kotva.cz* Ⓜ *Line B: Náměstí Republiky.*

TOYS
Hugo chodí bos
TOYS | FAMILY | This almost impossibly cute toy store was founded in the last few years by a parent-led team who wanted to bring traditional Czech toys back to Czech children. Its name means "Hugo goes barefoot," and it sells a range of lovely toys and gifts, many wooden, which hark back to a more innocent age. ⊠ *Vodičkova 35, Nové Město* ☎ *775–407–298* ⊕ *hugochodibos. cz* Ⓜ *Line B: Karlovo náměstí.*

Sparkys
TOYS | FAMILY | This is Prague's preeminent toy store chain, with goodies for babies, toddlers, and older children. Let the little ones run wild among the Legos, puzzles, and games. Sparkys also stocks an adorable array of stuffed animals, including Krtek, the cute Czech cartoon character whose popularity spread across the communist world in the second half of the 20th century. ⊠ *Václavské nám. 22, Nové Město* ☎ *777–722–085* ⊕ *sparkys.cz* Ⓜ *Lines A and B: Můstek.*

Chapter 7

SMÍCHOV AND VYŠEHRAD

Updated by
Joseph Reaney

● Sights	🍴 Restaurants	🛏 Hotels	🛍 Shopping	🍸 Nightlife
★★★★☆	★★★★☆	★★★★☆	★★★☆☆	★★★★☆

NEIGHBORHOOD SNAPSHOT

TOP EXPERIENCES

■ **Vyšehrad Cemetery:** Spot famous names like Antonín Dvořák and Alfons Mucha on the tombs and headstones in this historical burial place.

■ **Live Theater:** Take in a show (with English subtitles) at the superb Švandovo divadlo (Švanda Theater), or catch an alternative art performance at MeetFactory.

■ **Gorlice Hall:** Navigate through Vyšehrad's tunnels to reach this barrel-vaulted hall, home to the original baroque statues from the Charles Bridge.

■ Brown-Nosers : Interact with art as never before by enjoying a unique rear view of local enfant terrible David Černý's infamous sculpture.

■ **Sky-High Swimming:** Practice your breaststroke while enjoying stunning city panoramas at the Corinthia Hotel Prague's 24th-floor pool.

PLANNING YOUR TIME

Vyšehrad's main attractions are open only during the day, and you should plan at least four hours to see them all. However, the park can be visited at any time, and the view down the river to the castle is spectacular day or night. Due to its array of excellent restaurants, cinemas, and theaters, Smíchov is best visited after dark.

TAKE A BREAK

Hospůdka Na hradbách. This large beer garden is one of Prague's most popular after-work hangouts during the summer months, and it's no wonder with those stunning city views. ⊠ *V Pevnosti 2, Vyšehrad* ⊕ *facebook.com/hospudkanahradbachm* Ⓜ *Line C: Vyšehrad.*

GETTING HERE

■ Smíchov is a major transport hub. All attractions are within walking distance of one of two Metro stations—Smíchovské nádraží and Anděl (both Line B)—while there are regular tram connections to Malá Strana (Lesser Quarter) and Nové Město (New Town). The neighborhood is also home to Praha-Smíchov railway station, which offers easy train connections to Karlštejn and Plzeň. Vyšehrad is easily accessible by the Metro station of the same name (Line C)—though expect a 15-minute walk from here to the main attractions—or by climbing the steep staircase up from the riverside near Výtoň tram stop. There's also parking available just outside Táborská brána (the entrance gate into the fortress).

Separated by the Vltava River, Smíchov and Vyšehrad are like night and day. In fact, that's when these two neighborhoods are best experienced: spend a morning and afternoon exploring Vyšehrad, then head to Smíchov for your evening entertainment.

The high-top Vyšehrad Citadel once rivaled Prague Castle in size and importance, but much of its historic architecture was leveled during the Hussite wars of the 15th century. The area got a new lease on life in the 18th century as a military fortress, and the casements remain one of the leading attractions. There's also a grand neo-Gothic cathedral and the country's most important cemetery. For many Prague residents, a trip here means simply a chance to enjoy the fresh air and stunning views of Prague Castle in the distance.

Smíchov, meanwhile, really comes to life after the sun goes down. When the city had walls, the neighborhood was on the outside, and all manner of people could live there, making it a colorful, cosmopolitan area. Today, it's known for its top-drawer dining options, excellent craft beer and cocktail bars, and world-class theaters and live music venues. There are also a few good hotels, allowing you to enjoy all Smíchov has to offer at a more leisurely pace. Connections from here to the city center are regular, quick, and easy.

Smíchov

Sights

Smíchov is less about sightseeing and more about food, drink, and entertainment. Nevertheless, there are a couple of sights worth seeing, including the Staropramen Brewery, which has been sitting proudly on the river since 1869.

★ Galerie Futura
ART GALLERY | This free-to-enter (donations welcome) art gallery, set within a labyrinthine, brick-walled basement, houses an eclectic range of quirky, contemporary, and occasionally downright creepy artworks, from oil paintings to audiovisual installations. But it's one particular provocative sculpture that takes the headlines: David Černý's *Brown-Nosers*. Head through the rotating window out into the garden to see two giant, naked, lower halves of bodies, bent over at 90 degrees. Climb one of the two rickety ladders and peer "into" the sculptures to watch a video. In one of the videos—spoiler alert!—former president Václav Klaus is being clumsily spoon-fed human waste to the soundtrack of Queen's "We Are the Champions." In the other, he's the one doing the feeding. The scenes are a metaphor for the state of Czech politics, apparently.

Smíchov and Vyšehrad

0   1/4 mi

0   1/4 km

Museum Kampa

Vítězná

most Legií

Střelecký ostrov

Janáčkovo nábř.

Kinského zahrada

Štefánikova

Elišky Peškové

Zborovská

Slovanský ostrov

Masarykovo nábřeží

Dětský ostrov

Národopisné Muzeum
(Kinsky Summerhouse)

Ortinova

Arbesovo náměstí

Strahovský tunel

Holečkova

V Botanici

Jiráskův most

Resslova

Matoušova

Vltava

Dittrichova

Václavská

Trojanova

Gorazdova

Na Moráni

Park Sacré Coeur

Kartouzská

SMÍCHOV

Plešova

Palackého most

Plzeňská

Lidická

Svornosti

Pod Slovany

Trojická

Podskalské

Duškova

Štrupežnického

Nádražní

Mrázovka

Hořejší nábř.

Vltavská

Plavecká

Vyšehradská

Ostrovského

Radlická

Skatepark Smíchov

Na Výtoni

Pivovarská

Svobodova

Tunel Mrázovka

Na Valentince

Železniční most

Libušina

Vratislavova

Rašínovo nábř.

Na Václavce

Sady Na skalce

Vyšehrad

Santoška

Vltava

Paví Vrch

Nádražní

Radlická

Strakonická

Český Yacht Klub

Pechlátova

Dobříšská

Křížová

Císařská louka

Veslařský ostrov

K Závěrce

Pod Děvínem

Sights ▼

1 Galerie Futura **A4**
2 Království Železnic **C5**
3 Pivovar Staropramen.............. **D5**
4 Vyšehrad Casemates.............. **G6**
5 Vyšehrad Citadel.................. **G7**

Restaurants ▼

1 Bockem **C3**
2 Fortel **D4**
3 Gourmet Pauza..................... **D4**
4 Na Kopci **C9**
5 Taro................................. **D5**
6 U Kroka **F6**

Quick Bites ▼

1 Artic Bakehouse.................... **C2**
2 Hospůdka Na hradbách **G7**
3 Kavárna co hledá jméno........... **C5**

Hotels ▼

1 Corinthia Hotel Prague............. **I7**
2 Mamaison Riverside
   Hotel Prague **D4**
3 Vienna House Andel's Prague.....**C5**

■TIP→ The gallery is a 15-minute uphill walk from Anděl Metro station. Ring the buzzer at the door to be let in. ⊠ *Holečkova 49, Smíchov* ☏ *608–955–150* ⊕ *www. futuraprague.com* ✉ *Free* ⊙ *Closed Mon. and Tues.* Ⓜ *Line B: Anděl.*

Království Železnic

CHILDREN'S MUSEUM | FAMILY | This family-friendly attraction is home to Prague's most extensive model railway, comprising more than 600 meters of track and literally thousands of toy trains. There are several different sets, representing different regions of the Czech Republic (complete with intricately re-created, scaled-down sights), although they are mostly kept at an arm's length and behind glass. Luckily, there are also plenty of interactive sights, including remote control cars, train and tram simulators, and themed play areas. ⊠ *Stroupežnického 23, Smíchov* ☏ *257–211–386* ⊕ *www. kralovstvi-zeleznic.cz* ✉ *260 Kč* Ⓜ *Line B: Anděl.* Railway Kingdom

Pivovar Staropramen (Staropramen Brewery)

FACTORY | The slogan for this brewery on the riverside in Smíchov could be "For beer, go directly to the source." *Staropramen* literally means "old source," and it's definitely one of the most ubiquitous beers in the city—and beyond. This visitor center offers 50-minute "guided" tours every day, where a video projection of early brewmaster Josef Paspa (well, a suitably ruddy-cheeked actor) takes you through the history of the site, the beer brewing method, and how far and wide the beer is exported. It all culminates in a tasting of four different Staropramen brews, from the excellent unfiltered lager to the dark beer. If you're feeling peckish afterward, one of the brewery's chain of Potrefená Husa restaurants, serving classic Czech food and beer, is just around the corner. ⊠ *Staropramen Visitor Center, Pivovarská 9, Smíchov* ☏ *251–553–389* ⊕ *www.centrumstaropramen.cz* ✉ *Tour 299 Kč* ⊙ *Closed Mon.* Ⓜ *Line B: Anděl.*

🍴 Restaurants

Smíchov is a former working-class neighborhood that was thrust into upscale territory in the late 1990s, when several banks decided to locate their headquarters near the Metro station Anděl. Now the de facto center of the neighborhood, there are a handful of very good restaurants dotted around Anděl, as well as in the northern part of the district, near Malá Strana.

Bockem

$$$$ | CZECH | It may not look too salubrious from outside, but this tucked-away fine-dining restaurant has a wonderfully warm and welcoming interior, all roughly plastered walls, sturdy wooden furniture, soft golden lighting, and autumnal wall hangings. What's more, the food is great: the seasonal, five-course degustation menu (1,590 Kč) has a mix of influences but really comes to life with main courses built around classic Czech ingredients like rabbit, pork, dumplings, and cabbage. **Known for:** seasonal menu of delicious and inventive dishes; distinctive non-alcoholic pairing option; beautiful interior with limited seating. ⑤ *Average main: Kč1590* ⊠ *Elišky Peškové 5, Smíchov* ☏ *770–101–223* ⊕ *www.bockem.cz* ⊙ *Closed Mon. and Tues. No dinner Wed. and Sun.* Ⓜ *Line B: Anděl plus Tram 9, 12, 15, or 20 to Arbesovo náměstí.*

Fortel

$$ | INTERNATIONAL | On the site of a historic Smíchov theater but now a paean to industrial-chic design, this hip restaurant and bar combines eye-catching decor with an excellent menu of modern Czech and international cuisine. Regular main dishes are available, but order instead from the extensive tapas menu, where highlights include duck parfait with cognac, beet hummus with whipped goat's cheese, and crispy pork belly in hoisin sauce. **Known for:** art-filled and industrial space; great food and drinks; friendly service. ⑤ *Average main: Kč275*

✉ *Lidická 29, Smíchov* ☎ *702–040–808* ⊕ *www.fortel-smichov.cz* ◔ *Closed Sun.* Ⓜ *Line B: Anděl.*

Gourmet Pauza

$$ | **MEDITERRANEAN** | This small and stylish bistro, run by mother-and-daughter team Zuzana and Pavlína, offers a casual, family-friendly atmosphere in which to enjoy a delicious meal. Open from breakfast to dinner, the place is busiest at lunch, where the good-value daily menus feature some of the restaurant's best dishes (like the gnocchi with salmon and sun-dried tomatoes) at half the usual price. **Known for:** stylish but unfussy ambience; quality Mediterannean-inspired food; slightly high prices. ⑤ *Average main: Kč325* ✉ *Lidická 19, Smíchov* ☎ *608–800–077* ⊕ *www.gourmetpauza. cz* ◔ *No dinner Sun.* Ⓜ *Line B: Anděl.*

★ Na Kopci

$$$ | **CZECH** | Although a little out of the way, this lovely restaurant overlooking Smíchov (the name means "On the Hill") serves exceptional, high-end Czech and international cuisine within a comfortable and casual setting. The menu is completely overhauled every three months, making the best use of seasonal, locally sourced ingredients—from rabbit and wild boar to porcini mushrooms—to create surprising and satisfying dishes. **Known for:** sublime seasonal dishes; warm and welcoming decor; good value for high quality. ⑤ *Average main: Kč450* ✉ *K Závěrce 20, Smíchov* ☎ *251–553–102* ⊕ *www.nakopci.com* Ⓜ *Line B: Radlická.*

★ Taro

$$ | **VIETNAMESE** | This extraordinary Asian fusion restaurant, which consists of just 17 bar stalls arranged around an open kitchen, offers an interactive dining experience combining traditional Vietnamese cuisine with European techniques and flavors. It's a combination inspired by owners Khanh's and Giang's personal experiences as Vietnamese men growing up in Prague. **Known for:** kitchen spectacle with chef interaction; flavor-packed seasonal dishes; great quality-to-value ratio. ⑤ *Average main: Kč275* ✉ *Nádražní 100, Smíchov* ☎ *777–446–007* ⊕ *www. taro.cz* ◔ *Closed Sun. and Mon.* Ⓜ *Line B: Anděl.*

☕ Coffee and Quick Bites

Artic Bakehouse

$ | **BAKERY** | The home-baked sourdough bread, the huge selection of delicious pastries, and the lovingly brewed coffee make this café-bakery a local favorite. It's so popular that there are now two other branches in Prague, including a second one in Smíchov (at Štefánikova 31). **Known for:** delicious almond croissants; three-day rye bread; good (and cheap) coffee. ⑤ *Average main: Kč100* ✉ *Újezd 11, Smíchov* ☎ *771–140–048* ⊕ *www. articbakehouse.cz* Ⓜ *Tram 9 to Újezd.*

★ Kavárna co hledá jméno

$$ | **CAFÉ** | Literally translated as "A Coffee Shop Looking for a Name," this achingly hip café-cum-gallery serves great coffee, tempting cocktails, and excellent food—including top-notch breakfasts and brunches until midday on weekdays and 3 pm on weekends. The gallery space showcases work by local artists and hosts pop-up events. **Known for:** no reservations possible; setting in a former joiner's workshop; Smíchov's best brunch place. ⑤ *Average main: Kč190* ✉ *Stroupežnického 10, Smíchov* ⊕ *kavarnacohledajmeno.czm* Ⓜ *Line B: Anděl.*

🛏 Hotels

With a host of entertainment options on your doorstep, as well as easy access—via tram, Metro, or on foot—to the city's historical center, Smíchov is a great place to stay.

Mamaison Riverside Hotel Prague

$$ | HOTEL | True to its name, the Riverside is situated right above the Vltava across from Frank Gehry's Tančící dům (Dancing House). **Pros:** clever art nouveau design; incredible river views; great value if booked early. **Cons:** no fitness facilities; interior rooms are dark; a little tired in places. ⑤ *Rooms from: Kč4500* ✉ *Janáčkovo nabř. 15, Smíchov* ☎ *225–994–611* ⊕ *www.mamaisonriverside.com* ⮌ *80 rooms* ⦿ *Free Breakfast* Ⓜ *Line B: Anděl.*

Vienna House Andel's Prague

$$ | HOTEL | Located next to one of the city's best shopping malls, this simple, modernist hotel may be built for business, but it's also where many of the young, up-and-coming, and mostly German-speaking trendsetters stay. **Pros:** chic and pared-back interior design; good choices at breakfast; great tram and Metro connections to the center. **Cons:** breakfast room can be busy; mall area is lacking personality; not walkable to any major sights. ⑤ *Rooms from: Kč2500* ✉ *Stroupežnického 21, Smíchov* ☎ *296–882–302* ⊕ *www.viennahouse. com* ⮌ *239 rooms* ⦿ *No Meals* Ⓜ *Line B: Anděl.*

 Nightlife

This neighborhood is jam-packed with cool beer and wine bars, cocktail joints, and live music venues. Stroll around and see what takes your fancy.

BARS AND PUBS

Brothers Bar & Cafe

BARS | This small but stylish American-style bar serves beers, wines, spirits, and a wide range of excellent cocktails. It also has, somewhat unexpectedly, some of Prague's best coffee. Whether serving a Tom Collins or a latte macchiato, the bartenders really know their stuff. ■**TIP→ Cash only.** ✉ *Lidická 12, Smíchov* ☎ *735–343–535* ⊕ *www.brothersbar.cz* Ⓜ *Line B: Anděl.*

Craft Beer Spot

BARS | This side-street taproom has an enormous, arching bar with an ever-changing selection of 10 Czech and international beers on tap. There are fridgefuls of bottles, too; the enthusiastic and knowledgeable staff will be happy to help you make a selection. Beer-friendly food, from cheddar-smothered nachos to beer-marinated ribs, is served throughout the day. ✉ *Plaská 5, Smíchov* ☎ *257–219– 855* ⊕ *www.thebeerspot.cz* Ⓜ *Line B: Anděl plus Tram 9, 12, 15, or 20 to Újezd.*

JAZZ CLUBS

★ Jazz Dock

LIVE MUSIC | If you missed your boat tour, don't despair. You can still hear notes and beats wafting across the water while sipping a cocktail in a decadent venue. This extremely cool, glass-enclosed nightclub and jazz bar—built, as the name suggests, on a dock—offers a view of the passing boat traffic and lit-up landmark buildings like the National Theater, while you enjoy the strains of world-class live music acts. There are typically two concerts per night; it's worth reserving a table in advance for weekend shows. ✉ *Janáčkovo nábř. 2, Smíchov* ☎ *774– 058–838* ⊕ *www.jazzdock.cz* Ⓜ *Line B: Anděl.*

LIVE MUSIC CLUBS

Futurum

LIVE MUSIC | The decor at this stalwart Smíchov club could be described as odd but cool. Think 1950s sci-fi crossed with art deco, and you're on the right track. It all makes for a fun, casual night out. Video parties, complete with '80s, '90s, and '00s music, draw big crowds every Friday night. There are occasional live performances, too, usually from punk or goth bands, or DJs playing electronic music. ✉ *Zborovská 7, Smíchov* ☎ *257–328–571* ⊕ *futurum.musicbar.cz* Ⓜ *Line B: Anděl.*

Phenomen Music Bar
DANCE CLUBS | This upmarket dance club has regular themed nights with energetic DJs and, occasionally, live music acts. There's a large dance floor, but also a good-size seating area for enjoying a cocktail, a glass of Champagne, or some pick-me-up chicken wings. ☒ *Nádražní 84, Smíchov* ☎ *774–366–636* ⊕ *www. phenomen.cz* Ⓜ *Line B: Anděl.*

 Performing Arts

THEATER AND DANCE
Švandovo divadlo (*Švanda Theater*)
THEATER | If you want to join the theater-loving masses and there's nothing on in English, Švanda Theater is your best bet. The plays shown here—a rotating mix that can include everything from Shakespeare to Ibsen to contemporary theater—are supertitled above the stage in English. The theater also occasionally hosts live concerts and serves as a major venue for the Prague Pride festival, held every August.

■ TIP➔ **For the best view, sit in the balcony, on the right side, facing the stage.** ☒ *Štefánikova 6, Smíchov* ☎ *234–651–111* ⊕ *www.svandovodivadlo.cz* Ⓜ *Line B: Anděl plus Tram 9, 12, 15, or 20 to Švandovo divadlo.*

VENUES
MeetFactory
ARTS CENTERS | If you want to take the pulse of Prague's contemporary arts scene, get yourself down to MeetFactory. This spot really is too cool for school. Established more than a decade ago by leading Czech modern artist David Černý as a place for cultural and artistic collaboration, the space houses a gallery, concert hall, and theater, so it offers regular art, theater, dance, and music performances. To get here, cross over the railway tracks on a little bridge and keep an eye out for the car sculptures driving up the side of the building. ☒ *Ke Sklárně 15, Smíchov* ☎ *251–551–796* ⊕ *meetfactory.cz* Ⓜ *Line B: Smíchovské nádraží.*

⬛ Shopping

This area offers a reasonable range of modern shops and international brands. They're mainly within or around Nový Smíchov, the big daddy of shopping centers.

SHOPPING MALLS AND DEPARTMENT STORES
OC Nový Smíchov
MALL | This bright and airy mall is one of Prague's largest, but it's still manageable. It has a convenient mix of shops, including brands like Zara, H&M, Humanic, Levi's, and Clinique. There's also a large Tesco, a multiscreen movie theater, and a varied food court. ☒ *Plzeňská 8, Smíchov* ☎ *251–511–151* ⊕ *novy-smichov. klepierre.cz* Ⓜ *Line B: Anděl.*

Vyšehrad

 Sights

The district of Vyšehrad is dominated by the Vyšehrad Citadel and its many attractions, the most visible of which is the Bazilika sv. Petra a Pavla (Basilica of Sts. Peter and Paul). But the neighborhood also incorporates the area around and below the castle, where there are a handful of other interesting sights.

★ **Vyšehrad Casemates**
CAVE | Buried deep within the walls of Vyšehrad Citadel, this series of long, dark passageways was built by the French army in 1742 and later improved by other occupying forces, including the Prussians and the Austrians. A guided tour leads through several hundred meters of military corridors into Gorlice Hall, once a gathering place for soldiers and now a storage site for six of the original, pollution-scarred statues from Charles Bridge. Tours start at the information center, near the Táborská brána entrance gate. ☒ *V Pevnosti 5B, Vyšehrad* ⊕ *www.praha-vysehrad.cz* 🎫 *90 Kč* Ⓜ *Line C: Vyšehrad.*

A Cubist Walk

Fans of 20th-century architecture should head below the rocky outcropping that's crowned by Vyšehrad Citadel to find a satisfying smattering of cubist gems. Prague's cubist architecture followed a great Czech tradition: embracing new ideas, while adapting them to existing artistic and social contexts to create something sui generis. Between 1912 and 1914, Josef Chochol (1880–1956) designed several of the city's dozen or so cubist projects, and you'll find a number of them in Vyšehrad.

Stroll down the staircase that leads from the citadel to the riverside, then peel off from the crowds by heading left and walking around 200 yards. Here, you'll find an eye-catching three-family house at Rašínovo nábřeží 6–10. This cubist masterpiece was completed early in Chochol's career, when his cubist style was still developing, so you can see a design touched with baroque and neoclassical influences, with a mansard roof and end gables. Cross the road for the best view of the properties.

Once you've taken it all in, walk along the riverside back the way you came, then cross back over the road at the second pedestrian crossing. You're now looking into the garden of another great work of cubist architecture, Chochol's villa. The wall and gate of the house use triangular moldings and metal grating to create an effect of controlled energy. Head around to the front of the building (the street address is Libušina 3) to appreciate the property's full, undulating effect, created by smoothly articulated forms.

From here, walk around the corner to Neklanova 2, another apartment house that is attributed to Chochol. It uses pyramidal shapes and a suggestion of Gothic columns. Finally, walk just down the street and you'll come to Chochol's own apartment house. Situated at Neklanova 30 (on the corner of Přemyslova), it's a masterpiece in concrete. The pyramidal, kaleidoscopic window moldings and roof cornices make an expressive link to the baroque yet are wholly novel; the faceted corner balcony column, meanwhile, alludes to Gothic forerunners.

★ **Vyšehrad Citadel** (*Vyšehrad Fortress*) **CASTLE/PALACE** | Bedřich Smetana's symphonic poem *Vyšehrad* opens with four bardic harp chords that echo the legends surrounding this ancient fortress. Today the flat-top bluff stands over the right bank of the Vltava as a green, tree-dotted expanse showing few signs that splendid medieval monuments once made it a landmark to rival Prague Castle.

The Vyšehrad, or "High Castle," was constructed by Vratislav II (ruled 1061–92), a Přemyslid duke who became the first king of Bohemia. He made the fortified hilltop his capital. Under subsequent rulers it fell into disuse until the 14th century, when Charles IV transformed the site into an ensemble including palaces, the main church, battlements, and a massive gatehouse whose scant remains are on V Pevnosti ulice. By the 17th century royalty had long since departed, and most of the structures they built were crumbling. Vyšehrad was turned into a fortress.

Vyšehrad's place in the modern Czech imagination is largely thanks to the

7

Smíchov and Vyšehrad VYŠEHRAD

Many of Prague's greats lie buried in the cemetery adjacent to the Basilica of Sts. Peter and Paul. Most notable are the graves of Antonín Dvořák, Bedřich Smetana, and Alfons Mucha.

National Revivalists of the 19th century, particularly writer Alois Jirásek. Jirásek mined medieval chronicles for legends and facts to glorify the early Czechs, and that era of Czech history is very much in the popular consciousness today.

Today, the most notable attraction within the fortification walls is the Basilica of Sts. Peter and Paul, the landmark neo-Gothic church that can be seen from the riverside. Head inside to see the rich art nouveau decorations, including carvings, mosaics, and figural wall paintings. Beside the church is the entrance to Hřbitov Vyšehrad (Vyšehrad Cemetery), the final resting place of some of the country's leading artists and luminaries, including composers Antonín Dvořák and Bedřich Smetana.

Traces of the citadel's distant past can be found at every turn and are reflected even in the structure chosen for the visitor center, the remains of a Gothic stone fortification wall known as Špička, or Peak Gate, at the corner of V Pevnosti

and U Podolského Sanatoria. Farther ahead is the sculpture-covered Leopold Gate, which stands next to brick walls enlarged during the 1742 occupation by the French. Out of the gate, a heavily restored Romanesque rotunda, built by Vratislav II in the 11th century, stands on the corner of K Rotundě and Soběslavova. It's considered the oldest fully intact Romanesque building in the city. Down Soběslavova are the excavated foundations and a few embossed floor tiles from the late-10th-century Basilika sv. Vavřince (St. Lawrence Basilica, closed to the public). The foundations, discovered in 1884 while workers were creating a cesspool, are in a baroque structure at Soběslavova 14. The remains are from one of the few early medieval buildings to have survived in the area and are worth a look.

On the western side of Vyšehrad, part of the fortifications stand next to the surprisingly confined foundation mounds of a medieval palace overlooking a ruined

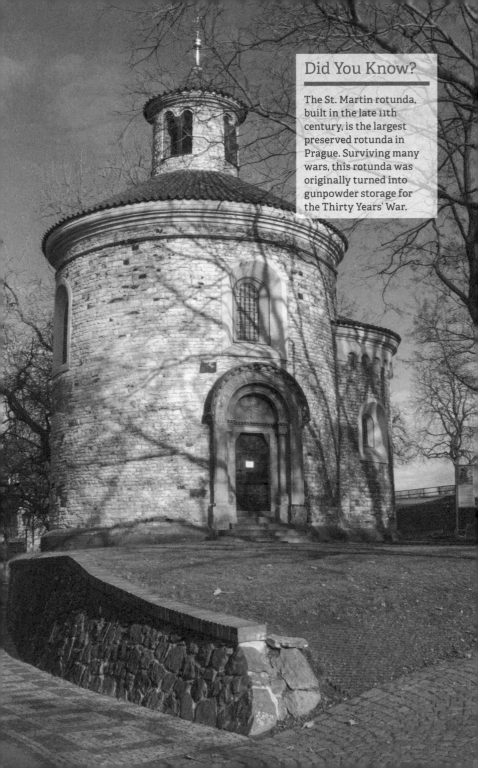

watchtower called Libuše's Bath, which precariously juts out of a rocky outcropping over the river. A nearby plot of grass hosts a statue of Libuše and her consort Přemysl, one of four large, sculpted images of couples from Czech legend by J. V. Myslbek (1848–1922), the sculptor of the St. Wenceslas monument. ⊠ *V Pevnosti 5B, Vyšehrad* ⊕ *www.praha-vysehrad.cz* ⊠ *Grounds and cemetery free, Gothic cellar 70 Kč* Ⓜ *Line C: Vyšehrad.*

🍴 Restaurants

Vyšehrad is best enjoyed with a picnic in the park. However, if this doesn't appeal, there are a handful of cafés and pubs dotted around the fortress and more in the streets below.

★ U Kroka

$$ | CZECH | This traditional pub, which sits below the walls of Vyšehrad Citadel, serves up traditional, meaty Czech fare—think beef goulash, pork knuckle, and duck leg confit—with freshly poured beer. The interior is warm and welcoming, the staff are unfailingly friendly, and the prices are very competitive. **Known for:** good-quality Czech food; pleasant industrial-chic interior; more locals than tourists. ⑤ *Average main: Kč175* ⊠ *Vratislavova 12, Vyšehrad* ☎ *775–905–022* ⊕ *www.ukroka.cz* Ⓜ *Line B: Karlovo náměstí plus Tram 2 or 3 to Výtoň.*

Hotels

Vyšehrad has a very limited choice of accommodations. If you want to stay near the citadel, the Corinthia Hotel Prague is your best option.

Corinthia Hotel Prague

$$ | HOTEL | An ideal accommodation option for business travelers, Corinthia Prague combines modern interiors, spacious rooms, and a choice of good restaurants with a convenient location; it sits on Metro Line C and is right opposite

Prague Congress Center. **Pros:** right by Prague Congress Center; top-floor spa with panoramic city views; great value option. **Cons:** rooms a little corporate; reception sometimes understaffed; breakfast room gets busy. ⑤ *Rooms from: Kč3300* ⊠ *Kongresová 1, Vyšehrad* ☎ *261–191–111* ⊕ *www.corinthia. com/prague* ⊋ *539 rooms* ⑪ *No Meals* Ⓜ *Line C: Vyšehrad.*

🎭 Performing Arts

VENUES

Kongresové centrum Praha (*Congress Center*)

ARTS CENTERS | Somehow, this former Palace of Culture, built in 1981, has never found a place in people's hearts. The large, functionalist, multipurpose building has several performance spaces that can seat thousands, but overall it has a very sterile feel. Plays (usually musicals), stand-up comedians, circus shows, and more come here. As the largest venue in the city, it also hosts the majority of conferences. ⊠ *5. května 65, Vyšehrad* ☎ *261–171–111* ⊕ *www.praguecc.cz* Ⓜ *Line C: Vyšehrad.*

Chapter 8

VINOHRADY AND VRŠOVICE

8

Updated by
Joseph Reaney

👁 Sights	🍴 Restaurants	🛏 Hotels	🛍 Shopping	🍸 Nightlife
★★★☆☆	★★★★☆	★★★☆☆	★★★★☆	★★★★☆

NEIGHBORHOOD SNAPSHOT

TOP EXPERIENCES

■ **Fine Dining:** Enjoy a meal in one of Prague's top-drawer restaurants, such as Vinohrady's Blue Wagon or Vršovice's Benjamin.

■ **St. Wenceslas Church:** Stroll around this weird and wonderful 20th-century church, with its sky-high clock tower visible from far and wide.

■ **Craft Beer:** Set off on an epic pub crawl around the countless craft beer bars and microbreweries in this part of town.

■ **Indie Boutiques:** Shop for boho vintage clothes and designer accessories in a host of small, independent boutiques.

■ **Slavia Prague:** Watch one of the country's most famous soccer teams in full flow during a game at the Sinobo Stadium.

GETTING HERE

Metro Line A bisects Vinohrady, so most sights are within easy reach of three stations: Náměstí Míru, Jiřího z Poděbrad, and Flora. Vršovice does not have any Metro stations, but Tram 22 offers a direct connection to Nové Město (New Town), Malá Strana (Lesser Quarter), and Prague Castle. There is limited (mostly paid) parking available in both neighborhoods.

PLANNING YOUR TIME

As they are mainly residential, Vinohrady and Vršovice make for pleasant, quiet neighborhoods to visit during weekdays. But if you want to make the most of the restaurants and nightlife—and meet some locals—come during evenings and weekends.

QUICK BITES

■ **Pavilon Grébovka.** This historic pavilion in pretty Havlíčkovy sady (Havlíček Gardens) serves sweet and savory breakfasts, tasty lunches, and all-day snacks. There's also a grill in summer. ⊠ *Havlíčkovy sady 2188* ⊕ *www.pavilon-grebovka.czm* Ⓜ *Tram 13 to Ruská*

Dotted with pretty green parks, charming turn-of-the-20th-century houses, and some of Prague's best cafés and restaurants, Vinohrady and Vršovice are two of Prague's most appealing—yet mercifully crowd-free—neighborhoods.

Vinohrady is centered on Vinohradská, the main street that extends eastward from the top of Václavské náměstí (Wenceslas Square) to a belt of enormous cemeteries. Named for the vineyards that once dominated the area, it retains an air of upper crustiness thanks to its splendid 19th-century apartment buildings, pleasant tree-lined streets, and handsome church- and market-filled squares, as well as its extraordinarily high concentration of upmarket cafés and restaurants. Vinohrady also boasts two of Prague's most popular green spaces: the English garden–style Riegrovy sady (Rieger Park) and the Italian Renaissance–style Havlíčkovy sady (Havlíček Gardens).

Neighboring Vršovice, to the south and east of Vinohrady, is equally charming, if a little rougher around the edges. Its art nouveau town houses may be a little more faded and its hip coffee shops less ubiquitous, but its incredible choice of bars (from craft beer hangouts to down-to-earth *hospody,* traditional Czech pubs), its quirky modernist churches, and its buzzing atmosphere during Slavia Prague match days more than make up for it.

Vinohrady

◉ Sights

Havlíčkovy sady (*Havlíček Gardens*)
CITY PARK | Arguably Prague's prettiest park, Havlíček Gardens is best known for its Italian-style grotto and its rows of verdant vineyards. But it also manages to pack in plenty of other attractions, from placid lakes to cascading fountains, and expansive green lawns to narrow woodland trails. It also has two excellent drinking and dining options: the charming garden café Pavilon Grébovka, which serves sweet and savory breakfasts, tasty lunches, and all-day snacks (there's also a grill in summer); and the hilltop gazebo wine bar Viniční Altán, which offers stunning views of the surrounding area. Getting to the park involves a short walk, either from tram stop Krymská (five minutes) or Metro stop Náměstí Míru (10 minutes). ⊠ *Vinohrady* ⊕ *www.pavilongrebovka.cz* ⊠ *Free* Ⓜ *Line A: Náměstí Míru.*

★ **Kostel Nejsvětějšího Srdce Páně**
(*Church of the Most Sacred Heart*)
CHURCH | If you've had your fill of Romanesque, Gothic, and baroque, this church offers a startlingly modernist alternative. Designed in 1927 by Slovenian architect Jože Plečnik—the same architect who

Vinohrady

KEY

- ➊ Sights
- ➊ Restaurants
- ➊ Quick Bites
- ➊ Hotels
- Ⓜ Metro Station

0 — 1/4 km
0 — 1/4 mi

Sights ▶

1	Havlíčkovy sady	C3
2	Kostel Nejsvětějšího Srdce Páně	D2
3	Nový židovský hřbitov	H1

Restaurants ▶

1	Aromi	B2
2	Bílá Kráva	A2
3	Blue Wagon	B2
4	Bruxx	B2
5	Lal Qila	B1
6	Pho Vietnam	A2
7	The Tavern	C1

Quick Bites ▶

1	Cafefin	D2

Hotels ▶

1	Hotel Anna	C2
2	Le Palais Art Hotel Prague	A3

updated Prague Castle and who almost single-handedly designed the modern city of Ljubljana—the art deco edifice of this church resembles a luxury ocean liner more than a place of worship, topped by a tower with an enormous glazed clock. The effect was purposeful, as during the 1920s and 1930s the avant-garde imitated mammoth objects of modern technology. The interior decor is equally striking, particularly the altar, overlooked by a 10-foot-high gilded figure of Christ, flanked by six Czech patron saints. It's hard to miss the structure, which looms as you exit the Metro.

■ TIP→ **While the front door (with a view of the interior) is open 9 to 5 every day, entrance is allowed only 45 minutes before and after mass.** ⊠ *Nám. Jiřího z Poděbrad, Vinohrady* ☎ *222–727–713* ⊕ *srdcepane. cz* ⊡ *Free* Ⓜ *Line A: Jiřího z Poděbrad.*

Nový židovský hřbitov (*New Jewish Cemetery*)
CEMETERY | In this, the newest of the city's half-dozen Jewish burial grounds, you can find the modest **tombstone of Franz Kafka,** which seems grossly inadequate to Kafka's fame but oddly in proportion to his own modest sense of self. The cemetery is usually open, although guards sometimes inexplicably seal off the grounds. Men may be required to wear a yarmulke (you can buy one here if you need to). Turn right at the main cemetery gate and follow the wall for about 100 yards. Kafka's thin white tombstone lies at the front of section 21. City maps may label the cemetery "Židovské hřbitovy." ⊠ *Izraelská 1, Vinohrady* ☎ *226–235–248* ⊕ *www.kehilaprag.cz* ⊡ *Free* Ⓜ *Line A: Želivského.*

🍴 Restaurants

Vinohrady has some of the capital's best restaurants. The neighborhood has two main dining hubs: the area surrounding Náměstí Miru, particularly south along

Americká ulice; and the streets around the Metro station Jiřího z Poděbrad. However, you'll find some of the very finest dining experiences tucked away on less well-trodden avenues. For tasty, down-to-earth Czech food, you're better off heading to a pub.

★ Aromi
$$$ | **ITALIAN** | Gracious, gregarious, and extremely confident, Aromi is easily among the top tier of Italian restaurants in the city and proud of it. Classic pastas made in-house and fresh seafood shown off tableside are two of the crowd favorites, as are the superb salads and well-chosen Italian wines. **Known for:** sumptuous seafood dishes; extensive choice of wines and grappas; faultless service. ⑤ *Average main: Kč650* ⊠ *Nám. Míru 6, Vinohrady* ☎ *222–713–222* ⊕ *aromi.lacollezione.cz* ۞ *Closed Sun. No lunch Sat.* Ⓜ *Line A: Náměstí Míru.*

★ Bílá Kráva
$$$ | **STEAKHOUSE** | Meat lovers will be in their element at this French countryside-inspired steak restaurant, situated just behind the National Museum. Take a seat beneath the wood-beamed ceiling and choose from a menu dominated by dishes of expertly aged Charolais beef, from steak tartare and tenderloin carpaccio to juicy rump steaks and hearty beef bourguignon. **Known for:** delicious aged beef dishes; charming countryside-style setting; good value for such high quality. ⑤ *Average main: Kč450* ⊠ *Rubešova 10, Vinohrady* ☎ *603–397–367* ⊕ *www. bilakrava.cz* ۞ *Closed Sun. No lunch Sat.* Ⓜ *Lines A and C: Muzeum.*

Blue Wagon
$$$ | **CZECH** | This appealing Vinohrady restaurant serves up innovative, high-quality, and beautifully presented cuisine in a soothing and unstuffy setting. The à la carte menu is all about fresh and flavorful Czech dishes with occasional French, Italian, or Asian twists (and added seafood): think duck breast with parsnip

Did You Know?

Havlíčkovy sady, known as Grébovka to locals, is a wonderful park for a stroll, views, and a leisurely glass of wine at the top of the vineyard.

and cranberries, shrimp and carrot cream soup with yellow curry, and pan-fried sea bass with *fregola* and bok choy. **Known for:** outdoor seating in summer; phenomenal chocolate fondant dessert; piped-in pop music that adds little to the atmosphere. ⑤ *Average main: Kč500* ✉ *Uruguayská 19, Vinohrady* ☎ *222–561–378* ⊕ *www.bluewagon.cz* ⊙ *Closed Sun. and Mon.* Ⓜ *Line A: Náměstí Míru.*

Bruxx

$$ | **BELGIAN** | **FAMILY** | For an alternative to pilsner in the Czech capital, this superb Belgian brasserie offers a choice of half a dozen Belgian beers on draft, and more than 60 others in bottles. The beers, which are often tinged with fruit or nut flavors, are served alongside kettles of mussels (cooked in wine or beer), golden frites with mayo sauce, and ridiculously tasty waffles. **Known for:** Belgian beers on draft; fine fish and seafood dishes; outdoor seating in summer. ⑤ *Average main: Kč400* ✉ *Nám. Míru 9, Vinohrady* ☎ *224–250–404* ⊕ *www.bruxx.cz* Ⓜ *Line A: Náměstí Míru.*

Lal Qila

$$ | **INDIAN** | Vinohrady has several very good Indian restaurants, but this corner restaurant along one of the area's prettiest streets may just be the best. Those familiar with Indian cooking can expect all of the standard curries, tandoori dishes, samosas, naans, and other staples of Indian cuisine. **Known for:** delicious lamb dishes; fast and friendly service; lunch buffet available for 220 Kč. ⑤ *Average main: Kč285* ✉ *Italská 30, Vinohrady* ☎ *774–310–774* ⊕ *www.lalqila.cz* Ⓜ *Lines A and C: Muzeum.*

Pho Vietnam

$$ | **VIETNAMESE** | Prague's large and long-established Vietnamese community means the city is littered with cheap Southeast Asian dining options, but this cellar restaurant is one of the very best. While it's certainly no-frills—order at the counter and then find a table; in a few minutes someone brings around your food—the dishes are unfailingly fresh and delicious. **Known for:** satisfying fare in big portions; excellent value; can get very warm inside. ⑤ *Average main: Kč180* ✉ *Anglická 15, Vinohrady* ☎ *606–707–880* ⊕ *www.pho-vietnam.cz* ⊙ *Closed Sun.* Ⓜ *Line C: I. P. Pavlova.*

★ The Tavern

$$ | **BURGER** | A hopping burger bar on the fringe of Riegrovy Park in Vinohrady, the Tavern arguably serves the city's best hamburgers and cheeseburgers. The restaurant began as the dream of an American couple to use classic U.S. combinations, like bacon-cheddar or blue cheese and caramelized onion, and then re-create them with locally sourced beef and toppings. **Known for:** the city's best burgers; intimate cellar setting; extensive cocktail menu. ⑤ *Average main: Kč240* ✉ *Chopinova 26, Vinohrady* ⊕ *www.thetavern.cz* Ⓜ *Line A: Jiřího z Poděbrad.*

☕ Coffee and Quick Bites

Cafefin

$$ | **CAFÉ** | This popular Vietnamese-Czech coffee shop offers a real mix of Western and Asian coffee culture, from cappuccinos, espresso tonics, and hot chocolates to Vietnamese coffee, matcha lattes, and kombucha. The food is great, too: come for the excellent Western-style breakfasts and brunches (things like granola, scrambled eggs, and banana bread), or the tasty Asian-influenced lunches and dinners (like *bun bo nam bo,* Penang curry, and bibimbap). **Known for:** delicious pan-Asian menu; wide choice of hot drinks; friendly service. ⑤ *Average main: Kč250* ✉ *Nám. Jiřího z Poděbrad 4, Vinohrady* ☎ *606–707–199* ⊕ *facebook.com/cafefin-vpraze* Ⓜ *Line A: Jiřího z Poděbrad.*

Hotels

With its excellent restaurants and pretty tree-lined streets, ideal for meandering after an exhausting day in the center, Vinohrady is the perfect place to stay for those looking to avoid the crowds.

Hotel Anna

$ | **HOTEL** | The bright neoclassical façade and art nouveau details have been lovingly restored on this 19th-century building on a quiet residential street. **Pros:** top-floor suites have views of the historic district; helpful English-speaking staff; affordable for city center. **Cons:** some guests find walls to be thin; very small elevator; parking fee. ⑤ *Rooms from: Kč1750* ✉ *Budečská 17, Vinohrady* ☎ *222–513–111* ⊕ *www.hotelanna.cz* ⇌ *26 rooms* ⦿| *Free Breakfast* Ⓜ *Line A: Náměstí Míru.*

★ Le Palais Art Hotel Prague

$$$ | **HOTEL** | This venerable 19th-century mansion served as the home and shop of Prague's main butcher. **Pros:** gorgeous hotel in nice neighborhood; some rooms have fireplaces; excellent breakfast. **Cons:** requires public transit to get anywhere; basic rooms are small for the price; beds a little hard for some. ⑤ *Rooms from: Kč5900* ✉ *U Zvonařky 1, Vinohrady* ☎ *234–634–111* ⊕ *www.lepalaishotel.eu* ⇌ *72 rooms* ⦿| *Free Breakfast* Ⓜ *Line C: I. P. Pavlova.*

Nightlife

Vinohrady has a great local scene of trendy bars and clubs, as well as laid-back traditional pubs, popular with locals and expats alike.

BARS AND PUBS

★ BeerGeek Bar

BARS | This popular craft beer bar serves uncommon brews from the Czech Republic, across Europe, and the United States. It has an impressive 32 taps, with the choice of beers changing daily

(though usually including at least one from its in-house Sibeeria Brewery label). There's also a good selection of beer snacks; opt for the excellent chicken wings. If you don't have time to stop, there's also a BeerGeek Pivoteka (bottle shop) a five-minute walk away, which stocks more than 500 bottled beers. ✉ *Vinohradská 62, Vinohrady* ☎ *776–827–068* ⊕ *beergeek.cz* Ⓜ *Line A: Jiřího z Poděbrad.*

Bonvivant's

COCKTAIL LOUNGES | The cocktail maker's cocktail bar of choice in Prague, and still probably one of the absolute best, Bonvivant's has a nostalgic feel and fantastic staff, who ask you what drinks and tastes you like and then whip you up something bespoke. Upmarket but not pricey, this is a perfect place for an adventure in mixology and some tasty tapas in a refined setting. ✉ *Mánesova 55, Vinohrady* ☎ *775–331–862* ⊕ *bonvivants.cz* ⊗ *Closed Sun. and Mon.* Ⓜ *Line A: Jiřího z Poděbrad.*

Vinohradský pivovar

BREWPUBS | This popular neighborhood hangout brews a range of traditional and well-regarded Czech pilsners, including unpasteurized and unfiltered versions, as well as an increasing number of IPAs and other ales. You can pop in for a beer or two, or make a whole evening of it with a meal in the restaurant (expect classic Czech pub food at good prices) followed by some live entertainment in the music hall (there's everything from jazz concerts to improv comedy). ✉ *Korunní 106, Vinohrady* ☎ *222–760–080* ⊕ *www.vinohradskypivovar.cz* Ⓜ *Line A: Flora.*

CLUBS

Retro Music Hall

DANCE CLUBS | With its location just a bit out of the center, this fun club provides an escape from the hassle of downtown. The street-level part is a pleasant functionalist-style café with outdoor seating, and the lower level houses a club with a big dance floor. The name is a bit misleading; there are some '80s nights, but the bulk of the schedule is hip-hop, dance music, and other more contemporary sounds. Friday and Saturday nights only. ⊠ *Francouzská 4, Vinohrady* ☎ *606–824–005* ⊕ *www.retropraha.cz* ☾ *Closed Sun.–Thurs.* Ⓜ *Line A: Náměstí Míru.*

LGBTQ
Club TERMAX
DANCE CLUBS | It claims to be the largest gay club in the Czech Republic, and with three floors it's a reasonable claim. There's a disco, multiple bars, seating areas with Wi-Fi, and other attractions for a male crowd. It's open only on Friday and Saturday night, but the party continues right through till 5 am. Not to be confused with the similarly named Club TerMIX, another gay club situated nearby. ⊠ *Vinohradská 40, Vinohrady* ☎ *222–710–462* ⊕ *facebook.com/clubmax.cz* ☾ *Closed Sun.–Thurs.* Ⓜ *Line A: Náměstí Míru.*

★ The Saints
BARS | This small British-owned pub and cocktail bar is centrally located near several other gay and gay-friendly establishments in Vinohrady. But unlike many of those other places, it's open all week long. The owners also run a gay-friendly travel and accommodations service. ⊠ *Polská 32, Vinohrady* ☎ *222–250–326* ⊕ *www.praguesaints.cz* Ⓜ *Line A: Jiřího z Poděbrad.*

🛍 Shopping

As a local neighborhood with less tourist footfall, Vinohrady's shopping scene is less about crystal trinkets and touristy tchotchkes and more about local fashion boutiques.

CLOTHING
BOHO Vintage Concept Store
WOMEN'S CLOTHING | One of Prague's hippest shopping experiences, BOHO has in recent years morphed from perennially popular pop-up to Vinohrady mainstay. The center of the space is dominated by a cool café-bar serving brunches and booze, while the vintage fashion items and other designer trinkets fill shelves on the walls. ⊠ *Ondříčkova 6, Vinohrady* ☎ *222–946–162* ⊕ *boho.cz* ☾ *Closed Sun. and Mon.* Ⓜ *Line A: Jiřího z Poděbrad.*

Pour Pour
WOMEN'S CLOTHING | Can't bear the thought of leaving Prague without something completely unique? Stop by this little shop filled with eclectic creations—from underwear to funny diaries—by young, up-and-coming Czech designers. With a rotating collection, the shop is all about originality and unexpected fashions, reminding you that getting dressed can be an adventure. ⊠ *Vinohradská 74, Vinohrady* ☎ *777–830–078* ☾ *Closed weekends* Ⓜ *Line A: Jiřího z Poděbrad.*

Thrift Store
MARKET | Prague's got good game when it comes to thrift and retro stores, and this emporium in Vinohrady is one of the oldest and best. Moreover, a percentage of the profits goes to charity. ⊠ *Budečská 13, Vinohrady* ☎ *608–623–339* ⊕ *www.thriftshop.cz* Ⓜ *Line A: Náměstí Míru.*

Vršovice

👁 Sights

Kostel sv. Václava (*St. Wenceslas Church*)
CHURCH | It's hard to miss this church—a striking constructivist work of art that, at 164 feet high, dominates the Vršovice skyline. Built in 1930 to commemorate 1,000 years since the death of St. Wenceslas, the building's most striking feature is its skyscraping white clock tower, topped by a 23-foot-high gold cross. It's worth a visit to see the exterior alone (and the lovely surrounding park), but for a peek inside, doors are usually open between 8 and 1 on Sunday for services.

8

Vinohrady and Vršovice VRŠOVICE

There are also occasional morning and evening services during the week; check the website in advance for more information. ✉ *Nám. Svatopluka Čecha 3, Vršovice* ☎ *607–084–855* ⊕ *www.farnostvrsovice.cz* 🎟 *Free* ⊙ *Closed Mon.–Sat. (excl. services)* Ⓜ *Line A: Náměstí Miru plus Tram 4, 13, or 22 to Čechovo náměstí.*

🍴 Restaurants

The rapidly gentrifying Vršovice has an increasing number of good restaurants and a few excellent ones. The most convenient Metro station for accessing the neighborhood is Náměstí Miru, but from there you'll have to take Tram 4, 13, or 22.

★ Benjamin

$$$$ | **CZECH** | Since opening in 2017, Benjamin has consistently been one of Prague's most sought-after fine-dining experiences. Well, with just 10 seats set around a horseshoe-shaped table, it's a very exclusive ticket—so make sure you book far in advance. Each boldly flavored dish on the eight-course tasting menu exhibits oodles of imagination, innovation, and inspiration—and when combined with the unique communal setup, makes for a one-of-a-kind meal. **Known for:** beautifully presented and flavorful dishes; interactive and communal dining experience; booking up months in advance. ⓢ *Average main: Kč2190* ✉ *Norská 14, Vršovice* ☎ *774–141–432* ⊕ *www.benjamin14.cz* ⊙ *Closed Sun.–Tues. No lunch.* Ⓜ *Line A: Náměstí Míru plus Tram 4, 13, or 22 to Ruská.*

Slavia Prague is holder of a world record: since 1892 the players of the club have traditionally been wearing their red and white colors.

Coffee and Quick Bites

The Conductor

$ | INTERNATIONAL | Famed for its soft and squishy cinnamon rolls (some of the best in town), this takeout spot also serves perfect pulled-pork sandwiches and lip-smacking vegan wraps. **Known for:** location right by Krymská tram stop; friendly service; delicious cinnamon rolls. ⑤ *Average main: Kč120* ✉ *Francouzská 78, Vršovice* ⊕ *facebook.com/streetfood-maestro* ⊘ *Closed weekends* Ⓜ *Line A: Náměstí Míru plus Tram 4, 13, or 22 to Krymská.*

La Focacceria

$ | BAKERY | A tiny bakery with a big reputation, this place allows you to take your pick from dozens of different focaccias, as well as delicious arancini (small balls of rice stuffed with a savory filling), fresh ciabattas, crispy Italian biscuits, and various pastries and cakes. **Known for:** local favorite; authentic Sicilian bread; friendly English-speaking owner Sergio.

⑤ *Average main: Kč60* ✉ *Krymská 30, Vršovice* ☎ *774–741–416* ⊕ *lafocacce-ria-bakery.business.site* ⊘ *Closed Sun.* Ⓜ *Line A: Náměstí Míru plus Tram 4, 13, or 22 to Ruská.*

🛏 Hotels

Vršovice has only limited accommodation options, but what's here is generally great value for money. It's also convenient if you're catching an evening soccer match or concert at the Sinobo Stadium.

Iris Hotel Eden

$$ | HOTEL | Set within the Sinobo Stadium, home of Czech soccer club Slavia Prague and a regular venue for concerts, Iris Hotel Eden is a modern, comfortable city hotel. **Pros:** modern and spacious rooms; good breakfast buffet; free parking available. **Cons:** limited dining options around; Wi-Fi connections can be patchy; a little out of the way. ⑤ *Rooms from: Kč2500* ✉ *Vladivostocká 2, Vršovice* ☎ *702–033–159* ⊕ *www.irishoteleden.cz*

⇨ *150 rooms* ⦿ *Free Breakfast* Ⓜ *Line A: Námesti Míru plus Tram 4 or 22 to Slavia.*

Nightlife

Vršovice has an enjoyable mix of swanky cocktail joints, hipster craft beer bars, and traditional Czech *hospody* (pubs).

Bad Flash Bar

BARS | One of Prague's best craft beer bars, Bad Flash has 12 taps serving a constant rotation of brews from its own stable as well as other Czech and international microbreweries. The minimalist, shabby-chic interior and simple menu of beer snacks (try the pickled cheese) attract a young and cosmopolitan crowd. The bar doesn't take reservations, so it's best to come early and stay late. ⊠ *Krymská 2, Vršovice* ☎ *273–134–609* ⊕ *www. badflash.cz* Ⓜ *Line A: Námesti Míru plus Tram 4, 13, or 22 to Krymská.*

★ Pivnice pivovaru Trilobit

BREWPUBS | From the street, this Vršovice taproom appears entirely unremarkable, but step inside to find one of Prague's true after-dark gems. The beer is exceptional, with four home brews on tap—the award-winning 12° pale lager plus three seasonal beers—while the service is friendly and the interior is cozy. In the summer, you can enjoy your beer out on the terrace. ⊠ *Francouzská 112, Vršovice* ☎ *734–525–843* ⊕ *pivovartrilobit.com* Ⓜ *Line A: Námesti Míru plus Tram 4, 13, or 22 to Krymská.*

Activities

SOCCER
Fortuna Arena

SOCCER | Home to Slavia Prague, one of the country's "big two" soccer teams along with Sparta Prague, the 21,000-seater Fortuna Arena shows Slavia games throughout the season (July to May). There are league matches every other weekend, as well as occasional midweek European fixtures. Outside of home games, you can find out more about the club (and Czech football in general) at the stadium's Slavia Museum. As one of Prague's biggest seated venues, the stadium also hosts regular concerts. ⊠ *U Slavie 2A, Vršovice* ☎ *725–875–438* ⊕ *www.slavia.cz* ⊗ *Museum closed weekends* Ⓜ *Line A: Námesti Míru plus Tram 4 or 22 to Slavia.*

Chapter 9

ŽIŽKOV AND KARLÍN

Updated by
Joseph Reaney

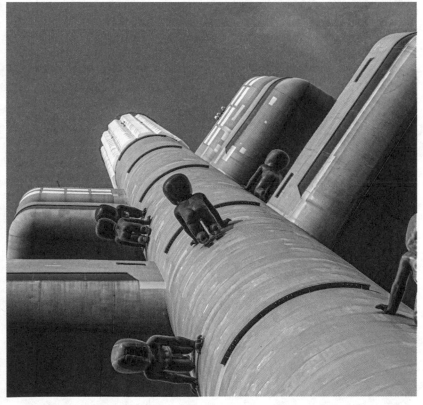

◉ Sights	🍴 Restaurants	🛏 Hotels	🛍 Shopping	🍸 Nightlife
★★★☆☆	★★★★☆	★★★☆☆	★★★☆☆	★★★★★

NEIGHBORHOOD SNAPSHOT

TOP EXPERIENCES

- **Žižkov Pub Crawl:** Line your stomach and roll up your sleeves for the bar crawl to end all bar crawls in this impossibly pub-packed district.

- **Karlín Musical Theater:** From *West Side Story* to *Jesus Christ Superstar,* catch a musical theater production at this grand old Karlín venue.

- **National Monument:** Delve into 20th-century Czech history, from pre–World War II to post–Velvet Revolution, at this Vítkov Hill exhibition.

- **Žižkov TV Tower:** Take the elevator up to 305 feet for a unique panorama of Prague—or stay at the one-room hotel to wake up to the view.

- **Fine Hipster Dining:** Eat your way around Karlín. Hip, high-end restaurants include meat maestro Nejen Bistro and sourdough savant Eska.

GETTING HERE

Žižkov is not directly served by any Metro line, though the Line A stop at Jiřího z Poděbrad will bring you within about 10 minutes' walking distance. Alternatively, any tram heading east from Hlavní nádraží (just north of the main train station) will take you into the heart of the neighborhood. Karlín, by contrast, has two Metro stops—Florenc (Lines B and C) and Křižíkova (Line B)—as well as trams running the length of Sokolovská ulice.

PLANNING YOUR TIME

Both Žižkov and Karlín are pretty quiet during weekdays, so this is a good time to come and see the museums. But if you want to make the most of the neighborhoods' after-dark attractions, including restaurants, bars, and theaters, come during evenings and weekends.

QUICK BITES

- **UGO Freshbar.** With a wide array of freshly made juices pressed to order and light sandwiches and snacks, UGO Freshbar is a great place to stop by before heading to Riegrovy sady. ⊠ *Seifertova 39, Žižkov* ⊕ *ugo.cz* Ⓜ *Tram 9 to Viktoria Žižkov*

- **Pivo Karlín.** This industrial chic neighborhood brewpub, in a quiet corner of Karlín facing the leafy slopes of Vítkov Hill, serves a good choice of home-brewed beers (the dark ones beat the light ones) as well as hearty pub food. A good stop before or after taking in a show at Forum Karlín. ⊠ *Pernerova 42, Karlín* ⊕ *www.pivokarlin. czm* Ⓜ *Line B: Křižíkova*

- **Veltlin.** This modish wine bar offers a wide selection of natural and organic wines by the glass, with a particular focus on Central and Eastern European wine regions. You can also order cheeses and cured meats to accompany your drink. ⊠ *Křižíkova 115, Karlín* ⊕ *www.veltlin.cz* Ⓜ *Line B: Křižíkova*

For Prague residents, Žižkov and Karlín are synonymous with good times. The two neighborhoods, which border the New Town on its northeastern edge, are renowned for their after-dark adventures, from no-nonsense *hospody* (pubs) to sweaty live music clubs. But that's just the beginning of the story.

There are more places to knock back a Pilsner Urquell or a shot of Fernet Stock per square inch along Žižkov's run-down streets than anywhere else in the city (or, according to many, anywhere else in Europe). But alongside these traditional pubs are some of the city's coolest cafés, cinemas, and cocktail joints. The area is also home to the Národní památník na Vítkově (National Monument on Vítkov Hill) and the inescapable Žižkovská televizní věž (Žižkov TV Tower), offering one of the best panoramas in the city—and one of its most exclusive hotel rooms.

In Karlín, the entertainment scene is even more varied, with everything from fine-dining restaurants to craft beer bars and time-honored theaters. Come earlier in the day and you'll also enjoy its lovely parks, decorative churches, and fascinating museums.

Žižkov

Sights

Národní památník na Vítkově (*National Monument on Vítkov Hill*)

MONUMENT | Vítkov Hill is among the highest points in the city, and is topped by one of the world's largest equestrian statues—a 16½-ton metal sculpture of one-eyed Hussite leader Jan Žižka on horseback. The 20th-century memorial was originally built to honor the war heroes of World War I but was used for a time during the communist period (1953–62) to display the mummified body of the country's first communist leader, Klement Gottwald. Now, the building is part of the Národní muzeum (National Museum), home to a permanent exhibition of 20th-century Czech history. There are moving displays on the founding of Czechoslovakia in 1918, the Nazi occupation in 1939, the communist coup d'etat in 1948, the Warsaw Pact invasion in 1968, and finally the fall of communism in 1989. There's a great view over the city from the top of the building, or enjoy the view with a drink or snack in the first-floor Café Vítkov.

■ TIP➔ **To get to the monument, walk from Metro stop Florenc (15 minutes) or from bus stop Tachovské náměstí (10 minutes). Both require a climb. For a longer but gentler approach, walk from tram stop Ohrada (20 minutes).** ✉ *U Památníku 1900, Žižkov* ☎ *224–497–600* ⊕ *www.nm.cz* 💰 *120 Kč* 🕙 *Closed Mon. and Tues.* Ⓜ *Lines B and C: Florenc.*

Žižkov and Karlín

KEY

- 🅐 Sights
- 🅐 Restaurants
- 🅐 Quick Bites
- ⬤ Hotels
- Ⓜ Metro Station
- 🄸 Tourist Information

Sights ▶

1 Kostel sv. Cyrila a Metoděje E1
2 Lilit E1
3 Muzeum hlavního města Prahy C1
4 Národní památník na Vítkově E2
5 Žižkovská televizní věž E3

Restaurants ▶

1 Eska F1
2 Hanil D3
3 Lavička E3
4 Nejen Bistro D1
5 U Slovanské Lípy E2

Quick Bites ▶

1 Café Pavlač E3
2 Žižkovská štrúdlárna F2

Hotels ▶

1 Hilton Prague C1
2 Pentahotel Prague F1
3 Sky Suite E3

0 — 1/4 km
0 — 1/4 mi

★ **Žižkovská televizní věž** (*Žižkov TV Tower*)

NOTABLE BUILDING | Looking like a freakish, futuristic rocket ready to blast off, the Žižkov TV Tower is easily visible from around the city and commonly makes it onto Top 10 World's Ugliest Buildings lists. The upper-floor observatory platform, reached by a high-speed elevator and open until midnight, gives a bird's-eye view of the numerous courtyards and apartment blocks that make up the city and has a selection of exhibits on the history and architecture of the building. There's also a bar, restaurant, and luxury one-room hotel up there. Once back down on the ground, look up its 709-foot gray steel legs at the bronze statues of babies crawling on the structure, which were created by local provocateur artist David Černý. ⊠ *Tower Park Prague, Mahlerovy sady 1, Žižkov* ☎ *210–320–081* ⊕ *www.towerpark.cz* ⊟ *250 Kč* Ⓜ *Line A: Jiřího z Poděbrad.*

🍴 Restaurants

Scruffy Žižkov is better known for its pubs and dives than for its dining experiences, yet the southern part of the district abutting Vinohrady has some good snack stops, cafés, and restaurants. The best way to get here is to take the Metro to Jiřího z Poděbrad and walk north along Slavíkova.

Hanil

$$ | **KOREAN** | A nice counterpoint to the heavy, meaty cuisine found in most Prague diners, Hanil serves good-quality sushi as well as Korean and other Asian dishes at premium but affordable prices. The open, casual setting, which is accented with elegant light and dark woods, burnt-orange chair cushions, and curves galore, attracts a largely local crowd of young professionals who appreciate the blend of high-quality food with a lack of pretension. **Known for:** delicious Korean and Japanese cuisine; elegantly understated interior; slightly high prices for Žižkov. Ⓢ *Average main: Kč350* ⊠ *Slavíkova 24, Žižkov* ☎ *222–715–867* ⊕ *www.hanil.cz* ☼ *Closed Sun.* Ⓜ *Line A: Jiřího z Poděbrad.*

Lavička

$$ | **CZECH** | A mini-oasis in the heart of Žižkov, this family-owned restaurant sits on a busy street but has a hidden garden terrace and conservatory around the back. The menu features a mix of Czech staples (like beef goulash) and lesser-spotted dishes (like salmon fillet with pumpkin purée), as well as lots of vegetarian options. **Known for:** away-from-it-all atmosphere; premium Bernard beer on tap; slightly small portions. Ⓢ *Average main: Kč270* ⊠ *Seifertova 77, Žižkov* ☎ *222–221–350* ⊕ *www.restaurace-lavicka.cz* Ⓜ *Line C: Hlavní nádraží plus Tram 5, 9, 15, or 26 to Lipanská.*

★ **U Slovanské Lípy**

$$ | **CZECH** | One of the oldest pubs in Žižkov, this classic Czech pub offers a warm and inviting setting, great beers, and authentic Czech food. The name means "At the Linden Trees," a Czech and Slovak emblem, and while there are tourists here, it's also a meeting place for locals. **Known for:** typical Czech meals; sharing plates; wooden benches and other period decor. Ⓢ *Average main: Kč225* ⊠ *Tachovské náměstí 6, Žižkov* ☎ *734–743–094* ⊕ *uslovanskelipy.cz* Ⓜ *Line C: Hlavní nádraží plus Tram 5, 9, 15, or 26 to Lipanská.*

☕ Coffee and Quick Bites

Café Pavlač

$$ | **CAFÉ** | This lovely little sit-down spot on a sloping street serves excellent coffee, tasty homemade soups, and an impressive choice of vegan dishes. In the summer months, there's a pleasantly green courtyard garden. **Known for:** good-value lunch menu; quiet spot away from the crowds; regular themed food and drink events. Ⓢ *Average main: Kč185* ⊠ *V. Nejedlého 23, Žižkov*

Palác Akropolis is a palace of entertainment with a café, restaurant, smaller bar upstairs, a theater, and a club with two stages downstairs.

☎ *702–124–556* ⊕ *www.cafepavlac.cz*
Ⓜ *Tram 9 to Viktoria Žižkov.*

★ Žižkovská štrúdlárna

$ | **BAKERY** | This unexpected pastry paradise—essentially, a service hatch set within a regular apartment block—offers whole strudels (repeat: not a single slice, but a WHOLE strudel) for just 60 Kč. You can choose from three fillings: apple, *tvaroh* (curd cheese), or poppy seed.
Known for: special seasonal flavors; delicious strudel at an incredibly low price; easy-to-miss location. ⑤ *Average main: Kč60* ⊠ *Jeseniova 29, Žižkov* ☎ *222–590–912* ⊕ *www.strudl-zizkov.czm* ⊘ *Closed weekends* Ⓜ *Tram 9 to Lipanská.*

Hotels

Although Prague is a safe city where anyone can amble about alone, this is one of its grittier, seedier parts. That said, it's also a great neighborhood for extroverts who like student bars, music clubs, and hangouts where a fashion parade of people with piercings, tattoos,

dreadlocks—and sometimes all three—come to socialize. It's also home to one of Prague's most exclusive hotel rooms.

★ Sky Suite

$$$$ | **HOTEL** | Perhaps the most unique hotel in Prague, a night in this luxuriously decked-out, 80-square-meter capsule room at the top of the communist-era Žižkov TV Tower is quite an experience.
Pros: beautiful wood-paneled interior; amazing city panoramas; Prague's top bucket-list stay. **Cons:** gritty Žižkov an unlikely place for such glamour; incredibly expensive; no view of castle (but see it from the restaurant). ⑤ *Rooms from: Kč28000* ⊠ *Tower Park Prague, Mahlerovy sady 1, Žižkov* ☎ *210–320–081* ⊕ *towerpark.cz* ⇥ *1 room* ⦿ *Free Breakfast* Ⓜ *Line A: Jiřího z Poděbrad.*

Nightlife

This edgy neighborhood offers a lot to the discerning, thirsty traveler who ventures out of the city center. It's said to have the densest cluster of pubs in

Europe, so if you end up here, it's best to try out the random places that catch your eye.

BARS AND PUBS

Bukowski's Bar

COCKTAIL LOUNGES | This crowd-pleasing drinking establishment, named for the American writer–cum–bar fly Charles Bukowski, serves top-quality cocktails, beer, wine, and spirits. The candlelight makes for a cool (if slightly seedy) atmosphere, and bar staff are unfailingly friendly. In summer, patrons tend to spill out into the street. ⊠ *Bořivojova 86, Žižkov* ☎ *222–212–686* ⊕ *facebook. com/bukowskisbar* Ⓜ *Line A: Jiřího z Poděbrad.*

★ U Vystřelenýho oka

BARS | Literally translated as "At the Shot-Out Eye"—it's an homage to the one-eyed Jan Žižka, for whom the neighborhood is named (he's also the guy on the horse atop Vítkov Hill)—this poky, perennially popular pub has been a local favorite for years. As well as perfectly poured Czech beers (always three fingers of foam), the pub does a great line in traditional no-frills food, from cold pickled herring to fried Camembert cheese. Sit inside to enjoy the warm open fire and, often, the live music accompaniment, or head out onto the log-lined terrace. ⊠ *U Božích bojovníků 3, Žižkov* ☎ *222–540–465* ⊕ *www.uvoka.cz* ☉ *Closed Sun.* Ⓜ *Lines B and C: Florenc plus Bus 133, 175, or 207 to Tachovské náměstí.*

Vlkova 26

BARS | The cool kids hang out at this out-of-the-way Žižkov basement bar to drink and chat late into the night. It's cozy, with dim lights, candles, wooden benches, and the bare brick walls. There are DJs and themed music nights, when everyone gets up to dance. ⊠ *Vlkova 26, Žižkov* ⊕ *facebook.com/Vlkova26* ☉ *Closed Sun.* Ⓜ *Line A: Jiřího z Poděbrad.*

LIVE MUSIC CLUBS

★ Palác Akropolis

LIVE MUSIC | Housed in a funky art deco–esque building, this is arguably the city's best live music club. When shows are sold out, the place is pretty packed. While the main room closes at 10 due to noise concerns, DJs play in the two side bars until much later. ⊠ *Kubelíkova 27, Žižkov* ☎ *299–330–911* ⊕ *www.palacak-ropolis.com* Ⓜ *Line A: Jiřího z Poděbrad.*

🎭 Performing Arts

Žižkov has a couple of good theaters (including one dedicated solely to the adventures of fictional polymath Jára Cimrman) as well as an excellent indie cinema and arts center.

Kino Aero

FILM | Tucked away on a quiet residential street, Kino Aero is one of Prague's best independent movie theaters. It screens a mix of mainstream Hollywood and international fare, indie art-house darlings, and 20th-century cult classics. On-site, there's also a cocktail bar and café, which regularly hosts events ranging from stand-up comedy to film quizzes. Kino Aero is part of a minichain of indie Prague cinemas, along with BIO OKO in Holešovice and Kino Světozor off Václavské náměstí (Wenceslas Square). ⊠ *Biskupcova 31, Žižkov* ☎ *271–771–349* ⊕ *www.kinoaero.cz* Ⓜ *Line C: Hlavní nádraží plus Tram 5 or 9 to Ohrada.*

🛍 Shopping

This rough-and-tumble area may be most famous for its pubs, but it also has some good shopping, from cool boutiques to one of Prague's largest shopping malls.

CLOTHING AND ACCESSORIES

Bohemian Retro

MIXED CLOTHING | This vintage clothes shop, tucked down a Žižkov side street, sells retro womenswear, antique jewelry, leather and fabric bags, and more. It also has some random Czechoslovakian curios, from ceramics to clocks. It's only open from 12 to 5, and only five days a week, so plan your visit in advance. ✉ *Chvalova 8, Žižkov* ☎ *607–914–992* ⊕ *bohemianretro.com* ⊗ *Closed Sun. and Mon.* Ⓜ *Line A: Jiřího z Poděbrad.*

SHOPPING MALLS
Atrium Flora
MALL | Home to hundreds of stores, a well-stocked food court, and an IMAX movie theater, the Atrium Flora is hardly the cobblestoned-street boutique dream you might have in mind. But for shopping junkies, it's a good bet for finding some local and international brands that are hard to hunt down elsewhere. ✉ *Vinohradská 151, Žižkov* ☎ *255–741–704* ⊕ *www.atrium-flora.cz* Ⓜ *Line A: Flora.*

Karlín

◉ Sights

Kostel sv. Cyrila a Metoděje (*Church of Sts. Cyril and Methodius*)
CHURCH | A Karlín landmark and one of the largest religious buildings in Prague, this unmistakable black-and-white church is dedicated to the Orthodox missionary brothers Cyril and Methodius, who are credited with spreading the Christian faith through the Slavic lands. It was consecrated in 1863, exactly 1,000 years after the brothers started their important work. Head inside the neo-Romanesque basilica to discover decorative pillars, intricately painted ceilings, and an art nouveau baptismal chapel. The church is on the neighborhood's main square, Karlínské náměstí, which regularly hosts farmers' markets, festivals, and cultural events. ✉ *Karlínské nám., Karlín* ☎ *222–743–517* ⊕ *farnost-karlin.cz* 🎟 *Free* Ⓜ *Line B: Křižíkova.*

★ Lilit
PUBLIC ART | Located at the eastern edge of Karlín, this giant metallic female figure is the latest creation from Prague's master of modern sculpture David Černý, perhaps best known for the faceless babies climbing Žižkov TV Tower. Standing more than 24 meters high and weighing 35 tons, the figure is hugging—or seemingly holding up—the side of a modern apartment block. Take a stroll around to see other Černý artworks in a similar style, including giant arms and legs "propping up" elements of the building. For a uniquely strange experience, come at midnight to see Lilit's head rotate 180 degrees. ✉ *Rohanské náb., Karlín* Ⓜ *Line B: Invalidovna.*

Muzeum hlavního města Prahy (*City of Prague Museum*)
HISTORY MUSEUM | Set inside a grand, turn-of-the-20th-century building, this excellent yet often overlooked museum tells the story of Prague through the ages, from the earliest prehistoric settlers, through the city's golden medieval and baroque periods, to the Velvet Revolution of 1989. The big-ticket exhibit is the extraordinary Langweil model of Prague, an intricate, handmade model of the city circa 1826–37. There are more than 2,000 buildings at a scale of 1:480, some of which are still standing today, and some of which are long gone (including swathes of the Jewish Town). In fact, this model provides the only proof of how some of these buildings looked. As well as the permanent collection, there are also ever-changing temporary exhibitions, often focused on aspects of modern-day Prague. The museum is closed for renovation until autumn 2023. ✉ *Na Poříčí 52, Karlín* ☎ *221–709–674* ⊕ *www.muzeumprahy.cz* 🎟 *150Kč* ⊗ *Closed Mon.* Ⓜ *Lines B and C: Florenc.*

🍴 Restaurants

Once a blighted testament to the fates of state-controlled industry, Karlín is now on the up and up. Nowhere is that more apparent than in its ever-increasing choice of fashionable eating options.

Housed in former military barracks, Karlin Studios is a unique complex of art studios and galleries showcasing contemporary Czech art.

Eska

$$ | CZECH | An upmarket restaurant with a casual carefree vibe, Eska has been a big hit since opening its doors in 2016. The restaurant is located within a converted fabric factory, and it maintains the original industrial aesthetic through bare brick walls and exposed pipework, while also adding modern touches like Scandi-style furniture and a gleaming open kitchen. **Known for:** industrial-chic decor; delicious and innovative dishes; excellent bakery with good coffee. ⑤ *Average main: Kč300* ✉ *Pernerova 49, Karlín* ☎ *731–140–884* ⊕ *eska.ambi.cz* Ⓜ *Line B: Křižíkova.*

Nejen Bistro

$$ | EUROPEAN | This trendy bistro, on the corner of the neighborhood's main square, Karlínské náměstí, is all about light and space, with high ceilings, big windows, and an open kitchen, as well as muted colors throughout. It's also about great food, with particular pride taken in its array of meat dishes—from duck breast to pork loin to sirloin steak—cooked on the charcoal-fueled Josper grill. **Known for:** juicy charcoal-grilled burgers; great wine and beer selection; cool Scandi-chic interior. ⑤ *Average main: Kč360* ✉ *Křižíkova 24, Karlín* ☎ *721–249–494* ⊕ *www.nejenbistro.cz* ⊘ *Closed Sun.* Ⓜ *Line B: Křižíkova.*

Hotels

Karlín has several cheap and cheerful accommodation options. Higher-end hotels are a little thinner on the ground, but they do exist.

Hilton Prague

$$ | HOTEL | From the outside, this gigantic, 11-floor, glass-and-steel building looks like a throwback to communist Czechoslovakia, but step inside and you'll find a pleasant, modern, and stylish business hotel. **Pros:** great breakfast buffet and all-day dining options; large indoor swimming pool; quiet and alternative part of town. **Cons:** not the most inviting exterior; shower pressure could be better; a little way out of the center.

⑤ *Rooms from: Kč3500* ✉ *Pobřežní 1, Karlín* ☎ *224–841–111* ⊕ *www.hilton.com* ⇱ *791 rooms* ⑪ *Free Breakfast* Ⓜ *Lines B and C: Florenc.*

Pentahotel Prague

$$$ | **HOTEL** | Since opening in 2013, this trendy design hotel has been one of Karlín's hippest sleeping options, offering stylish, contemporary rooms with quirky, vintage touches. **Pros:** action-packed common area; nearby Metro and tram stops; parking spaces available. **Cons:** odd mixed hipster-business vibe; breakfast not included; 30-minute walk from the Old Town. ⑤ *Rooms from: Kč4750* ✉ *Sokolovská 112, Karlín* ☎ *222–332–800* ⊕ *www.pentahotels.com* ⇱ *227* ⑪ *No Meals* Ⓜ *Line B: Křižíkova.*

Nightlife

It may not be as renowned for nightlife as neighboring Žižkov, but Karlín still has its fair share of good after-dark options, from sky-high cocktail bars to basement brewery bars.

Cloud 9 Sky Bar

COCKTAIL LOUNGES | This chic, lounge-style bar, situated on the rooftop of the Hilton Prague hotel, offers glorious views of the Czech capital (including parts you don't usually see). There's an extensive menu of innovative cocktails, as well as some beautifully presented snack food; try the chicken lollipops and prawn popcorn. The music can be very loud in the evening so it's not the place to come for a quiet conversation. ✉ *Hilton Prague, Pobřežní 1, Karlín* ☎ *224–842–999* ⊕ *www.cloud9.cz* ☾ *Closed Sun.* Ⓜ *Lines B and C: Florenc.*

★ Dva Kohouti

BREWPUBS | When it comes to beer buzz, nothing in recent years has come close to Dva Kohouti (translation: "Two Roosters"). This joint brewery and taproom— the beer is brewed there in the mornings then served to thirsty patrons later the same day—has quickly established itself as a neighborhood favorite. There's

only one permanent local beer, but it's excellent: crisp, malty, and incredibly fresh (it's poured from a tank that is filled directly from the brewery). Alternatively, choose from one of their seasonal brews or the many other Czech lagers and ales on tap. You can also get a one-liter can to take away. Feeling peckish? Order a tasty slider and fries from Bufet (owned by the same group) just across the courtyard. ✉ *Sokolovská 55, Karlín* ☎ *604–611–001* ⊕ *www.dvakohouti.cz* Ⓜ *Line B: Křižíkova.*

Pivovarský Klub

PUBS | With literally wall-to-wall bottles— there are around 250 different brands of beer lining the walls—as well as six ever-changing brews on tap, there's nowhere better to take a deep dive into the Czechs' favorite pastime. The food's pretty good, too. ✉ *Křižíkova 17, Karlín* ☎ *222–315–777* ⊕ *www.pivo-klub.cz* Ⓜ *Lines B and C: Florenc.*

🎭 Performing Arts

Whether you are looking for big-name live music acts or high-quality musical theater, Karlín has you covered.

Forum Karlín

ARTS CENTERS | This 3,000-seater events space plays host to several touring live music acts. Recent years have seen performances from the likes of Thom Yorke, Bullet for My Valentine, Yes, and Simply Red. ✉ *Pernerova 51, Karlín* ⊕ *www.forumkarlin.cz* Ⓜ *Line B: Křižíkova.*

Hudební divadlo Karlín (*Karlín Musical Theater*)

THEATER | FAMILY | This beautiful, baroque-revival building plays host to all manner of song-and-dance performances, from high-art operas to cheesy musicals. Shows are usually performed in Czech but with a screen showing English subtitles. ✉ *Křižíkova 10, Karlín* ☎ *221–868–666* ⊕ *www.hdk.cz* Ⓜ *Lines B and C: Florenc.*

LETNÁ, HOLEŠOVICE, AND TROJA

Updated by
Jennifer Rigby

⦿ Sights	⦿ Restaurants	🛏 Hotels	👜 Shopping	🍸 Nightlife
★★☆☆☆	★★★★☆	★☆☆☆☆	★★★★★	★★★☆☆

NEIGHBORHOOD SNAPSHOT

TOP EXPERIENCES

■ **Vnitroblock and Veverkova Ulice:** Shop the modern way, in this former factory and cultural collective, or wander along the street currently vying for the title of Prague's coolest, with a handful of shoe, book, design, and cosmetics boutiques.

■ **DOX:** Prague's answer to New York's MoMA.

■ **Mama Shelter:** The city's—and one of Europe's— coolest hotels in this communist-era tower block (and at a reasonable price).

■ **Bistro 8:** Join Prague's growing brunch crowd at this relaxed, impossibly hip little bistro.

■ **Letná Park:** Take a break in this gorgeous hilltop green space, sip a beer at the beer garden, and cast your eyes over to the plain at the back of the park, where historically the city's biggest protests have taken place (after Václavské náměstí, or Wenceslas Square).

■ **Vineyards:** For a break from the city within the city, head to Troja and the beautiful Vinotéka sv. Klára (St. Claire's Vineyard).

QUICK BITES

■ **Mr. HotDog.** It's almost sacrilegious to describe these U.S.-style dogs as the best sausage in town, but their greatness cannot be denied (make sure you grab a Czech-style *klobasa*, or sausage, while in Prague, too, though). ⊠ *Kamenická 24 Letná* ⊕ *mrhotdog.cz* Ⓜ *Line C: Vltavská.*

■ **Gelateria Amato.** A perfectly located ice-cream parlor for taking a sweet, cold treat into Letná or Stromovka Park. Their slogan is "There's always a good time for an ice-cream," and frankly, when the gelato is this good, we agree. ⊠ *Kamenická 30, Letná* ⊕ *gelateriaamato.cz* Ⓜ *Line C: Vltavská*

GETTING HERE

By Metro, take Line A to Hradčanská station and then nearly any tram (No. 1, 5, 25, or 26) heading east two stops to Letenské náměstí (Letná Square). For Holešovice, the best Metro stations are both on Line C (Nádraží Holešovice and Vltavská), then various trams take you farther into the district (Nos. 1, 2, 6, 12, 14, 15, 17, and 24).

PLANNING YOUR TIME

Letná is a good place to visit on a weekend, to join Prague's locals in browsing, brunching, and soaking up the park during their downtime, while Troja works better on a weekday, particularly in summer, when there are fewer crowds of families hitting up the zoo or gardens.

All three of these neighborhoods are up and coming (and in some cases, particularly genteel Letná, they have up and come already), with new cultural and dining attractions popping up weekly. Come here to get away from the tourist masses and witness the rapid pace of the city's post–Velvet Revolution evolution.

From above the Vltava's left bank, the large, grassy plateau called Letná gives you one of the classic views of Staré Město and the many bridges crossing the river. Beer gardens, tennis, and Frisbee attract people of all ages, while amateur soccer players emulate the professionals of Prague's top team, Sparta, which plays in the stadium just across the road. The Národní technické muzeum (National Technical Museum) is also located near here, as well as a host of new brunch and coffee places.

The rapidly gentrifying former indusrial neighborhood of Holešovice features many urban riches of its own, including perhaps the city's most underrated museum, Veletržní palác (Trade Fair Palace), which houses the National Gallery's permanent exhibition of modern art, as well as the Centrum současného umění DOX (DOX Center for Contemporary Art). It also boasts extremely cool cultural centers, restaurants, and shopping and a recently opened hotel that finally meets the demand from the cool cats to stay somewhere in this neighborhood. Arguably, Letná is part of Holešovice, but the easiest thing to do to fit in with the locals

is to refer to both districts as "Prague 7," the postal code that spans both and that has become the shorthand for Prague's hippest and most creative area.

Troja is a remote, green district situated north of Holešovice on the bank of the Vltava. There are several attractions in this part of town, including the Prague City Gallery's branch at Trojský zámek (Troja Château), the Botanická zahrada (Botanical Gardens), and the zoo. Most visitors are unlikely to make it there on a first trip, but its "day-trip within the city" vibes could entice second- or third-time visitors or those desperate for greenery in the height of summer.

Letná

Sights

★ **Letenské sady** (*Letná Park*)
CITY PARK | This large, shady park offers a pretty view of Prague's bridges. From the enormous concrete pedestal at the center of the park—now occupied by a giant working metronome, which some say is marking time since the 1989 Velvet

Letná, Holešovice, and Troja

Sights ▼

1 Botanická zahrada **B1**
2 DOX........................ **H5**
3 Letenské sady............ **C7**
4 Národní technické
   muzeum................... **C7**
5 Trojský zámek **A1**
6 Veletržní palác **E6**
7 Vinotéka sv. Klára....... **B1**
8 Zoologická zahrada
   v Praze **A1**

Restaurants ▼

1 Big Smokers............. **H6**
2 Bistro 8................... **E7**
3 Curry Palace **C6**
4 The Eatery **H4**
5 Home Kitchen **I4**
6 Lokál Nad
   Stromovkou.............. **B5**
7 Restaurace
   Na Mělníku **D6**
8 Salabka **B1**

Quick Bites ▼

1 Café Domeček **C9**
2 Cafe Hrnek.............. **D6**
3 Dos Mundos............. **D6**
4 Erhartova cukrárna...... **C6**
5 The Farm................ **B6**
6 Gelateria Amato **D6**
7 Mr. HotDog **D6**
8 Ouky Douky.............. **E6**

Hotels ▼

1 Absolutum
   Boutique Hotel **G4**
2 Art Hotel **B6**
3 Hotel Belvedere......... **D6**
4 Mama Shelter
   Prague **E5**

KEY

1 Sights
1 Restaurants
1 Quick Bites
1 Hotels
M Metro Station

0   1/4 mi
0   1/4 km

The expansive Letná Park dominates the northern edge of the Vltava River that divides the city in half.

Revolution—the world's largest statue of Stalin once beckoned to citizens on Staroměstské náměstí (Old Town Square) below. The statue was blown up in 1962, just seven years after it was completed. In nice weather, there's a large and popular beer garden at the park's eastern end and Czechs and expats playing games on the grass. Walk east along Milady Horákové ulice after exiting the Metro or take the tram, or head up the hill from Staré Město if you want some exercise. At the back of the park, toward the home of the football club Sparta at the Generali Arena, there's a huge open space that is often used for the Czech Republic's largest protests (it's even bigger than famous Wenceslas Square), including those heralding the end of communism in 1989. ⊠ Letná M Line A: Hradčanská plus Tram 1, 25, or 26.

Národní technické muzeum (*National Technical Museum*)
SCIENCE MUSEUM | FAMILY | This thoroughly renovated and kid-friendly museum is dedicated to the fun aspects of science, technology, and industry. There are full-sized steam locomotives, historic automobiles, and old aircraft on display. There are also engrossing exhibits on photography and astronomy and an active program of rotating temporary shows. ⊠ *Kostelní 42, Letná* 🕿 *220–399–111* ⊕ *ntm.cz* 🖂 *280 Kč* ⊘ *Closed Mon.* M *Line A: Hradčanská plus Tram 1, 5, 25, or 26 to Letenské náměstí.*

🍽 Restaurants

This residential area, north of Staré Město and across the river, is arguably one of the most desirable places in Prague to live, and as such its dining and coffee scene is ever expanding. Most, but not all, of these places aren't necessarily worth the trip from the center alone, but if the green spaces surrounding them appeal, they represent solid options for some sustenance. The neighborhood is popular with students, and prices here tend to be lower than in the center.

Bistro 8

$$ | INTERNATIONAL | Located on what is among Prague's coolest streets, this hip little spot combines a retro aesthetic— black walls, a mix of chairs, and lots of plants—with tasty international food and unique touches. **Known for:** fun design, such as bright monster sculptures and cracked pots in the window; great brunch; huge sandwiches. $ Average main: Kč160 ⊠ Veverkova 8, Letná ☎ 730–511–973 ⊕ bistro8.cz Ⓜ Line C: Vltavská.

Curry Palace

$$ | INDIAN | Just behind Letná Park, Curry Palace is a bit off the beaten path, but it's *the* place for Indian and Bangladeshi food. You'll find the usual mix of tandoori dishes and curries, and staff are happy to recommend more unique options. **Known for:** excellent rezela, a specialty made with varyingly spicy chicken or lamb, with garlic-ginger paste and yogurt; relaxed family atmosphere; affordable lunch menu. $ Average main: Kč250 ⊠ Jirečková 13, Letná ☎ 233–378–342 ⊕ currypalace.cz Ⓜ Line A: Hradčanská.

Lokál Nad Stromovkou

$$ | CZECH | The same talented team behind Lokál Dlouhááá and Café Savoy refurbished this long-standing Czech pub near Stromovka Park in 2013. Not only did they add a fresh coat of paint to the walls, but, true to form, they refreshed and reintroduced some traditional tavern classics alongside great beer. **Known for:** modern takes on classics, like steak tartare served with toast; convivial vibe; popularity with locals. $ Average main: Kč190 ⊠ Nad Královskou oborou 31, Letná ☎ 220–912–319 ⊕ lokal-nadstromovkou.ambi.cz Ⓜ Line A: Hradčanská plus Tram 1, 25, or 26 to Letenské náměstí.

🅒 Coffee and Quick Bites

Café Domeček

$ | CAFÉ | This sweet "Little House" perched in a community center in the other park bordering Letná district, Stromovka, is a very pleasant option for a coffee in summer, particularly ahead of a leafy walk across the park. There are grilled foods, too, some cakes, some sandwiches, homemade ice cream and lemonade, and (of course) beer. **Known for:** decent coffee and cakes; board games; lovely setting in a listed former railway building in Stromovka Park. $ Average main: Kč70 ⊠ Královská obora 74, Letná ☎ 731–142–109 ⊕ www.domusvitae.cz/kavarna ⊟ No credit cards Ⓜ Tram 1, 2, 8, 12, 25, or 26 to Sparta.

Cafe Hrnek

$ | CAFÉ | With its bare plaster walls and laid-back vibe, uber-cool Cafe Hrnek is a fab spot for great coffee, tasty brunches, and decadent sweet treats. **Known for:** food and drink served in lovely retro blue porcelain; delicious cinnamon rolls; warm, welcoming staff. $ Average main: Kč90 ⊠ Veletržní 49, Letná ☎ 771–203–034 ⊕ facebook.com/cafehrnek Ⓜ Line C: Vltavská.

Dos Mundos

$ | CAFÉ | Come for the swings, stay for the coffee: this small coffee shop has swing seats (a bit of a gimmick, but actually quite a cute one), lovely cakes, and excellent coffee. It's more of a daytime place than an evening bar, although it is open until 9. **Known for:** having its own roastery; rotating house coffee choices; unusual options like an espresso-flavored tonic water. $ Average main: Kč100 ⊠ Milady Horákové 38, Letná ☎ 736–454–762 ⊕ dos-mundos.cz Ⓜ Line C: Vltavská.

Erhartova cukrárna

$ | **BAKERY** | There are retro vibes and delicious pastries in this mini-chain, which now has three branches around town. The company dates back to 1937, so it's authentic, with good coffee and more than 20 cake choices. **Known for:** the Erhart cake—chocolate cake, pumpkin seed cream, and marzipan; excellent value; more than 70 years of history in the functionalist style building and interior, much of which is original. ⑤ *Average main: Kč50* ⊠ *Milady Horákové 56, Letná* ⊕ *erhartovacukrarna.cz* Ⓜ *Line C: Vltavská.*

The Farm

$ | **CAFÉ** | Locals love this buzzing café that focuses on local ingredients and serves generous brunches, delicious bread, and excellent coffee. Chleba a máslo, next door, is a similarly unpretentious neighborhood bakery that's owned by the same crew. **Known for:** weekend brunch; delicious (but pricey) juices; live music in the evenings. ⑤ *Average main: Kč120* ⊠ *Korunovační 923/17, Letná* ☎ *774–863–999* ⊕ *farmletna.cz* Ⓜ *Tram 1, 2, 8, 12, 25, 26 to Sparta.*

 Hotels

Staying in Letná can offer some bargains in a leafy part of town, with long boulevards, tall trees, and an authentic local feel. It doesn't offer the fairy-tale beauty of Staré Město, but it is a refined, attractive area, and it's a quick tram ride or 20-minute walk over to the main tourist sights (or a pleasant walk through greenery to the area around Prague Castle). Plus, there are increasing numbers of trendy cafés opening up, making it a great spot for brunch.

Art Hotel

$ | **HOTEL** | This family-run little hotel has art on the walls by the grandfather and great-grandfather of the owner, as well as other Czech artists, and is otherwise clean, comfortable, and modern. **Pros:** mostly quiet, leafy neighborhood; reasonably priced; hotel garden. **Cons:** by Sparta Praha FC stadium so there can be crowds after games; showers weirdly low; elevator small and some stairs still necessary to reach certain rooms. ⑤ *Rooms from: Kč1500* ⊠ *Nad Královskou oborou 53, Letná* ☎ *777–008–778* ⊕ *arthotel.cz* ⇆ *24 rooms* ⥾ *Free Breakfast* Ⓜ *Tram 1, 2, 8, 12, 25, or 26 to Sparta.*

Hotel Belvedere

$ | **HOTEL** | Located in one of the early-20th-century constructivist-style buildings dotted around this district, the Hotel Belvedere is an unremarkable but reliable hotel with good prices and a prime location, in the middle of Letná and Holešovice (the districts kind of blend into one around here). **Pros:** surrounded by hip cafés and restaurants; decent hotel restaurant and breakfast; still only 20 minutes' walk from Old Town Square. **Cons:** away from the main sights; some street noise; a little dated. ⑤ *Rooms from: Kč1600* ⊠ *Milady Horákové 19, Letná* ☎ *220–106–111* ⊕ *hotelbelvedere-prague.cz* ⇆ *149 rooms* ⥾ *Free Breakfast* Ⓜ *Line C: Vltavská.*

⦿ **Nightlife**

Once a sleepy part of town, Letná now has a burgeoning coffee and bar scene, and the whole of Prague 7 is probably one of the best districts to visit as a tourist if you want to drink with cool young Czechs.

BARS AND PUBS

Café Letka

CAFÉS | This gorgeous café-bar, all distressed walls and high ceilings, is open from 8 am till midnight, and manages to transition nicely from coffee stop by day to funky bar by night. The owners reclaimed an old Austro-Hungarian café space for their modern version, and the update is pitched perfectly, with tasty food as well as drinks, including beer from the well-regarded Matuška brewery. ✉ *Letohradská 44, Letná* ☎ *777–444–035* ⊕ *cafeletka.cz* Ⓜ *Line A: Hradčanská plus Tram 1, 5, 25, or 26 to Letenské náměstí.*

★ Cobra

CAFÉS | The owners set up this exceedingly cool bar when bemoaning the fact that Letná used to be entirely dead after midnight. Almost single-handedly, they've changed that, with cool, modern food, a brilliant cocktail list, a disco ball or two, no proper sign (of course: the right people know where to come), industrial-chic decor, and a welcoming attitude at all hours of the day and late into the night. A gem. ✉ *Milady Horákové 8, Letná* ☎ *777–355–876* ⊕ *barcobra.cz* ⊘ *Closed Sun.* Ⓜ *Line C: Vltavská.*

★ Letenské sady

BEER GARDENS | Gaze over the river and the breathtaking rooftops of Staré Město in this beer garden at the top of Letná Park. The beer is cold and the atmosphere is fantastic. Facilities, however, (chiefly, toilets) are a little basic. ✉ *Letná* ☎ *233–378–200* ⊕ *letenskyzamecek.cz* Ⓜ *Line A: Hradčanská.*

CLUBS

★ Stalin parties

GATHERING PLACES | This open-air party at the top of Letná Park in summer is the hottest ticket in town, for a nominal "recommended" fee of 50 Kč at some events. There are concerts, film screenings, and even secondhand clothes nights through the week, electronic music shindigs on Friday and Saturday, and a "musical siesta" on Sunday. The bar and DJs are located right next to the huge metronome monument, which marks the spot that once housed the world's largest statue of Stalin. Chill vibes, a young, international crowd, and great views over the sparkling city lights make this a cool option on warm nights. Beer is for sale, but lines can be long—good thing bringing a can of your own is acceptable. Currently it's open only May–September. ✉ *Letenské sady, Letná* ⊕ *stalinletna.cz* ⊘ *Closed Oct.–Apr.* Ⓜ *Line A: Hradčanská.*

Shopping

BEAUTY

★ Liška Mazaná

COSMETICS | A unique, 100% natural, zero-waste, eco-friendly cosmetics shop that not only sells products, from lotions to lip balms, but also runs classes teaching customers how to make their own. From the moss growing in the cupboard (for decoration) to the friendly owners, Petra and Tereza, who are happy to help with any queries, it's a delight. The name is cute, too: cunning fox. ✉ *Veverkova 10, Letná* ☎ *737–948–223* ⊕ *liskamazana.cz* ⊘ *Closed Fri.–Sun.* Ⓜ *Line C: Vltavská.*

BOOKS

Page Five

BOOKS | This wonderful modern bookshop specializes in art books, magazines, and prints, from gorgeous coffee-table photography books to Czech poetry. Page Five is also a publishing house, with a few of its own books available, as well as a meeting place and exhibition space. Plus, there's a friendly shop dog welcoming customers. ✉ *Veverkova 5, Letná* ☎ *771–147–600* ⊕ *pagefive.com* Ⓜ *Line C: Vltavská.*

Both Letná and Holešovice have a lot to offer shoppers, from high-concept design stores to warren-like traditional hardware shops. While the boundaries of the districts blur a bit, we've included most of the shops on the main streets here, with a few farther-afield markets and the amazing Vnitroblock in Holešovice. The main treat in Letná is a wander down Veverkova ulice, currently one of the holders of the unofficial title of Prague's coolest street: it's a small strip, and there are intriguing new additions all the time.

CLOTHING

Sisters Conspiracy

MIXED CLOTHING | This light-filled boutique in a historic building, with a gorgeous tiled floor, showcases clothes that are easily as lovely as the surroundings. Chic, light, and individual, for men and women, this is modern, sustainable Czech fashion at its most understated and elegant. ✉ *Dobrovskeho 24, Letná* ☎ *732–644–122* ⊕ *sistersconspiracy.cz* ⊘ *Closed Fri.–Sun.* Ⓜ *Line A: Hradčanská plus Tram 1, 5, 25, or 26 to Letenské náměstí.*

HOME

Coverover

HOUSEWARES | The shop logo (it looks more like (C)over than Coverover) should give you a clue: this is an interiors shop with design chops that's not afraid to have fun. Set up by a French man and his Czech wife, products are available from across Europe and are varied and interesting, from the fig room scent by Geodesis that also gives the boutique its fragrance to the parrot earrings from Nach, among the cool bags, coasters, rugs, and cushions. ✉ *Milady Horákové 24, Letná* ☎ *222–096–011* ⊕ *coverover.cz* ⊘ *Closed weekends* Ⓜ *Line C: Vltavská.*

Holešovice

◉ Sights

★ **DOX** (*DOX Center for Contemporary Art*)

ART GALLERY | This giant modern art hub makes up the trio of big-beast artistic institutions in Prague 7 that have seen the district christened the city's most creative, alongside the Trade Fair Palace and the Academy of Fine Arts college next to Stromovka Park. This one is arguably the most fun, from its witty slogans (emblazoned on the building and sold as postcards) to its often flamboyant modern art collection, via a discussion space located in a life-size suspended airship. Housed in a former factory, DOX is more than just a brilliant modern art gallery, though; it is also a cultural center aiming to put art at the forefront of modern ways of thinking about the world. ✉ *Poupětova 1, Holešovice* ☎ *295–568–123* ⊕ *dox.cz* 🎫 *Free* ⊘ *Closed Mon. and Tues.* Ⓜ *Line C: Nádraží Holešovice.*

★ **Veletržní palác** (*Trade Fair Palace*)

ART GALLERY | This sometimes overlooked gallery, boasting the National Gallery's *The Art of a Long Century* (1796–1918), as well as the art of *The First Republic* (1918–38), has a real claim to being the city's best. Touring the vast spaces of this 1920s functionalist exposition hall filled to the brim with quirky, stimulating, comprehensive modern and contemporary local art is the best way to see how Czechs surfed the forefront of the avant-garde wave until the cultural freeze following World War II. Keep an eye out for works by František Kupka, credited as one of the first-ever abstract artists, and other Czech giants like Josef Čapek. Also on display are works by Western European—mostly French—artists from Delacroix to the present, with paintings by Gauguin, Picasso, and Braque an unexpected bonus. But painting is only the beginning—also occupying the many levels of the museum are collages, cubist sculptures, vintage gramophones, futuristic architectural models, art deco furnishings, and an exhaustive gathering of work from this new century, some of which is just as engrossing as the older stuff. Also, watch the papers and posters for information on traveling shows and temporary exhibits. ✉ *Dukelských hrdinů 47, Holešovice* ☎ *224–301–122* ⊕ *ngprague.cz* 🎫 *220 Kč* ⊘ *Closed Mon.* Ⓜ *Line C: Vltavská or Tram 6 or 17 to Veletržní palác.*

Restaurants

This is a gentrifying, formerly scruffy area that is becoming something of a dining mecca. As well as the new clutch of hip places, though, there are still plenty of low-cost pizzerias and pubs that serve food at an acceptable level of quality at prices that are much lower than in areas more popular with tourists.

Big Smokers
$$ | BARBECUE | This recently opened joint brings modern barbecue to the Czech capital, in a big way. The meats are glorious, the vibe is industrial-cool, and the welcome is friendly. **Known for:** trays of perfectly flamed meat; piquant accompaniments; cheap sandwich-based lunch menu. $ *Average main: Kč180* ⊠ *Dělnická 40, Holešovice* ☎ *737–070–373* ⊕ *bigsmokers.cz* ⊙ *Closed Mon.* Ⓜ *Tram 1, 2, 7, 11, 12, 14, or 25 to Dělnická.*

★ The Eatery
$$ | CZECH | This fantastic destination restaurant, with thoughtful, delicate twists on modern Czech food in a shiny-steel-and-concrete industrial setting, is certainly the district's best and even holds its own against the rest of the city. Run by the former Michelin-starred chef at Alcron, in the center of town, the Eatery is a more informal but no less delicious venture, with all the extras you'd expect from an establishment of this quality, from a chef's table to delicious wines and an open kitchen. **Known for:** Czech and European food, with fresh, local ingredients; theatrical cooking in the open kitchen; regularly buzzing. $ *Average main: Kč350* ⊠ *U Uranie 18, Holešovice* ☎ *603–945–236* ⊕ *theeatery.cz* ⊙ *Closed Sun. and Mon. No lunch Sat.* Ⓜ *Line C: Nádraží Holešovice.*

Home Kitchen
$$ | BAKERY | A popular café-bistro-bar with a homey feel (per its name), the menu here changes daily, taking inspiration from a mix of the owners' grandmothers and U.K. superchef Gordon Ramsay. There's also a shop for fresh vegetables and pastries. **Known for:** crusty home-baked bread and fluffy pancakes; lively spot, often packed; chill international feel. $ *Average main: Kč150* ⊠ *Jankovcova 14A, Holešovice* ☎ *605–263–812* ⊕ *homekitchen.cz* Ⓜ *Lines A and B: Můstek.*

Restaurace Na Mělníku
$$ | CZECH | Rub shoulders with locals at this pub that serves up fantastic, authentic local cuisine. Expect rib-sticking Czech favorites—there's a large selection of dumplings—that are perfect on cold days, and perfect cold draft beers. **Known for:** great schnitzel; visiting is like stepping back in time; down-to-earth, historic atmosphere. $ *Average main: Kč175* ⊠ *Františka Křížka 745/28, Holešovice* ☎ *233–378–731* ⊕ *namelniku.cz* Ⓜ *Line C: Vltavská, Tram 6 or 17 to Veletržní palác, or Tram 26 to Kamenicka.*

◉ Coffee and Quick Bites

Ouky Douky
$ | CAFÉ | A Prague original, this combination Czech bookstore and coffeehouse draws a mix of students, intellectuals, and vagabonds. The coffee is very good, as are the homemade daily soups and breakfast specials. **Known for:** eclectic setting; always lively; homemade soups. $ *Average main: Kč140* ⊠ *Janovského 14, Holešovice* ☎ *266–711–531* ⊕ *oukydouky.cz* Ⓜ *Line C: Vltavská.*

⊟ Hotels

Holešovice used to be a cheap, slightly grimy alternative to staying in the city center. That is still available; but now that the area has sealed its reputation as Prague's most arty neighborhood, the accommodation options are catching up.

Mama Shelter Prague offers well-designed rooms, excellent service and amenities, and a bar and a lobby you'll want to hang out in.

Absolutum Boutique Hotel

$ | **HOTEL** | This modern hotel in a somewhat industrial part of town doesn't exactly live up to its "boutique" name, but it's not a bad option nevertheless. **Pros:** some luxurious touches such as marble bathrooms and in-floor heating; clean and comfortable; very close to Nádraží Holešovice for getting around the city. **Cons:** breakfast could be better; uninspiring exterior; little to do in the immediate surroundings. $ *Rooms from: Kč1500* ✉ *Jablonského 4, Holešovice* ☎ *222–541–406* ⊕ *absolutumhotel.cz* ➥ *45 rooms* ❍❘ *Free Breakfast* Ⓜ *Line C: Nádraží Holešovice.*

★ Mama Shelter Prague

$ | **HOTEL** | Stand up and take a bow, Mama Shelter: finally, this hip district has the hip lodging it deserves, in this revitalized communist-era tower block right by the National Gallery. **Pros:** cool rooms with large windows and fun design touches, like Looney Tunes lamps; huge bar and terrace to see and be seen; reasonable prices. **Cons:** no gym; breakfast can get packed; not central to main attractions. $ *Rooms from: Kč1635* ✉ *Veletržní 1502/20, Holešovice* ☎ *225–117–111* ⊕ *mamashelter.com* ➥ *238 rooms* ❍❘ *Free Breakfast* Ⓜ *Line C: Vltavská, Tram 6 or 17 to Veletržní palác, or Tram 26 to Kamenicka.*

Nightlife

Going out in Holešovice, whether to one of the bars listed below or an experimental art performance listed in the Performing Arts section, is often a uniquely memorable, distinctly Czech event. Shake off your apprehensions and get involved.

BARS

Kavárna Liberál

CAFÉS | This very traditional, welcoming gathering spot offers a convivial drinking place from morning to midnight, following in the tradition of the grand cafés of Prague's past, where literary greats would gather and debate till morning. To get a hit of that vibe, head in, take a seat at one of the dark wood tables, order a beer, and start setting the world to rights. There are dance, art, and theater performances, too. ⊠ Heřmanova 6, Holešovice ☎ 732–355–445 ⊕ facebook. com/kavarnaliberal Ⓜ Line C: Vltavská.

Pivovar Marina
BREWPUBS | An old-school Czech microbrewery with views of the river in summer and a cozy beer-hall vibe in the winter. There's also some surprisingly fancy Italian food at the restaurant. Try the wheat beer in particular. ⊠ Jankovcova 1059, Holešovice ☎ 607–453–036 ⊕ pivovarmarina.cz Ⓜ Line C: Nádraží Holešovice plus Tram 6 to Maniny.

CLUBS
Cross Club
DANCE CLUBS | If you're a fan of alternative culture and really memorable nights, Cross Club will not let you down. It's a glorious mixture of many different things: otherworldly metal sculptures; floors and floors of different music, including lots of drums and bass; interesting artistic happenings, such as poetry readings, theater shows, film screenings, author readings, and an afternoon kids' theater; and a gorgeous garden lit in a variety of bright colors. But, it all comes together for a great night out, if not one for the fainthearted. Its closing hours are listed as "??," which should give you some idea of its general ethos. ⊠ Plynární 1096/23, Holešovice ☎ 736–535–010 ⊕ crossclub. cz Ⓜ Line C: Nádraží Holešovice, Tram 6, 12, or 17, or Night Tram 53 or 54.

SaSaZu
DANCE CLUBS | A restaurant and nightclub and music venue in a warehouse in the middle of a market isn't really the place you'd expect to draw Prague's high-heeled glitterati, but SaSaZu often does.

The gorgeous restaurant serves delicious and inventive pan-Asian fusion cuisine, and the vast club can be fun, too: it hosts performances by big international names, from Kesha to Public Enemy, and diners get their own doorway to the club, making an evening here—involving dinner and tickets to see a global music star—a pleasingly swanky experience. ⊠ Pražská tržnice, Bubenské nábř. 306/13, Holešovice ☎ 284–097–455 ⊕ sasazu.com Ⓜ Line C: Vltavská.

🎭 Performing Arts

For modern, experimental performances, this neighborhood is the place to be.

THEATER AND DANCE
Divadlo Alfred ve dvoře (Alfred in the Courtyard Theater)
THEATER | Most of the programming for this small, out-of-the-way theater is physical, nonverbal theater and dance, along with some music. It's a great place to see cutting-edge, unconventional productions; each year has a different theme. It's also home to Motus, a not-for-profit organization, set up by young local artists, producers, and presenters to promote and produce interesting and inventive new art. ⊠ Fr. Křížka 36, Holešovice ☎ 233–376–985 ⊕ alfredvedvore.cz Ⓜ Line C: Vltavská.

Jatka78
THEATER | This experimental theater is based in a market hall, complete with a cavernous bar and bistro bisected by a huge, twisting plywood sculpture. It's worth checking out Jatka78's program online to see what new and often thrilling Czech or European performances are on, from comedy to cabaret to circus. ⊠ Pražská tržnice, Bubenské nábř. 13, Halls 7 and 8, Holešovice ✛ Inside market, toward back ☎ 222–703–070 ⊕ jatka78.cz Ⓜ Line C: Vltavská.

Studio Alta

ARTS CENTERS | A creative hub that in some ways defies description, combining theater, dance, teaching, artists' studios, and a "living room" café. Alta is an artistic, exciting place to spend a few hours or take in some cutting-edge contemporary dance. ⊠ *Sokolovská 24, Holešovice* ⊕ *In the west wing of the Invalidovna* ⊕ *altart. cz* Ⓜ *Tram 17 to Výstaviště Holešovice.*

🛍 Shopping

Shopping in this district, once you have exhausted the boutiques at the Letná end of town, can be a bit hit or miss, but a wander is often rewarding (particularly around the market and the area near the DOX gallery), and Vnitroblock in particular is a must-see.

Pražská tržnice (*Prague Market*)

MARKET | This large, industrial-style market by the river offers some great deals and scope for bargaining, as well as a pleasant art nouveau market hall selling fruits, vegetables, and fresh flowers (Hall 22). Known locally as Holešovická tržnice, there are also some restaurants, bars, and bakeries, including a Slovakian deli, plus the experimental theater Jatka78.

■TIP➔ **There's an Asian market section here, too, but if you are looking for Prague's famous Vietnamese market, head to Sapa, or "Little Hanoi," on the edge of town (Metro Line C to Chodov, then Bus 197).** ⊠ *Bubenské nábř. 306/13, Holešovice* ☎ *220–800–592* ⊕ *prazska-trznice.cz* ⊗ *Closed Sun.* Ⓜ *Line C: Vltavská.*

★ **Vnitroblock**

WINE/SPIRITS | A cultural center in a former factory that's also a foodie mecca with a cinema, plus a hub for workshops, galleries, and hip boutiques, Vnitroblock resembles a shopping center as imagined by the coolest kids in town. From rotating pop-ups, including a favorite selling falafel and rosé wine, the gorgeous reclaimed industrial spaces, and the chill café vibe at the heart of the project, it's worth a trip here regardless where you are staying in Prague. ⊠ *Between Tusarova 31 and Dělnická 32, Holešovice* ☎ *732–373–069* ⊕ *vnitroblock.cz* Ⓜ *Line C: Vltavska or Nádraží Holešovice plus Tram 1, 12, 24, or 25 to Tusarova or Dělnická.*

Winegeek

WINE/SPIRITS | Part bar, part wine shop, this is a great addition to this neighborhood, offering wines from across Europe. It includes Czech producers as well as all-natural wines. There are tastings too. ⊠ *Řezáčovo nám., Holešovice* ☎ *776–708–090* ⊕ *winegeek.cz* ⊗ *Closed weekends* Ⓜ *Line C: Nádraží Holešovice.*

Troja
👁 Sights

Botanická zahrada (*Botanical Gardens*)

GARDEN | Not far from Zoologická zahrada v Praze (Prague Zoo), the public garden has a path in a greenhouse that first takes you through a semidesert environment, then through a tunnel beneath a tropical lake and into a rain forest; you end up cooling off in a room devoted to plants found in tropical mountains. Sliding doors and computer-controlled climate systems help keep it all together. The impressive Fata Morgana, a snaking 429-foot greenhouse that simulates the three different environments, has been drawing large crowds since it opened in 2004. There are lots of other areas in the huge outdoor gardens to explore, too, including beehives, a Japanese ornamental garden, and hilly areas with good views. The trails, including a scented trail and a nature trail, are pleasant as well. And don't miss the vineyard. ⊠ *Trojská 196, Troja* ☎ *234–148–122* ⊕ *botanicka.cz* 🎫 *150 Kč* Ⓜ *Line C: Nádraží Holešovicé plus Bus 112.*

Trojský zámek (Troja Château) is a luxurious baroque château surrounded by beautiful gardens and vineyards in Prague's northwest borough.

Trojský zámek (*Troja Château*)
NOTABLE BUILDING | Built in the late 17th century for the Czech nobleman Count Šternberg, this sprawling summer residence, modeled on a classical Italian villa, had the first French-style gardens in Bohemia. Inside, rich frescoes that took more than 20 years to complete depict the stories of emperors. Outside, there's plenty of pomp and ceremony, with a red-and-white baroque façade and a sweeping staircase adorned with statues of the sons of Mother Earth.

■**TIP→ The château is closed from November through March.** ⊠ *U trojského zámku 1, Troja* ☎ *283–851–614* ⊕ *ghmp. cz/zamek-troja* ⛟ *150 Kč, gardens free* ⊙ *Closed Mon. and Nov.–Mar.* Ⓜ *Line C: Nádraží Holešovice plus Bus 112.*

Vinotéka sv. Klára (*St. Claire's Vineyard*)
WINERY | This vineyard perched on a hill within the Botanical Gardens is a rewarding stop on a visit to Troja's zoo, the gardens, or the château. Well priced and lively, with delicious hyperlocal vintages, of course, it's a beautiful and relaxed spot for sunset among the vines. Note: you have to pay admission to the Botanical Gardens to go to the vineyard. ⊠ *Botanická zahrada, Trojská 196, Troja* ✛ *Entrance through Botanical Gardens* ☎ *234–148–153* ⊕ *facebook. com/vinotekasvklara* ⛟ *150 Kč* Ⓜ *Line C: Nádraží Holešovice plus Bus 112.*

Zoologická zahrada v Praze (*Prague Zoo*)
ZOO | **FAMILY** | Flora, fauna, and fresh air are the main things you can find in Prague's zoo. Hit hard by the floods in 2002, when some 134 animals perished, and again in 2013, when much of the zoo's grounds were inundated with water, Prague's zoo gets a periodic clean-up and offers a welcome break from the bustle of the city, particularly for those traveling with kids. Covering 160 acres on a slope overlooking the Vltava River, the zoo has thousands of animals representing 500 species. Take the chairlift for an

outstanding view of the area, and look into arriving via boat: either, in summer, on a steamboat from the center of town or on the simple daily passenger ferry between Podbaba and Podhoří. ⊠ *U trojského zámku 3, Troja* ☎ *296–112–230* ⊕ *zoopraha.cz* ✉ *250 Kč* Ⓜ *Line C: Nádraží Holešovice plus Bus 112.*

🍴 Restaurants

Salabka

$$$ | EUROPEAN | Residential, semirural-seeming Troja is hardly a dining hot spot, but this vineyard restaurant with rooms is a real treat if you are in the area or looking for something a bit different for a special-occasion lunch or dinner. High-end dining, a stylish setting, and delicious wines combine to make visitors forget, or maybe remember, that they are in the bustling Czech capital. **Known for:** excellent wines, particularly the historic Riesling; inventive tasting menus (no à la carte), with standout freshwater fish dishes; exclusive feel. Ⓢ *Average main: Kč600* ⊠ *K Bohnicím 2, Troja* ☎ *778–019–002* ⊕ *salabka.cz* ⊗ *Closed Sun.–Tues.* Ⓜ *Line C: Nádraží Holešovice plus Bus 112.*

Chapter 11

DAY TRIPS FROM PRAGUE

Updated by
Joseph Reaney

👁 **Sights**
★★★★★

🍴 **Restaurants**
★★★☆☆

🛏 **Hotels**
★★★☆☆

👜 **Shopping**
★★☆☆☆

🍸 **Nightlife**
★★☆☆☆

WELCOME TO DAY TRIPS FROM PRAGUE

TOP REASONS TO GO

★ **Find a storybook come to life:** A true medieval castle—babbling brook and all—can be found in Karlštejn.

★ **Take a historic tour:** The home of Archduke Franz Ferdinand, whose assassination started World War I, is remarkably well preserved in Konopiště; look for the bear living in the moat.

★ **Visit spooky Sedlec:** The *kostnice* (ossuary) on the edge of Kutná Hora is a mesmerizing church decorated with human bones.

★ **Sample the wine:** It's not all about beer. Try the excellent, locally produced wine at pretty Mělník.

★ **Pay remembrance to the past:** In Terezín, a baroque fortress turned into a concentration camp is both powerful and chilling.

1 Český Šternberk. An enormous family-owned fortification perched high over the river.

2 Karlštejn. The quickest castle excursion ticks all the European fairy-tale fortress boxes.

3 Konopiště Castle. A castle with a moat of bears, a hall of horns, and an untamed park.

4 Křivoklát. An evocative 12th-century fortress, complete with a torture-chamber tour.

5 Kutná Hora. Home to a macabre bone church and a majestic cathedral.

6 Lidice. A haunting memorial to the horrors of World War II.

7 Litomyšl. This pretty town is dominated by a UNESCO-listed Renaissance château.

8 Mělník. Toast this beautiful medieval town with a glass (or two) of delicious local wine.

9 Terezín. A glimpse into a former World War II Jewish ghetto and concentration camp.

10 Czech Switzerland. Excellent hiking opportunities in mystical landscapes.

As the saying goes, the world is a book, and those who don't travel read only one page. The same applies to visitors who come to the Czech Republic but visit only Prague. Don't get us wrong: it's a great page to read. But if you want the whole story, you need to get out of the capital and embrace the adventures beyond.

You can stay overnight or for a whole weekend, but it's not essential; there's plenty to do with just a few hours set aside.

The UNESCO-listed Kutná Hora is worth a visit for its bone church alone; one of the most memorable, and strangely beautiful, attractions close to Prague. The surrounding town is charming, too, and offers plenty of options if you do plan an overnight stay. There's more charm to be found in the myriad castles that dot the landscape around Prague. Karlštejn is a typical fairy-tale château atop a mountain; Křivoklát is a wonderfully secluded and quiet fortification; and Konopiště is the one-time hunting lodge of the doomed Archduke Franz Ferdinand. All the castles offer great hiking opportunities, but if walking is your thing, it's worth going farther afield to the breathtaking Pravčická brána (Pravčická Archway) rock bridge. Here, you can roam through the forest or take a guided boat ride through gorges. If you want to sample some Czech wine, Mělník has vineyards aplenty. And there are more sobering—in every sense—sights, too, such as Lidice and Terezín, which both tell terrible tales of the horrors of World War II.

Traveling may not come as easy as in Prague, with fewer tourist facilities, fewer English speakers, and fewer nightlife and entertainment options. But the trade-off will be more bang for your buck and a genuine feel for the country and its people, plus a real sense of adventure.

Planning

When to Go

Many of the Czech Republic's castles and monuments are closed November through March. Some, especially those closer to Prague, stay open year-round although with shortened hours. The busiest time for a visit is June through August; April and October are less crowded. When school is in session, expect school groups during the week.

Getting Here

When traveling around the Czech Republic, buses are typically faster and cheaper, while trains are easier to navigate and more comfortable. Bus drivers don't typically announce the stops, so when boarding, ask the driver to let you know when you should get off. If you are planning a trip, it's worth knowing your options ahead of time; search the best connections to and from Prague (covering all forms of public transport) at ⊕ *www.idos.idnes.cz/en.* If you are taking a bus from Florenc, buy your tickets online or at the station a day or two before your trip. People with tickets board first, and you'll get an assigned seat (so you won't have to stand).

Guided Tours from Prague

Guided bus tours are available from several companies for Karlštejn, Konopiště, Kutná Hora, Český Šternberk, and Terezín. The ease of booking and traveling (compared with figuring out the train and bus schedules or renting a car) are often worth the time constraints and extra cost. There are also special-interest tours available, from guided bicycle day trips to Jewish-focused bus tours.

Biko Adventures Prague
BICYCLE TOURS | **FAMILY** | Biko offers a gentle and family-friendly full-day tour by e-bike through small villages (with stops for beer and baked goods) to Hrad Karlštejn (Karlštejn Castle). It's around 65 km (40 miles) there and back; about seven hours including stops. Others options include a bike tour of "Green Prague," which covers city parks like Petřín and Letná as well as the nearby nature reserve of Divoká Šárka. ⊠ *Vyšehrad* ⊕ *www.bikoadventures.com.*

Premiant City Tour
GUIDED TOURS | This company has knowledgeable guides and a wide range of day trips, from Karlštejn to Kutná Hora. Standard tours, which are available in several languages, are in small groups, but individual or private groups are also available on request. Book online or at the easy-to-find booths on Na příkopě. ⊠ *Na příkopě 23, Nové Mesto* ☎ *606–600–123* ⊕ *www.premiant.cz.*

Wittmann Tours
GUIDED TOURS | This company offers interesting and informative trips with a particular focus on Jewish sites and history. As well as offering day trips to the former Jewish ghetto of Terezín (with an optional add-on of Lidice) the company has a full-day tour to Kutná Hora and Kolín, once the country's second main Jewish center. ⊠ *Novotného lávka 5, Staré Mesto* ☎ *603–426–564* ⊕ *www. wittmann-tours.com.*

Restaurants and Hotels

In general, food and lodging should be cheaper than in Prague, but some restaurants, especially those close to a town center or near a tourist attraction, can be just as pricey. You won't find the same range of options either, and be prepared for fewer English speakers—but people will probably be friendlier than in the big city. Anyway, that's all part of the adventure.

Restaurant and hotel reviews have been shortened. For full information, visit Fodors.com.

What It Costs in koruny			
$	$$	$$$	$$$$
RESTAURANTS			
under 175 Kč	176 Kč–300 Kč	301 Kč–500 Kč	over 500 Kč
HOTELS			
under 3,500 Kč	3,500 Kč–5,000 Kč	5,001 Kč–7,000 Kč	over 7,000 Kč

Český Šternberk

48 km (30 miles) southeast of Prague.

A quintessentially Czech castle, complete with descendants of its 13th-century founders still living inside, Český

Český Šternberk, or the "Star on the Hill," lives up to its name.

Šternberk may not be the easiest day trip from Prague, but for history, atmosphere, and authenticity, it's hard to beat.

GETTING HERE

There are daily trains to Český Šternberk, but it isn't the easiest trip. Trains leave from Hlavní nádraží (Prague's main train station) and stop in many small towns on the way; you have to change trains in Čerčany, about one hour out of Prague. The good news is that the last leg, which runs alongside the Sázava River, is very scenic. Also, in summer you may be lucky enough to score a ride on an old-fashioned steam train; ask at the main station for the *parní vlak* (steam train). Whichever trains you end up taking, expect a 2 to 2.5-hour journey time.

Alternatively, if time is of the essence, you can save up to half an hour by continuing on the first train from Prague to Benešov, then switching to Bus 791 for Český Šternberk.

If you're driving, you will take the D1 highway out of Prague (the main highway

to Brno) and take the turnoff to Český Šternberk, following Route 111 to the castle, which perches over the highway. The drive takes around 45 minutes.

TIMING

Summer sees the most tourists at Český Šternberk, and it can get very busy June through August. Nevertheless, the daily falconer displays can make a peak-time visit worthwhile. May and September are a little quieter yet still warm, while October has a historical festival that features "live" characters from the castle's history. From November to March, as well as midweek in April and October, the castle is open only by appointment.

Sights

Český Šternberk

CASTLE/PALACE | Dramatic Český Šternberk looms over the Sázava River and surrounding countryside and looks positively forbidding at night. Perched on an outcropping of rock, this 13th-century castle is not only striking from the exterior; it has the period interiors to match.

Founded in 1241 by Zdeslav of Divišov, it was originally built as a fortress. Amazingly, descendants of Zdeslav have remained in the castle, making it their residence through the centuries and up to the present day. Šternberk is the Czech spelling of the German composite word Sternberg (it was customary to use German names at the time), which roughly translates to "star on the hill." Look out for the eight-pointed gold star on the family coat of arms, which can be found throughout the property.

The exterior of the castle retains a late Gothic look, while the interiors were mainly redone in a baroque style. The latest major work was done in 1911, when electricity and water were added. Guided tours lasting around 45 minutes are required to see the interior, but the rooms are gorgeous and the guides are excellent. There are regular English-language tours in summer, but out of peak season it's best to call or email in advance to book your place.

Furnishings date back to the Renaissance and are either original from the castle or brought from other Šternberk properties around Europe. Beautiful frescoed walls and stucco ceilings can be found throughout, including the Knight's Hall lined with paintings. You'll see items in the rococo and Czech baroque style, Louis XVI furnishings, and an amazing collection of copper engravings dating back to the 17th century.

Look out for a (literal) family tree, with portraits of generations of the Šternberk family. Its members included scientists, bishops, officers, and government employees, all of whom left their mark on aspects of the country's history. One even helped found the Národní muzeum (National Museum) in Prague.

During the nationalization period under communism, the castle was seized and became government property; however Jiří Šternberk agreed to stay on as caretaker and guide, thus keeping the family's connection to the castle. The Šternberks received the property back in 1992.

There are some lovely walks in the woodlands around the castle. One route leads to Hladomorna, a stand-alone fortress tower you can climb during the summer for a fine view of the castle, river, and surrounding forest. ⊠ Český Šternberk 1, Ceský Šternberk ☎ 317–855–101 ⊕ www.hradceskysternberk.cz ⊠ Guided tour in English 260 Kč, night tour 350 Kč ⊗ Closed Mon. Closed weekdays in Apr. and Oct. Open Nov.–Mar. by appointment only.

Karlštejn

29 km (18 miles) southwest of Prague.

If you've only a few hours to spend outside of Prague, going to Karlštejn is an easy and delightful half-day trip. The town itself seems to exist mainly to support visitors to the castle, so if you are looking for some Czech authenticity this probably isn't the one to choose. But for castle and nature lovers, it's a lovely outing.

GETTING HERE

There's no bus service to Karlštejn from Prague, but it's a quick, simple, and scenic train journey (around 65 Kč) from the main station. Many trains leave every day from Hlavní nádraží—look on the schedule for trains heading to Beroun. When you arrive at Karlštejn station, simply follow the crowds across the river and up to the castle. On the very rare occasions where there's no one else around, here's what you need to do: Exit the station, turn right, and walk back along the small lane parallel to the railway tracks to find the town. Follow the signs reading "Hrad." After a few minutes, cross a bridge over the river, and turn right onto the main road, which resembles a small highway (the absence of a pedestrian sidewalk doesn't bother the locals). Be wary of traffic, but continue for another two or three minutes until you reach a road going up the hill to your left. This is the main road up to the village and castle.

A visit to Karlštejn can also be combined with a challenging 13-km (8-mile) hike through beautiful forests and along a small wooded waterfall from Beroun. Get off at Beroun train station, walk toward town, and make a right just before an underpass. Follow the red-marked trail through the hills and dales, passing through the tiny village of Svatý Jan pod Skalou (with its unusual cave chapel and rocky hilltop viewpoint) before arriving in Karlštejn—just above the village—about three hours later. Don't set out without water, good shoes, and, above all, a decent local hiking map, available at the visitor center.

By car from Prague, take Highway 4—on the western side of the Vltava—to the edge of the city, then go right on Highway 115, southwest through Radotín. Take the Karlštejn exit, which puts you on Highway 116, and after a few more minutes you end up beside the Berounka River. You can find a large parking lot at the bottom of the hill below Karlštejn. No vehicles are allowed on the road up to the castle.

TIMING

It's possible to visit Karlštejn all year round, but peak season is from Easter to October. In September, there's a *burčák* (young wine) festival, complete with tastings, craft booths, artistic displays, and a visit from Charles IV himself (sort of). December is also a good time to visit, as there are often Christmas concerts on weekends—and far fewer crowds than in summer.

◉ Sights

★ **Hrad Karlštejn** (*Karlštejn Castle*)

CASTLE/PALACE | If it's a picture-book European castle you're after, look no further. Perched atop a wooded hillside, Karlštejn comes complete with battlements, turrets, and towers. Once Charles IV's summer palace, Karlštejn was originally built to hold and guard the crown jewels (which were moved to Prague Castle's Katedrála sv. Víta, or St. Vitus Cathedral, in 1619). There is a fairly strenuous hike up to the castle—lined with souvenir stands and overpriced snack bars—but it's worth the journey. Once you've reached the top, take time to walk the ramparts and drink in the panorama of the village and countryside below. There's a slightly bewildering list of different interior tours, but the pick of the bunch is Tour 2, which includes the castle's greatest treasure, the Chapel of the Holy Cross, which once held the crown jewels. Tours of the chapel are limited (and more expensive than the other tour route), so you must book in advance. On sunny days, there's also an exterior tour, or you can simply take a stroll around the courtyards at no cost. Because of its proximity to Prague, it is the most-visited site outside of the Czech capital, so be prepared for crowds, especially in the high summer months. ⊠ *Karlštejn 18, Karlštejn* ☎ *311–681–617* ⊕ *www.hrad-karlstejn.cz* ☜ *Tours from 190 Kč* ⊗ *Closed Mon. Tower closed Oct.–Apr., chapel closed Nov.–Apr.*

◉ Restaurants

Pod dračí skálou

$$ | CZECH | This traditional hunting lodge–style restaurant is the most rustic and fun of Karlštejn's eateries. To find it, follow the main road uphill out of the village about a third of a mile from town. **Known for:** large portions of good food; hit-or-miss service; accommodation

Karlštejn Castle is a 45-minute train ride from Prague, and one of the most convenient and popular escapes from the Czech capital city.

also available. $ *Average main: Kč220* ✉ *Karlštejn 130, Karlštejn* ☎ *311–681–177* ⊕ *www.poddraciskalou.eu.*

U Janů

$ | **CZECH** | The best of the many touristy restaurants in the town proper, this spot is just on the upper edge of the village, not far from where the castle path starts. It also offers a nice big terrace with slight views of the castle. **Known for:** good food at a reasonable price; location right on the main street; option of three suites and a double room. $ *Average main: Kč140* ✉ *Karlštejn 28, Karlštejn* ☎ *725–805–965* ⊕ *www.ujanukarlstejn.cz.*

Hotels

Hotel Karlštejn

$ | **HOTEL** | The best "proper" hotel in town, the Karlštejn offers 11 modern but pared-down rooms. **Pros:** clean and modern rooms; outdoor pool with view of castle; free parking spaces. **Cons:** no restaurant for dinner; some rooms are

poky; lacking an elevator. $ *Rooms from: Kč2800* ✉ *Karlštejn 7, Karlštejn* ☎ *311–600–900* ⊕ *www.hotel-karlstejn.cz* ➪ *11 rooms* ⦾ *Free Breakfast.*

Konopiště Castle

45 km (27 miles) southeast of Prague.

Bears, hunting trophies, and history are found at the country residence of the doomed Archduke Franz Ferdinand, whose 1914 assassination ignited World War I and changed the course of modern history.

GETTING HERE

For being so close to Prague, Konopiště can feel quite remote. Trains leave from Hlavní nádraží to Benešov u Prahy (1 hour; 90 Kč), but from here it's still another 2½ km (1½ miles) to Zámek Konopiště (Konopiště Castle). You can either walk the last leg (30 minutes; simply follow the signs) or hop on bus 438 (5 minutes;

14 Kč). By car, it's 30 minutes from Prague: join the D1 highway southwest toward Brno, taking exit 21 to Benešov. Signs along this road will lead you to Konopiště.

VISITOR INFORMATION

CONTACTS Turistické informační centrum. (*Tourist Information Center*) ⊠ *Konopiště, Benešov* ☎ *317–726–004 for main tourist office in Benešov.*

Sights

Zámek Konopiště (*Konopiště Castle*)
CASTLE/PALACE | Set in a huge, beautiful park, Konopiště Castle dates from the 14th century and is best known as the hunting lodge of Archduke Franz Ferdinand. He no doubt had a whale of a time hunting on the grounds before he met his untimely end, and now visitors can wander the forests, gaze at the lake, and even watch plays in summer. In a suitably historic touch, there's also a bear who lives in the castle moat. The castle itself is also worth a look, with a carefully preserved interior including many original furnishings from Ferdinand's time. The rooms reflect his incredible opulence as well as his fondness for hunting—there are animal trophies and weapons everywhere. You can even stay inside the castle walls at a little pension. Getting to the castle usually involves a ⅓-mile walk through the woods. It can be seen only on a guided tour; book in advance for an English-speaking guide. ⊠ *Benešov* ☎ *317–721–366* ⊕ *www.zamek-kono-piste.cz* 🎫 *Tours from 240 Kč* ⊗ *Closed Mon. and Dec.–Mar.*

Hotels

Pension Konopiště
$ | **B&B/INN** | Konopiště is near enough to Prague that you don't really need to stay overnight, but if you fancy a night in the countryside, this pension inside the castle walls and attached to a motorcycle museum is a lovely option. **Pros:** great

location; free activities like table tennis and pétanque; surrounded by nature. **Cons:** no restaurant; narrow staircases; some rooms small. ⑤ *Rooms from: Kč2200* ⊠ *Konopiště 30, Benešov* ☎ *317–702–658* ⊕ *www.penzion-konopiste.cz* 🍴 *6 apartments* ⏐⊙⏐ *Free Breakfast.*

Křivoklát

43 km (27 miles) west of Prague.

One of the most evocative castles in the country, Křivoklát is the real deal. A brisk walk up the hill to the top feels like a trip back in time as you leave the trappings of modern life behind.

GETTING HERE

A train is the best, and prettiest, way to reach Křivoklát. The scenic ride from Hlavní nádraží, with a change in Beroun, takes about 1½ hours and costs around 100 Kč. Trains aren't all that regular, so check your return options before setting off. If you plan to visit over a summer weekend, the heritage train "Rakovnický rychlík" offers irregular but direct services from Prague; check ⊕ *kzc.cz* for details and timetables.

If you're driving, the fastest way to Křivoklát is to follow Route 6 from Prague toward Karlovy Vary, then take exit 25 onto Route 236. The trip is about an hour. For a beautiful drive (and an extra 15 minutes) take the E50 Highway from Prague toward Plzeň, then exit at Beroun to Route 116. Follow this highway, which goes along a river before veering up into the hills, to Route 201, which winds back south toward Křivoklát. There's free parking just beneath the castle or paid parking just above it.

TIMING

In summer you'll see cyclists zooming around the region and locals visiting the castle in swarms. At the beginning of December, Křivoklát holds an Advent fair, complete with musicians, performances, and lots of crafts.

VISITOR INFORMATION
CONTACTS Křivoklát Tourist Information.
✉ *Nám. Svatopluka Čecha 82, Krivoklát* ☎ *313–558–101* ⊕ *www.is-krivoklat.cz.*

◉ Sights

★ Křivoklát

CASTLE/PALACE | A man dressed as a monk asleep in the corner; children practicing archery; traditional craftsmen offering their wares—close your eyes in Křivoklát's strangely atmospheric courtyard and you can easily imagine the scene with hunters clattering back atop their horses. Because the castle is a little farther from Prague, it's much less crowded and more authentic, so you can let your imagination run wild as you wander the walls and gaze out on the surrounding forest and the Berounka river winding lazily by below. The evocative name helps as well, even if it's a little hard to pronounce (it means "twisted branches" in Czech). There also aren't many signs, which helps with the feeling that you are having an adventure. You'll meet a lot of locals, rather than tourists, enjoying the castle, mainly because it's a national favorite thanks to its many romantic references in Czech literature. The river area is also popular with hikers and cyclists.

Křivoklát began life as a humble hunting lodge back in the 12th century. Greater things were to come, thanks to King Wenceslas I, who commissioned the first castle here. Future inhabitants expanded and beautified the place, including Charles IV and his son, Wenceslas IV. A number of fires significantly damaged the buildings, and toward the end of the 16th century it lost its importance and fell into disrepair. Following the Thirty Years' War, the Schwarzenbergs took over and revived it. It's been in state hands since 1929.

A Pagan Spring

Spirits swing to life in Křivoklát on April 30, when many Czech villages celebrate something called *Čarodejnice*. Roughly translated as "witch-burning"—a pagan-rooted festival to ward off the winter spirit and welcome the bounty of spring—it turns Křivoklát into a gleeful scene of Slavic festivities and mock Celtic battles. Hundreds of Czechs from all over come to enjoy the music, merriment, and cheap wine into the wee hours.

Today, Křivoklát offers some of the more interesting castle tours around. There are five to choose from, with Tour 3 ("The Grand Tour"; 390 Kč in English) the most comprehensive. Over the course of 1 hour and 40 minutes, visitors will see the Great Hall, one of the largest Gothic halls in Central Europe (second only to the one at Prague Castle), the beautiful chapel, the castle library, a prison complete with torture instruments, and lots of hunting trophies. Tours of the castle are offered regularly in Czech and less regularly in English (check the website for times), but you can always join a Czech tour and purchase a pamphlet with information in English.

Even without a tour, the castle is well worth a visit. You can walk along the castle ramparts, climb the tower (for great views of the surrounding countryside), or simply sit and nurse a beer in the beautiful courtyard. There's also a lovely 2-km (1-mile) woodland walk from the castle to a viewpoint above the river; follow the path marked with yellow paint, which starts across the road from the castle entrance. ✉ *Křivoklát 47, Krivoklát* ☎ *313–558–440* ⊕ *www.hrad-krivoklat. cz* 🎫 *Tours from 240 Kč* ⊘ *Closed Mon. Closed weekdays Nov.–Mar. (except festivals; check website for details).*

Kutná Hora

70 km (44 miles) east of Prague.

Kutná Hora is a UNESCO World Heritage Site, and the town proudly boasts of its "10 centuries of architecture" that run the gamut from Gothic to cubist. The town is worth a visit any time, but the tourist season really starts in April. Historical peddlers, dancers, and fencers celebrate the city's silver-mining history at the Královské stříbření (Royal Silvering) festival held every June. There are also some traditional Czech eateries, a great silver-mining museum, and the stunning Chrám sv. Barbory (St. Barbara's Cathedral), which dates from 1388.

A little out of the town center, Sedlec Ossuary, or the "Bone Church," is one of the Czech Republic's most famous sights. The small chapel is decorated floor to ceiling with human bones. The shapes, chandeliers, and sculptures are strangely, hauntingly beautiful, adding up to a breathtaking and morbid memento mori.

GETTING HERE

Both buses and trains make the short trip to Kutná Hora, but the train is a better bet. The journey takes less than an hour and a ticket costs around 125 Kč. You will most likely be dropped off at the Kutná Hora main station, which is in the suburb of Sedlec, about 3 km (almost 2 miles) from the center. But that's fine, as you're only a 10-minute walk from the bone church; signs point the way and there's a map in the station. From here, you can then walk into the town center along the main road in about 30 minutes. Alternatively, wander down to Kutná Hora–Sedlec train station (passing the Church of the Assumption of the Virgin on your left) and cross the tracks to follow the riverside path west; it takes five minutes longer but it's infinitely more pleasurable.

Bus 381 leaves from Háje at the end of Metro Line C (red). It's a little cheaper than the train, but takes almost twice as long. By car, follow Vinohradská třída west out onto the E65, then take the D11 to Route 38 into Kutná Hora. If the traffic is clear, the drive should take an hour.

VISITOR INFORMATION

There are four official tourist information centers in Kutná Hora. The main one is at Kollárova 589, just off Palackého náměstí, but there are also offices at the main train station, in the courtyard beside St. Barbara's Cathedral, and just down the street from Sedlec Ossuary. Each sell tickets and provide free maps and information all year-round.

CONTACTS Info-Centre Kutná Hora.
✉ *Kollárova 589, Kutná Hora* ☎ *327–512–378* ⊕ *www.kutnahora.cz.*

 Sights

České Muzeum Stříbra (*Czech Museum of Silver*)
FACTORY | FAMILY | A silver mine is a little more romantic than a run-of-the-mill coal mine, and this silver museum combines all manner of period mining and minting equipment with the chance to tour an actual medieval silver mine. With the first tunnels dug in the 1300s, by the 1500s Kutná Hora had some of the deepest mines in the world. The trek nowadays—through low, narrow, and claustrophobic tunnels—will probably make you glad you weren't a miner. The 90-minute guided tours (with around 30 minutes spent underground) start roughly every half hour during the summer months, with English-language tours once or twice a day; check the website for timings. In late spring and early autumn, English-language tours are only on request.

■**TIP→ Taller people may struggle with some of the lower sections of the mines, while wider people will find some tighter sections a challenge. For those who are both, this is probably an experience to skip.** ✉ *Barborská 28, Kutná Hora* ☎ *327–512–159* ⊕ *www.cms-kh.cz* 🎟 *From 70*

The looming St. Barbara's Cathedral is a tribute to Kutná Hora's miners.

Kč, foreign-language explanation 20 Kč ⊘ *Closed Dec.–Mar. and in particularly bad weather.*

★ Chrám sv. Barbory (*St. Barbara's Cathedral*)
CHURCH | Getting to this beautiful cathedral is pleasurable enough; it's about a 10-minute walk from the main Palackého náměstí along a road lined with baroque statues. But the church itself is the jewel in Kutná Hora's crown, resembling a grand circus tent more than a religious center. St. Barbara's was started in the late 1300s; it drew on the talents of the Peter Parler workshop as well as two luminaries of the late 15th century, Matyáš Rejsek and Benedikt Ried.

Upon entering, look up. The soaring ceiling is one of the church's most impressive features. It was added in 1558 and replaced and restored in the late 1800s. Take the stairs up to the elevated section for closer views of the ceiling and the lavish organ. There are also some interesting casts of reliefs and other decorative church elements here, including a

sculpture of angels carrying the miners' guild coat of arms. The balcony has lovely views over the garden and the town center, including the visibly leaning tower of the Kostel sv. Jakuba (Church of St. James).

■ TIP → **Avoid paying an extra 50 Kč for opera glasses; you get close enough to the ceiling that you don't need them.** ⊠ *Barborská, Kutná Hora* ☎ *327–515–796* ⊕ *www.khfarnost.cz* 🖾 *160 Kč, combo ticket 300 Kč (incl. Sedlec Ossuary and Church of the Assumption).*

Katedrála Nanebevzetí Panny Marie
(*Church of the Assumption of the Virgin*)
CHURCH | The Cathedral of the Assumption of Our Lady and Saint John the Baptist, to give it its full name, sits across the street from the ossuary at the former Sedlec Monastery. It exemplifies the work of one-of-a-kind architect Giovanni Santini (1667–1723), a master of expressive line and delicate proportion who fathered a bravura hybrid of Gothic and baroque.

Kutná Hora

KEY

- 1 Sights
- 1 Restaurants
- 1 Hotels
- *i* Tourist Information

0 ——— 200 yd
0 ——— 200 m

Sights ▼

1 České Muzeum Stříbra **B5**
2 Chrám sv. Barbory **A6**
3 Katedrála Nanebevzetí Panny Marie.............. **C1**
4 Kostel sv. Jakuba **C5**
5 Kostnice Sedlec **E3**
6 Národní hřebčín Kladruby nad Labem **E3**
7 Vlašský dvůr.............. **C5**

Restaurants ▼

1 Dačický **B5**
2 Factory **B4**
3 Harmonia **C5**

Hotels ▼

1 Hotel U Vlašského dvora **C5**

■ TIP → **Tickets must be purchased from the nearby ticket office at Zámecká 279.** ✉ *U Zastávky 280, Sedlec* ☎ *326–551–049* ⊕ *www.sedlec.info* 🖅 *160 Kč (incl. Sedlec Ossuary); 300 Kč (also incl. St. Barbara's Cathedral).*

★ **Kostnice Sedlec** (*Sedlec Ossuary*)
RELIGIOUS BUILDING | This is the reason many people outside the Czech Republic have heard of, and make the trip to, Kutná Hora. Forget all that beautiful baroque architecture and descend into the darkness with some bones. The skeletal remains of around 40,000 people have been lovingly arranged in the Kaple Všech svatých (All Saints Chapel), more commonly called the Bone Church. Built in the 16th century, this church forced the movement of a nearby graveyard, so monks from the nearby Sedlec Monastery decided to use the displaced cemetery bones to decorate the church with beautiful, weird, and haunting results. Look out for the chandelier, which is made with every bone in the human body, as well as the Schwarzenberg coat of arms, which includes a raven (assembled from various small bones) pecking the eye of a Turkish warrior. ✉ *Zámecká, Sedlec* ☎ *326–551– 049* ⊕ *www.sedlec.info* 🖅 *160 Kč (incl. Church of the Assumption); 300 Kč (also incl. St. Barbara's Cathedral)* ⊙ *Closed Mon. Nov.–Jan.*

★ **Národní hřebčín Kladruby nad Labem** (*National Stud at Kladruby nad Labem*)
FARM/RANCH | Located 15 miles northeast of Kutná Hora, this national stud farm was established in the 16th century to breed and train ceremonial horses for the Habsburg court. In 2019, it was named a UNESCO World Heritage Site—the first stud farm anywhere to be listed—in recognition of its vital role in protecting and promoting the rare but ancient Kladruber breed. Covering 1,310 hectares (3,240 acres) of flat, sandy land and fenced pastures near the Elbe, the site includes fields and forests along

with its horse breeding and training grounds. Visitors can take a guided tour of the stables, home to a mix of gray and black horses—in the past, the former were used for royal ceremonies and the latter for high-ranking clergy—as well as explore the coach room, the château, the forester's lodge, and the observation tower. ✉ *Kladruby nad Labem 1, Kladruby nad Labem, Kutná Hora* ☎ *601–191–580* ⊕ *www.nhkladruby.cz/en* 🖅 *Tours from 180 Kč* ⊙ *Closed Mon. and Oct.–Mar.*

Vlašský dvůr (*Italian Court*)
HISTORY MUSEUM | Coins were first minted here in 1300, made by Italian artisans brought in from Florence—hence the mint's odd name. The Italian Court was where the Pražský groš (Prague groschen), one of the most widely circulated coins of the Middle Ages, was minted until 1726. The regular, self-guided tour (120 Kč) takes you through the Royal Mint museum, where you can see the development of the groschen and other Bohemian coins throughout the centuries, from the tiny halíř of the mid-1400s to the giant, pocket-filling Tolar of 1630. A more extensive tour (300 Kč) includes a visit to the cellar and the Royal Palace. ✉ *Havlíčkovo nám. 552, Kutná Hora* ☎ *327–512–873* ⊕ *www.pskh.cz* 🖅 *From 120 Kč* ⊙ *Closed Mon. in Nov.–Mar.*

🍴 Restaurants

★ **Dačický**
$$ | **CZECH** | A medieval tavern feel and big plates of Czech food make Dačický a warm, authentic experience. The yellow walls decorated with cartoon-style murals, the long (shared) wooden tables, and the massive chandelier also add to the ambience. **Known for:** popularity with locals; good choice of draft beers; giant kebab with meat skewered on a sword. ⑤ *Average main: Kč240* ✉ *Rakova 8, Kutná Hora* ☎ *603–434–367* ⊕ *www. dacicky.com.*

Did You Know?

Morbid, marvelous, or both? The ossuary outside Kutná Hora uses thousands of ancient bones for decorative purposes creating chalices, chandeliers, and even this family coat of arms.

Factory

$$ | AMERICAN | This popular, modern bistro-café serves fairly standard European-American fare, but everything is freshly and expertly made. That means pizzas cooked crispy Neapolitan style, steaks that have been matured for 14 days, and fresh pasta that's firmly al dente. **Known for:** great burgers and fries; cozy cellar setting; friendly English-speaking staff. $ *Average main: Kč225* ✉ *Česká 1, Kutná Hora* ☎ *721–323–145* ⊕ *www.factorybistro.cz.*

Hotels

Hotel U Vlašského dvora

$ | HOTEL | Lovely views from this hotel make it a nice option for an overnight stay in Kutná Hora. **Pros:** great views from room; nice breakfast; convenient central location. **Cons:** lots of steps; lack of a/c makes rooms hot in summer; some furniture a bit dated. $ *Rooms from: Kč2100* ✉ *28. října 511, Kutná Hora* ☎ *771–226–021* ⊕ *www.hotelykh.cz* ⤢ *10 rooms* ⦿ *Free Breakfast.*

Lidice

18 km (11 miles) northwest of Prague.

No more than a speck on the map to the northwest of Prague, this tiny village became a part of the tragic history of World War II. Adolf Hitler ordered Lidice to be razed to the ground as a lesson to the Czechs and a representation of what would happen to anyone who opposed his rule. The act was a retaliation for the assassination of the Nazi leader Reinhard Heydrich by Czech patriots. On the night of June 9, 1942, a Gestapo unit entered Lidice. The entire adult male population was shot, nearly 200 men; about the same number of women were sent to the Ravensbrück concentration camp. The children were either sent to Germany to be "Aryanized" or accompanied the

women to the death camp. By June 10, the entire village was completely wiped out.

The name Lidice soon became an example around the world of the brutality of Nazi rule. A group of English miners from Stoke-on-Trent took up the cause and formed Lidice Must Live, an initiative to build a new village of Lidice. The city is adjacent to the memorial, which is an amazing and beautiful site, albeit one that is usually visited only by school groups.

GETTING HERE

It's a shame that an important memorial so close to Prague can be a bit tricky to reach by public transportation, although it's a quick trip once you are on board. There's no train service to Lidice, but there is a regular bus service from Zličín, at the end of the Metro Line B (yellow)— the same place you can get the airport bus. Tickets (30 Kč) are purchased directly from the driver and the journey takes around 30 minutes. You can also get Bus 300, Prague–Kladno, from the stop above Metro station Nádraží Veleslavín (Line A); this route takes about 20 minutes. Either way, you'll be let off at an intersection across from the memorial itself.

By car, Lidice is an easy 30-minute journey. From the Dejvice area, follow Evropská třída out of Prague past the airport, then continue west on D7 until you see the well-marked memorial, with a parking lot, beside the highway. If you're driving, it's ideal to combine this with a trip to Terezín, about 30 km (18 miles) farther along in the same direction from Prague.

Sights

★ **Památník Lidice** (*Lidice Memorial*)
HISTORIC SIGHT | There is an eerie silence at Lidice. The lovely green rolling hills, small pond, babbling brook, and groves of trees are typical of the Czech countryside, but somehow the events that happened here remain in the air. It's

incredibly moving to walk around the empty area, constantly reminding yourself that this was a thriving village before the Nazis effectively erased it from the map.

You'll first enter the colonnade that houses a small museum. Inside you're introduced, through a series of films and photographs, to the original inhabitants of the city. German documentation from the time describes the horror of the mass murder in a disturbingly straightforward fashion. From here, the grounds of the memorial are free to wander, or you can secure an English-speaking guide to escort you around the entire area for 500 Kč (book in advance through the website).

The most visited and evocative sight in Lidice is the Monument to Child Victims of War. This life-size sculpture of the 82 children gassed by the Nazis is haunting in its detail, particularly the delicate facial expressions. Sculptor Marie Uchytilová dedicated two decades of her life to the project. On the opposite side of the path is a stark cross, which marks the place where the men were executed.

Walk to the end of the field to see the former location of the town's cemetery, or head back toward the entrance to a vast rose garden; the west portion of the garden is planted with light-colored roses to honor the children.

The museum entrance fee also includes access to Lidická galerie, home to a permanent exhibition of contemporary art donated by artists from around the world, and Rodinný dům č. 116, an example of the typical 1950s houses that make up the new, thriving village of Lidice. Both are around a 10-minute walk west of the rose garden. ⊠ *Tokajická 152, Lidice* ☎ *312–253–088* ⊕ *www.lidice-memorial. cz* ⊠ *150 Kč, guided tour (in English) 500 Kč.*

Litomyšl

160 km (100 miles) east of Prague.

This small Eastern Bohemian city is renowned for its picture-perfect, UNESCO-listed arcade castle. It also has one of the country's prettiest town squares, as well as the annual summer opera festival **Smetanova Litomyšl** (⊕ *www.smetanovalitomysl.cz*), named for renowned composer and local boy Bedřich Smetana.

GETTING HERE

It's possible to get from Prague to Litomyšl with public transport, but it's a little complicated. You'll need to take a *rychlík* (fast train) from Prague's main station to Choceň (about 1½ hours), then switch to a local bus (28 or 34, about 30 minutes). The whole journey will cost around 225 Kč and take just over two hours.

For drivers, it's also a little complicated. Take the E67 east, then turn off at junction 84 (signed to Pardubice). You'll join Route 35 towards Časy, then switch to Route 36 to Holice, before rejoining Route 35 all the way into Litomyšl. The journey takes around two hours on a clear day.

Sights

★ **Státní zámek Litomyšl** (*Litomyšl Castle*) **CASTLE/PALACE** | Built in 1568, this towering Renaissance château is a rare example of the "arcade" castle style in northern Europe. As you approach, the white-walled exterior appears to be made from thousands of bricks, but on closer inspection, it becomes clear the pattern has been achieved through intricate *sgraffito*. Each "brick" is etched into the plaster and has its own design, often incorporating imagery from the Old Testament or from classical mythology. Head into the courtyard to find even grander and more elaborate wall frescoes. While the exterior has remained largely unchanged for the last 450 years, the interior has a number of high baroque architectural additions. To see them, two guided tours are available: the first takes in a set of 12 castle rooms plus the perfectly preserved 18th-century baroque theater, complete with original stage machinery and decorations; the second takes in another set of 12 rooms as well as the elegant, vaulted castle chapel. Each tour lasts just 50 minutes, but if you have time for only one, choose the first. Tours are in Czech, but an English transcript is provided. It's also possible to visit the castle cellars—home to a permanent exhibition of contemporary sculptures by Olbram Zoubek—for a wine tasting and to stroll around the pretty castle gardens. ⊠ *Jiráskova 93* ☎ *461–615–067* ⊕ *www.zamek-litomysl. cz* 🎫 *Tours 190 Kč each* ☾ *Closed Mon. and Nov.–Mar.*

Mělník

40 km (23 miles) north of Prague.

This pretty town, on the confluence of the Vltava and Elbe Rivers, is the closest place to Prague to go for homegrown Czech wine. Every autumn, usually in late September, the town celebrates what is likely the region's best Vinobraní, an autumn festival held when barrels of young, still fermenting wine, called *burčak*, are tapped. If you happen to come at this time, look for the rare red-wine version. Even outside of wine season, Mělník has plenty of reasons to visit, with a historic center featuring a hilltop château, a baroque church with a bone-filled crypt, and a hidden underground network.

GETTING HERE
The best way from Prague to Mělník is by bus. Take bus 400 from Střížkov on Metro Line C (red), which takes around 30 minutes, or bus 369 from Ládví (one

stop closer to the center on Metro Line C), which takes around 45 minutes. Either way, tickets cost 60 Kč and can be bought from the driver. You'll be dropped off at the bottom of the hill, and it's a short, signposted walk up to the town center with all the sights. If you're coming by car, take Highway 9 from Prague's northern tip, which heads all the way to Mělník. Park on the small streets just off the main square (head in the direction of the towers to find it).

In the summer, an all-day boat trip along the Vltava River is a lovely option. Check out Prague Steamboat Company's website for sailing times.

BOAT TRAVEL Prague Steamboat Company. ⊠ *Rašínovo nábř., Staré Mesto* ☎ *734–761–003* ⊕ *www.praguesteamboats. com.*

VISITOR INFORMATION
CONTACTS Turistické informační centrum Mělník. (*Tourist Information Center Mělník*) ⊠ *Legionářů 51, Mělník* ☎ *602–679–552* ⊕ *ticmelnik.cz.*

Sights

Chrám sv. Petra a Pavla (*Church of Sts. Peter and Paul*)
CHURCH | With origins dating back around 1,000 years, this is one of the oldest churches in Bohemia, with a dramatic Gothic interior. But it's what lies beneath, and what rises above, that's really of interest. Below the church is a crypt with an ossuary, containing the skeletal remains of 10,000 to 15,000 people. Like a smaller-scale version of Kostnice Sedlec in Kutná Hora (but without the tourist hordes), bones and skulls are arranged into various sculptures, including an anchor, a cross, and a heart to symbolize hope, faith, and love. The remains date from between the 13th and 18th centuries, and have been used by academics to learn about diseases in medieval Europe.

The town of Mělník lies on a high ridge overlooking the junction of Bohemia's two greatest rivers, the Labe and the Vltava.

Above the church soars the 127-foot tower. Climb to the top, through rooms of exposed stone walls and wooden beams, past the three 15th-century bells and the intricate clock mechanism, and you'll emerge onto an open-air platform. From here, you can enjoy the best panorama in Mělník, with views of the town in one direction and vistas of the rivers, vineyards, and rolling hills in the other.

If you are visiting outside of summer, email to arrange access to the crypt and tower. ⊠ Na Vyhlídce, Mělník ☎ 731–518–750 ✉ farnost.melnik@dltm.cz ⊕ www.farnostmelnik.cz 🎫 Church free, ossuary 40 Kč, tower 50 Kč ⊙ Closed Mon. Closed Nov.–Mar. except by appointment.

★ **Mělnické podzemí** (*Underground Mělník*)
OTHER ATTRACTION | Under the historic center of Mělník lies a secret: a network of underground passages leading to a medieval well. Half-hour guided tours from the Tourist Information Center take you down into the tunnels, which were

dug out of the sandstone rock in the 13th and 14th centuries and used as storage rooms, wine cellars, and shelters during times of war. After a short walk, you'll come to the beautiful and unique medieval well. At 184 feet deep and 15 feet wide, it's the largest well in the Czech Republic—yet from above ground in the main square, you wouldn't even know it exists. ⊠ Turistické informační centrum Mělník, Legionářů 51, Mělník ☎ 602–679–552 ⊕ ticmelnik.cz 🎫 60 Kč.

Zámek Mělník (*Mělník Château*)
CASTLE/PALACE | The town's castle may be petite but it hovers grandly over the confluence of the Labe (Elbe) and Vltava Rivers. On entering, the courtyard's three dominant architectural styles jump out at you, reflecting alterations to the castle over the years. On the north side, note the typical arcaded Renaissance balconies, decorated with *sgraffiti*. To the west, a Gothic touch is still easy to make out. The southern wing is clearly baroque (although also decorated with arcades).

Inside the castle, you can walk through 10 ornate rooms filled with paintings, furniture, and porcelain belonging to the old aristocratic Lobkowicz clan, as well as a vestry chapel. In particular, look out for the Big Hall, which is decorated with 17th-century European maps and *vedute* (views) of cities including London, Paris, and Madrid.

Day-tripping wine lovers can also tour the wine cellars under the castle and book a wine tasting. The town is known best for its special Ludmila wines made from local grapes. As the locals tell it, Emperor Charles IV was responsible for bringing wine production to the area. Having a good eye for favorable growing conditions, he encouraged vintners from Burgundy to come here and plant their vines.

The castle also has a good restaurant, looking out on the vineyards, river, and fields beyond, as well as a café and wine bar. ⊠ *Svatováclavská 16, Mělník* ☎ *315–622–121* ⊕ *www.lobkowicz-melnik.cz* ⊠ *Castle 110 Kč, wine cellar tour 50 Kč, wine tasting from 140 Kč.*

🍴 Restaurants

Němý Medvěd

$$ | BURGER | Although billing itself primarily as a microbrewery and beer bar, this lovely cellar restaurant also serves the city's best burgers. Choose your beer (there are usually eight options on tap: a mix of home brews and beers from other Czech breweries), then dive into the extensive burger menu, including delicious vegetarian and vegan options. **Known for:** atmospheric cellar with vaulted ceilings; great selection of Czech beers; monster 21-oz. "Grizzly Daddy Burger". $ *Average main: Kč250* ⊠ *Nám. Míru 27, Mělník* ☎ *773–898–122* ⊕ *www.nemymedved.cz.*

Terezín

48 km (30 miles) northwest of Prague.

Just the word "Terezín" (Theresienstadt in German) immediately recalls the horrors of the Jewish Holocaust for Czechs. Originally built as a military city in the 18th century, Nazis quickly saw its potential and removed the 7,000 original inhabitants to turn the city into a Jewish ghetto and the fortress into a prison. Terezín was the main Nazi concentration camp in Bohemia, but it wasn't designed as a death camp, even though in the end more than 38,000 people died in either the ghetto or the prison. The city was supposed to be a "model" Jewish settlement, part of a humane façade the Nazis presented to the Red Cross in 1944.

GETTING HERE

There's no train service directly to Terezín. Several buses (Bus Line no. 550909) leave the Nádraží Holešovice station daily, and weekends offer a bit more choice. The trip lasts an hour and typically costs 105 Kč each way.

If you're driving, take the E55 north out of Prague (this is the main highway going to Dresden and Berlin) and head toward Lovosice. You can either take Exit 35 at Doksany and follow the country road straight to Terezín or continue to Lovosice, and from there turn right; the road leads directly into Terezín. There's a large parking lot next to the Malá Pevnost. The trip takes about 50 minutes.

VISITOR INFORMATION

CONTACTS Terezín Tourist Information. ⊠ *Dukel. hrdinů 43, Terezín* ☎ *775–711–881* ⊕ *www.terezin.cz.*

👁 Sights

Památník Terezín – Magdeburská kasárna (*Terezín Memorial – Magdeburg Barracks*)

HISTORY MUSEUM | Under the Nazis, this unassuming building was primarily used for administration offices, but today it is a fascinating and important education facility. There's an excellent re-creation of how a former dormitory would have looked, plus exhibits detailing the arts in Terezín. Inspiring displays show how people in the ghetto continued to hold literary, musical, theatrical, and artistic happenings. ✉ *Tyršova 204, Terezín* ☎ *416–782–225* ⊕ *www.pamatnik-terezin.cz* 🎫 *210 Kč (incl. one of Small Fortress or Ghetto Museum), 260 Kč (incl. both).*

★ **Památník Terezín – Malá pevnost**
(*Terezín Memorial – Small Fortress*)
HISTORIC SIGHT | The most powerful aspect of Terezín is that you don't need much imagination to visualize how it looked under Nazi rule. When it was a Jewish ghetto, more than 59,000 people were crammed into this camp. Terezín was actually an exception among the many Nazi concentration camps in Central Europe. The Germans, for a time, used it as a model city in order to deflect international criticism of Nazi policy toward the Jews. In the early years of the war—until as late as 1944—detainees had a semblance of a normal life, with limited self-rule, schools, a theater, and even a library. (Pictures drawn by the children at Terezín are on display in Prague's Jewish Museum.) As the Nazi war effort soured, the conditions for the people in Terezín worsened. Transports to Auschwitz and other death camps were increased to several times a week, and eventually 87,000 Jews were murdered in this way. Another 35,000 died from starvation or disease.

The enormity of Terezín's role in history is most starkly illustrated at this former military fortress. From 1940 to 1945, it functioned as a jail, mainly for political prisoners and others resisting the German occupation, holding them in abject conditions. Around 30,000 prisoners came through here during the war. A tour through the fortress is chilling; you'll first visit the administrative area, where new prisoners were brought, and then glimpse their cells, crudely furnished with stone floors and long wooden beds. Not much has been done to spruce up the place for visitors, leaving the original atmosphere intact. As a military prison, 150 people could be held in the cells; under the Nazis, it was typical to have 1,500 prisoners held in the same space. There was no gas chamber here, but the appalling hygienic conditions led to many deaths, and about 300 prisoners were executed. Many of the juxtapositions are deeply cruel, such as the swimming pools for guards and their families, which prisoners would pass on their way to their execution.

Those who did not die in detention were shipped off to other concentration camps. Above the entrance to the main courtyard stands the horribly false motto "Arbeit macht Frei" (Work Brings Freedom). At the far end of the fortress, opposite the main entrance, is the special wing built by the Nazis when space became tight. These windowless cells display a brutal captivity. ✉ *Principova alej 304, Terezín* ☎ *416–782–225* ⊕ *www.pamatnik-terezin.cz* 🎫 *210 Kč (incl. Magdeburg Barracks); 260 Kč (also incl. Ghetto Museum)* 🕑 *Crematorium closed Sat.*

Památník Terezín – Muzeum ghetta (*Terezín Memorial – Ghetto Museum*)
HISTORY MUSEUM | Told in words and pictures, the town's horrific story is depicted at the Museum of the Terezín Ghetto, just off the central park in town. A short documentary is also shown in many languages. Tell the staff that you speak English; they'll let you roam the building and flag you down when the next English-language video is being shown. ✉ *Komenského 148, Terezín* ☎ *416–782–225* ⊕ *www.pamatnik-terezin.cz* 🎫 *210 Kč (incl. Magdeburg Barracks); 260 Kč (also incl. Small Fortress).*

🍴 Restaurants

Terezín has very little in the way of services for visitors. There are a couple of depressing haunts, serving mostly inedible pub standards from menus run off on mimeograph machines. Duck out of town to nearby Litoměřice down the road about 2 km (1 mile). Buses run regularly from the main square, and it's barely a five-minute ride. After the heavy atmosphere of Terezín, it's refreshing to walk down the tree-lined main street between colorful buildings bustling with shops and people.

Radniční Sklípek

$$ | CZECH | This spot is a local favorite, and it's easy to see why. Here the setting, a Gothic cellar with arched ceilings, is as pleasant as the food. **Known for:** deliciously hearty Czech food; summer terrace on lovely city square; occasional wine-tasting events. $ *Average main: Kč275* ⊠ *Mírové nám. 12, Litomerice* ☎ *731–422–013* ⊕ *www.radnicni-sklipek.cz.*

Czech Switzerland

110 km (68 miles) northwest of Prague.

Czech Switzerland, also known as Bohemian Switzerland, is a picturesque region with towering sandstone cliffs, fairy-tale landscapes, quaint villages, and excellent hiking and biking opportunities, all just 90 minutes' drive from Prague. It lies on the Czech side of the Elbe Sandstone Mountains north of Děčín on both sides of the Elbe River. Confusingly, you are not in Switzerland; the name was inspired by the Swiss artists Adrian Zingg and Anton Graff, who were reminded of their homeland by the geography of northern Bohemia. While you cannot cross into Switzerland here, you may find yourself in Narnia—several scenes of *The Chronicles of Narnia: The Lion, the Witch and the Wardrobe* were filmed at the Pravčická Archway here.

GETTING HERE

Czech Switzerland may seem like a bit of a hike from Prague, but it can be done in a day with some forward planning. Take the train to Děčín, which takes just more than 90 minutes (and costs just under 200 Kč), followed by the local bus to Hřensko, the nearest village, which takes another 35 minutes or so. The driver, or the tourists getting off, will let you know where the best stop is for the hike to Pravčická Archway. If you're driving, head north on the E55 to Ústí nad Labem, then switch to Route 62. There are plenty of paid parking lots in Hřensko.

👁 Sights

★ **Pravčická Brána** (*Pravčická Archway*)
NATURE SIGHT | The largest natural rock bridge in Europe, Pravčická Archway is the symbol of the gorgeous national park that is Czech Switzerland, which sits on the border with Germany. To reach the archway, you can either start walking from Hřensko (follow the red hiking route) or take a local bus to a stop called Tři Prameny. From here, it's a lovely and atmospheric walk up through the forest to reach the rock formation, which comes complete with a museum and restaurant called Falcon's Nest—supplies are brought in via pulley. This being the Czech Republic, there's also a pub where you can order fine beer in the shadow of the bridge itself. For an entrance fee of 95 Kč, you can scramble around nearby rock formations, which have a similarly alien appeal, for a better vantage point.

A series of gentle, well-marked hikes on pretty forest trails and mossy gorges will take you on a circular route back, ending up in Hřensko. The highlight of these trails is being punted along the river—when the paths run out—in a precarious boat with a ferryman who tells you (in German and Czech and hand gestures) how the rocks over your head look like different animals and monsters. Each boat trip costs around 50 Kč. ✉ *Hrensko* ⊕ *www.pbrana.cz* 📧 *95 Kč* ☾ *Closed weekdays Nov.–Mar.*

Krkonoše

129 km (80 miles) northeast of Prague.

Known as the Giant Mountains, this lofty range of craggy peaks stretches across the Czech Republic–Poland border, with dedicated national parks on both sides. The Czech side is immensely popular with locals in the winter months for its array of pristine ski slopes, and from spring to autumn for its well-marked hiking and mountain biking trails. The biggest draw of all is Sněžka, the country's highest point at 5,259 feet (1,603 meters). But that's just one of dozens of stunning peaks to explore here, so strap on your hiking boots or jump on your bike to discover a world of gentle river valleys, flower-filled meadows, tumbling waterfalls, dense green forests, and unforgettable mountain vistas.

GETTING HERE

The edge of Krkonoše National Park is around a two-hour drive from Prague, so it's possible to start early and come for a day's hiking. Alternatively, you can stay in a resort town for a night or two and really lose yourself in the mountains. Either way, most people use three main towns as their base for exploring the park: quiet and green Harrachov in the west, charming and characterful Špindlerův Mlýn in the center, and bustling but well-located Pec pod Sněžkou in the east (right at the foot of Sněžka).

Buses to Krkonoše leave from Prague's Černý Most station, at the eastern end of Metro Line B (yellow). It's a little over two hours to Harrachov (FlixBus), 2.5 hours to Špindlerův Mlýn (Arriva bus 690290), and about three hours to Pec pod Sněžkou (Arriva bus 690250).

By car, start by heading northeast on the D10 from Prague. For the central and eastern parts of the park (including Sněžka), you will continue to Mladá Boleslav, then switch to Route 16 heading northeast. Continue on Routes 293/295 for Špindlerův Mlýn or Routes 325/14/296 for Pec pod Sněžkou. For the western edge of the park, stay on the D10 until Turnov, at which point you'll "turnov" to Route 10 all the way up to Harrachov.

 Sights

Sněžka

MOUNTAIN | Straddling the border between the Czech Republic and Poland—with one side belonging to each country—Sněžka is by far the most popular mountain ascent in Krkonoše. Luckily, the routes are long enough for the hiking groups to be spread out, so it rarely feels like you're part of a big crowd. Most visitors from the Czech side start and end in the resort town of Pec pod Sněžkou: a strenuous hike leads up through blueberry-filled forests and across gentle waterfalls to the summit, where you can stop to soak up the sweeping panoramic views with a cold beer (from the bistro or cafe), before heading back down the other side of the mountain and across the slopes of Růžová hora into town. The route is around 8.5 miles (13.5 km) altogether, so plan for around six hours including stops. For non-hikers, there's also a cable car running from Pec up to the summit; it takes around 15 minutes and costs 330 Kč each way (620 Kč return) in peak season.

Chapter 12

SOUTHERN BOHEMIA

Updated by
Raymond Johnston

 Sights
★★★★★

 Restaurants
★★★☆☆

 Hotels
★★★★☆

 Shopping
★★☆☆☆

 Nightlife
★★☆☆☆

WELCOME TO SOUTHERN BOHEMIA

TOP REASONS TO GO

★ **Sense the enchantment:** Feel like a storybook character strolling through Český Krumlov.

★ **Loop around the streets:** Get lost among the tiny streets of Tábor.

★ **Take the bike lane to lunch:** Bike around and eat the fresh carp caught from the fishponds of Třeboň.

★ **Go for baroque:** Experience rustic baroque with a visit to the 19th-century living-museum village of Holašovice.

★ **Sip the suds:** Drink the local brew in České Budějovice, Český Krumlov, or Třeboň.

Southern Bohemia is one of the most popular regions in the Czech Republic. Chock-full of castles and pretty cities with well-preserved squares, it's a favorite weekend getaway for many Prague locals. Well-marked hiking and biking trails encourage lots of sporty times, and it's easy for visitors to take part, since even some of the train stations rent bicycles. The towns themselves are active, too, and many hold a variety of festivals throughout the year.

Being so close to Prague, several of these cities can be done in a day-trip; but to get a true flavor of the town and its inhabitants, it's worth your time to stay over or spend a couple of days jumping between a few of the outer areas. The attractiveness of the landscape combined with cultural pursuits makes Southern Bohemia an amazing place to explore.

1 Český Krumlov. A fanciful city with a stunning castle and gardens: Český Krumlov is *the* must-see in Southern Bohemia.

2 Tábor. With streets designed to thwart invading armies, Tábor will lose you in its beauty and friendliness.

3 **Písek.** Strung along the river, the city with the oldest Gothic bridge in the country is also home to some great museums.

4 **Třeboň.** The spas of Southern Bohemia can be found in Třeboň. Peat-moss bath, anyone?

5 **Jindřichův Hradec.** Authentic and attractive, Jindřichův Hradec is the perfect example of a true Southern Bohemian town: interesting castle, beautiful architecture, and real people.

6 **Hluboká nad Vltavou.** A castle to die for. The fairy-tale hulk of turreted white can be seen for miles around.

7 **České Budějovice.** Southern Bohemia's largest city, with a beautiful medieval square and lots of outdoor activities.

Southern Bohemia calls itself the "pearl of the Czech Republic," and it's not just a clever nickname. The richness and beauty of this corner of the country bordering Germany and Austria are undisputable.

The natural landscape is lovely—soft rolling hills crisscrossed with rivers and dotted with ponds mark most of the territory—and the Šumava Mountains to the southwest are a popular ski destination. Coming from Prague, you'll cross the border somewhere north of Tábor; heading east, the indiscernible crossing to Moravia comes near to Telč. Forestry and fishing make up most of the area's important industry, with tourism and beer brewing more fun runners-up.

The history of the cities is intertwined with many an aristocratic name. The Habsburgs, Rosenbergs, and Schwarzenbergs all had a large influence on the region, and their nobility is reflected in the area's many castles and beautifully preserved historic squares. The 15th century saw the territory wrapped up in the religious wars sparked by Jan Hus, whose reformist ways angered the Catholic Church and eventually led to his martyrdom. Evidence of the Hussite Wars in the mid-1400s is visible in Tábor.

Český Krumlov is the one must-see destination and often the only stop for visitors, which means huge crowds on summer weekends. The castle here rivals any monument in Prague.

Planning

When to Go

Southern Bohemia is a nature lover's paradise, and in nice weather it seems that the whole country heads here for cycling and hiking trips. Most of the main attractions are closed November through March, as well as Monday year-round, so winter is quiet but no less lovely in its snowy way. Many towns host weekend Christmas markets, so December is a particularly pretty time. Note: roads get congested with weekenders on Friday and Sunday.

Getting Here

Trains from Prague normally depart from the Hlavní nádraží main station, while buses leave from either the main Florenc station or the southern Roztyly station, accessible from a Metro stop on Line C (red). When exploring your transport options, look into private bus lines like RegioJet (formerly called Student Agency, but its services are not just for students). It offers more direct routes, plus free hot drinks and videos on board. Tickets must be purchased ahead of time; the company has a window at the Florenc station.

Guided Tours to Southern Bohemia

Guided bus tours are available from several companies covering several of the destinations in Southern Bohemia. Most need to be booked at least a day in advance. These are only two of many organizers.

Čedok

BUS TOURS | The country's original tour operator offers a variety of longer trips through the region. Experiences include Český Krumlov, a spa visit in Třeboň, and combinations of other cities and even regions. ⊠ *Brno* ⊕ *www.cedok.com.*

Martin Tours

GUIDED TOURS | Information can be found at the company's booths at Staroměstské náměstí (Old Town Square) and Republiky náměstí. It offers a bus tour to Český Krumlov. ⊠ *Staré Mesto* ⊕ *www. martintour.cz.*

Restaurants and Hotels

Outside of Prague, prices for food and hotels are lower, but service—especially in functional English—sometimes lags behind. With Austria so close, you are much more likely to find German-language menus in restaurants and German-speaking staff in both restaurants and hotels.

Restaurant and hotel reviews have been shortened. For full information, visit Fodors.com.

What It Costs in Koruny

	$	$$	$$$	$$$$
RESTAURANTS				
	under 150 Kč	150 Kč–350 Kč	351 Kč–500 Kč	over 500 Kč
HOTELS				
	under 2,200 Kč	2,200 Kč–4,000 Kč	4,001 Kč–6,500 Kč	over 6,500 Kč

Český Krumlov

48 km (29 miles) southwest of Třeboň; 186 km (112 miles) south of Prague.

It's rare that a place not only lives up to its hype but exceeds it. Český Krumlov, the official residence of the Rožmberk (Rosenberg) family for some 300 years, is such a place. It's the only must-see in Southern Bohemia, with a storybook landscape so perfect it resembles a movie set. Hordes of other tourists pass through, but if you stay overnight you can experience the city after the tour buses have departed, and in the evening when quiet descends, the town is twice as spellbinding.

Český Krumlov's lovely looks can be put down to a castle and a river. Hrad Český Krumlov (Český Krumlov Castle) is one of the most gorgeous in the country, perched on a hill and watching over its quaint village with the Vltava River doing its picturesque winding best. The castle area offers plenty of sightseeing, and the extensive gardens are worth an hour or two. Down in the town, the medieval streets are beyond charming.

As in the rest of Southern Bohemia, outdoor activities are plentiful here. Check with the local tourist information office about places to rent bikes or rafts, or pick up an area hiking map.

12

Southern Bohemia ČESKÝ KRUMLOV

GETTING HERE

A direct bus to Český Krumlov leaves Prague from both the Florenc and the Na Knížecí stations. The trip lasts a hair under three hours, and costs 215 Kč. There's no direct train; with a change at České Budějovice, a train trip clocks in at usually more than three hours and costs around 189 Kč. Note that the train station is a 20-minute hike from the main square, while the bus station is much closer. Your best choice would be to purchase a bus ticket at least a day or two before travel; Český Krumlov is a popular destination.

Car travel from Prague is fairly straightforward and takes three hours. Simply follow the directions to České Budějovice, and once there follow the signs to Český Krumlov. When you arrive in Český Krumlov you'll be confronted by a confusing array of public parking areas, with no indication of how close the parking lot is to the Old Town. One safe bet is to use Parking Lot No. 2, which, if you follow the tiny lanes as far as they go, will bring you to just behind the town brewery and an easy 10-minute walk from the main square.

TIMING

Wintertime can be lonely in Český Krumlov, and most of the sites are closed, including the castle. On the flip side, avoid weekends in the summer; hordes of tourists, both Czech and German, flood the streets. Also, midday when the tour buses arrive can be a bit overwhelming. The city holds a Renaissance festival called the Five-Petaled Rose Celebration every June; an Early Music Festival and an International Music Festival in July; an Autumn Fair at the end of September; and a number of holiday events in December.

VISITOR INFORMATION

Český Krumlov's tourist information office is on the main square. Well versed and extremely helpful, the staff can assist you in everything from what to see to where to go. They can recommend restaurants and hotels as well as book tickets and assist with bus and train schedules, or even boat and bike travel.

The Vltava travel agency is a solid bet if you're considering outdoor activities. It will rent boats and bikes as well as arrange excursions.

A discount pass called **Český Krumlov Card** is available at information centers and offers reduced admission to several attractions.

INFORMATION Infocentrum Český Krumlov. ✉ Nám. Svornosti 2, Český Krumlov ☎ 380–704–622 ⊕ www.ckrumlov.cz. **Vltava.** ✉ Hradební 60, Český Krumlov ☎ 380–711–988 ⊕ www.ckvltava.cz.

 ## Sights

Egon Schiele Center

OTHER MUSEUM | A large and rambling former brewery now showcases the work of Austrian painter Egon Schiele, along with other modern and contemporary Czech and European artists. The Renaissance building, built in three phases in the early 1600s, is a wonder, with soaring ceilings in some places and wooden-beamed rooms in others. Schiele often painted landscapes of Český Krumlov from the castle's bridge. The museum does close unexpectedly on occasion in winter but is one of the only sites in town normally open year-round. ✉ Široká 71, Český Krumlov ☎ 380–704–011 ⊕ www.schieleartcentrum.cz ⬚ 200 Kč; discount with Český Krumlov Card ⊘ Closed Mon.

Hotel Růže

HOTEL | Gorgeous sgraffiti façades decorate this former Jesuit school, now the Hotel Růže. Abundant Renaissance flourishes point to the fact that the city used to be on the Bavarian-Italian trade route. Be sure to visit the parking area (really!); the view is perfect. ✉ Horní 154, Český Krumlov ⊕ www.hotelruze.cz.

★ **Hrad Český Krumlov** (*Český Krumlov Castle*)

CASTLE/PALACE | FAMILY | Like any good protective fortress, the castle is visible from a distance, but you may wonder how to get there. From the main square, take Radniční ulice across the river and head up the staircase on your left from Latrán ulice. (Alternatively, you can continue on Latrán and enter via the main gateway, also on your left.) You'll first come across the oldest part of the castle, a round 13th-century **tower** renovated in the 16th century to look something like a minaret, with its delicately arcaded Renaissance balcony. Part of the old border fortifications, the tower guarded Bohemian frontiers from the threat of Austrian incursion. It's now repainted with an educated guess of its Renaissance appearance, since the original designs have long been lost. From dungeon to bells, its inner secrets can be seen climbing the interior staircase. Go ahead and climb to the top; you'll be rewarded with a view of the castle grounds and across the countryside.

Next up is the moat, fearlessly protected by a pair of brown bears—truthfully not really much help in defending the castle; their moods range from playful to lethargic. But bears have been residents of this moat since 1707. In season, the castle rooms are open to the public. Crossing the bridge, you enter the second courtyard, which contains the ticket office. The Route 1 tour will parade you past the castle chapel, baroque suite, and Renaissance rooms. The highlights here are the 18th-century frescoes in the delightful **Maškarní sál** (Masquerade Hall). Route 2 takes you through the portrait gallery and the seigneurial apartments of the Schwarzenbergs, who owned the castle until the Gestapo seized it in 1940. (The castle became state property in 1947.) In summer you can visit the Lapidarium, which includes statues removed from the castle for protection, and the dungeon.

A succession of owners all had the same thing in mind: upgrade the castle a bit more opulently than before. Vilém von Rožmberk oversaw a major refurbishment of the castle, adding buildings, heightening the tower, and adding rich decorations—generally making the place suitable for one of the grandest Bohemians of the day. The castle passed out of the Rožmberks' hands, however, when Vilém's brother and last of the line, the dissolute Petr Vok, sold both castle and town to Emperor Rudolf II in 1602 to pay off his debts. Under the succeeding Eggenbergs and Schwarzenbergs the castle continued to be transformed into an opulent palace. The Eggenbergs' prime addition was a **theater,** which was begun in the 1680s and completed in 1766 by Josef Adam of Schwarzenberg. Much of the theater and its accoutrements—sets, props, costumes, stage machinery—survive intact as a rare working display of period stagecraft. Theater buffs will appreciate a tour, and tickets should be reserved in advance.

Continuing along outside, the third courtyard bears some beautiful Renaissance frescoes, while the fourth contains the Upper Castle, whose rooms can be visited on the tours. From here you'll arrive at a wonderfully romantic elevated passageway with spectacular views of the huddled houses of the Old Town. The Austrian expressionist painter Egon Schiele often stayed in Český Krumlov in the early 1900s and liked to paint this particular view over the river; he titled his Krumlov series *Dead City.* The middle level here is the **most Na plášti** (Cloaked Bridge), a massive construction spanning a deep ravine. Below the passageway are three levels of high arches, looking like a particularly elaborate Roman viaduct. At the end of the passageway you come to the theater, then to the nicely appointed **castle garden** dating from the 17th century. A cascade fountain, groomed walking paths, flower beds, and manicured lawns are a restful delight. The famed open-air

Český Krumlov

Vltava

Český Krumlov
Castle Tower

Náměstí
Svornosti

Vltava

0   300 feet

0   100 m

KEY

- **1** Sights
- **1** Restaurants
- **1** Hotels
- **i** Tourist Information

Revolving Theater is here, as is the **Musical Pavilion**. If you continue walking away from the castle, the park grows a bit wilder and quieter. Unlike the castle, the courtyards and passageways are open to the public year-round.

■ **TIP→ If visiting between October and April, check the website for detailed opening hours, as these vary for different parts of the castle and for different tours.** ⊠ *Zámek 59, Český Krumlov* ☎ *380–704–721* ⊕ *www.castle.ckrumlov.cz* ✉ *Castle tours (in English) from 210 Kč, theater tour (in English) 280 Kč, castle museum and tower 180 Kč (discount only on museum and tower with Český Krumlov Card), garden free* ☉ *Garden closed and no tours Nov.–Mar.*

Kostel sv. Víta (*Church of St. Vitus*)
RELIGIOUS BUILDING | This neo-Gothic church with its octagonal tower provides a nice contrast with the castle's older tower across the river. Step inside to see the elaborate baptismal font and frescoes. Much reconstruction took place in the 17th and 18th centuries but some earlier features remain; the Gothic entrance portal dates to 1410. ⊠ *Kostelní ul., Český Krumlov* ⊕ *www.farnostck. bcb.cz* ✉ *Free.*

Museum Fotoatelier Seidel (*Seidel Photographic Studio Museum*)
OTHER MUSEUM | Head across the other side of the river from the castle and explore a more lived-in side of the city. This refurbished home used to belong to photographer Josef Seidel and is now a museum dedicated to his work and the history of photography. The exhibit is a fascinating mix of home and workplace, with period furnishings plus a photographic studio. The building itself is lovely and includes a picturesque garden, and photography lovers will enjoy the historic camera collection plus samples of Seidel's work. ⊠ *Linecká 272, Český Krumlov* ☎ *380–712–354* ⊕ *www.seidel. cz* ✉ *140 Kč; discount with Český Krumlov Card* ☉ *Closed Mon. Oct.–Mar.*

Náměstí Svornosti (*Unity Square*)
PLAZA/SQUARE | A little oddly shaped, yes, but a "square" nonetheless; Náměstí Svornosti should be home base for your explorations. Pick a street and head off into the tiny alleys that fan out in all directions. There's no real sense in "planning" your route, simply choose a direction and go—you'll end up where you started eventually. Each turn seems to bring a new charming vista, and cute buildings and shops will amuse and keep shutterbugs busy. Don't forget to look up in the direction of the castle every once in a while; it pokes through in some amazing places. The actual square has a couple of notable buildings, including the town hall with its Renaissance friezes and Gothic arcades. ⊠ *Český Krumlov.*

Regionální muzeum (*Regional Museum*)
HISTORY MUSEUM | From the main square, a street called Horní ulice leads off toward the regional museum. A quick visit gets you acquainted with the history of the region from prehistoric times. A ceramic model of the city is one of the highlights. ⊠ *Horní 152, Český Krumlov* ☎ *380–711–674* ⊕ *www.muzeumck.cz* ✉ *60 Kč; discount with Český Krumlov Card.*

 Restaurants

★ **Na louži**
$$ | CZECH | Czech comfort food is served up every day and every night at Na louži. Lovingly preserved wood furniture and paneling lend a traditional touch to this warm, inviting, family-run pub. **Known for:** hearty traditional food; lovely wood-paneled interior; occasionally brusque service. ⑤ *Average main: Kč300* ⊠ *Kájovská 66, Český Krumlov* ☎ *380–711–280* ⊕ *www.nalouzi.cz* ⊟ *No credit cards.*

🛏 **Hotels**

It seems you can't walk two blocks in Český Krumlov without stumbling over a pension or place offering private rooms.

Spooky Side Trip

About 20 km (12 miles) south of Český Krumlov, the sprawling Hrad Rožmberk (Rosenberg Castle) overlooks the Vltava River. Inside, on the main tour, you'll see a mix of romantic and Renaissance interiors; portraits of crusaders; and the Rosenberg Hall, dedicated to the family's history. The second route shows the apartments of aristocrats. The English Tower is a 200-step climb and rewards with beautiful vistas of the countryside. English-language tours on Routes 1 and 2 are available for groups only. The basement has a Museum of Capital Justice, but the information is only in Czech. Buses run from Český Krumlov's main depot but are infrequent on weekends. Legend has it that the ghost of a White Lady appears from time to time. ⊕ *www.hrad-rozmberk.cz/en*

Even with this plethora, you'll need to book ahead May through September, when it's high season. Prices can be on a level with some Prague hotels and definitely more expensive than in neighboring cities.

Bellevue

$$ | **HOTEL** | The façade of a 16th-century bakery gives way to a modern hotel with all the standard accessories. **Pros:** close to the castle; sauna and massage service; good restaurant and wine cellar. **Cons:** small breakfast room; rooms a bit cramped; no air conditioning because it is a historical building. ⑤ *Rooms from: Kč3690* ⊠ *Latrán 77, Český Krumlov* ☎ *380–720–177* ⊕ *www.bellevuehotelkrumlov.cz* ⇨ *65 rooms* ⏏⧫️ *Free Breakfast.*

Hotel Dvořák

$$ | **HOTEL** | Wonderful views of the castle and river are the main selling points of this centrally located and quaint hotel. **Pros:** nice views; smack-dab-central location; large rooms. **Cons:** old-fashioned interior design; elevator does not reach fifth floor; noise from street performers. ⑤ *Rooms from: Kč3619* ⊠ *Radniční 101, Český Krumlov* ☎ *380–711–020* ⊕ *www. hoteldvorak.com* ⇨ *22 rooms, 4 apartments* ⏏⧫️ *Free Breakfast.*

★ Hotel Růže

$$$ | **HOTEL** | Converted from a Jesuit school, this excellent, centrally located hotel with spacious rooms is a two-minute walk from the main square. **Pros:** central location; magnificent castle views; quality restaurant. **Cons:** inconsistent bed layouts; baroque decorations are a bit overdone; service doesn't always come with a smile. ⑤ *Rooms from: Kč4157* ⊠ *Horní 154, Český Krumlov* ☎ *380–772–100* ⊕ *www.hotelruze.cz* ⇨ *71 rooms* ⏏⧫️ *Free Breakfast.*

Hotýlek & Hospoda u malého Vítka

$$ | **HOTEL** | Rooms are cleverly named after Czech fairy tales, with simple wooden furniture and fittings, and the folklore spirit extends throughout this hotel located between the main square and the castle. **Pros:** whimsical spirit; great value for the money; great location and views. **Cons:** limited in-room amenities; rooms are simple and pared down; cramped bathrooms. ⑤ *Rooms from: Kč2277* ⊠ *Radniční 27, Český Krumlov* ☎ *380–711–925* ⊕ *www.vitekhotel.cz* ⇨ *20 rooms* ⏏⧫️ *Free Breakfast.*

Nightlife

Zapa Bar

BARS | A rare cocktail bar in the middle of beer country features historical arches and stone walls, as well as a large array of whiskies and other liquors. The staff is friendly and knowledgable in mixology. Some drinks feature typical Czech ingredients for those who want to try something different. ✉ *Latrán 15, Český Krumlov* ⊕ *www.zapa-bar.cz.*

Performing Arts

Český Krumlov is a hotbed of cultural activity in summer. Events range from Renaissance fairs to music festivals. Activities to note include the International Music Festival held at the castle in July and August and summer performances at the open-air Revolving Theater. Opera and theater companies from České Budějovice perform here. Tickets can be pre-booked (almost a necessity) by visiting or check with the tourist information offices in either Český Krumlov or České Budějovice. The website also has information on an app called Overtekst that allows people to follow a translation of the show's dialogue on a phone or tablet that runs an Android OS. The Český Krumlov office can also tell you about any other concerts or events happening while you are in town.

Tábor

90 km (54 miles) south of Prague.

Looking at Tábor now, it's hard to believe that this was once a counterculture utopia and fortress. Lucky for visitors a few centuries later, the town has retained all this turbulent history in its design and buildings.

In the 15th century, the town began as an encampment for religious reformers centered on the teachings of the anti-Catholic firebrand preacher Jan Hus. After Hus was burned at the stake in Constance, his followers came here by the thousands to build a society opposed to the excesses of Rome and modeled on the primitive communities of the early Christians. Tábor quickly evolved into the Hussites' symbolic and spiritual center and, along with Prague, served as the bulwark of the religious reform movement.

The 1420s in Tábor were heady days for the reformers. Private property was denounced, and the many poor who made the pilgrimage to Tábor were required to leave their possessions at the town gates. Some sects rejected the doctrine of transubstantiation (the belief that the Eucharistic elements become the body and blood of Christ), turning Holy Communion into a bawdy, secular feast of bread and wine. Other reformers considered themselves superior to Christ—who by dying had shown himself to be merely mortal.

War fever in Tábor ran high, and the town became one of the focal points of the Hussite Wars (1419–34), which pitted reformers against an array of foreign crusaders, Catholics, and noblemen. Military general Jan Žižka led the charge fairly successfully, but the Church proved to be stronger and wealthier. Many of the reformists' victories were assisted by the strategic location of Tábor, which with its hilltop position and river boundary made it virtually impregnable. And what nature didn't provide, the residents did. The town was well fortified and there was an ingenious system of underground tunnels (whether they were used to hide in or to store food is disputed). The streets were purposely laid out in a crooked and confusing manner to thwart invaders. Glimpses of this past can still be seen and make Tábor one of the more interesting places to visit.

GETTING HERE

Direct buses and trains to Tábor are available, and both take about 1½ hours. Buses from Prague leave from the Florenc station and cost about 95 Kč; trains cost about 150 Kč and depart from Hlavní nádraží station. By car, the distance is about 90 km (56 miles) and should take a little more than an hour. You'll take the E55 heading south toward České Budějovice.

TIMING

Tábor is rarely overrun with tourists, which makes it a relaxing place to see. It's a popular spot with cyclists, and summers always bring a few more people. Music festivals are held in the summer and there's also a Christmas market in December. The big event is the Tábor Meeting Days, held at the beginning of September. This fun medieval festival is incredibly popular. Crafts, music, entertainers, and food all pack into the main square; there's even a parade.

VISITOR INFORMATION

CONTACTS Tábor Tourist Information.
⊠ Žižkovo nám. 2, Tábor 🕿 381–486–230 ⊕ www.visittabor.eu.

 Sights

Hrad Kotnov (*Kotnov Castle*)
CASTLE/PALACE | Rising above the river in the distance, this castle dates to the 13th century and was part of Tábor's earliest fortifications. After a fire in the early 1600s the castle was rebuilt as a brewery. You can visit the tower, which the Hussites used for storing artillery, as well as Bechyňská brána (Bechyně Gate). This is the last city gate still standing and has been preserved in its original High Gothic style. Inside is a new permanent exhibition of the history of Tábor opened in early 2020. ⊠ Klokotská, Tábor 🕿 381–252–242 ⊕ www.husitskemuzeum.cz 🎫 Tower and gate 80 Kč ⊙ Closed Oct.–Apr.

Husitské muzeum (*Hussite Museum*)
OTHER MUSEUM | You can find out all you ever wanted to know about the Hussite movement and the founding and history of the city. The museum is housed in the Old Town Hall, a building that dates back to the early 1500s. You can also enter the extensive labyrinth of tunnels below the Old Town here. A tour of the tunnels takes about 20 minutes. The Gothic Hall was renovated in 2018–20. ⊠ Žižkovo nám. 1, Tábor 🕿 381–252–242 ⊕ www.husitskemuzeum.cz 🎫 Museum tour 80 Kč, tunnel tour 80 Kč, combined tour 150 Kč ⊙ Closed Sun.–Tues. Oct.–May.

Pražská ulice
STREET | The main route to the newer part of town, this street is delightfully lined with beautiful Renaissance façades. If you turn right at Divadelní and head to the Lužnice River, you can see the remaining walls and fortifications of the 15th century, evidence of the town's function as a vital stronghold. ⊠ Tábor.

Žižkovo náměstí (*Žižka Square*)
PLAZA/SQUARE | There's no doubt who this square belongs to—a bronze statue of Jan Žižka dominates the area and clearly points to its Hussite past. The stone tables in front of the Gothic town hall and the house at No. 6 date to the 15th century, used by the Hussites to give daily communion to the faithful. Many fine houses that line the square bear plaques describing their architectural style and original purpose. Be sure to stroll the tiny streets around the square, as they curve around, branch off, and then stop; few lead back to the main square. This bemusing layout, created in the 15th century, was designed to thwart incoming invaders. ⊠ Tábor.

🍴 Restaurants

Havana
$$ | **AMERICAN** | Right on the square, this café-bar has a superb atmosphere, if oddly resembling an English pub, and serves

up tasty plates of steaks, grilled meat, burgers, and chicken. **Known for:** outdoor seating; setting on historic town square; good burgers and beers. ⑤ *Average main: Kč250* ✉ *Žižkovo nám. 17, Tábor* ☎ *381–253–383* ⊕ *www.kafehavana.cz.*

Hotels

Dvořák

$$ | **HOTEL** | A bit outside the city center, this former brewery building has been thoroughly renovated into one of the nicest places in town. **Pros:** modern rooms; free parking; on-site beer spa. **Cons:** can be busy during conferences; weak Wi-Fi at times; swimming pool very small. ⑤ *Rooms from: Kč2690* ✉ *Hradební 3037, Tábor* ☎ *381–212–221* ⊕ *www.lhdvoraktabor.cz* ⇔ *84 rooms* ⦿*l Free Breakfast.*

★ Nautilus

$$ | **HOTEL** | This tasteful boutique hotel on the edge of Tábor's charming central square exhibits touches of Bohemian craftsmanship in the architecture, beautiful antiques in the rooms, and elegant, original art on the walls (think shells). **Pros:** great eats; best address in town; rooms with genuine Bohemian flair. **Cons:** some rooms are a little dark; breakfast spread not as great as the food at the restaurant; paid parking is separate from hotel. ⑤ *Rooms from: Kč2846* ✉ *Žižkovo nám. 20, Tábor* ☎ *380–900–900* ⊕ *www.hotelnautilus.cz* ⇔ *22 rooms* ⦿*l Free Breakfast.*

Písek

44 km (28 miles) west of Tábor; 103 km (62 miles) south of Prague.

Písek is a bit of a surprise. It used to be that people came for one thing: Písek's 700-year-old Gothic bridge peopled with baroque statues. But an infusion of European Union funds has introduced some beautiful upgrades. The former mill and power station is now a museum

dedicated to electricity, and a former malt house is a cultural house and art museum. There's a promenade that runs along the river beside the old city wall, and the square around the church is nothing short of lovely. They've changed the former Gothic moat into a tiny park, and even the city museum displays some interesting finds.

GETTING HERE

Buses leave from Prague's Na Knížecí station and will take you there for around 149 Kč in approximately 90 minutes. Trains leave from Prague's Hlavní nádraží and cost 145 Kč, with the trip taking more than 2½ hours. If you drive, the trip should take no more than 90 minutes.

TIMING

Písek means "sand," and back before the city was a city, people used to pan for gold in the river. From mid-May to the beginning of June the city displays sand sculptures honoring its namesake. There's a town festival every June and a folklore festival at the end of August.

VISITOR INFORMATION

CONTACTS Písek Tourist Information. ✉ *Velké nám. 113, Písek* ☎ *387–999–999* ⊕ *www.pisek.eu.*

Sights

Gothic Bridge

BRIDGE | Once the city's only claim to fame, this bridge is a site to see. It was built in the 1260s—making it the oldest bridge in the Czech Republic, surpassing Prague's Charles Bridge by 90 years. Not too shabby. Přemysl Otakar II commissioned it, seeking a secure crossing for his salt shipments over the difficult-to-ford Otava River. As early as the 9th century, Písek stood at the center of one of the most important trade routes to the west, linking Prague to Passau and the rest of Bavaria. In the 15th century it became one of five major Hussite strongholds. The statues of saints weren't added to the bridge until the 18th

Písek's stone bridge crosses the Otava River and was built before the end of the 13th century.

century. During the devastating floods of 2002 one of the statues was damaged, and all the paving stones washed away, but divers recovered most of the lost pieces. The statues on the bridge are not the originals. You can reach the bridge from třída Národní svobody on the left bank or Karlova ulice from the right bank. ⊠ *Karlova ul., Písek.*

Mariánský chrám (*Church of the Virgin*) **CHURCH** | Just off the main square, this church is the highlight of Bakaláře náměstí. You can't miss the 240-foot tower, which is open for a climb. Construction began in the late 1200s, about the time the bridge was built. The lone surviving tower was completed in 1487. On the inside, look for the *Madonna of Písek*, a 14th-century Gothic altar painting. On a middle pillar is a rare series of early-Gothic wall paintings dating from the end of the 13th century.

■ **TIP→ Ask about a tower visit at the Písek Tourist Information Center.** ⊠ *Bakaláře at Leoše Janáčka, Písek* ⊕ *www.farnost-pisek.cz* 🖾 *Free.*

Prácheňské muzeum
HISTORY MUSEUM | Inside a 13th-century castle's frescoed medieval halls, this museum documents the history of Písek and its surroundings, including the Czech fishing industry (with the additional original touch of live fish in a large aquarium) and the history of local gold panning and mining in the nearby hills. There are two galleries devoted to temporary exhibits. Everything is in Czech, but ask for an info sheet in English. ⊠ *Velké nám. 114, Písek* ☎ *382–201–111* ⊕ *www.prachen-skemuzeum.cz* 🖾 *40 Kč, photography fee 20 Kč* ⊘ *Closed Mon. and Jan.–Feb.*

Sladovna
OTHER MUSEUM | FAMILY | Písek has a brewing history dating back to the Middle Ages. This malt house was built in the 19th century and continued producing malt for 100 years. In 2008, the city opened Sladovna, a cultural facility that houses two permanent exhibitions and five playrooms for kids. There's a spot for inspired kids to color, a reading area, plus an igloo that shows fairy tales. It's all in

Czech, but children should appreciate the bright colors and great graphics. ⊠ *Velké nám. 113, Písek* ☎ *387–999–999* ⊕ *www. sladovna.cz* ✉ *Kids playrooms 80 Kč to 100 Kč, exhibitions 30 Kč* ⊙ *Closed Mon.*

🛏 Hotels

Hotel Biograf

$ | HOTEL | A design-conscious hotel with an award-winning restaurant is a rare find in Písek. **Pros:** large rooms; good location; all amenities. **Cons:** exterior low on charm; not a lot in the area to keep you overnight; near church bells that ring in the night. ⑤ *Rooms from: Kč1550* ⊠ *Gregorova 124, Písek* ☎ *380–425–510* ⊕ *www.hotelbiograf.com* ⤴ *47 rooms* ⦿ *Free Breakfast.*

Třeboň

48 km (28 miles) south of Tábor; 138 km (83 miles) south of Prague.

Třeboň, like Tábor, is off the international tourist trail, but it's a favorite with cyclists. And the town offers an appealing mix of adorable old buildings and authentic workaday local life.

Třeboň itself is a charming jewel box of a town. It was settled during the 12th century by the Wittkowitzes (later called the Rožmberks, or Rosenbergs), once Bohemia's noblest family. You can see their emblem, a five-petal rose, on castles, doorways, and coats of arms all over the region. Their official residence was 40 km (25 miles) to the southwest, in Český Krumlov, but Třeboň was an important second residence and repository of the family archives, which still reside in the town's château. The main square, Masarykovo náměstí, is a pleasing arrangement of baroque and Renaissance structures. Various markets pop up here all through the summer, and the Town Hall has notable frescoes.

To Czechs, Třeboň and carp are almost synonymous. If you're in the area in late autumn, you may be lucky enough to witness the great carp harvests, when tens of thousands of the glittering fish are netted from ponds in the surrounding area. Traditionally, they are served breaded and fried as the centerpiece of Christmas Eve dinner. But regardless of the season, you'll find carp on every menu in town. Don't be afraid to order it; the carp here are not the notorious bottom-feeders they are elsewhere but are raised in clean ponds and served as a fresh catch with none of that muddy aftertaste.

One of the most pleasant activities here is a walk around the **Rybník Svět** (World Pond), an easy 12-km (7½-mile) trail that takes you through grassy fields and forests. When taking the walk (or as a destination itself), visit the Schwarzenberg Family Vault. Built in English Gothic style; it's a bit startling at first but then seems to blend into its woody environs. If you'd rather not walk, 45-minute boat tours go around the lake about once an hour (in season and weather permitting). There's a variety of other walks and lots of cycle paths in the region; ask at the tourist information office for recommended routes and maps.

GETTING HERE

Direct bus service to Třeboň is infrequent but costs around 70 Kč and departs from the Roztyly Metro stop in Prague. Trains depart from the main station and cost around 233 Kč. Be sure to ask to go to the Třeboň lázné station and not the main Třeboň station, and save yourself a 20-minute walk into town.

VISITOR INFORMATION

CONTACTS Třeboň Tourist Information.
⊠ *Masarykovo nám. 103, Trebon* ☎ *384–721–169* ⊕ *www.itrebon.cz.*

Sights

Bílý koníček (*Little White Horse*)
HOTEL | Look for the Little White Horse, the best-preserved Renaissance house on the square, dating to 1544. It's now a modest hotel and restaurant—the perfect spot to enjoy some excellent local beer. ⊠ *Masarykovo nám. 97, Trebon* ☎ *792–314–606* ⊕ *bilykonicekhotel.cz.*

Kostel sv. Jiljí (*Church of St. Giles*)
CHURCH | The Gothic style of Southern Bohemia is exemplified in this curious church. The unassuming exterior gives no clue to the vastness inside or the treasures it holds. Paintings in the Czech Gothic style can be found by the main altar, along with other artwork and frescoes dating as far back as the late 15th century. ⊠ *Husova, Trebon* 🎫 *Free.*

Zámek Třeboň (*Třeboň Château*)
CASTLE/PALACE | The entrance to this château lies at the southwest corner of the square. From the outside the white walls make it appear restrained, but the inner courtyard is covered with *sgraffito*. There's a variety of tours of the interior, which boasts sumptuous re-creations of the Renaissance lifestyle enjoyed by the Rožmberks and apartments furnished in late-19th-century splendor. The gardens adjacent to the castle are well maintained and free to stroll in. The last of the Rožmberks died in 1611, and the castle eventually became the property of the Schwarzenberg family, who built their family tomb in a grand park on the other side of Svět Pond. It's now a monumental neo-Gothic destination for Sunday-afternoon picnickers. It's well worth the easy stroll along the lake to visit this tomb; summer concerts are held here occasionally. In the summer you can tour a kitchen for preparing dogs' meals, a stable, and casemates (part of the fortifications) with tunnels. The dogs' kitchen is a rarity and was for the noble family's pampered pets and working dogs. ⊠ *Masarykovo nám., Trebon* ☎ *384–721–193* ⊕ *www.zamek-trebon.cz* 🎫 *Tours from 100 Kč* ⊗ *Closed Mon. and Nov.–Apr. Stable, dogs' kitchen, and casemates closed Sept.–June.*

SPAS

Along with its ponds, the Třeboň area is known for its peat bogs. This has given rise to a local spa industry, and wellness weekends are popular attractions at the city's two main spas. A variety of treatments are on offer, but both do peat massages. A dip in the iron-rich squishy substance is supposed to help with arthritis and other joint problems. Be prepared: the sensation and smell are acquired tastes.

Bertiny Lázně
HEALTH CLUB | Treatments with peat at Bertiny Lázně began in 1883, though the current modern facility, sporting a pool, sauna and wellness center, is much more recent, and was renovated in the first half of 2020. People can stay at the spa for multiday programs or a spa weekend. Services include baths with peat, herbs, Dead Sea salt, and iodine, among others. Massages and various types of motion therapy are also offered. The spa is located close to Třeboň's historical center, next to a park and small waterway. ⊠ *Tylova 171, Trebon* ☎ *384–754–111* ⊕ *www.berta.cz.*

Lázně Aurora

HEALTH CLUB | The socialist-style high-rise complex at the western edge of Třeboň may not be inviting at first glance, but inside it has a spa for treatment stays and relaxation weekends. The mud baths in peat are the main attraction. A range of other baths, massages, and therapies can also be found. There is a saltwater pool, an aqua center, and a sauna. ✉ *Lázeňská 1001, Trebon* ☎ *384–750–333* ⊕ *www.laznetrebon.cz/en/spa-houses/aurora-spa.*

Restaurants

Šupinka

$$$ | EUROPEAN | In a city full of fish, this is where the locals come to enjoy theirs. A stylish interior with floor-to-ceiling wooden arches and a small terrace serve as the backdrops to some creative cooking. **Known for:** fresh carp dishes from nearby fisheries; rustic vibe; locally made Regent beer. $ *Average main: Kč375* ✉ *Valy 56, Trebon* ☎ *384–721–149* ⊕ *www.supina.cz* ◔ *Closed Mon.–Wed.*

Hotels

The tourist information center on the square is very helpful when it comes to booking rooms. It also offers a catalog of hotel options that includes amenities and prices to help narrow your choices.

Romantick

$ | HOTEL | "Flower power" is the theme at this boutique hotel, as each room is named and designed after a flower; some also offer nice views of the city. **Pros:** lots of amenities for this area; lovely views from some rooms; water heated with solar energy. **Cons:** on the outskirts of the city, in an unattractive area; not all rooms have air-conditioning; some rooms very small. $ *Rooms from: Kč2090* ✉ *K Bertě 183, Trebon* ☎ *725–135–888* ⊕ *www.romantick.cz* ⇗ *26 rooms* ⦿ *Free Breakfast.*

Jindřichův Hradec

28 km (17 miles) southwest of Třeboň; 158 km (95 miles) south of Prague.

The ancient town of Jindřichův Hradec, which dates to the end of the 12th century, is mirrored in the reflective waters of the Vajgar Pond right in the town's center. Originally a market colony near the border between Bohemia and Moravia, the town acquired a castle to protect it, and it's the main attraction here as the third-largest castle in the country. (The interior, now an administrative center, is less interesting.) Other attractions include a town square with Gothic, Renaissance, and some baroque aspects, a regional museum, and excursions into the countryside.

Like other Southern Bohemian towns, this region is a popular spot for cyclists and hikers. If the countryside appeals to you but you're lacking the footpower to explore it, hitch a ride on the Narrow Gauge Railway. Trains depart daily in July and August from the city's main train station. The rails are a mere 30 inches apart, and the route winds south nearly to the border with Austria.

GETTING HERE

Jindřichův Hradec is about three hours from Prague. The train from Prague's Hlavní nádraží station requires a change at Veselí. It costs about 189 Kč. There is no good direct bus connection.

TIMING

A laid-back vibe flows through Jindřichův Hradec. Winter feels isolated, but summer brings lots of cyclists to the area. The Day of the City festival is held at the castle every June, while the big summertime festivities happen during the Folk Rose Festival in mid-July.

VISITOR INFORMATION

CONTACTS Jindřichův Hradec Tourist Information. ✉ *Panská 136, Jindřichův Hradec* ☎ *384–363–546* ⊕ *infocentrum.jh.cz.*

Jindřichův Hradec has a cluster of historic buildings including a castle that features the European mannerism style.

Sights

Kostel Nanebevzetí Panny Marie (*Church of the Ascension of Our Lady*)
CHURCH | Dating to the second half of the 14th century, this church and its tower are the other dominating features of the city's skyline besides the castle. It's a Gothic triple-nave church with some interesting elements, including a Gothic Madonna from the beginning of the 15th century. By coincidence, the church straddles the 15th meridian, and you'll see a line marking the point. The city tower is also open for those wishing to scale 157 steps for an extensive view of the surrounding area. ⊠ *Za kostelem, Jindřichův Hradec* ☎ *Church free, tower 30 Kč* ☺ *Tower closed Oct.–Mar. and weekdays Apr., May, and Sept.*

Kostel sv. Jana Křtitele (*Church of St. John the Baptist*)
RELIGIOUS BUILDING | The oldest church in town, built between the 13th and 16th centuries, this is an excellent example of Bohemian Gothic architecture. Inside, extensive frescoes in the clerestory date to the first half of the 14th century and portray scenes from the lives of Christ, the Apostles, and various Czech saints. They also demonstrate the medieval necessity for pictorial narratives in educating the illiterate population. On the south side of the sanctuary you can see the Chapel of St. Nicholas, built in 1369. The vaulted ceiling is supported by a single central pillar; this is one of the earliest buildings using this construction in Bohemia. The church and monastery are part of the municipal museum and sometimes have exhibitions. ⊠ *Štítného, Jindřichův Hradec* ☎ *384–363–660* ⊕ *www.mjh.cz* ☺ *Church and cloister 50 Kč, exhibitions 30 Kč* ☺ *Closed Oct.–May.*

Muzeum Jindřichohradecka
OTHER MUSEUM | Founded in 1882, this museum's big draw is its impressive Nativity scene. The huge, mechanical créche was built by one committed craftsman, Mr. Krýza, who dedicated more than 60 years to its creation in the latter part of the 19th century. The

scene has recently been restored to its original design showing the primitive charm of the moving figures. Amazingly, the scene contains 1,398 figures. Other exhibitions in the former Jesuit seminary include an apothecary. ⊠ *Balbínovo nám. 19, Jindřichův Hradec* ☎ *384–363–660* ⊕ *www.mjh.cz* ▨ *80 Kč, exhibitions 30 Kč* ⊘ *Closed Jan. 6–Mar., Mon. Apr.– June, and Mon. Sept.–mid-Dec.*

Národní muzeum fotografie (*National Photography Museum*)
ART MUSEUM | This former Jesuit college now houses the foremost photography institution in the country. Reconstructed interiors rival the photos on display—the wall and ceiling frescoes have been lovingly restored. The permanent collection includes more than 200 photos donated by Czech photographers. Attached to the museum is the Chapel of St. Mary Magdalene, which occasionally hosts concerts. ⊠ *Kostelní 20, Jindřichův Hradec* ☎ *384–362–459* ⊕ *www.mfmom.cz* ▨ *90 Kč* ⊘ *Closed weekends Jan.–Mar., Mon. Apr.–June, and Mon. Sept.–Dec.*

Zámek v Jindřichově Hradci (*Jindřichův Hradec's Castle*)
CASTLE/PALACE | As the third-largest castle in the Czech Republic, this is the dominant structure in town, holding 300 rooms and 10,000 pieces of art. Behind the courtyard and its elegant Italian arcades, the castle's core is pure Gothic splendor, reflected not only in its thick defensive walls and round tower but also in the **frescoes** covering interior corridors. Colorful examples of medieval coats of arms and a panorama depicting the legend of St. George date to 1338. Over the course of centuries, buildings of an adjoining Renaissance-era château were added to the early Gothic castle, together forming a large complex. There are three different marked routes through the castle for visitors to follow. Tour A is best for design lovers: you'll visit the Adam building, which includes glimpses of Renaissance, baroque, rococo,

Empire, and classical styles, as well as see numerous paintings from a previous owner's vast collection. Tour B takes you to the castle's Gothic and medieval core, the Chapel of the Holy Spirit, and the Royal Hall. Tour C offers the opportunity to visit 18th- and 19th-century apartments as well as the Rondel, a bit of an architectural oddity set in this Gothic scene, designed by an Italian in the 16th century. The official term for the decor is "European mannerism," but it really resembles a big pink cake with confectionary images of aristocratic dancers and musicians. Built as a ballroom, this space still hosts the occasional concert. Wander the exterior courtyards for free, or simply climb the Black Tower for a view of the castle and surrounding area. ⊠ *Dobrovského 1, Jindřichův Hradec* ☎ *384–321–279* ⊕ *www.zamek-jindrichu-vhradec.cz/en* ▨ *Castle tours (in Czech) from 80 Kč, exhibitions from 100 Kč* ⊘ *Closed Mon. and Nov.–Apr.*

 Hotels

Hotel Bílá paní
$ | HOTEL | Situated next to the castle, this cozy hotel takes its name (The White Lady) from a ghost legend—and its otherwise comfortable rooms are alleged to be haunted. **Pros:** cheap and cheerful; castle views; historical building. **Cons:** rooms are sweet but spare; bathroom size and placement is a bit unorthodox; the promised ghost never appears. ⑤ *Rooms from: Kč1340* ⊠ *Dobrovského 5, Jindřichův Hradec* ☎ *384–363–329* ⊕ *www.hotelbilapani.cz* ⮌ *11 rooms* ❍ *Free Breakfast.*

Hotel Concertino
$ | HOTEL | Right on the town square, this historical-looking hotel with a modern interior lets you spring directly into sightseeing action. **Pros:** near the town square; expressive furnishings; plentiful services for business travelers. **Cons:** decor is expressive but not necessarily cohesive; restaurant is hit or miss; rooms

can be noisy in summer due to open windows. $ *Rooms from: Kč1800* ✉ *Nám. Míru 141, Jindřichův Hradec* ☎ *384–362–320* ⊕ *www.concertino.cz* ⬎ *37 rooms* ❍❙ *Free Breakfast.*

Hluboká nad Vltavou

17 km (11 miles) southwest of Třeboň; 155 km (94 miles) south of Prague.

Yes, Hluboká has a massive fairy-tale castle that can be seen for miles around. But active outdoorsy types should come here for the excellent sport center that offers tennis, golf, an adrenaline center, and more. Cycling is easy for a brief nature break.

GETTING HERE

The journey from Prague to Hluboká—either by train from the Hlavní nádraží station or by bus from the Roztyly station—is 2½ hours unless you get one of the local connections that stops in every small town (in which case the trip takes 3½ hours). The train ticket costs about 224 Kč and requires a change in České Budějovice; the bus ticket is 145 Kč. There are also frequent buses from Florenc that require a change. You may find it more convenient to stay overnight in České Budějovice and see the castle in the morning after a 10-minute train trip. Alternatively, there's a 10-km (6-mile) cycle path.

VISITOR INFORMATION

CONTACTS Hluboká nad Vltavou Tourist Center. ✉ *Zborovská 80, Hluboká nad Vltavou* ☎ *387–966–164* ⊕ *www.hluboka.cz.*

 Sights

Galerie Mikoláše Alše (*Aleš Art Gallery*)
ART MUSEUM | Located near the château, the region's museum for art history displays a variety of works including sculpture, paintings, and porcelain. It's one of the most extensive collections of Gothic art in the country, and temporary exhibitions range from modern to contemporary. ✉ *Hluboká nad Vltavou 144, Hluboká nad Vltavou* ☎ *387–967–120* ⊕ *www.ajg.cz* ✆ *190 Kč.*

Lovecká chata Ohrada (*Ohrada Hunting Lodge*)
OTHER ATTRACTION | FAMILY | Care for a brisk walk? Follow the yellow trail signs 2 km (1 mile) to the Lovecká chata Ohrada, which houses a museum of hunting and fishing and is near a small children's zoo.

■ **TIP**→ **The lodge and the zoo have the same entrance.** ✉ *Zamék Ohrada 1, off Rte. 105, Hluboká nad Vltavou* ☎ *728–328–304* ⊕ *www.nzm.cz/en/ohrada* ✆ *120 Kč (incl. zoo)* ⊘ *Closed Nov.–Mar.*

Sportovně relaxačni areál (*Sport-Relax Area*)
SPORTS VENUE | Hluboká is working hard to offer visitors something beyond its castle, and this extensive sports complex is a complete change of pace. Here you can golf, play tennis or volleyball, rent Rollerblades or other sports equipment, test your bravery (and fitness level) in the "adrenaline park" (think a massive ropes course, unicycles, and a bungee trampoline), watch the local hockey team play in the stadium, or even catch a baseball or soccer game. The park offers a playground for kids, plus a restaurant with a huge terrace. It backs up to the woods, so you can take off for a short hike as well. There's also a hotel. ✉ *Sportovní 1276, Hluboká nad Vltavou* ☎ *606–096–326 restaurant and accommodations* ⊕ *www.areal-hluboka.cz* ⊘ *Some parts closed Nov.–Feb.; weekdays Mar., Apr., and Oct.; and Mon. May, June, and Sept.*

★ **Státní zámek Hluboká** (*State Château Hluboká*)
CASTLE/PALACE | Hluboká's main focus is its castle, with a cluster of white towers flanking its walls, and tour groups pop in and out regularly. Although the structure dates to the 13th century, what you see is pure 19th-century excess, perpetrated by the wealthy Schwarzenberg family

Endear yourself to locals by referring to the city of České Budějovice as "Budějce," pronounced "boo-dyay-tse."

attempting to prove their good taste. If you think you've seen this castle somewhere before, you're probably thinking of Windsor Castle, near London, which served as the template. Take a tour; the happy hodgepodge of styles in the interior reflects the no-holds-barred tastes of the time. On Tour A you'll see representative rooms, including the stunning morning salon and library. Tour B brings you into the private apartments and hunting salon, while Tour C takes in the kitchen. Tour D is available daily only in July and August, and weekends only in June and September, and shows off the tower and chapel. Check out the wooden Renaissance ceiling in the large dining room, which was removed by the Schwarzenbergs from the castle at Český Krumlov and brought here. Also look for the beautiful late-baroque bookshelves in the library. The gardens are free to wander in. ✉ *Zamék 142, Hluboká nad Vltavou* ☎ *387–843–911* ⊕ *www.zamek-hluboka. cz/en* ✆ *Tours from 130 Kč (audio headsets available with English commentary)* ☉ *Closed Mon. Sept.–June.*

České Budějovice

26 km (16 miles) southwest of Třeboň; 164 km (99 miles) south of Prague.

České Budějovice is the largest city in Southern Bohemia, but it's more of a transportation hub and not nearly as charming as the neighboring towns. Still, a couple of interesting spots ensure that you won't be bored if you have a stopover, and you probably will. Schedule a couple of extra hours for a wander through the Old Town and a lunch break, and pause to sip the locally brewed Budvar.

The enormously proportioned main square, named after King Přemysl Otakar II, is lined with arcaded houses. The stunning Old Town Hall is from the 16th century. Designed by an Italian, it has bells in the tower that chime old Southern Bohemian tunes at the top of every hour. Another attraction is the central fountain from the 18th century. Be sure to look for the "magic stone," the lone cobblestone in the brick-covered square. Legend has it that if you step on this stone after 10 pm, you'll become lost. But the town's real claim to fame is its beer—the slightly sweetish Budvar.

GETTING HERE
The trip from Prague takes about two hours by either bus or train. Be careful to choose a *rychlík* (express train), not an *osobní* (passenger train), which would make your journey four hours. Trains leave from Prague's Hlavní nádraží station and cost about 219 Kč; buses leave from both Florenc and Na Knížecí stations and cost 159 Kč–193 Kč. Car travel (about 2½ hours) affords the greatest ease and flexibility. České Budějovice lies on the main artery through the region, the two-lane E55 south from Prague, which, though often crowded, is in relatively good shape.

VISITOR INFORMATION
CONTACTS České Budějovice Tourist Center. ⊠ *Nám. Přemysla Otakára II 2, České Budějovice* ☎ *386–801–413* ⊕ *www.budejce.cz/en/information-center.*

Sights

Budějovický Budvar Brewery
BREWERY | Tours of the brewery start at the modern glass-enclosed visitor center. On the 60-minute route, you'll see the wells that source the water, the brewhouse, and other parts of the process up to the bottling plant. A beer tasting is included at the end of the tour. Advanced booking (online) is required for tours outside the normal times. ⊠ *Karolíny Světlé 4, České Budějovice* ☎ *387–705–347* ⊕ *www.visitbudvar.cz* ⊠ *180 Kč* ☾ *Closed Sun.–Mon. in Jan.–Feb.*

Černá věž (*Black Tower*)
NOTABLE BUILDING | To get a good view over the city, climb the 225 steps up to the Renaissance gallery of the Black Tower at the northeast corner of the square

next to St. Nicholas's Cathedral. Don't look for a black tower; it's actually white but got the nickname after a fire left some charred marks. ⊠ *Nám. Přemysla Otakara II, České Budějovice* ⊠ *50 Kč* ☾ *Closed Nov.–Mar., Mon. Apr.–June, and Mon. Sept. and Oct.*

Holašovice
TOWN | Peppered with small country homes and farmsteads, this traditional Czech village is so well preserved it's been designated a UNESCO World Heritage Site. Hardly touched by reconstruction or modern meddling, some of the houses date back to the town's founding in the 13th century. Don't expect grand châteaux or extensive decoration; this is "rural baroque" but every bit as picturesque with custard-yellow façades. The information center at No. 43 has a small exhibit about rural life. Budget about an hour for a visit or longer if you'd like to enjoy traditional fare at Špejchar u Vojty (⊠ *Holašovice 3* ☎ *777–621–221*). Every July a "peasant" festival, Selské slavnosti, is held with traditional crafts and entertainment. ⊠ *Holašovice* ☎ *387–982–145 for tourist office* ⊕ *www.holasovice.eu* ☾ *Tourist Information Office closed Nov.–Mar. and Mon. and Tues. Apr.–Oct.*

Jihočeské muzeum (*Museum of Southern Bohemia*)
OTHER MUSEUM | You can't miss the imposing neo-Renaissance building of the Museum of Southern Bohemia. It was originally founded in 1877 in a small building next to the town hall, but generous donors flooded the facility with so many artifacts that the space had to be expanded. The major exhibits include theme collections portraying the history of the town and the region through an extensive variety of artifacts including metalwork, ceramics, glass, and furniture. A fascinating large-scale model shows the Old Town and its picturesque medieval walls and towers. A regular series of temporary exhibits also runs alongside the permanent

ones. ⊠ *Dukelská 1, České Budějovice*
☎ *391–001–531* ⊕ *www.muzeumcb.cz*
☒ *90 Kč* ⊙ *Closed Mon.*

Koněspřežka

NOTABLE BUILDING | A source of pride for České Budějovice, Koněspřežka is the oldest railway station on the continent. Designed to transport salt to Bohemia from Linz in Austria, a horse-drawn railway was built between 1825 and 1832. One of the first major industrial developments in Europe, it reduced the journey between Linz and České Budějovice from two weeks to four days. Public transport was introduced soon afterward. The station is now a part of the city museum and houses an exhibit dedicated to the horse-drawn railroad. You can also pick up a brochure from the tourist office that details other buildings throughout town that played a role in the transport. ⊠ *Mánesova 10, České Budějovice* ☎ *386–354–820* ⊕ *www. muzeumcb.cz/navstivte-nas/pobocky/ muzeum-konesprezky/* ☒ *30 Kč* ⊙ *Closed Oct.–Apr. and Mon. May–Sept.*

 Restaurants

Masné krámy

$$ | **CZECH** | Operated by the Budvar brewery, the restaurant—a former butcher's market—aims for an upscale yet casual atmosphere with reasonably priced food and is now one of the best restaurants in town. It specializes in great Czech food and serves unpasteurized Budvar beer; fish and game are also on the menu. **Known for:** fresh tank beer; relaxed atmosphere; locally sourced trout. ⑤ *Average main: Kč299* ⊠ *Krajinská 13, České Budějovice* ☎ *387–201–301* ⊕ *www. masne-kramy.cz.*

 Hotels

Hotel Budweis

$$ | **HOTEL** | Situated next to the river in a former mill, this beautifully restored grand hotel has exposed wooden beams, polished floors, and loads of natural light. **Pros:** nicest hotel in town; central location with good views; rooms adapted for people with disabilities. **Cons:** cheaper options available; modern room design doesn't match historical exterior; showers are a bit tricky to use. ⑤ *Rooms from: Kč2650* ⊠ *Mlýnská 6, České Budějovice* ☎ *389–822–111* ⊕ *www.hotelbudweis.cz* ⤴ *60 rooms* ⦿ *Free Breakfast.*

Performing Arts

The city has its own theater, ballet, opera, and orchestra that put on a variety of performances throughout the year. The Jihočeské divadlo (South Bohemian Theater) is also the group that organizes the July and August performances at the Revolving Theater in Český Krumlov. Tickets sell out fast. You can reserve online at ⊕ www.cbsystem.cz. ⊠ Dr. Stejskala 19 ☎ 386–356–925 ⊕ www.jihoceskedivadlo.cz.

Chapter 13

WESTERN BOHEMIA

Updated by
Raymond Johnston

⊙ Sights 🍴 Restaurants 🛏 Hotels 🛍 Shopping 🍸 Nightlife

WELCOME TO WESTERN BOHEMIA

TOP REASONS TO GO

★ **Take the waters:** Wind through the Vřídlo Colonnade, where adventurous souls can sip the waters.

★ **Book a spa day:** Try the spa treatments, either old-school health-oriented treatments or more familiar pampering.

★ **Catch the stunning view:** Head up to Stag's Leap for a sweeping vista.

★ **Walk the "main streets":** Picturesque spa towns Františkovy Lázně and Mariánské Lázně make a quaint stroll.

★ **Drink a Pilsner Urquell:** Try this brew in the town where it was born—Plzeň.

The natural springs of hot mineral water that dot the lands of Western Bohemia have made this region one of Europe's most important spa centers. These facilities near neighboring Germany have been renovated inside to meet international expectations during the last 25 years, but the exteriors of the colonnades and pavilions still reflect the styles of the 19th century. Because access to much of the border area was highly restricted in the communist era, the hills and forests still provide unspoiled natural settings for hiking and biking. The area also has a rich history of manufacturing luxury glassware and porcelain, which can be seen in downtown shops and factory stores. Farther south is the city of Plzeň, famous for inventing pilsner.

1 Karlovy Vary. Better known to many as Karlsbad, the largest of the spa towns also hosts the country's biggest film festival every July.

2 Cheb. Proximity to the German border brings many bargain hunters for shopping, while castle ruins and a historical center add some diversion.

3 Františkovy Lázně. The smallest of the spa towns in Western Bohemia offers a quiet escape to hotels with mud baths and old-world pampering.

4 Mariánské Lázně. In this town's heyday, everyone from Thomas Edison to Czar Nicholas II came to take the waters. Today visitors can also enjoy golf and hiking.

5 Plzeň. The only major Czech city to have been liberated by U.S. forces at the end of World War II, it's also home to the country's largest brewery.

GERMANY

Litvínov

0   20 miles

0   30 km

Vejprty

D7

D13 E442 Most

Chomutov

D27

D25

E442 D13

Ostrov

Žatec

Obře

Karlovy Vary **1**

D7

Sokolov

E48

Františkovy Lázně **3**

D6

E49

D20

E49

D6

Bochov

D27

D6 E48

Cheb **2**

Bečov

Toužim

D21

Mariánské Lázně **4**

Kralovice

D27

Berounka

Chodová Planá

D20

E49

Tachov

Stříbro

E50 D5

Plzeň **5**

D5 E50

Rokycany

Bor

D5

GERMANY

E50

Dobřany

D20

E49

D26

Horšovský Týn

D27

E53

Nepomuk

Domažlice

D26

D22

Klatovy

D22 Horažd'ovice

D27

E53

Otava

Once upon a time, Western Bohemia was known as the playground of Central Europe's rich and famous. Its three well-known spas, Karlovy Vary, Mariánské Lázně, and Františkovy Lázně (also known by their German names, Karlsbad, Marienbad, and Franzensbad, respectively), were the annual haunts of everybody who was anybody: Johann Wolfgang von Goethe, Ludwig van Beethoven, Karl Marx, and England's King Edward VII, to name but a few.

The spas suffered dramatically, however, in the decades after World War II. The concept of a luxurious health spa was anathema to the ruling communist government, and many of the spa facilities were transformed into hospitals—in fact, the idea that these towns are where the sick should recuperate remains today. Pre-1989, some of the nicest properties were transformed into recuperation centers for workers.

The years since 1989 have been kinder to the spa resorts, and now the cities are home to the rich and famous once again. Karlovy Vary, as always, has the most recognition, and rebounded best of all. Helped by its annual international film festival and a heavy infusion of Russian private capital, Karlovy Vary is back on the map as an international spa destination. Františkovy Lázně, too, is on the comeback trail. The city officials have used bucketloads of Kaiser-yellow paint to spruce up those aging Empire façades, and the city's parks have gotten a much-needed makeover. Mariánské Lázně benefits from hordes of German day-trippers from just over the border.

In the Czech Republic spas have traditionally been seen as serious health treatments first, complete with physical examinations, blood tests, and various infusions to complement the waters, relaxation, and massage. This means for many visitors that the local concept of a spa differs from what they are used to back home (and explains in part the large number of elderly tourists shuffling about). Many hotels have added treatments—from Thai massages to pedicures—that fit the modern concept of a spa resort. For many places, though, "spa" still primarily means doctors, nurses, and lab coats, but this is changing as beer spas, wine spas, and other less traditional places pop up. The best place to inquire is at your hotel or the tourist information center.

Aside from the spas, the area is full of historic features stemming from the wealth it accrued as the district's important trade route into Germany and Italy. A strong Germanic influence can still be seen, particularly in towns like Cheb and Mariánské Lázně. Everywhere in the region you'll see Germans, mostly pensioners on coach tours dropping by for a walk around town and a slice of apple strudel before hitting the road back to Deutschland.

Planning

When to Go

The region's key cultural event is the Karlovy Vary International Film Festival, held in the first week in July. As strolling on the promenades of the spa towns is de rigueur, the summer months are the season. The winter months are fine if you want to spend all your time indoors getting massages and other luxury treatments. Most hotels do stay open during this season. But promenading around the colonnade will be a bit of a letdown in the cold, and there's less hobnobbing with fellow spa goers due to much smaller crowds.

Getting Here

By car, the D5 (E50) highway leads directly to Plzeň, while the R6 (E48) goes to Karlovy Vary and the spa towns in the northern part of the region. Some towns lack direct train connections, making a direct bus a better choice. Buses to major hubs such as Plzeň are also faster and less expensive than trains.

Guided Tours from Prague

Guided one-day bus tours from Prague are available from several companies to the larger spa towns.

Martin Tours
One of the country's larger tour operators, Martin Tours offers regular trips to Karlovy Vary, including a glass factory, for 1,800 Kč. ⊕ www.martintour.cz.

Restaurants and Hotels

The quality of hotels in Western Bohemia is on a par with those in Prague (something that can't be said about some other parts of the country) and three- and four-star establishments have standard amenities, including satellite TV, room phones, and private bathrooms (and sometimes even Wi-Fi). One difference from the hotels in Prague: the peak season is shorter, running from May through September. Another difference: the staff tend to speak a very limited amount of English—German and Russian (particularly in Karlovy Vary) are much more common, in keeping with the majority of visitors. Prices have risen dramatically in recent years, making private accommodations a more attractive offer.

■TIP→ **Be sure to read the fine print, as many spa hotels quote rates per person per night, rather than for double occupancy.**

The local tourist offices usually keep lists of pensions and private rooms. In addition to value-added tax (V.A.T.), there is also a "spa tax" of about 15 Kč per day for accommodations in spa facilities.

Hotel reviews have been shortened. For full information, visit Fodors.com.

What It Costs in Koruny

	$	$$	$$$	$$$$
RESTAURANTS				
	under 150 Kč	150 Kč–350 Kč	351 Kč–500 Kč	over 500 Kč
HOTELS				
	under 2,200 Kč	2,200 Kč–4,000 Kč	4,001 Kč–6,500 Kč	over 6,500 Kč

Karlovy Vary

132 km (79 miles) west of Prague on R6 (E48).

Karlovy Vary—often known outside the Czech Republic by its German name, Karlsbad—is the most famous of the Bohemian spas. It's named for the omnipresent Emperor Charles IV, who allegedly happened upon the springs in 1358 while on a hunting expedition. As the story goes, the emperor's hound fell into a boiling spring and was scalded. Charles had the water tested and, familiar with spas in Italy, ordered the village of Vary to be transformed into a haven for baths. The spa reached its golden age in the 19th century, when aristocrats from all over Europe came for treatments. The long list of those who "took the cure" includes Peter the Great, Goethe, Schiller, Beethoven, and Chopin. Even Karl Marx, when he wasn't decrying wealth and privilege, spent time at the wealthy and privileged resort; he wrote some of *Das Kapital* here between 1874 and 1876.

Pulling off an extraordinary comeback after decades of communist neglect that left many buildings crumbling into dust behind beautiful façades, Karlovy Vary drips with luxury once again. Much of the reconstruction was led not by Czechs, but by Russians. Since the days of Peter the Great, Karlovy Vary has held a deep fascination for Russians, and many of them poured their newly gained wealth into properties here—so much so that Karlovy Vary's sleepy airport boasts non-stop service from Moscow several times a week, and four-fifths of the properties are actually Russian-owned. Don't be surprised to hear Russian spoken widely in the streets or see it used as the second language, after Czech, on restaurant menus.

Karlovy Vary's other vehicle in luring attention and investment has been its international film festival, which began in 1946. Every year during the first week of July, international stars and film fans flock here. Recent attendees include Oliver Stone, John Travolta, and Helen Mirren. If you're planning on visiting during the festival, line up your hotel room well in advance. Unless you're a true film buff, you're better off coming on a different week.

Whether you're arriving by bus, train, or car, your first view of the town approaching from Prague will be of the run-down section on the banks of the Ohře River. Don't despair: continue along the main road, following the signs to the Grand-hotel Pupp, until you are rewarded with a glimpse of the lovely main street in the older spa area, situated gently astride the banks of the little Teplá ("Warm") River. (Drivers, note that driving through or parking in the main spa area is allowed only with a permit obtained at your hotel.) The walk from the new town to the spa area is about 20 minutes.

The Historická čtvrt (Historic District) is still largely intact. Tall 19th-century houses, with decorative and often eccentric façades, line the spa's proud riverside streets. Throughout, you can see colonnades full of people sipping the spa's hot sulfuric water from funny drinking cups with piped spouts.

Like Prague, Karlovy Vary also has a central river: the swirling Teplá.

GETTING HERE

Frequent bus service between Prague and Karlovy Vary makes the journey only about two hours each way, and the ticket costs about 169 Kč to 199 Kč. The Prague–Karlovy Vary train takes longer—more than three hours by the shortest route—and costs about 215 Kč. If you're driving, you can take the E48 directly from Prague to Karlovy Vary, a drive of about 1½ hours in light traffic.

VISITOR INFORMATION Karlovy Vary Tourist Information. ✉ *Husovo nám. 2, Karlovy Vary* ☎ *355–321–171* ⊕ *www. karlovyvary.cz.*

Sights

Hotel Thermal

HOTEL | Built in the late 1960s as the communist idea of luxury, this oversize modern hotel is the main venue of the Karlovy Vary International Film Festival in early July. Many people, though, consider it an eyesore that's out of step with the rest of the city. ✉ *I. P. Pavlova 11, Karlovy Vary* ☎ *359–001–111* ⊕ *www.thermal.cz.*

★ Jelení skok (*Stag's Leap*)

VIEWPOINT | From Kostel svatého Lukáše, take a sharp right uphill on a redbrick road, then turn left onto a footpath through the woods, following signs to Jelení skok (Stag's Leap). After a while, steps lead up to a bronze statue of a deer looking over the cliffs, the symbol of Karlovy Vary. From here a winding path threads toward a little red gazebo opening onto a mythical panorama that's worth the strenuous hike to the top. ✉ *Sovava trail in Petrova Výšina park, Karlovy Vary.*

Kostel Maří Magdaleny (*Church of Mary Magdalene*)

CHURCH | To the right of the Vřídlo Colonnade, steps lead up to the white Church of Mary Magdalene. Designed by Kilian Ignaz Dientzenhofer (architect of the two churches of St. Nicholas in Prague), this is the best of the few baroque buildings still standing in Karlovy Vary.

Karlovy Vary

KEY

- 1 Sights
- 1 Restaurants
- 1 Quick Bites
- 1 Hotels
- i Tourist Information

0 ——— 200 yd
0 ——— 200 m

■ **TIP➜ If it's open, try to visit the crypt.**
✉ *Moravská ul., Karlovy Vary* ☎ *No phone*
⊕ *www.farnost-kv.cz* 🖾 *Free.*

Kostel svatého Lukáše (*St. Luke's Church*)
CHURCH | A five-minute walk up the steep
Zámecký vrch from the Market Colonnade brings you to the Victorian, redbrick
St. Luke's Church, once a gathering
point for the local English community.
✉ *Zámecký vrch at Petra Velikého, Karlovy Vary* 🖾 *Free.*

Kostel svatých Petra a Pavla (*Church of
Sts. Peter and Paul*)
RELIGIOUS BUILDING | Six domes top this
splendid Russian Orthodox church. It
dates to the end of the 19th century, and
is decorated with paintings and icons
donated by wealthy Russian visitors.
■ **TIP➜ You can usually peek inside, daily
9–6.** ✉ *Třída Krále Jiřího 26, Karlovy Vary*
🖾 *Free.*

Mlýnská kolonáda (*Mill Colonnade*)
NOTABLE BUILDING | This neo-Renaissance
pillared hall, along the river, is the town's
centerpiece. Built from 1871 to 1881, it
has four springs: Rusalka, Libussa, Prince
Wenceslas, and Millpond. ✉ *Mlýnské
nábř., Karlovy Vary.*

Rozhledna Diana
VIEWPOINT | Give your feet a rest. You
won't need to walk to one of the best
views of the town. Even higher than
Stag's Leap sits this observation tower,
accessible by funicular from behind the
Grandhotel Pupp. There's an elevator to
the top of the tower, and a restaurant
at the tower's base. ✉ *Výšina přátelství,
Karlovy Vary* ⊕ *www.dianakv.cz* 🖾 *Funicular from 100 Kč in main season; tower
free.*

Sadová kolonáda (*Park Colonnade*)
NOTABLE BUILDING | Laced with white
wrought iron, this elegant colonnade at
the edge of Dvořákovy sady was built in
1882 by the Viennese architectural duo

Fellner and Helmer, who sprinkled the
Austro-Hungarian Empire with many
such edifices during the late 19th century. They also designed the town's theater,
the quaint wooden Tržní kolonáda (Market
Colonnade) next to the Vřídlo Colonnade,
and one·of the old bathhouses. ✉ *Dvořákovy sady, Karlovy Vary.*

Vřídelní kolonáda (*Vřídlo Colonnade*)
HOT SPRING | Shooting its scalding water
to a height of some 40 feet, the Vřídlo is
indeed Karlovy Vary's hottest and most
dramatic gusher. Built around it is the
jarringly modern Vřídlo Colonnade. Walk
inside the arcade to watch patients take
the famed Karlsbad drinking cure. The
waters (30°F–72°F) are said to be especially effective against diseases of the
digestive and urinary tracts. They're also
good for gout (which probably explains
the spa's former popularity with royals).
If you want to join the crowds and take
a sip, you can buy your own spouted
cup from one of the souvenir vendors
throughout the town. ✉ *Vřídelní ul., near
Kosterní nám., Karlovy Vary.*

🍴 Restaurants

The food in Karlovy Vary has improved
due to the influx of foreign tourists with
money to spend. Pork and beer pubs are
still the rule, though. Hotel food tends to
be better.

Promenáda
$$$ | CZECH | Although it's pricey,
Promenáda is unquestionably the best
place to eat in Karlovy Vary. The starchy
vibe is "'70s French fussy," and meals
are on the heavy side. **Known for:** modern
haute cuisine; central location near the
colonnades; old World charm. ⑤ *Average
main: Kč500* ✉ *Tržíště 31, Karlovy Vary*
☎ *353–225–648* ⊕ *hotel-promenada.cz.*

U Švejka

$$ | CZECH | Usually when a restaurant has the name "Schweik" in it—from the novel *Good Soldier Schweik*—it means one thing: tourist trap. But this local Schweik incarnation is a cut above its brethren. **Known for:** attentive staff; selfie-friendly statue out front; large portions. ⑤ *Average main: Kč300* ✉ *Stará Louka 10, Karlovy Vary* ☎ *353–232–276* ⊕ *www.svejk-kv.cz* ▭ *No credit cards.*

Hotels

Carlsbad Plaza

$$$ | HOTEL | A luxury hotel a stone's throw from the Grandhotel Pupp, Carlsbad Plaza is aimed at Karlovy Vary's wealthiest visitors. **Pros:** quiet location just off the main street; everything you could ever want; great wellness center. **Cons:** lots of things you probably don't want—and you're paying for it all; spa services can be fully booked; some might find it fussy or distant. ⑤ *Rooms from: Kč6242* ✉ *Mariánskolázeňská 23, Karlovy Vary* ☎ *352–441–111* ⊕ *www.carlsbad-plaza.com* ⤴ *126 rooms, 26 suites* ❍| *Free Breakfast.*

★ Grandhotel Pupp

$$$ | HOTEL | The granddaddy of them all, this is one of Central Europe's most famous resorts, going back some 220 years. **Pros:** large rooms; living history; a sleek casino. **Cons:** costly extras; easy to get lost in the maze of halls; rooms are opulent but not that modern. ⑤ *Rooms from: Kč6500* ✉ *Mírové nám. 2, Karlovy Vary* ☎ *353–109–631* ⊕ *www.pupp.cz* ⤴ *Grandhotel Pupp Riverside: 111 rooms; Grandhotel Pupp Parkside: 117 rooms* ❍| *Free Breakfast.*

★ Hotel Embassy

$$ | HOTEL | On a peaceful bend in the river, this family-run hotel includes spacious, well-appointed rooms. **Pros:** intimate and private ambience; perfect for duffers; rooms offer a great value.

Cons: small; restaurant is a bit cramped; no spa. ⑤ *Rooms from: Kč2550* ✉ *Nová Louka 21, Karlovy Vary* ☎ *353–221–161* ⊕ *embassy.cz/en* ⤴ *29 rooms* ❍| *Free Breakfast.*

Hotel Heluan

$ | HOTEL | A clean, safe bet if you've arrived in town without reservations and don't want to spend your savings on a room. **Pros:** inexpensive; friendly staff; completely no-smoking hotel. **Cons:** a bit of a hike uphill; less opulent than other options; parking is distant. ⑤ *Rooms from: Kč1782* ✉ *Tržíště 41, Karlovy Vary* ☎ *353–321–111* ⊕ *heluan.marianskelaznehotels.com/en/* ⤴ *25 rooms* ❍| *Free Breakfast.*

Promenáda

$$ | HOTEL | The family-operated hotel is another good last-minute option right in the center of town, with pastel yellow rooms that are brightened by the occasional exposed wooden beam or windowsill flower box. **Pros:** American-style spa; great restaurant; large rooms. **Cons:** dated fixtures; some rooms have poor views; street noise on weekends. ⑤ *Rooms from: Kč3479* ✉ *Tržíště 31, Karlovy Vary* ☎ *353–225–648* ⊕ *www.hotel-promenada.cz* ⤴ *22 rooms* ❍| *Free Breakfast.*

Růže Hotel

$ | HOTEL | More than adequately comfortable and well-priced given its location in the center of the spa district, the Růže also offers an array of modern spa services like bubble baths and massage. **Pros:** nice views; good for large groups; new rooms. **Cons:** the modern interior lacks character; limited spa services; can be noisy due to traffic. ⑤ *Rooms from: Kč1881* ✉ *I. P. Pavlova 1, Karlovy Vary* ☎ *355–324–111* ⊕ *www.hotel-ruze.com* ⤴ *54 rooms* ❍| *Free Breakfast.*

Wellness Hotel Jean de Carro

$$ | HOTEL | Framed on a hilltop off a side street above the spa, the Jean de Carro

The town of Karlovy Vary is famed for bubbling hot springs and spa experience and for its cast-iron colonnade.

sits comfortably above the fray. **Pros:** one suite designed for guests with disabilities; great views; friendly staff. **Cons:** a bit of a hike; weak Wi-Fi in some rooms; small rooms. [$] *Rooms from: Kč3100* ✉ *Stezka Jeana de Carro 4–6, Karlovy Vary* ☎ *353–365–160* ⊕ *www.jeandecarro.com* ⇦ *32 rooms* ⏍ *Free Breakfast.*

Windsor Spa Hotel
$ | HOTEL | Neo-Gothic in style—on the outside, anyway—this spa hotel has fairly spartan rooms and a slight hospital vibe (it takes treatment rather seriously), but the location is excellent and treatments are gently priced. **Pros:** beautiful building; clean, minimalist rooms; great location. **Cons:** austere rooms; limited amenities; medical feel. [$] *Rooms from: Kč2188* ✉ *Mlýnské nábř. 5, Karlovy Vary* ☎ *353–242–500* ⊕ *windsor-carlsbad.cz* ⇦ *36 rooms* ⏍ *Free Breakfast.*

Performing Arts

Lázně III
MUSIC | If you're looking to get your high-culture fix, the Karlovy Vary Symphony Orchestra plays regularly at this hotel, a spa facility that doubles as an important cultural center for the town. Head to the Antonín Dvořák Concert Hall on the first floor of the building to catch the concerts. The same building is also now home to Windsor Spa Hotel. ✉ *Mlýnské nábř. 5, Karlovy Vary* ☎ *353–242–500* ⊕ *www.windsor-carlsbad.cz/events-celebrations/concert-hall/.*

Městské divadlo
THEATER | Restored to its opulent 1890s glory, the Municipal Theater is home to live concerts of many kinds as well as theater performances. Interior paintings were done by well-known artists including a young Gustav Klimt. ✉ *Divadelní nám. 21, Karlovy Vary* ☎ *351–170–015* ⊕ *www.karlovarske-divadlo.cz.*

🛍 Shopping

A cluster of exclusive stores huddles around the Grandhotel Pupp and back toward town along the river on Stará Louka. Lesser-known, high-quality makers of glass and porcelain can also be found on this street. If you're looking for an inexpensive but nonetheless singular gift from Karlovy Vary, consider a bottle of the bittersweet (and potent) Becherovka, a liqueur produced by the town's own Jan Becher distillery. Another thoughtful gift would be one of the pipe-shape ceramic drinking cups used to take the drinking cure at spas; you can find them along the colonnades. Boxes of tasty *oplatky* wafers, with various sweet fillings, can be found at shops in all the spa towns. (The most famous, Kolonáda, is actually made in Mariánské Lázně.) The challenge is stopping yourself from eating it all before you give it as a gift.

Moser

GLASSWARE | To glass enthusiasts, Karlovy Vary is best known as the home of Moser, one of the world's leading producers of crystal and decorative glassware. ✉ *Tržiště 7, Karlovy Vary* ☎ *353–235–303* ⊕ *www.moser-glass.com.*

Moser Visitors Center

GLASSWARE | For people who want to see more of the process of glassmaking, the Moser Visitors Center has a museum and offers factory tours along with shopping. ✉ *Kapitána Jarose 19, Karlovy Vary* ☎ *353–416–242* ⊕ *www.moser.cz* ⌖ *180 Kč combined admission for museum and glassworks.*

🏃 Activities

Karlovy Vary is a town made for staying active in the outdoors. Exercise was often part of the treatment during the heyday of the resort, and the air quality here is markedly superior to that of Prague or other industrialized towns in

Sip with Caution

The waters from natural springs are loaded with minerals, which means they often have a sulfuric smell and taste—not necessarily the most appetizing thing. What's more, many of the waters speed the digestive process. You may want to sip at first as you get used to the flavor, and plan your day accordingly.

the Czech Republic. Hiking trails snake across the beech-and-pine-covered hills that surround the town on three sides. If you walk past the Grandhotel Pupp, away from the center, and follow the paved walkway that runs alongside the river for about 10 minutes, you'll discover a Japanese garden.

Karlovy Vary Golf Club

GOLF | This course, opened in 1904, has been extensively modernized since 2004 to include a new clubhouse and redesigned holes, including two water traps. The clubhouse has a relaxation center and an indoor golf simulator. The club requires a golf association membership and a minimum handicap of 36 to make a reservation to use the course. Electric carts and clubs can be rented. The European ground squirrel, listed as a vulnerable species, lives on the course. ✉ *Pražská 125, Karlovy Vary* ☎ *353–331–001* ⊕ *www.golfresort.cz* 🏌 *1200 Kč for 9 holes; 2000 Kč for 18 holes* 🏌 *18 holes; 6773 yards; par 72* ⊗ *Closed Nov.–Mar.*

Thermal Hotel

SWIMMING | Karlovy Vary's recently renovated warm, open-air public pool on top of the Thermal Hotel offers the experience of swimming at a cozy bathtub temperature even in the coolest weather; the view over the town is outstanding.

Even if you are not staying at the hotel, you can still take a dip in the waters for 390 Kč per three hours. ✉ *I. P. Pavlova, Karlovy Vary* ⊕ *www.thermal.cz* ☻ *Closed Oct.–Mar.*

Cheb

42 km (26 miles) southwest of Karlovy Vary; 174 km (105 miles) southwest of Prague.

Known for centuries by its German name of Eger, the old town of Cheb tickles the German border in the far west of the Czech Republic. The town has been a fixture of Bohemia since 1322 (when it was handed over to King Jan as thanks for his support of a Bavarian prince), but as you walk around the beautiful medieval square it's easy to forget you're not in Germany. The tall merchants' houses surrounding the main square, with their long, red-tile, sloping roofs dotted with windows like droopy eyelids, are more Germanic in style than anything else in Bohemia. You will also hear a lot of German on the streets from the day-trippers coming here from across the border.

Germany took possession of the town in 1938 under the terms of the notorious Munich Agreement. Following World War II, virtually the entire German population was expelled, and the Czech name of Cheb was officially adopted. During the Cold War, Cheb suffered as a communist outpost along the heavily fortified border with West Germany. Since then, thanks to German tourist dollars, Cheb has made an obvious economic comeback. The town center, with a lovely pedestrian zone, merits a few hours of strolling.

GETTING HERE

The journey from Prague to Cheb is about 3½ hours each way, whether you are taking the bus or the train; expect to pay more for the ride by train. The price for the bus trip is 229 Kč or 243 Kč; the price for the train ride 298 Kč and up, depending on the type of train. The high-speed Pendolino train service goes to Cheb in 2½ hours, but seat reservations are required. Look for special deals on the Czech Railways website (⊕ *www.cd.cz*) that sometimes make the seat reservations free. If you're driving, you can take the E50 and then the 21 from Prague to Cheb, a drive of about 2½ hours, though traffic can sometimes be heavy.

VISITOR INFORMATION Tourist Info Cheb. ✉ *Jateční 2, Cheb* ☎ *354–440–302* ⊕ *tic.cheb.cz/en/.*

Sights

Chebské muzeum (*Cheb Museum*)
OTHER MUSEUM | The building that houses this museum is just as interesting at its collection; it's known as the Pachelbel House, the setting for a murder during the Thirty Years' War. In 1634, General Albrecht von Wallenstein was executed in this house on the orders of Habsburg emperor Ferdinand II. He was provoked by Wallenstein's increasing power and rumors of treason. According to legend, Wallenstein was on his way to the Saxon border to enlist support to fight the Swedes when his own officers barged into his room and stabbed him through the heart with a stave. Wallenstein's stark bedroom has been left as it was with its four-poster bed and dark red velvet curtains. (The story also inspired playwright Friedrich Schiller to write the *Wallenstein* trilogy; he planned the work while living at the top of the square at No. 2.) The museum is also interesting in its own right, with a Wallenstein family picture gallery, a section on the history of Cheb, and a collection of minerals (including one discovered by Goethe). There's also the stuffed remains of Wallenstein's horse. ✉ *Nám. Krále Jiřího z Poděbrad 4, Cheb* ☎ *601–122–664* ⊕ *www.muzeum-cheb.cz* 🎫 *100 Kč* ☻ *Closed weekdays*

in Jan. and Feb., Mon. and Tues. in Mar., Apr., and Oct.–Dec., and Mon. May–Sept.

Chebský hrad (*Cheb Castle*)
CASTLE/PALACE | Built with blocks of lava taken from the nearby Komorní Hůrka volcano, this castle stands on a cliff overlooking the Ohře River. The castle—now a ruin—was built in the late 12th century for Holy Roman Emperor Frederick Barbarossa. Redbrick walls are 17th-century additions. Inside the castle grounds is the carefully restored double-decker **Romanesque chapel,** notable for the many lovely columns with heads carved into their capitals. The rather dark ground floor was used by commoners. A bright, ornate top floor was reserved for the emperor and his family, who entered via a wooden bridge leading to the royal palace. ✉ *Dobrovského 21, Cheb* ☎ *602–169–298* ⊕ *www.hrad-cheb. cz* 💰 *100 Kč* ⊙ *Closed weekdays in Nov.–Mar., and Mon. Apr.–Oct.*

Komorní Hůrka
NATURE SIGHT | Red markers indicate a path from Cheb's main square westward along the river and then north past this extinct volcano, now a tree-covered hill. Excavations on one side have laid bare the rock, and one tunnel remains open. Goethe instigated and took part in the excavations, and you can still—barely—make out a relief of the poet carved into the rock face.

■ TIP→ **The volcano is about 2 miles out of town.** ✉ *Komorní dvůr, Cheb.*

Kostel svatého Mikuláše (*Church of St. Nicholas*)
RELIGIOUS BUILDING | The plain but imposing Church of St. Nicholas was begun in 1230, when it belonged to the Order of Teutonic Knights. Tinkering over the centuries added an impressive Gothic portal and a baroque interior. Just inside the Gothic entrance is a wonderfully faded plaque commemorating the

diamond jubilee of Habsburg emperor Franz Joseph in 1908. The church was restored in 2016, and you can now visit the crypt, which has exhibitions, and the south tower, which has a panoramic view of the city. ✉ *Kostelní nám., Cheb* ☎ *354–422–458* ⊕ *www.farnostcheb.cz* 💰 *Tower and crypt 20 Kč donation (put coins in the turnstile)* ⊙ *Closed Mon. except for Easter Monday.*

"Roland" Statue
PUBLIC ART | In the middle of the central square, Náměstí Krále Jiřího z Poděbrad, this statue is similar to other Roland statues seen throughout Bohemia, attesting to the town's royal privileges. (Roland is a figure in medieval and Renaissance literature; his statues are found throughout Europe.) This one represents the town hero, Wastel of Eger. Look carefully at his right foot, and you can see a small man holding a sword and a head—this shows the town had its own judge and executioner. ✉ *Nám. Krále Jiřího z Poděbrad, Cheb.*

Špalíček
NOTABLE BUILDING | In the lower part of Náměstí Krále Jiřího z Poděbrad stand two rickety-looking groups of timbered medieval buildings (11 houses in all) divided by a narrow alley. The houses, forming the area known as Špalíček, date to the 13th century, and were once home to many Jewish merchants. Židovská ulice (Jews' Street), running uphill to the left of the Špalíček, served as the actual center of the ghetto. The small, unmarked alley running to the left off Židovská is called ulička Zavražděných (Lane of the Murdered). It was the scene of an outrageous act of violence in 1350: pressures had been building for some time between Jews and Christians. Incited by an anti-Semitic bishop, the townspeople chased the Jews into the street, closed off both ends, and massacred them. Now only the name attests to the slaughter. ✉ *Nám. Krále Jiřího z Poděbrad, Cheb.*

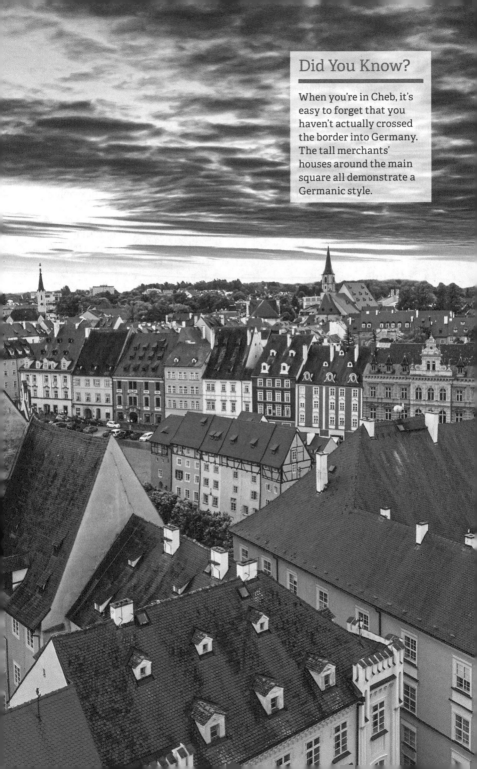

🍴 Restaurants

Kavárna-Restaurace Špalíček

$$ | CZECH | The sameness of the restaurants lining the square can be a bit numbing, but this one offers a reasonably priced selection of standard pork and chicken dishes, with the added charm of being in the ancient Špalíček complex. **Known for:** historic building; great spot to people watch; traditional Bohemian food. ⑤ *Average main: Kč230* ⊠ *Nám. Krále Jiřího z Poděbrad 50, Cheb* ☎ *777–203–013* ⊕ *restaurace-spalicek.cz* ▭ *No credit cards.*

Hotels

Barbarossa

$ | HOTEL | One block from the main square, this charming family-run hotel is a favorite among visiting Germans, so book ahead, especially on weekends. **Pros:** near the main square; parking available; friendly staff. **Cons:** gets crowded; staff can be abrupt; few amenities. ⑤ *Rooms from: Kč2000* ⊠ *Jateční 7, Cheb* ☎ *354–423–446* ⊕ *www.hotel-barbarossa.cz* ⇥ *21 rooms* ⦿ *Free Breakfast.*

Františkovy Lázně

6 km (4 miles) north of Cheb; 180 km (109 miles) southwest of Prague.

Františkovy Lázně, or Franzensbad, is the smallest of the three main Bohemian spas. It isn't really in the same league as Karlovy Vary. The main spa area is only a few blocks, and aside from a dozen or so cafés in which to enjoy an apple strudel or ice cream, there isn't much to see or do. That said, the charm of its uniform, Kaiser-yellow Empire architecture grows on you. Gardens surrounding the main spa area—both the manicured "French" gardens and the wilder "English" parks—grow on you, too. They're as perfect for strolling now as they were 200 years ago.

Mother and Child

Františkovy Lázně has long been known as a refuge for women seeking help in fertility problems. Evidence of that can be seen in the main spring's statue of a small cherub holding a fish. In keeping with the fertility theme, women are encouraged to touch the fish to ensure their own fertility. You'll notice the statue is shiny from so many years of being rubbed.

Summer is particularly pleasant, when a small orchestra occupies the gazebo in the Městkské sady (City Park) and locals and visitors sit in lawn chairs and listen.

The healing properties of the waters here were recognized as early as the 15th century, but Františkovy Lázně came into its own only at the start of the 19th century. Like Bohemia's other spas, Františkovy Lázně drew from the top drawer of European society, including one Ludwig Van Beethoven, who came here in 1812. But it remained in Cheb's shadow, and the spa stayed relatively small. In the years following World War II the spa declined. Most of the buildings were given over to factories and organizations to use as convalescent centers. Františkovy Lázně also developed a reputation for helping women with fertility problems, and Milan Kundera used it as the humorous, small-town backdrop for his novel *The Farewell Party.* Since 1989 the town has worked hard to restore the yellow façades to their former glory.

The best way to approach Františkovy Lázně is simply to find Národní ulice, the main street, and walk.

GETTING HERE

Expect to spend about four hours each way traveling between Prague and Františkovy Lázně via bus or train. As with other destinations, you'll pay more for riding the rails, and also make a few changes as there is little direct service. Costs are about 229 Kč one-way for the bus, about 310 Kč for a train with a change or 344 Kč without a change. If you're driving, you can take the E50 and then the 21 from Prague to Františkovy Lázně, a drive of about three hours.

VISITOR INFORMATION Františkovy Lázně Tourist Information. ✉ *Máchova 8, Františkovy Lázně* ☎ *778–736–298* ⊕ *www.frantiskovy-lazne.info.*

Sights

Františkův pramen

HOT SPRING | Under a little gazebo filled with brass pipes sits the town's main spring. The colonnade to the left once displayed a bust of Lenin that was replaced in 1990 by a memorial to the American liberation of the town in April 1945. To the right, in the garden, you'll see a statue of a small cherub holding a fish. The oval neoclassical temple just beyond the spring (amazingly, *not* painted yellow and white) is the **Glauberova dvorana** (Glauber Pavilion), where several springs bubble up into glass cases. ✉ *Národní ul. at Nám. Miru, Františkovy Lázně.*

Mětské muzeum (*Town Museum*)

OTHER MUSEUM | A fascinating peek into spa culture is housed in this small museum, just off Národní ulice. There's a wonderful collection of spa-related antiques, including copper bathtubs and a turn-of-the-20th-century exercise bike called a Velotrab. The guest books provide insight into the cosmopolitan world of pre–World War I Central Europe. The book for 1812 contains the entry "Ludwig van Beethoven, composer from Vienna." Texts are in Czech and German, but not

Marienbad with a French Twist

If the name "Marienbad" rings a bell, it may recall the groundbreaking 1961 French film *Last Year at Marienbad*. A collection of surreal vignettes, the movie explores the possible affair one French couple had in Marienbad through new-wave tricks like jarring jump cuts. But don't expect the manicured lawns and estates of this movie to reflect the landscape of the real Marienbad; it was shot in southern Germany.

English. ✉ *Dlouhá 4, Františkovy Lázně* ☎ *354–544–308* ⊕ *www.muzeum-frantiskovylazne.cz* ✑ *50 Kč* ⊘ *Closed Mon., and mid-Dec.–mid-Jan.*

Hotels

Most of the lodging establishments in town depend on spa patients, who generally stay for several weeks. Spa treatments usually require a medical checkup and cost substantially more than the normal room charge. Walk-in treatment can be arranged at some hotels or at the information center. Signs around town advertise massage therapy and other treatments for casual visitors.

Rossini

$ | **HOTEL** | An alternative to the upscale spa hotels in the center, this small family-operated pension is in a more residential area and offers nine rooms, two with balconies. **Pros:** affordable and clean; free coffee throughout the day. **Cons:** no spa; outside of the town's main area. ⑤ *Rooms from: Kč1500* ✉ *Lidická 5, Františkovy Lázně* ☎ *727–834–602* ⊕ *www.rossini.cz* ➷ *9 rooms* ⦿ *Free Breakfast.*

Mariánské Lázně

30 km (18 miles) southeast of Cheb; 47 km (29 miles) south of Karlovy Vary.

Once Bohemia's star spa town, Mariánské Lázně now plays second fiddle to Karlovy Vary. Whereas the latter, with its glitzy international film festival and wealthy "New Russian" residents, has succeeded in luring investors, Mariánské Lázně seems to survive largely on the decidedly less glamorous (and much older) crowd coming over from Germany. Busloads of German retirees arrive daily. They walk the promenades and repair over ice cream and cake before boarding the coach to head back home. This trade keeps the properties in business but hardly brings the capital influx needed to overhaul the spa facilities.

The grounds have remained lush and lovely, especially the upper part of the town's spa area near the Grandhotel Pacifik. Here you'll find the colonnades and fountains and river walks you expect from a once-world-famous spa. And the woods surrounding the town are magnificent.

A hundred years ago Mariánské Lázně, or Marienbad as it was known, was one of Europe's finest resorts. It was a favorite of Britain's King Edward VII. Goethe and Chopin also came. Mark Twain, on a visit in 1892, couldn't get over how new everything looked. Twain—who had a natural aversion to anything too salubrious—labeled the town a "health factory."

The best way to experience the spa—short of signing up for a weeklong treatment—is simply to buy a spouted drinking cup (available at the colonnades) and join the rest of the sippers taking the drinking cure. Be forewarned, though: the waters from the Rudolph, Ambrose, and Caroline springs, though harmless, all have a noticeable diuretic effect. For this reason they're used extensively in treating disorders of the kidney and bladder. Unlike Karlovy Vary, the springs here are all cold water, and may be easier to stomach.

Walking trails of varied difficulty surround the resort in all directions, and one of the country's best golf courses lies about 3 km (2 miles) to the east of town. Hotel staff can also help arrange activities such as tennis and horseback riding. For the less intrepid, a simple stroll around the gardens, with a few deep inhalations of the town's clean air, is enough to restore a healthy sense of perspective.

GETTING HERE

Train service between Prague and Mariánské Lázně takes about three hours each way. There is no direct bus service. Expect to pay 288 Kč one way for the train. From Karlovy Vary, there is regular regional bus service for about 50 Kč. If you're driving, you can take the E50 and then the 21 from Prague to Mariánské Lázně, a drive of about two hours.

VISITOR INFORMATION Mariánské Lázně Tourist Information. *(Cultural and Information Center)* ✉ *Hlavní 47, Mariánské Lázně* ☏ *354–622–474* ⊕ *www.marianskelazne.cz.*

 Sights

Chodová Planá

BREWERY | Need a break from the rigorous healthiness of spa life? Chodovar Beer Wellness Land is a few miles south of Mariánské Lázně and offers a wellness hotel, two restaurants, and an underground complex of granite tunnels that have been used to age beer since the 1400s. Generous servings of Czech dishes can be ordered to accompany the strong, fresh Chodovar beer tapped directly from granite storage vaults. You can tour the brewery, but don't expect much English commentary. The brewery also offers a beer bath and spa services starting at 690 Kč. The brewery promises it will cause a mild and gradual rise in heart activity and "scour away any unhealthy substances that may have accumulated."

■ **TIP→ There are brewery tours daily at 2 pm.** ⊠ *Pivovarská 107, Chodová Planá* ☎ *374–617–100 spa* ⊕ *www.chodovar.cz* ⊠ *Tour 140 Kč.*

Restaurants

Česká hospůdka

$$ | CZECH | The simple rustic-type setting with a fireplace and lots of wooden details complements the classic Czech menu of duck, goose, fish, and *guláš.* Service is informal and friendly. **Known for:** informal ambience; attentive service; classic Czech food. ⑤ *Average main: Kč250* ⊠ *Klíčová 179, Mariánské Lázně* ☎ *720–121–500* ⊕ *www.ceskahospud-kaml.cz.*

Restaurace Poštovní Dvůr

$$ | CZECH | Just off the main street, this former postal building offers Czech and international cuisine in an uncluttered setting filled with dark wood. In good weather, there is seating on the outdoor terrace. **Known for:** quiet location; large portions; efficient service. ⑤ *Average main: Kč250* ⊠ *Hlavní 15, Mariánské Lázně* ☎ *777–811–647* ⊕ *www.postovnid-vur.eu.*

Hotels

Hotel prices have risen in recent years, and many properties are terribly overpriced for what is offered. Despite the glorious Empire and neoclassical façades of many of the hotels and spas, the rooms are a bit on the blah side—typical Central European bland for the most part—with a few exceptions listed below. Most of the hotels have ready-made packages with treatments, and if you plan to indulge in the spas anyway, they can offer some level of savings. Check the hotel's website for current offers.

Private accommodations are usually cheaper than hotels, although with more limited amenities. The best place to look for a private room is along Paleckého ulice and Hlavní třída, south of the main spa area, or look in the neighboring villages of Zádub and Závišín.

Centrální Lázně

$$ | HOTEL | Near the colonnade and Ambrose Spring, this eggshell-white spa hotel offers unusual treatments such as magnetotherapy and peat packs. **Pros:** some rooms have excellent views; extensive therapies; central location (hence the name). **Cons:** not exactly a jumping scene; noisy, especially in the summer; rooms are a bit spartan. ⑤ *Rooms from: Kč2600* ⊠ *Goethovo nám. 1, Mariánské Lázně* ☎ *354–635–300* ⊕ *www.ensan-ahotels.com/centralni-lazne/en* ⤣ *99 rooms* ⦿ *Free Breakfast.*

Falkensteiner Spa Resort Marienbad

$$$$ | HOTEL | Formerly the Grand Spa Marienbad, this Austrian-owned hotel is made up of three interconnected buildings and boasts the most rooms and the biggest wellness center in Mariánské Lázně. **Pros:** huge spa; excellent spa services; sleek rooms. **Cons:** expensive; officious staff; overly Teutonic vibe. ⑤ *Rooms from: Kč7100* ⊠ *Ruska 123, Mariánské Lázně* ☎ *354–929 399* ⊕ *www.falkensteiner.com/en/spa-re-sort-marianske-lazne* ⤣ *164 rooms* ⦿ *Free Breakfast.*

Grandhotel Pacifik

$$ | HOTEL | This regal hotel at the top of Hlavní Street has a full range of spa and wellness facilities including a pool and a sauna. **Pros:** great views; prime location; extensive treatments. **Cons:** pricey; food is a bit lackluster; common areas a bit down at the heels. ⑤ *Rooms from: Kč3350* ⊠ *Mírové nám. 84, Mariánské Lázně* ☎ *354–651–300* ⊕ *www.ensan-ahotels.com/pacifik/en* ⤣ *102 rooms* ⦿ *Free Breakfast.*

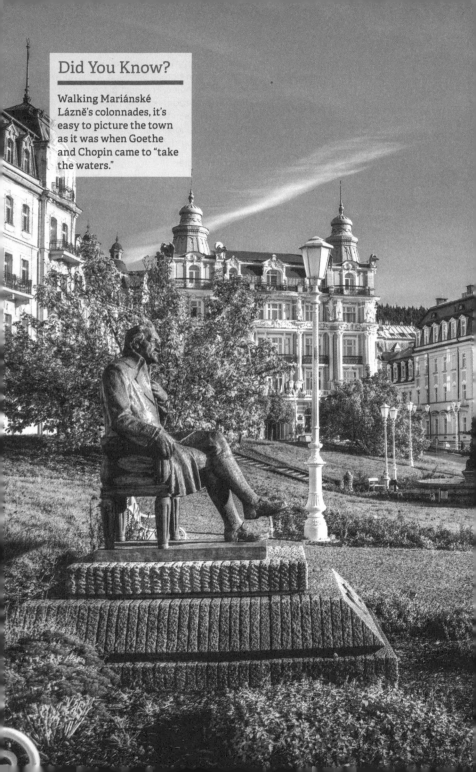

Did You Know?

Walking Mariánské Lázně's colonnades, it's easy to picture the town as it was when Goethe and Chopin came to "take the waters."

Hotel Nové Lázně

$$ | HOTEL | This neo-Renaissance hotel and spa—opened in 1896—boasts an opulent façade and public spaces, but these give way to slightly austere rooms. **Pros:** above-average café; beautiful façade; two pools. **Cons:** spa services cost extra; rooms are a bit dated; maintains a slight institutional feel. ⑤ *Rooms from: Kč2850* ⊠ *Reitenbergerova 53, Mariánské Lázně* ☎ *354–644–300* ⊕ *www.ensanahotels.com/nove-lazne* ⤳ *98 rooms* ⦿⧵ *Free Breakfast.*

Performing Arts

The West Bohemian Symphony Orchestra performs regularly in the ornate Společenský dům Casino. The town's annual Chopin Festival each August brings in pianists from around Europe to perform the Polish composer's works.

Plzeň

92 km (55 miles) southwest of Prague.

Plzeň—or Pilsen in German, as it's better known abroad—is the industrial heart of Western Bohemia and the region's biggest city. To most visitors the city is known as a beer mecca. Anyone who loves the stuff must pay homage to the enormous Pilsner Urquell brewery, where modern Pils-style beer was first developed more than 150 years ago. Brewery tours are available and highly recommended. There's even a brewing museum here for intellectual beer aficionados.

Another item of interest—particularly for Americans—is historical. Whereas most of the Czech Republic was liberated by Soviet troops at the end of World War II, Plzeň was liberated by the U.S. Army, led by General George S. Patton. Under the communists this fact was not widely acknowledged. But since 1989

the liberation week celebrations held in May have gotten bigger and bigger each passing year. If you're traveling in the area at this time, it's worth stopping by to take part in the festivities. To this day Plzeň retains a certain "pro-American" feeling that other towns in the Czech Republic lack. There's even a big statue here emblazoned with an enthusiastic "Thank You, America!" written in both English and Czech. You'll find it, naturally, at the top of Americká street near the intersection with Klatovská. You can learn all about the liberation at the Patton Memorial Museum.

GETTING HERE

Frequent bus and train service between Prague and Plzeň makes the journey about 1 hour 15 minutes each way. Expect to pay about 100 Kč for the bus, 155 Kč for the train. If you're driving, you can take the E50 directly to Plzeň, a drive of about one hour.

VISITOR INFORMATION Plzeň City Information Centre. ⊠ *Nám. Republiky 41, Plzeň* ☎ *378–035–330* ⊕ *www.pilsen.eu/ tourist.*

⊙ Sights

Náměstí Republiky (*Republic Square*) **PLAZA/SQUARE** | The city's architectural attractions center on this main square. Dominated by the enormous Gothic **Chrám svatého Bartoloměje** (Church of St. Bartholomew), the square is one of the largest in Bohemia. The church, at 335 feet, is among the tallest in the Czech Republic, and its height is rather accentuated by the emptiness of the square around it. There are a variety of other architectural jewels around the perimeter of the square, including the town hall, adorned with *sgraffiti* and built in the Renaissance style by Italian architects during the town's heyday in the 16th century. The **Great Synagogue,** which claims to be the second-largest in Europe, is a few blocks west of the square, just

The Pilsner Urquell Brewery is the birthplace of the world renowned lager Pilsner Urquell and the biggest brewery in the Czech Republic.

outside the green strip that circles the Old Town. Three very modern gold-color fountains were added to the square in 2011; however, not everyone is a fan, as the fountains don't really mesh with the historic surroundings. ⊠ *Plzeň*.

Pilsen Beer Spa & Wellness Hotel Purkmistr
HOT SPRING | While Plzeň lacks the bitter thermal waters that are a draw in the spa region, it is better known for bitter pilsner-style beer. So the opening of a beer spa was inevitable. You can bathe in a custom-made larchwood tub filled with warm beer for a 60-minute treatment. Potable beer is available from a barrel at the same time. The room is lined with stone tiles, and relaxing music plays in the background. The treatment can be combined with a beer massage, or a honey or chocolate massage. Other procedures are also available. The spa is a bit outside of the city center. ⊠ *Selská náves 21/2, Plzeň* ☎ *377–994–311* ⊕ *www. pilsenbeerspa.cz*.

★ **Pilsner Urquell Brewery**
BREWERY | This is a must-see for any beer lover. The first pilsner beer was created in 1842 using the excellent Plzeň water, a special malt fermented on the premises, and hops grown in the region around Žatec. (Hops from this area remain in great demand today.) Guided tours of the brewery, complete with a visit to the brewhouse and beer tastings, are offered daily. The brewery is near the railway station. There are also tours of the nearby Gambrinus brewery. ⊠ *U Prazdroje 7, Plzeň* ☎ *377–062–888* ⊕ *www.prazdroj-visit.cz* ✉ *Pilsner Urquell Brewery 300 Kč (in English); Gambrinus Brewery 200 Kč (in English)*.

Pivovarské muzeum (*Brewery Museum*)
HISTORY MUSEUM | In a late-Gothic malthouse, this museum sits one block northeast of Náměstí Republiky. All kinds of fascinating paraphernalia trace the region's brewing history, including the horse-drawn carts used to haul the kegs.

■ **TIP**→ **A phone app is available with info in English.** ✉ *Veleslavínova 6, Plzeň* ☎ *377–062–888* ⊕ *www.prazdrojvisit. cz* ⊠ *100 Kč unguided (English text available).*

Plzeň Historical Underground

NOTABLE BUILDING | Dating to the 13th century, this is a web of multilevel tunnels. Used for storing food and producing beer and wine, many of the labyrinthine passageways are dotted with wells and their accompanying wooden water-pipe systems. Tours last about 50 minutes. The entrance is in the Brewery Museum. ✉ *Veleslavínova 6, Plzeň* ☎ *377–235–574* ⊕ *www.plzenskepodzemi.cz* ⊠ *150 Kč (in English).*

U.S. General George S. Patton Memorial

HISTORIC SIGHT | With exhibits and photos, this memorial tells the story of the liberation of Plzeň from the Nazis by U.S. soldiers on May 6, 1945. As the story goes, Patton wanted to press on from Plzeň to liberate Prague, but was prevented from doing so by the Yalta agreement between the United States and the Soviet Union that said Czechoslovakia was to remain under Soviet influence. U.S. aid to Czechoslovakia is also documented. The museum was dedicated in 2005 on the 60th anniversary of Plzeň's liberation. ✉ *Pobřežní 10, Plzeň* ☎ *378–037–954* ⊕ *www.patton-memorial.cz* ⊠ *100 Kč* ⊘ *Closed Mon. and Tues.*

Restaurants

Anděl Café

$$ | CAFÉ | In the evenings, this café, which offers affordable lunches and snacks, becomes a trendy bar. The emphasis is on fair-trade items and food from local farmers who follow ecological practices. **Known for:** good value; eco-friendly menu; trendy hipster vibe. ⑤ *Average main: Kč150* ✉ *Bezručova 7, Plzeň* ☎ *777–022–235* ⊕ *www.andelcafe.cz.*

Caffe Fellini

$ | CAFÉ | This dessert spot is right across from the Church of St. Bartholomew. With an outdoor patio overlooking the square, it's a great place to cool down. **Known for:** simple but tasty Italian food; great cakes and pastries; good spot for watching the square. ⑤ *Average main: Kč80* ✉ *Nám. Republiky 7, Plzeň* ☎ *776–151–429* ⊕ *www.caffefellini.cz* ▤ *No credit cards.*

El Cid

$$$ | SPANISH | An extensive wine list complements the tapas at this Spanish-style restaurant along the old town walls, just across from the Continental hotel. Pictures of bullfighters line the yellow walls, while a large patio overlooks the sprawling Křižíkovy Park. **Known for:** central location; spanish theme and cuisine; attentive service. ⑤ *Average main: Kč380* ✉ *Křižíkovy sady 1, Plzeň* ☎ *377–224–595* ⊕ *www.elcid.cz.*

Na Spilce

$$ | CZECH | After a visit to the Pilsner Urquell Brewery, you can carry on drinking and find some cheap traditional grub at the large Na Spilce beer hall just inside the brewery gates. The pub is open daily from 11 am to 11 pm. **Known for:** great for beer fans; recently renovated; modern take on Czech classic dishes. ⑤ *Average main: Kč275* ✉ *U Prazdroje 7, Plzeň* ⊕ *www.naspilce.com.*

Rango

$$ | MEDITERRANEAN | Part of a hotel of the same name, the interior of Rango is a mash-up of medieval, baroque, and modern style—think Gothic arched ceilings and '60s modern light fixtures. Similarly, the cuisine ranges from Italy to Greece; in addition to panini, they serve excellent pasta dishes, pizzas, and grilled meat. **Known for:** friendly and quick service; superior pizza and pasta; historical space. ⑤ *Average main: Kč270* ✉ *Pražská 10, Plzeň* ☎ *377–329–969* ⊕ *www.rango.cz.*

U Mansfelda

$$ | CZECH | Fresh Pilsner Urquell and variations on classic Czech dishes draw diners to this Pilsner Urquell–sponsored restaurant. A gleaming copper hood floats above the taps in traditional pub style, and the patio invites visitors to spend the evening sipping cold beer and enjoying treats such as boar guláš with dumplings or roasted duck with red cabbage. **Known for:** large menu of classic dishes; well-poured beer; historical space. ⑤ *Average main: Kč260 ⊠ Dřevěná 9, Plzeň ☎ 377–333–844 ⊕ umansfelda.cz ◑ Wine bar closed Sun.–Wed.*

Hotels

Courtyard Pilsen

$$ | HOTEL | This sleek property offers all the amenities a visiting American could hope for, right down to the flat-screen televisions and ice machines in the hallways on each floor. **Pros:** central location; great amenities; a trusted name. **Cons:** doesn't feel especially local; rooms lack charm; extras such as breakfast are pricey. ⑤ *Rooms from: Kč4000 ⊠ Sady 5. kvetna 57, Plzeň ☎ 373–370–100 ⊕ www. marriott.com ⇥ 195 rooms ⦿ No Meals.*

Hotel Central

$$ | HOTEL | This angular 1960s structure is recommendable for its sunny rooms, friendly staff, and great location, right on the main square. **Pros:** rooftop restaurant; superlative staff; beautiful views of the main square. **Cons:** the square can echo noise at night; rooms have a retro feel; very small bathrooms. ⑤ *Rooms from: Kč2200 ⊠ Nám. Republiky 33, Plzeň ☎ 377–226–757 ⊕ www.hotelcentral.cz ⇥ 77 rooms ⦿ Free Breakfast.*

Hotel Gondola

$$ | HOTEL | A superb choice, the Gondola is clean and quiet with cozy brick-walled rooms and modern facilities, including air-conditioning—all just a few steps away from the central square. **Pros:** quiet location with parking; incredible value; chockablock with add-ons. **Cons:** slightly odd location; some rooms only have skylight windows; limited business facilities. ⑤ *Rooms from: Kč2390 ⊠ Pallova 12, Plzeň ☎ 377–994–211 ⊕ www.hotelgondola.cz ⇥ 20 rooms ⦿ Free Breakfast.*

Parkhotel Plzeň

$$ | HOTEL | A 10-minute tram ride from the center, this large hotel built in 2004 near the Borský Park is perfect for anyone passing through town with a car. **Pros:** sleek rooms; spa services; tennis court. **Cons:** outside the center; no elevator in the annex; breakfast options rather limited. ⑤ *Rooms from: Kč2400 ⊠ U Borského parku 31, Plzeň ☎ 378–772–977 ⊕ en.parkhotel-czech.eu ⇥ 150 rooms ⦿ Free Breakfast.*

Chapter 14

MORAVIA

Updated by
Raymond Johnston

👁 Sights	🍴 Restaurants	🛏 Hotels	👜 Shopping	🍸 Nightlife
★★★★★	★★★☆☆	★★★★☆	★★☆☆☆	★★☆☆☆

WELCOME TO MORAVIA

TOP REASONS TO GO

★ **Circle the square:** In a country of town squares, Telč's is far and away the most impressive.

★ **See a classic castle:** When people think of castles, they imagine something like Hrad Bouzov (Bouzov Castle).

★ **Spot colossal columns:** Olomouc's Morový sloup (Trinity Column) is so amazing, it's under UNESCO protection.

★ **See the Château Lednice:** A delightful castle, with huge gardens and even a minaret out back!

★ **Uncover some history:** It's exciting to watch Třebíč and Mikulov embrace their past by renovating and promoting their Jewish Quarters.

The most obvious difference between Bohemia and Moravia is that the former is beer country and the latter is wine country. The divisions, while amicable, run much deeper. The people are also more in touch with their past, embracing folk costumes and music for celebrations. In smaller towns, some older women still wear embroidered scarves and dresses, something you never see in Bohemia. The pace is also much slower, as agriculture and not industry has always been the driving force of life.

The castles and châteaus attest to the fact that the area was once quite wealthy, but in recent times development has been limited, leaving many areas still unspoiled. And because it's so far off the beaten path of Prague, you'll see far fewer tourists.

1 Třebíč. With one of the best-preserved Jewish Quarters in Central Europe, with a number of synagogues and a cemetery, this small town finds itself on the UNESCO World Heritage list. The city's dominant feature, however, is a looming Catholic basilica.

2 Telč. Time seems to have stopped several centuries ago in this town, almost unchanged since the Renaissance. Beautiful frescoes adorn the exteriors of most of the buildings in pastel colors or ornate black and white.

3 Mikulov. Moravia is wine country, and Mikulov is at its center. Castles, châteaus, and sculpted parks dot the area, and vineyards cover many of the hills. Small wine cellars serve the best of the local beverages plus regional cuisine.

4 Brno. The capital of Moravia, Brno is a busy hub and the modern counterpoint to Prague's Old World charm. That said, Brno also has a castle, a cathedral, and an Old Town Hall that are on par with attractions in other European capitals.

5 Olomouc. The central city of Moravia was a major base for occupying Russian soldiers. Parts still have an abandoned feel, but the city is slowly waking up. The main square offers a truly monumental baroque column not far from a curious socialist-realist town clock built after World War II.

The Czech Republic's other half, Moravia, is frequently overlooked by visitors. No cities here can compare with the noble beauty of Prague, and Moravia's gentle mountains suffer in comparison with the more rugged Tatras in Slovakia just to the east. Yet Moravia's colorful villages and rolling hills do merit a few days of exploration. Come here for good wine, good folk music, friendly faces, and the languid pace.

Despite sharing a common political union for more than 1,000 years with Bohemians, Moravians still consider themselves distinct from "Czechs" (though it must be said that those differences are not always apparent to visitors). The Moravian dialect of Czech is softer and—as Moravians insist—purer than that spoken in Bohemia. It's hard to generalize, but in a word the Moravians are "earthier" than their Bohemian cousins. They tend to prefer a glass of wine—or even better, fiery *slivovice* (plum brandy)—to beer. Folk music, all but gone in Bohemia, is still very much alive in Moravia. And Catholicism is still a part of life here— particularly in cities like Olomouc—in a way that died out long ago in much of Bohemia.

Historically, Olomouc is one of Moravia's main centers. And it is still impressive today. Long a bastion of the Austro-Hungarian Empire—the city boasts two enormous central squares, a clock tower, and the country's largest Trinity column.

In addition, southern Moravia has many small cities, including Mikulov, and a lovely wine region.

If your time is limited or you're just passing through, be sure to at least plan a stopover in the town of Telč in the south. Its enormous central square is like the backdrop of a film set.

Planning

When to Go

Wine harvest festivals, with the opportunity to taste the barely fermented young wine, hear folk songs, and eat local delicacies, are mainly in September. For some towns it is the only time they are truly crowded. But the summer months offer pleasant relaxation at outdoor cafés in an unhurried atmosphere. For cyclists, many trails have opened up in the wine region, with spring and early summer being ideal for a tour, but beware that intoxicated cycling is illegal. Winter should be avoided, especially in smaller towns, as many sights are closed, and many shops still close for the weekend throughout the year.

Getting Here

Bus and train service makes much of Moravia easily accessible. A high-speed train to Olomouc makes it possible to go there for a day trip from Prague, in just over two hours each way. And while trains do serve the smaller towns and cities, buses are usually more direct and faster. The D1 highway from Prague also leads into South Moravia and loops back up to end near Olomouc, but it gets heavy traffic at the start and end of the weekend.

Guided Tours

Only a few tour providers offer day trips from Prague to Moravia, as it is farther than places in Bohemia. Guided tours are often available from tourist information centers in individual towns but without transportation to and from Prague.

Wittmann Tours

Wittmann Tours focuses on Jewish culture and offers a private trip to Třebíč. The trip starts at 9,000 Kč for a group, plus entrance fees, and goes up depending on the group size. ⊕ www.wittmann-tours. com.

Restaurants and Hotels

Compared with Prague, change has been slow to arrive in Moravia since 1990, especially beyond the major towns. The good news: food and hotels are priced lower. Service has improved but still lags behind Prague's. Older hotel staff might not be proficient in English, but the younger generation has a functional level.

And you might find menus in Czech and German, rather than English, especially in the south near the border. On the plus side, hotel and restaurant workers tend to be friendlier in Moravia and a bit more attentive than they are in Prague.

Cuisine in Moravia leans toward the heavy and the old-fashioned. Choices are sometimes limited to pork, chicken, and duck dishes, usually with lots of gravy. Slowly, a few places with healthier food and modern international cuisine are opening. Pizza places are also widespread. In mountainous areas, inquire locally about the possibility of staying in a *chata* (cabin). These are abundant, and they often carry a bit more of the Moravian spirit than faceless modern hotels. Many lack modern amenities, though, so be prepared to rough it a bit.

Restaurant and hotel reviews have been shortened. For full information, visit Fodors.com.

What It Costs in koruny			
$	$$	$$$	$$$$
RESTAURANTS			
under 150 Kč	150 Kč–350 Kč	351 Kč–500 Kč	over 500 Kč
HOTELS			
under 2,200 Kč	2,200 Kč–4,000 Kč	4,001 Kč–6,500 Kč	over 6,500 Kč

Třebíč

35 km (21 miles) east of Telč; 151 km (91 miles) southeast of Prague.

UNESCO declared both the looping streets of the Židovská čtvrt' (Jewish Quarter) and an ornate basilica in Třebíč World Heritage Sites in 2003. The town is first mentioned in 1101, but it was almost completely destroyed in a war in 1468 and then rebuilt. Although known for its historic buildings, Třebíč also has a few modern ones in the art nouveau, cubist, and functionalist styles. Guided tours of the town are available in English from the information center at Karlovo náměstí 53. As in all small towns, very few shops are open on weekends.

If you arrive by bus or train from Prague, keep an eye out for the 19th-century windmill at the west edge of town. The town's tower, **Městská věz**, on Martinské náměstí provides a nice view of the whole city.

GETTING HERE
Ideally, you should combine Třebíč with a visit to Telč. Direct bus travel to Třebíč from Prague takes around 2½ hours and costs around 160 Kč. Train connections are not direct and are more expensive. Bus travel with a change in Jihlava, which has a nice square and town wall, is also possible; from Telč the bus trip takes less than 45 minutes and costs around 25 Kč.

Car travel from Telč is direct on Route 23 and takes about 20 minutes. From Prague, it's fastest to get back on Highway E50 and go east to Velké Meziříčí. Then go south on Route 360; the trip should take less than three hours.

TIMING
Out of respect for Jewish traditions, some sites are closed on Saturday.

VISITOR INFORMATION
CONTACTS Třebíč Tourist information. ✉ Karlovo nám. 47, Třebíč ☎ 568–610–021 ⊕ www.visittrebic.eu.

Sights

Bazilika sv. Prokupa (*St. Procopius Basilica*)
RELIGIOUS BUILDING | The late Romanesque and early Gothic St. Procopius Basilica remains true to its original layout from 1260. New sections were added as recently as the 1950s, but the oldest parts are easy to spot. Look for a very heavy style, with lots of stone and few windows. Two baroque towers at the front were added in the early 1700s by architect F. M. Kaňka. One of the oldest sections is the crypt, with Romanesque pillars and arches. The château next door has been fully renovated and houses the Vysočina Museum Třebíč. ✉ *Zámek 1, Třebíč* ☎ *568–610–022* ⊕ *www.visittrebic. eu/sights/basilica-of-st-prokopius* ✉ *Basilica 160 Kč (English tour), museum 80 Kč* ☉ *Museum closed Mon. Sept.–June.*

Rear Synagogue
RELIGIOUS BUILDING | The Rear Synagogue has an exhibition of Jewish religious items and a wooden model of the ghetto as it was in the 1800s. A touch screen attached to the model provides audio information about the various buildings, with English as an option. Guided tours to the synagogue are available and include a tour of the house of Seligmann Bauer. ✉ *Subakova 44, Třebíč* ☎ *568–610–023* ⊕ *www.visittrebic.eu/ sights/rear-synagogue-and-seligmann-bauer-apos-s-house* ✉ *160 Kč (tour in English); synagogue with no guide 40 Kč* ☉ *Closed Sat.*

Židovská čtvrť (*Jewish Quarter*)
HISTORIC DISTRICT | A spiraling maze of winding streets, the Jewish Quarter has two synagogues and other buildings formerly used by the town's Jewish community. The **Front Synagogue** on Tiché náměstí is now used for Protestant services. Several houses in the district are intriguing, including a pink Renaissance house with an overhanging second floor at Pokorný 5. A trail of signs in English points out the remarkable spots. Remember your manners—most houses in this area are not museums, and people actually live in them. ✉ *Tiché nám., Třebíč* ⊕ *www.visittrebic.eu.*

Židovský hřbitov (*Jewish Cemetery*)
CEMETERY | The Jewish Cemetery has 3,000 tombstones dating from the Renaissance up to the 20th century.

A unified style is what makes Telč so lovely.

It's free to enter, but guided tours can be arranged. The cemetery is closed on Saturday, but almost all of it can be seen from the gate and the low wall. ✉ *Hrádek 14, Třebíč* ☎ *737–180–813* ⊕ *www. visittrebic.eu/sights/jewish-cemetery* 🎫 *Free* ⏱ *Closed Sat.*

Telč

35 km (21 miles) west of Třebíč; 154 km (94 miles) southeast of Prague via Rte. 406.

Don't be fooled by the dusty approach to the little town of Telč or the unpromising, unkempt countryside surrounding the place. Telč is a knockout. What strikes the eye most here is not just its size but the unified style of the buildings. On the lowest levels are beautifully vaulted Gothic halls, just above are Renaissance floors and façades, and all the buildings are crowned with rich Renaissance and baroque gables.

GETTING HERE
A car is your best option and makes it easy to combine a trip to Telč with a stop in Třebíč. From Prague, take Highway E50 and E59 south to Route 23 and then west to Telč. The trip takes about two hours without stops. Třebíč is east on Route 23.

Direct bus service leaves from Prague's Florenc bus station and takes just under three hours; the fare is approximately 209 Kč. From Třebíč a direct bus can take 42 minutes and costs around 45 Kč.

Train service from Prague requires several changes and takes more than four hours, so it isn't a practical option. It's recommended only for those who want the scenic route.

VISITOR INFORMATION
CONTACTS Telč Tourist Information.
✉ *Nám. Zachariáše z Hradce 10, Telč* ☎ *567–112–407* ⊕ *www.telc.eu.*

👁 Sights

Kostel sv. Ducha (Church of the Holy Spirit)

RELIGIOUS BUILDING | A tiny street leading off the main square takes you to the 160-foot Romanesque tower of the Church of the Holy Spirit, a solid tower finished off in conical gray peaks. This is the oldest standing structure in Telč, dating to the first quarter of the 13th century. The interior, however, is a confused hodge-podge, as the style was fiddled with repeatedly, first in a late-Gothic makeover and then refashioned again because of fire damage.

■**TIP**→ **In the summer months, the tower is open for a small entrance fee.** ✉ *Palackého ul., Telč* ☎ *567–112–407 tower information* ⊕ *www.telc.eu/vez_sv_ducha* 🎟 *Free; tower 30 Kč* ⊙ *Tower closed Mon., closed Oct.–May.*

★ Náměstí Zachariáše z Hradce

PLAZA/SQUARE | This main square is so perfect you feel like you've stepped into a painting, not a living town. Zacharias of Neuhaus, the square's namesake, allegedly created the architectural unity. During the 16th century, so the story goes, the wealthy Zacharias had the castle—originally a small fort—rebuilt into a Renaissance château. But the town's dull buildings clashed so badly that Zacharias had the square rebuilt to match the castle's splendor.

From the south side of town, walk through the **Great Gate,** part of the original fortifications dating to the 13th century. As you approach on Palackého ulice, the square unfolds in front of you, graced with the château at the northern end and beautiful houses bathed in pastel ice-cream shades. Fans of Renaissance reliefs should note the *sgraffito* corner house at No. 15. The house at No. 61, across from the Černý Orel Hotel, also bears intricate details. ✉ *Telč.*

Statní zámek Telč (Telč Château)

CASTLE/PALACE | This Gothic castle was transformed into a refined Renaissance château by Italian masters between 1553 and 1568. Grouped in a complex with the former Jesuit college and Kostel sv. Jakuba (Church of St. James), the castle was built during the 14th century, perhaps by King John of Luxembourg, the father of Charles IV. In season you can tour the castle and admire the rich Renaissance interiors. The chastising *sgraffito* relief in the dining room depicting gluttony (in addition to the six other deadly sins) seems oddly placed. Other interesting rooms with *sgraffiti* include the Treasury, the Armory, and the Blue and Gold Chambers. There are two tours: the first, Tour A, goes through the Renaissance chambers and is available in English; the second, Tour B, displays the rooms that were used as recently as 1945 but is available only in Czech. The castle basement and gardens are also accessible. ✉ *Nám. J. Kypty, Telč* ☎ *567–243–943* ⊕ *www.zamek-telc.cz* 🎟 *Tours from 150 Kč (in Czech)* ⊙ *Tours currently limited due to renovations.*

☕ Coffee and Quick Bites

Cukrárna u Matěje

$ | **CAFÉ** | Indulge in good, freshly made cakes or an ice-cream cone at Cukrárna u Matěje, a little café and pastry shop at Na baště 2, on the street leading past the château to a small lake. **Known for:** good coffee; fresh ice cream; smoking permitted. 🟅 *Average main: Kč80* ✉ *Na baště 2, Telč* ☎ *777–162–160.*

 # Hotels

Celerin

$ | **HOTEL** | Occupying a tiny corner of the square on the opposite side from the castle, this is the nicest hotel in town. **Pros:** central location on square; historical details in rooms; children's playground.

Cons: some rooms have limited views due to small (but historically accurate) windows; no elevator; limited parking. $ *Rooms from: Kč1620* ✉ *Nám. Zachariáše z Hradce 1/43, Telč* ☎ *730–519–443* ⊕ *www.hotelcelerin.cz* 🛏 *12 rooms* ⦿ *Free Breakfast.*

Hotel U Černého orla

$ | HOTEL | A decent older lemon-yellow baroque hotel on the main square has suitably high standards. **Pros:** restored historic building right on the main square; romantic ambience; pets can stay for free. **Cons:** lacks modern features such as a/c; limited parking; only one room has barrier-free entrance. $ *Rooms from: Kč1999* ✉ *Nám. Zachariáše z Hradce 7* · ☎ *567–243–222* ⊕ *www.cernyorel.cz* 🛏 *33 rooms* ⦿ *Free Breakfast.*

Mikulov

60 km (37 miles) south of Brno; 283 km (174 miles) southeast of Prague.

In many ways Mikulov is the quintessential Moravian town, with pastel pink-and-yellow buildings and green rolling hills. For centuries it was one of the most important towns in the region—the seat of the Liechtenstein family in the late Middle Ages and then later the home to the powerful Dietrichstein family. The castle's size and splendor demonstrate Mikulov's onetime crucial position astride the traditional border between Moravia and Austria.

But Mikulov began an extended decline in the 19th century, when the main railroad line from Vienna bypassed the town in favor of Břeclav. Historically, Mikulov was the center of Moravia's Jewish community, growing to a population of several thousand at one point, but many Jews left to seek out life in bigger cities. The 20th century was especially cruel to Mikulov. The Nazis Aryanized many of the industries and deported remaining Jews.

After the war, many local industries—including the all-important wineries—were nationalized. Mikulov stagnated as a lonely outpost at the edge of the Iron Curtain.

Recent years have seen a slow revival. Much of the wine industry is back in private hands, and standards have been raised, thanks in part to European Union wine regulations. Day-trippers from Austria have spurred development of a nascent tourist industry. And after many decades of decline, the old Jewish Quarter is getting overdue attention. Although the Jewish community is still tiny—numbering just a handful of people—work is under way to try to preserve some of the remaining houses in the quarter. You can tour the quarter, where many of the houses are now marked with plaques explaining their significance. The Jewish cemetery is one of the largest in Central Europe and a must-see if you're passing through.

Grape-harvesting time in October provides an ideal moment to visit and enjoy the local pastoral delights. Head for one of the many private *sklípky* (wine cellars) built into the hills surrounding the town. If you visit in early September, try to hit Mikulov's renowned wine-harvest festival that kicks off the season with traditional music, folk dancing, and much guzzling of local Riesling.

GETTING HERE

Mikulov is easily reached by bus from Prague with a change at Brno's Zvonařka bus station. The trip takes a little more than four hours and costs about 360 Kč.

Train service from Prague requires a change at Břeclav. It takes about 4½ hours and costs about 453 Kč.

By car, the trip is south of Brno on Highway E65 to Břeclav and then east on Route 40 and takes a little more than 30 minutes from Brno.

Main Square with the fountain and Holy Trinity Statue in Mikulov

VISITOR INFORMATION

CONTACTS Mikulov Tourist Information.
✉ *Nám. 1, Mikulov* ☎ *519–510–855*
⊕ *www.infomikulov.cz.*

👁 Sights

★ Státní zámek Lednice na Moravé (*Château Lednice na Moravé*)

CASTLE/PALACE | The Château Lednice na Moravé, 12 km (7 miles) east of Mikulov, is a must-see. The dining room alone, with resplendent blue-and-green silk wall coverings embossed with the Moravian eagle, makes the visit memorable. The grounds have a 200-foot-tall minaret and a massive greenhouse filled with exotic flora. The minaret halls have been recently restored. A horse-drawn carriage ride and a romantic boat ride are available and are a great way to see the grounds. The absolute splendor of the palace and gardens contrasts sharply with the workaday reality of the town of Lednice. Tickets can be bought online to save time. ✉ *Zámek 1, Lednice* ☎ *519–340–128* ⊕ *www.zamek-lednice.com* ✉ *Main tours 240 Kč; Museum of Marionettes from 220 Kč; greenhouse 100 Kč; grotto 100 Kč; minaret 100 Kč; minaret halls 180 Kč; castle ruin 110 Kč* ⊗ *Closed weekdays Nov.–May and Mon. June–Sept.*

Zámek Mikulov (*Mikulov Château*)

CASTLE/PALACE | The château holds the **Regionální Muzeum** (Regional Museum), exhibiting period furniture and local wine-making items, including a remarkable wine cask, made in 1643, with a capacity of more than 22,000 gallons. Built as the Gothic-era residence of the noble Liechtenstein family in the 13th century, this château later served as the residence of the powerful Dietrichsteins. Napoléon Bonaparte also stayed here in 1805 while negotiating peace terms with the Austrians after winning the Battle of Austerlitz (Austerlitz is now known as Slavkov, near Brno). Sixty-one years later, Bismarck used the castle to sign a peace treaty with Austria. At the end of World War II, retreating Nazi SS units set fire to it. Much of what you see today was rebuilt after World War II.

■ TIP➡ There are several different tours that can be combined in various ways. ⊠ *Zámek 5, Mikulov* ☎ *519–309–019* ⊕ *www.rmm.cz* ⊠ *Tours from 90 Kč* ⊗ *Closed Dec.–Mar.; Mon.–Thurs. in Apr., Oct., and Nov.; and Mon. in May, June, and Sept.*

Zámek v Moravském Krumlově (Moravský Krumlov Château)

CASTLE/PALACE | Admirers of art nouveau master Alfons Mucha may want to take a 40-km (31-mile) detour off the main road linking Mikulov to Brno to visit the Moravský Krumlov Château, which is now the temporary home to one of Mucha's most celebrated works, his 20-painting *Slav Epic*. This enormous work took almost two decades to complete and tells the history of the Slav nation. The city of Prague won ownership of the paintings in a long legal battle but is lending them back until at least 2025. The château, built as a castle in the 13th century, also offers a tour of noble chambers and access to the château tower. It is next to a large park with a plague column (a monument built in thanksgiving for the end of a plague). ⊠ *Zámecká 2, Mikulov* ☎ *770–132–566* ⊕ *www. mucha-epopej.cz* ⊠ *Slav Epic 250 Kč; noble chambers 150 Kč; tower 100 Kč* ⊗ *Closed Mon.*

Židovská čtvrť (Jewish Quarter)

NEIGHBORHOOD | What's left of Mikulov's once-thriving Jewish Quarter can be seen on a stroll down Husova ulice, which was once its center. An information board near the corner with Brněnská ulice explains the significance of the community and what happened to it. The most important building still standing is the 16th-century Altschul. The community once numbered several thousand people, and the town was the seat of the chief rabbi of Moravia from the 17th to the 19th century. Several respected Talmudic scholars, including Rabbis Jehuda Loew and David Oppenheimer,

lived and taught here. ⊠ *Husova ul. 11, Mikulov* ⊕ *www.rmm.cz/index_en.html* ⊠ *Synagogue 50 Kč* ⊗ *Synagogue closed Dec.–Mar.; Mon.–Thurs. in Apr., Oct., and Nov.; and Mon. in May and June.*

★ Židovský hřbitov (Jewish Cemetery)

CEMETERY | Mikulov's massive cemetery with 4,000 tombs is not far from Husova ulice, just off Brněnská. The cemetery dates to shortly after 1421 when Jews were forced to leave Vienna and Lower Austria. The oldest legible stone is from 1605 and the most recent are from the 19th century, giving a wide range of stylistic flourishes. Step into the ceremonial hall to view an exhibit of the cemetery's history. Visits outside of opening hours and guided tours can be arranged at least two days in advance. ⊠ *Off Brněnská ul., Mikulov* ⊕ *www.jewishheritagemikulov. org* ⊠ *40 Kč* ⊗ *Closed Nov.–May; Sat. in Jun.–Sept.; and Mon.–Sat. in Oct.*

🛏 Hotels

Hotel Tanzberg

$ | HOTEL | Prim and nicely renovated, this hotel sits in the middle of the Jewish Quarter, on Husova ulice. **Pros:** central location; historic building; wine cellar for tastings. **Cons:** very narrow stairs and no elevator; parking lot distant from the hotel; furniture is basic and a bit worn. ⑤ *Rooms from: Kč2000* ⊠ *Husova ul. 8, Mikulov* ☎ *519–510–692* ⊕ *www. hotel-tanzberg.cz* ⮑ *17 rooms* ❌ *Free Breakfast.*

Brno

202 km (122 miles) southeast of Prague via Hwy. E65.

Nicknamed the "Manchester of Moravia," Brno (pronounced *burr*-no) has a different feel from other Czech or Moravian cities. Beginning with a textile industry imported from Germany, Holland,

and Belgium, Brno became a leading industrial center of the Austro-Hungarian Empire during the 18th and 19th centuries. Some visitors search in vain for an extensive Old Town, pining for the traditional arcaded storefronts that typify other historic Czech towns. Instead, you'll see fine examples of the Empire and neo-Renaissance styles, their formal, geometric façades more in keeping with the conservative tastes of the 19th-century middle class.

In the 1920s and '30s, the city became home to some of the best young architects working in the early-modern, Bauhaus, and "international" styles. The architectural rivalry with Prague continues to this day, with Brno now claiming the country's tallest building. The AZ Tower beats Prague's City Tower by a mere six feet. When Prague roundly rejected a modern library designed by famed architect Jan Kaplický, a scale model of the façade was built as a bus stop on Okružní ulice in Brno's Lesná district.

Experimentation wasn't restricted to architecture. Leoš Janáček, an important composer of the early modern period, lived and worked in Brno, as did Austrian novelist Robert Musil. That artistic support continues today, and the city is considered to have some of the best theater and performing arts in the country, as well as a small but thriving café scene. It has also become a high-tech development hub, with numerous software companies, several good science-oriented schools, and a government-backed support center.

And while the city has been reaching new heights with skyscrapers in its "Little Manhattan" area, it has also been reaching new depths by opening up an underground labyrinth as well as Europe's largest ossuary—a subterranean collection of human bones from several centuries.

Allow a couple of hours to fully explore the Hrad Špilberk (Spielberg Castle). Museum enthusiasts could easily spend a half day or more browsing through the city's many collections. Brno is relatively busy on weekdays and surprisingly slow on weekends. Avoid the city at trade-fair time (the biggest are in early spring and early autumn), when hotel and restaurant facilities are strained. If the hotels are booked, the tourist information center at the town hall will help you find a room.

GETTING HERE AND AROUND

Bus connections from Prague's Florenc terminal to Brno are frequent, and the trip is a half hour shorter than the train route. Most buses arrive at the main bus station, a 10-minute walk from the train station. Some buses stop next to the train station. Bus and train lines connect Brno and Vienna and run several times a day.

Brno—within easy driving distance of Prague, Bratislava, and Vienna—is 196 km (122 miles) from Prague and 121 km (75 miles) from Bratislava. The E65 highway links all three cities.

Comfortable EuroCity or InterCity trains run six times daily, making the three-hour run from Prague to Brno's station. They depart either from Prague's main station, Hlavní nádraží, or the suburban Nádraží Holešovice. Trains leaving Prague for Bratislava, Budapest, and Vienna normally stop in Brno (check timetables to be sure).

Trams are the best way to get around the city. Tickets start at 20 Kč for one zone with no transfer and go up to 27 Kč for 90 minutes of travel with changes. Tickets from the driver cost more. Single-day, three-day, and other long-term tickets are available. Most trams stop in front of the main station (Hlavní nádraží). Buses to the city periphery and nearby sights such as Moravský Kras in northern Moravia congregate at the main bus station, a

Saved by the Bell

During the Thirty Years' War, Brno faced a fierce attack by Swedish troops. Brno's resistance was determined, and the Swedish commander decided that if the town couldn't be taken by noon the next day, they would give up the fight. Word of this reached the cathedral's bell ringer, and just as the Swedish troops were preparing their final assault, they rang the noon bells—an hour early. The ruse worked, and the Swedes decamped. The cathedral bells proved to be the final defensive strategy that saved the town from being taken. The new bullet-shaped clock at Náměstí Svobody commemorates this by dropping a glass ball into a hole at 11 am every day.

10-minute walk behind the train station. To find it, simply go to the train station and follow the signs to *čsad*.

The tourist card Brnopas, available at tourist information centers, also works as a public transportation pass and allows entry to five main attractions, plus a chance to get last-minute tickets to Villa Tugendhat. The pass can be valid for between one and three days.

The nominal taxi fare is about 30 Kč per km (½ mile), on top of a 60 Kč initial fee. There are taxi stands at the main train station, at the Výstaviště exhibition grounds, on Joštova ulice at the north end of the Old Town, and at other locations. Brush up on your Czech—dispatchers sometimes don't understand English.

INFORMATION Hlavní nádražní.
✉ *Nádražní 1, Brno* ☎ *221–111–122* ⊕ *www.idos.cz.* **Main bus station.** (*ÚAN Zvonařka*) ✉ *Zvonařka 1, Brno* ☎ *543–217–733* ⊕ *idos.cz.*

VISITOR INFORMATION
CONTACTS Brno Tourist Information. ✉ *Old Town Hall, Radnická 8, Brno* ☎ *542–427–150* ⊕ *ticbrno.cz/en.*

◉ Sights

Chrám sv. Petra a Pavla (*Cathedral of Sts. Peter and Paul*)
RELIGIOUS BUILDING | Best admired from a distance, the silhouette of slim neo-Gothic twin spires—added in the 20th century—give the cathedral a touch of Gothic dignity. Up close, the interior is light and tasteful but hardly mind-blowing. The treasury and tower can be visited for a fee. The crypt can be visited on request if it is closed. This is the church pictured on the face of the 10 Kč coin. ✉ *Petrov at Petrská ul., Brno* ⊕ *www.katedrala-petrov.cz* ✉ *Free; treasury and tower 40 Kč* ☉ *Tower closed Sun. May–Sept.; crypt closed weekdays Oct.–Apr. and Sun.–Fri. May–Sept.*

Hrad Špilberk (*Spielberg Castle*)
CASTLE/PALACE | Once among the most feared places in the Habsburg Empire, this fortress-cum-prison still broods over Brno behind menacing walls. The castle's advantageous location brought the early lords of the city, who moved here during the 13th century from neighboring Petrov Hill. Successive rulers gradually converted the old castle into a virtually impregnable fortress. It withstood the onslaughts of Hussites, Swedes, and Prussians over the centuries; only Napoléon, in 1809, succeeded in occupying the fortress. But

Booming Brno, with its creativity, history, and subterranean mystery, is the perfect antidote to tourist-filled Prague.

the castle's fame comes from its gruesome history as a prison for enemies of the Austro-Hungarian monarchy and later for the Nazis' prisoners during World War II. The hardest offenders were shackled day and night in dank, dark catacombs and fed only bread and water. The castle complex is large, and the various parts generally require separate admission. The **casemates** (passages within the walls of the castle) have been turned into an exhibition of the late-18th-century prison and their Nazi-era use as an air-raid shelter. You can see the entire castle grounds as well as the surrounding area from the **observation tower.** Aboveground, a **museum** in the fortress starts off with more displays on the prison era with detailed English texts. Included in the tour of the museum are exhibitions of objects from Brno's history and art from the Renaissance to modern times from the city's collection.

■ TIP→ **Admission and opening hours vary according to what you want to see and where you want to go, that is, the entire complex, various combinations of exhibits, or individual castle sections.** ✉ *Špilberk 1, Brno* ☎ *542–123–611* ⊕ *www.spilberk.cz* 🎫 *From 60 Kč* ⊙ *Closed Mon. Oct.–Mar.*

Kostel Nalezení sv. Kříže (*Church of the Holy Cross*)

CHURCH | Formerly part of the Capuchin Monastery, the Church of the Holy Cross combines a baroque form with a rather stark façade. Enter the *krypta* (crypt) in the basement, and the mummified remains of some 200 nobles and monks from the late 17th and 18th centuries are displayed, ingeniously preserved by a natural system of air circulating through vents and chimneys. The best-known mummy is Col. František Trenck, commander of the brutal Pandour regiment of the Austrian army, who, at least in legend, spent several years in the dungeons of Spielberg Castle before finding his final rest here in 1749. A note of caution about the crypt: the graphic displays can be frightening to children (and even some adults), so ask at the admission desk for a small brochure with pictures that preview what's to come, or look at the postcards for sale. Locals refer to the building simply as the Capuchin Church. ⊠ *Kapucínské nám. 5, Brno* ☎ *511–140–053* ⊕ *www.hrobka.kapucini.cz* ✉ *120 Kč, photography fee 30 Kč.*

Kostnice u sv. Jakuba (*St. James Ossuary*)
CEMETERY | Several basement rooms in the tunnels next to the St. James Church are filled with neatly stacked bones, making it one of the largest ossuaries in Europe. Sealed up since the late 1700s, its contents were unearthed in 2001 and were cleaned after years of neglect before being opened to the public in 2012. Remains of some 50,000 people are estimated to be in the rooms, including victims of plagues, epidemics, and wars from the 13th to 18th centuries. It is much larger than the famous ossuary in Kutná Hora in Central Bohemia, which has bones in decorative designs. At one of the upper windows of the church, as seen from the street, there is a sculpture of a monk exposing his backside toward a rival church across town. ⊠ *Jakubské nám., Brno* ☎ *515–919–793* ⊕ *podzemibrno.cz* ✉ *160 Kč, video fee 50 Kč* ⊘ *Closed Mon.*

Labyrint pod Zelným trhem (*Labyrinth under the Cabbage Market*)
RUINS | Some 2,296 feet of underground passages are filled with exhibits relating to alchemy, medicine, medieval punishment, and the more mundane aspects of life—like storing wine. Some of the old passages were rediscovered in the 1970s and have undergone years of archeological research before opening to the public in 2011. Unfortunately, explanatory plaques are only in Czech. ⊠ *Zelný trh 21, Brno* ☎ *542–212–892* ⊕ *podzemibrno. cz* ✉ *180 Kč, video fee 50 Kč* ⊘ *Closed Mon.*

Místodržitelský palác (*Governor's Palace*)
CASTLE/PALACE | Moravia's strong artistic ties to Austria can be seen in the impressive collection of painting and sculpture found in this splendid palace. The museum is divided into sections, but the most impressive part—art from the Gothic period to the 19th century—is on the first floor. The short-term exhibits are often a bit disappointing. ⊠ *Moravské nám. 1A, Brno* ☎ *532–169–333* ⊕ *www.moravska-galerie.cz* ✉ *Permanent exhibits free, temporary exhibits vary* ⊘ *Closed Mon. and Tues.*

Muzeum romské kultury (*Museum of Romani Culture*)
RELIGIOUS BUILDING | A small but singular museum devoted to the culture of the Roma, as Gypsies prefer to be called, is halfway between Brno's historical center and the high-rise housing projects. To foster cross-cultural understanding (as Roma people are often the victims of discrimination), this museum is dedicated to their culture and history. Exhibits deal with traditional occupations, dress, and lifestyles. A study room has documents and photographs. ⊠ *Bratislavská 67, Brno* ☎ *545–581–206* ⊕ *www.rommuz.cz* ✉ *Main exhibit 80 Kč, temporary exhibits free* ⊘ *Closed Mon.*

Náměstí Svobody (*Freedom Square*)
PLAZA/SQUARE | The best place to start any walking tour, this is the focal point of the city and a centerpiece for the massive effort to modernize the area. The square underwent extensive renovation in 2006, and adjoining streets feature some of the city's best shopping. Anyone who has been to Vienna might experience déjà vu here, as many of the buildings were designed by 19th-century Austrian architects. Especially noteworthy is the stolid Klein Palace at No. 15, built by Theophil Hansen and Ludwig Foerster, both prominent for their work on Vienna's Ringstrasse. A highly controversial clock—it's supposed to look like a bullet and remind people of a battle that

happened in 1645—was added in 2010; most people, however, say it looks more like—ahem—a sex toy than a bullet. Also, you need a pamphlet to explain how to read the time on it. The clock drops a glass ball on the hour, which people try to catch. ⊠ *Brno.*

Pražákův palác (*Pražák Palace*)
ART GALLERY | The largest collection of modern and contemporary Czech art outside of Prague lines the walls of this handsome, 19th-century neo-Renaissance building. If you've already seen these same artists represented in Prague's major galleries, you may be tempted to adopt a been-there-done-that attitude. But the emphasis here is on Moravian artists, who tended to prefer rural themes—their avant-garde concoctions have a certain folksy flavor. Modern and contemporary art is on the second floor; other sections have temporary exhibits. ⊠ *Husova 18, Brno* ☎ *725–097–374* ⊕ *www.moravska-galerie.cz* ⊠ *Permanent exhibits free, temporary exhibits vary* ⊗ *Closed Mon. and Tues.*

Stará radnice (*Old Town Hall*)
GOVERNMENT BUILDING | Just inside the door of the oldest secular building in Brno, dating to the 13th century, are the remains of two famous Brno legends, the **Brno Dragon** and the **wagon wheel.** The dragon—actually an alligator—apparently turned up at the town walls one day in the 17th century and began eating children and livestock. As the story goes, a gatekeeper came up with the idea of stuffing a freshly slaughtered goat with limestone. The dragon devoured the goat, swallowing the limestone as well, and when it drank at a nearby river, the water mixed with the limestone and burst the dragon's stomach (the scars on the preserved dragon's stomach are still clearly visible). The story of the wagon wheel, on the other hand, concerns a bet placed some 400 years ago that a young wheelwright, Jiří Birek, couldn't

Old Refueling Spot

After climbing to Spielberg Castle and touring several museums, stop and relax awhile with a cold beer at Stopkova pivnice; if you're hungry, try the house *guláš* (goulash). Now part of the Kolkovna chain, there has been a pub on this site since the late 19th century. Its name comes from Jaroslav Stopka, who took over the existing pub in 1910. ⊕ *www.kolkovna.cz*

chop down a tree, form the wood into a wheel, and roll it from his home at Lednice (53 km [33 miles] away) to the town walls of Brno—all between sunup and sundown. The wheel stands as a lasting tribute to his achievement. (The townspeople, however, became convinced that Jiří had enlisted the help of the devil to win the bet, so they stopped frequenting his workshop; poor Jiří died penniless.)

No longer the seat of the town government, the Old Town Hall holds exhibitions and performances and the town's tourist information office. To find out what's on, ask in the information center just inside Pilgram's portal. The view from the top of the tower is one of the best in Brno, but the climb (five flights) is strenuous. ⊠ *Radnická 8, Brno* ⊕ *www.gotobrno. cz/en/place/old-town-hall* ⊠ *Tower 90 Kč* ⊗ *Tower closed Jan.–Mar.*

10-Z Fallout Shelter
RUINS | A Cold War–era relic, this highly classified (hence the "10-Z" code name) shelter was designed to protect the political elite of the region in the event of a nuclear attack. Built during the Nazi occupation in World War II as a bomb shelter, between 1945 and 1948 it was used by a wine wholesaler, after which it

served as a secret shelter until 1989. Up to 500 people could have stayed inside if needed, but fortunately no one had to. It was declassified and opened to the public in 2015. There is an exhibition about the Cold War at the entrance with English text. Guided group tours of the whole complex with a flashlight (provided) take place as well, with some at night. On the tour you can see underground offices, a phone switchboard, heavy doors, and other curious infrastructure. The entrance is across the street from Husova 12. Tour tickets are available at the Tourist Information Center at Panenská 1. ⊠ *Husova, Brno* ⊕ *10-z.cz/en/* ✉ *Tours from 180 Kč* ⊘ *Closed Mon.*

★ Uměleckoprůmyslové muzeum (*Museum of Applied Arts*)

ART MUSEUM | Arts and crafts shine in this museum, which is without a doubt the Czech Republic's best venue to see applied arts. It has an assemblage of artifacts far more extensive than the truncated collection in Prague's museum of the same name. The collection includes Gothic and art nouveau pieces, as well as an excellent, comprehensive overview of Bohemian and Moravian glass. Keep an eye out for the elegant furniture from Josef Hoffmann's Wiener Werkstätte (Vienna Workshop). Milan Knížák's jagged, candy-color table provides a striking example of contemporary work. ⊠ *Husova 14, Brno* ☎ *532–169–111* ⊕ *www.moravska-galerie.cz* ✉ *Permanent exhibits free, temporary exhibits vary* ⊘ *Closed Mon. and Tues.*

Villa Tugendhat

HISTORIC HOME | Designed by Ludwig Mies van der Rohe and completed in 1930, this austere, white Bauhaus villa counts among the most important works of the modern period and is now a UNESCO World Heritage Site. Function and the use of geometric forms are emphasized. The Tugendhat family fled before the Nazis, and their original furnishings vanished. Replicas of Mies's cool, functional designs have been installed in the downstairs living area. Some of the original exotic wood paneling and an onyx screen remain in place. The best way to get there is to take a taxi or Tram 3, 5, or 11 to the Dětská nemocnice stop and then walk up unmarked Černopolní ulice for 10 minutes or so; you'll be able to see the modernist structure up on the hill.

■ **TIP →** **Reservations for tours are highly recommended at least three months in advance and can be made online.**

Holders of the Brnopas have access to a limited number of last-minute tickets at the Tourist Information Center at Panenská 1 and can skip to the front of the line at the villa. The extended tour shows some of the building's infrastructure.

⊠ *Černopolní 45, Brno* ☎ *515–511–015* ⊕ *www.tugendhat.eu* ✉ *Extended tour 450 Kč, outside tour 150 Kč* ⊘ *Closed Mon.*

Zelný trh (*Cabbage Market*)

FOUNTAIN | Only in this Cabbage Market could Brno begin to look like a typical Czech town—not just for the many stands from which farmers still sell vegetables but also for the flamboyant **Parnassus Fountain** that adorns its center. This baroque outburst (inspiring a love-it-or-hate-it reaction) couldn't be more out of place amid the formal elegance of most of the buildings on the square. But when Johann Bernhard Fischer von Erlach created the fountain in the late 17th century, it was important for a striving town like Brno to display its understanding of the classics and of ancient Greece. Therefore Hercules slays a three-headed dragon, and Amphitrite awaits the arrival of her lover—all incongruously surrounded by farmers hawking turnips and onions. What could be more Czech? ⊠ *Brno.*

Restaurants

Atelier Cocktail Bar and Bistro

$$ | CONTEMPORARY | The menu is on the decidedly short side but offers a constantly changing list of modern takes on fish, meat, and pasta dishes, served in a relaxed but trendy environment. Tasting menus with seasonal dishes include a vegetarian option. **Known for:** seasonal tasting menus; modern casual dining; trendy cocktails. ⑤ *Average main: Kč250* ✉ *Kobližná 2, Brno* ☎ *739–401–086* ⊕ *www.atelierbar.cz.*

Pavillon

$$$ | CZECH | A contemporary re-creation of a landmark 1920s coffeehouse (the original was razed by the communists to make way for a theater), this spot is high on flapper flair. Everything from the light fixtures to the furniture was faithfully copied from the original interior. **Known for:** modern Bauhaus architecture; tasting menus; vegan options. ⑤ *Average main: Kč450* ✉ *Jezuitská 6, between Za Divadlem and Koliště, Brno* ☎ *541–213–497 for large events* ⊕ *www.restaurant-pavillon.cz.*

Restaurace Špalíček

$$ | CZECH | This homey pub has a terrific central location right on the edge of the Cabbage Market. The menu features the standard "roast pork and dumplings" kind of thing but in a comfortable and merry setting. **Known for:** old-fashioned Czech atmosphere; good view on a main square; reasonable prices for a restaurant with a view. ⑤ *Average main: Kč150* ✉ *Zelný trh 12, Brno* ☎ *542–211–526* ▭ *No credit cards.*

Výčep Na stojáka

$$ | CZECH | It is always standing room only, as this pub has no chairs—just high tables. This keeps the line at the tap moving. **Known for:** no seats; friendly vibe; glass of beer foam for a discount. ⑤ *Average main: Kč195* ✉ *Behounska 16, Brno* ☎ *702–202–048* ⊕ *www.vycepnastojaka. cz/en/v/vycep-na-stojaka-jakubak.*

Hotels

Grandhotel Brno

$$ | HOTEL | The hotel dates to 1870 but got a thorough face-lift in the late 1980s and another upgrade in recent years, making it both comfortable and convenient, especially if you're traveling to Brno by train, as it's just across the street from the station. **Pros:** close to main transportation hub; air-conditioning; sauna and fitness room. **Cons:** parking at the hotel is limited; breakfast costs extra; location can be noisy. ⑤ *Rooms from: Kč2920* ✉ *Benešova 18/20, Brno* ☎ *542–518–100* ⊕ *www.grandhotelbrno.cz* ⤴ *105 rooms* ⅋ *No Meals.*

Hotel Pegas

$$ | HOTEL | A little inn with a reasonable price and central location, Pegas has plain rooms that are snug and clean, with wood paneling and down comforters. **Pros:** on-site brewery; central location; air-conditioning. **Cons:** parking is separate from hotel and costs extra; elevator does not reach ground floor; rooms are very plain. ⑤ *Rooms from: Kč2500* ✉ *Jakubská 4, Brno* ☎ *542–210–104* ⊕ *www. hotelpegas.cz* ⤴ *14 rooms* ⅋ *Free Breakfast.*

★ Royal Ricc

$$ | HOTEL | Lovingly restored from a baroque town house, this boutique hotel retains period details, like exposed-beam ceilings. **Pros:** fine detail in furniture; stained-glass windows; historical wooden ceilings in some rooms. **Cons:** hard to access by car since it's at the edge of a pedestrian zone; busy street is noisy at night; hotel bar is very small. ⑤ *Rooms from: Kč2480* ✉ *Starobrněnská 10, Brno* ☎ *736–487–948* ⊕ *www.royalricc.cz* ⤴ *30 rooms* ⅋ *Free Breakfast.*

🌄 Nightlife

Klub Alterna

LIVE MUSIC | A few blocks north of the city center, Klub Alterna hosts good Czech jazz and folk performers. ⊠ *Kounicova 48, Brno* ☎ *541–212–091* ⊕ *www.alterna.cz.*

🎭 Performing Arts

Brno is renowned throughout the Czech Republic for its theater and performing arts. Jacket-and-tie cultural events take place at a few main venues slightly northwest of the center of town, a five-minute walk from Náměstí Svobody. Check posted schedules at the theaters or on their websites.

TICKETS

Předprodej vstupenek

CONCERTS | In Brno you can buy tickets for performing arts productions at individual theater box offices or at the central Předprodej vstupenek. ⊠ *Panenská 1, Brno* ⊕ *vstupenky.ticbrno.cz.*

VENUES

Divadlo Husa na provázku (*Goose on a String Theater*)

THEATER | One of the country's best-known fringe theater companies, the Goose on a String Theater, has its home in Brno. Visiting productions are occasionally in English. ⊠ *Zelný trh 9, at Petrská ul., Brno* ☎ *732–728–040* ⊕ *www.provazek.cz.*

Janáčkovo divadlo (*Janáček Theater*)

THEATER | Opera and ballet productions are held at the modern Janáček Theater. ⊠ *Rooseveltova 7, Brno* ☎ *542–158–120* ⊕ *www.ndbrno.cz.*

Mahenovo divadlo (*Mahen Theater*)

THEATER | The Mahen Theater is the city's principal venue for dramatic theater. Some productions have projected English subtitles. ⊠ *Rooseveltova 1, Brno* ☎ *542–158–120* ⊕ *www.ndbrno.cz.*

🛍 Shopping

Bright red, orange, and yellow flower patterns are the signature folk-pottery look in Moravia. You can find these products in stores and hotel gift shops throughout the region.

The shopping mall **Vaňkovka** (⊠ *Ve Vaňkovce 1* ☎ *533–110–111*), linking the main rail station and main bus station, has several restaurants and stores for clothing.

Antikvariát Alfa

ANTIQUES & COLLECTIBLES | For rare books, art monographs, old prints, and a great selection of avant-garde 1920s periodicals, stop by Antikvariát Alfa. ⊠ *Veselá 39, Brno* ☎ *542–211–947* ⊕ *www.antikalfa.cz* ⊘ *Closed weekends.*

Galerie AmbrosianA

ART GALLERIES | For sophisticated artwork, including paintings and photography, stop by Galerie AmbrosianA. ⊠ *Jezuitská 11, Brno* ☎ *542–214–439* ⊕ *www.ambrosiana.cz* ⊘ *Closed weekends.*

Olomouc

77 km (48 miles) northeast of Brno; 275 km (165 miles) east of Prague.

Olomouc (pronounced oh-loh-moats) is a handsome district capital, with some beautifully restored baroque houses along its broad central squares and the country's largest Trinity column, another UNESCO World Heritage Site. Its laid-back, small-town feel and the presence of a charming, inexpensive pension right in town make it an easy choice for an overnight stay.

Olomouc owes its relative prosperity to its loyalty to the Austro-Hungarian Empire. In the revolutionary days of the mid-19th century, when the rising middle classes throughout the empire were asserting their independence from the nobility, the residents of Olomouc remained true to the ruling Habsburgs. During the revolutions of 1848, the royal family even fled here from Vienna for protection. Mozart, Mahler, and other famous composers stopped by on occasion, leaving behind a musical heritage that is still alive today with an active classical music scene.

The most prominent open space in Olomouc is the triangular Horní náměstí (Upper Square). Four of the city's half dozen renowned baroque fountains, depicting Hercules (1687), Caesar (1724), Neptune (1695), and Jupiter (1707), dot the square and the adjacent other large square, Dolní náměstí (Lower Square) to the south.

A discount card called the Olomouc Region Card is valid for most tourist sights in and around the city, and for public transportation in the city, and is available for 240 Kč for 48 hours and 480 Kč for five days. Admission to the town hall tower, botanical gardens, zoo, Hrad Bouzov (Bouzov Castle), Hrad Šternberk, and other sites is included. The card also provides discounts at some restaurants, pools, fitness centers, and hotels. You can buy the card—and get more information on discounts and deals—at the main tourist information center at Horní náměstí 1 and at many hotels, travel agencies, and tourist venues. The information center also can tell you about local tour operators that organize half-day outings to the area's castles.

GETTING HERE
Traveling from Prague, in addition to driving, you can take either a train or a bus. By car, follow the D1 motorway south to Brno and then follow the signs and turnoffs to Olomouc from Brno. The trip will take about three hours in moderate traffic.

Direct train travel from Prague takes at least 2¾ hours and costs around 339 Kč

for the 250-km (150-mile) trip. High-speed Pendolino trains also serve Olomouc from Hlavní nádraží (the main train station); seat reservations are required. Privately operated trains by Regiojet and Leo Express also travel here, with tickets starting at 289 Kč.

Bus travel requires a change at Brno and takes over four hours.

VISITOR INFORMATION
CONTACTS Olomouc Tourist Information. ⊠ *Radnice, Horní nám., Olomouc* ☎ *585–513–385* ⊕ *tourism.olomouc.eu.*

◉ Sights

Arcidiecézní muzeum (*Archdiocesan Museum*)
HISTORIC HOME | This ornate complex is home to treasures from the collections of the archdiocese, including golden monstrances, religious paintings, carved ivory objects, and a full-sized gilded coach. Modern art is also displayed in part of the building complex and included in the same admission, but it is often a bit disappointing in comparison. In 1767 the young musical prodigy Wolfgang Amadeus Mozart, age 11, spent six weeks recovering from a mild attack of chicken pox and completed his Sixth Symphony here. The 16-year-old King Wenceslas III suffered a much worse fate here in 1306, when he was murdered, putting an end to the Přemyslid dynasty. ⊠ *Václavské nám. 3, Olomouc* ☎ *585–514–241* ⊕ *www.muo.cz/en/olomouc-archdiocesan-museum* ⊠ *Permanent exhibitions free; temporary exhibits vary.* ⊙ *Closed Mon.*

Chrám sv. Mořice (*Church of St. Maurice*)
CHURCH | Nothing is left of the original Church of St. Maurice that stood just north of Horní náměstí in 1257. This is a new church started in 1412 on the same site and remodeled many times. Its current fierce, gray exterior dates to the middle of the 16th century. A sculpture

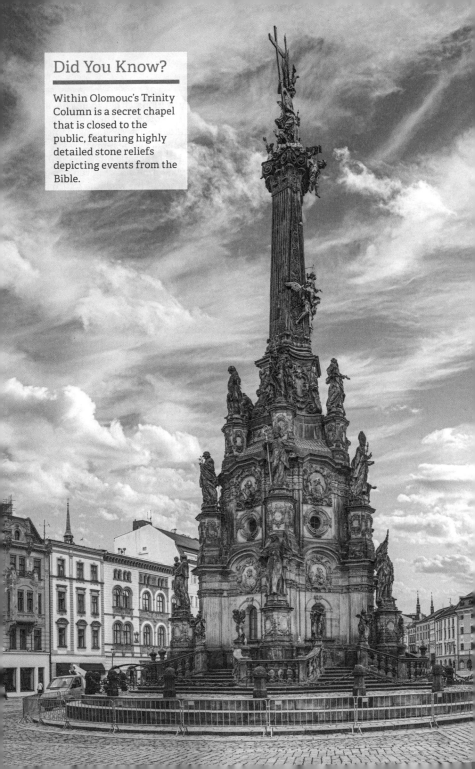

Off the Beaten Path

Hrad Bouzov (*Bouzov Castle*). One of Moravia's most impressive castles, 30 km (18 miles) west of Olomouc, has been featured in several fairytale films. Its present romanticized exterior comes from a remodeling at the turn of the 20th century, but the basic structure dates back to the 1300s. Owned by the Order of Teutonic Knights from the late 1600s up to the end of World War II, it was later confiscated by the state. Inside, the knights' hall has extensive carved-wood decorations and wall paintings that look old, even if many are reconstructions. Other rooms have collections of period furniture. The castle kitchen, which was used until 1945, is one of the best-preserved examples. The castle offers several tours, some aimed at children and one that shows off the wedding hall and knights' hall. You can easily arrange a tour from the tourist information office in Olomouc; the castle is included in the Olomouc Region Card. ⊠ *Bouzov 8, Bouzov* ☎ *775–888–960* ⊕ *www.hrad-bouzov.cz* ⊠ *Classic tours from 230 Kč; moat 80 Kč* ☉ *Closed Nov.–Mar.*

of Christ on the Mount of Olives dates to the 15th century. The baroque organ inside, the largest in the Czech Republic, originally contained 2,311 pipes until it was expanded in the 1960s to more than 10,000 pipes. An international organ festival takes place in the church every September. The tower is sometimes open to the public, depending on the weather. A large renovation was finished in 2021. ⊠ *8. května, Olomouc* ⊕ *www. moric-olomouc.cz* ⊠ *Free.*

Dóm sv. Václava (*Cathedral of St. Wenceslas*)

RELIGIOUS BUILDING | Between the main square and this cathedral lies a peaceful neighborhood given over to huge buildings, mostly belonging either to the university or the archbishop. The church itself is impressive, but its Gothic appearance comes only from a 19th-century makeover. A shrine has an ornate case with the relics of St. Jan Sarkander, a 17th-century priest who was tortured. A plaque marks the fact that Pope John Paul II celebrated mass there in 1995. The crypt, which has erratic hours depending on exhibitions, has a marble box with the heart of an archduke who otherwise is buried in Vienna. Some ecclesiastical treasures are also on display. ⊠ *Václavské nám., Olomouc* ⊕ *www.katedralaolomouc.cz* ⊠ *Free; crypt 50 Kč contribution* ☉ *Crypt often closed on weekdays.*

Kostel sv. Michala (*Church of St. Michael*)

CHURCH | The interior of this triple-domed church casts a dramatic spell. The frescoes, the high and airy central dome, and the shades of rose, beige, and gray trompe-l'oeil marble on walls and arches work in concert to present a harmonious whole. The decoration followed a fire in 1709, only 30 years after the original construction. Another renovation took place in the 1890s. The architect and builder are not known, but it's surmised they are the same team that put up the Church of the Annunciation on Svatý Kopeček (Holy Hill), a popular Catholic pilgrimage site just outside Olomouc. ⊠ *Žerotínovo nám., Olomouc* ⊹ *1 block uphill from Horní nám., along Školní ul.* ⊕ *www. svatymichal.cz.*

★ **Morový sloup** (*Trinity Column*)
NOTABLE BUILDING | In the northwest corner of Horní náměstí, the eccentric Trinity Column is one of the best surviving examples of the Olomouc baroque style, which was prevalent in this region of Moravia after the Thirty Years' War in the 17th century. At 115 feet, it's the tallest column devoted to victims of the plague in the Czech Republic. The column alone (not the rest of the square) is a UNESCO World Heritage Site. Its construction began in 1717, but it was not completed until 1754, long after the death of its principal designer, Václav Render, who left all his wealth to the city of Olomouc so that the column could be finished. Inside is a small chapel that, unfortunately, is never open. ⊠ *Horní nám., Olomouc.*

Radnice (*Town Hall*)
GOVERNMENT BUILDING | Olomouc's central square is marked by the bright, spire-bedecked Renaissance Town Hall with its 220-foot tower. The tower was constructed in the late 14th century. The modern socialist-realist mosaic decorations of the current clock on the face of the tower date to 1955. It replaced an astronomical clock built in 1422 that once rivaled the one in Prague. It was mostly destroyed by an artillery shell on the last two days of World War II. Be sure to look inside the Town Hall at the beautiful stairway. You can also visit a large Gothic banquet room in the main building, with scenes from the city's history, and a late-Gothic chapel. The Town Hall was renovated in late 2019 and early 2020, and the wooden interior of the tower was completely rebuilt. Tours of the tower are given several times daily; tours of the rest of the building are by appointment. An audio guide to the city can be borrowed from the information center in the Town Hall. ⊠ *Horní nám., Olomouc* ☎ *585–513–385 for tourist office* ⊕ *www. tourism.olomouc.eu* ⊠ *Tower tour free; audioguide 30 Kč per hour.* ☉ *Tower closed Nov.–Mar.*

Románský biskupský palace (*Romanesque Bishop's Palace*)
RELIGIOUS BUILDING | Next to the Cathedral of St. Wenceslas is a complex of buildings that for centuries were the center of the archdiocese. The oldest, commonly called Palác Přemyslovců (Přemyslid Palace), houses a museum where you can see early-16th-century wall paintings decorating the Gothic cloisters and, upstairs, a wonderful series of Romanesque windows and displays of sculpted stonework fragments. This part of the building was used as a schoolroom some 700 years ago, and you can still make out drawings of animals engraved on the walls by young vandals. ⊠ *Václavské nám. 4, Olomouc* ⊕ *www.muo.cz/roman-sky-biskupsky-palac–653* ⊠ *100 Kč, incl. Archdiocesan Museum* ☉ *Closed Mon. and Oct.–Mar.*

 Restaurants

Hanácká Hospoda
$$ | CZECH | A low-key, relatively cheap dining option, this popular local pub serves staples like pork, chicken, and duck but nicely turned out. The restaurant is located on the side of a palace but has an uncluttered, modern look inside. **Known for:** historical building; outdoor seating on a main square; above-standard food for a pub. ⑤ *Average main: Kč210* ⊠ *Dolní nám. 38, Olomouc* ☎ *774–033–045* ⊕ *www.hanackahospoda.com.*

Moravská restaurace a vinarná
$$$ | CZECH | Traditional Moravian dishes like roast duck with cabbage, chicken breast stuffed with almond butter, roast piglet, or fried Olomouc cheese are served in a rustic interior. The wine cellar, open weekdays, is a bit homier than the street-level restaurant. **Known for:** folkloric atmosphere; traditional Moravian dishes; local wines. ⑤ *Average main: Kč400* ⊠ *Horní nám. 23, Olomouc* ☎ *585–222–868* ⊕ *www.moravskarestaurace.cz.*

☕ Coffee and Quick Bites

Café Mahler

$$ | CAFÉ | Wooden paneling and floral upholstery in the Café Mahler recall the taste of the 1880s, when Gustav Mahler briefly lived around the corner while working as a conductor at the theater on the other side of Horní náměstí. It's a good spot for ice cream, cake, light meals, coffee, or simply for sitting back and taking in the lovely view. **Known for:** palačinke (crepes); leisurely spot for coffee; views of the main square. ⑤ *Average main: Kč160* ✉ *Horní nám. 11, Olomouc.*

🛏 Hotels

Arigone Hotel and Restaurant

$$ | HOTEL | A renovated historic building blends a nice façade with modern rooms that have modern furnishings. **Pros:** a good blend of historical and modern architecture; relaxation studio offering several types of massage; sauna and wellness facilities in some suites. **Cons:** parking is 300 yards away; hotel is three buildings, so reception and breakfast can require a trip; no elevator. ⑤ *Rooms from: Kč2484* ✉ *Universitní 20, Olomouc* ☎ *585–232–351* ⊕ *www.arigone.cz* ⇥ *59 rooms* ¶◎¶ *Free Breakfast.*

Hotel Flora

$ | HOTEL | The words "traditional communist-era hotel" don't generally evoke images of comfort, but this one was made much more inviting by a thorough makeover of the lobby and public areas. **Pros:** close to the main highways; lots of parking; barrier-free and allergy-free rooms. **Cons:** hotel might not suit modern tastes; relatively far from the center in a commercial zone; rooms have an institutional feel. ⑤ *Rooms from: Kč1357* ✉ *Krapkova 34, Olomouc* ☎ *585–422–200* ⊕ *www.hotelflora.cz* ⇥ *144 rooms* ¶◎¶ *Free Breakfast.*

U Dómu

$ | HOTEL | Each of the rooms in this quiet, family-run pension just off Vaclavské náměstí sleeps up to four and has a small kitchenette. **Pros:** quiet; near the center; breakfast is cooked to order. **Cons:** on a steep street; furniture has a 1980s vibe; parking is around the corner in a lot. ⑤ *Rooms from: Kč2000* ✉ *Dómská 4, Olomouc* ☎ *585–220–502* ⊕ *www.hotelu-domu.cz* ⇥ *6 rooms* ¶◎¶ *Free Breakfast.*

Index

314

Photo Credits

Front Cover: Tomekbudujedomek/GettyImages **[Description:** St.Nicoluas church in Prague]. **Back cover, from left to right:** Daliu/ Shutterstock. Kps1664/Shutterstock. Catarina Belova/Shutterstock. **Spine:** Alex Anton/Shutterstock. **Interior, from left to right:** Denis Poltoradnev/Shutterstock. (1). Scanrail/Dreamstime (2-3). **Chapter 1: Experience Prague:** Prague City Tourism/prague (6-7). Mitzo/shutterstock (8-9). David Marvan/CzechTourism (9). Petr Bonek/Shutterstock (9). CzechTourism (10). Jiri Alexander Bednar/nepijubrecky (10). Libor Svacek/CzechTourism (10). Bakotova/Prague City Tourism (10). Seqoya/Shutterstock (11). Jiří Kružík/CzechTourism (11). Plzeňský Prazdroj/ reservations (12). Irena Brozova/CzechTourism (12). Jakub Kynčl/CzechTourism (12). Prague City Tourism/k.bakotova (12). Michal Vitásek/ CzechTourism (13). Michal Fic/CzechTourism (14). Lukas Zentel/CzechTourism (14). Libor Svacek/CzechTourism (14). Filip Fuxa/Shutterstock (14). K.bakotova/Prague City Tourism (15). Dagmar Veselková/czechtourism (15). Kletr/Shutterstock (22). Ladislav Renner/ CzechTourism (22). Rhombur/Dreamstime (22). katerina/Zámek Loučeň (23). Aleš Motejl/CzechTourism (23). Beerspa-carlsbad.cz (24). Fotokon/Shutterstock (25). Ingrid Prats/Shutterstock (26). Paolo Gallo/Shutterstock (27). veronika/Filip Vido (28). Stefanik Observatory_telescope_ (28). Radek_Habada/ alfredvedvore (28). Mr. Jan Kolman/klementinum (29). Pragulic (29). Frantic00/Shutterstock (30). Hsunny/Shutterstock (31). **Chapter 3: Staré Město (Old Town) and Josefov:** Zoltan Gabor/Dreamstime (59). Marco Brivio/Dreamstime (65). Rglinsky/iStockphoto (68). Dmitry Agafontsev/Shutterstock (70-71). Israel dlrg/Flickr (78). Gabor Kovacs Photography/Shutterstock (87). Warren LeMay/Flickr (91). **Chapter 4: Malá Strana:** RossHelen/Shutterstock (97). Dorinmarius/Dreamstime (98). Millafedotova/Dreamstime (99). Adisa/Shutterstock (99). Courtyardpix/Shutterstock (106-107). Nataliya Hora/Shutterstock (112). Cafe Savoy (114). Kirillm/iStockphoto (118). **Chapter 5: Prague Castle and Hradčany:** NaughtyNut/Shutterstock (121). dimbar76/Shutterstock (125). Grisha Bruev/Shutterstock (127). Tatiana Dyuvbanova/Shutterstock (130). **Chapter 6: Nové Město:** PytyCzech/iStockphoto (133). Mikecphoto/Shutterstock (140). Vladimir Sazonov/Shutterstock (143). Al Case Ashland Daily Photo (150). **Chapter 7: Smíchov and Vyšehrad:** Radomír Režný/Dreamstime (157). National Geographic Image Collection/Alamy Stock Photo (162). PhotoFires/Shutterstock (168). Slowcentury/Dreamstime (169). **Chapter 8: Vinohrady and Vršovice:** Gabriel Prehn Britto/Shutterstock (171). Islavicek/Shutterstock (176). Juanlu Fajardo/Shutterstock (181). **Chapter 9: Žižkov and Karlín:** Michal Fic/CzechTourism (183). Julien Chatelain/Flickr (188). Pavel Matejicek/Flickr (191). **Chapter 10: Letná, Holešovice, and Troja:** DaLiu/Shutterstock (193). Larysa Uhryn/Dreamstime (198). Francis Amiand (204). Alexey Osokin/Shutterstock (207). **Chapter 11: Day Trips from Prague:** Rpeters86/iStockphoto (209). Nikolai Sorokin/Dreamstime (214). Iakov Filimonov/Shutterstock (217). Muratart/Shutterstock (221). Lindrik/Dreamstime (224). Honzik7/Dreamstime (228). **Chapter 12: Southern Bohemia:** Nataliia Budianska/Shutterstock (233). Sergey Fedoskin/Dreamstime (242). Kapruk/Dreamstime (247). Jens Hertel/Dreamstime (251). Botond Horvath/Shutterstock (254). **Chapter 13: Western Bohemia:** Zdenek Bedus/Dreamstime (257). marchello/Shutterstock (263). lavendertime/ iStockphoto (267). Lukas Gojda/ Shutterstock (271). VanGeo/Shutterstock (276-277). Guteksk7/Shutterstock (279). **Chapter 14: Moravia:** Martin Mecnarowski/Shutterstock (283). Jirik V/Shutterstock (289). Prosiaczeq/Dreamstime (292). Steven Hatton/Dreamstime (296). nektofadeev/Shutterstock (303). **About Our Writers:** All photos are courtesy of the writers except for the following: Raymond Johnston courtesy of Claire van der Lee. Jennifer Rigby courtesy of Claire van der Lee.

*Every effort has been made to trace the copyright holders, and we apologize in advance for any accidental errors. We would be happy to apply the corrections in the following edition of this publication.

Notes

Notes

Fodor's PRAGUE

Publisher: Stephen Horowitz, *General Manager*

Editorial: Douglas Stallings, *Editorial Director;* Jill Fergus, Amanda Sadlowski, *Senior Editors;* Brian Eschrich, Alexis Kelly, *Editors;* Angelique Kennedy-Chavannes, *Assistant Editor*

Design: Tina Malaney, *Director of Design and Production;* Jessica Gonzalez, *Senior Designer;* Erin Caceres, *Graphic Design Associate*

Production: Jennifer DePrima, *Editorial Production Manager;* Elyse Rozelle, *Senior Production Editor;* Monica White, *Production Editor*

Maps: Rebecca Baer, *Senior Map Editor;* David Lindroth, Mark Stroud (Moon Street Cartography), *Cartographers*

Photography: Viviane Teles, *Senior Photo Editor;* Namrata Aggarwal, Neha Gupta, Payal Gupta, Ashok Kumar, *Photo Editors;* Eddie Aldrete, *Photo Production Intern;* Kadeem McPherson, *Photo Production Associate Intern*

Business and Operations: Chuck Hoover, *Chief Marketing Officer;* Robert Ames, *Group General Manager*

Public Relations and Marketing: Joe Ewaskiw, *Senior Director of Communications and Public Relations*

Fodors.com: Jeremy Tarr, *Editorial Director;* Rachael Levitt, *Managing Editor*

Technology: Jon Atkinson, *Director of Technology;* Rudresh Teotia, *Associate Director of Technology;* Alison Lieu, *Project Manager*

Writers: Raymond Johnston, Joseph Reaney, Jennifer Rigby

Editor: Angelique Kennedy-Chavannes

Production Editor: Jennifer DePrima

4th edition

ISBN 978-1-64097-577-4

ISSN 1554-3447

All details in this book are based on information supplied to us at press time. Always confirm information when it matters, especially if you're making a detour to visit a specific place. Fodor's expressly disclaims any liability, loss, or risk, personal or otherwise, that is incurred as a consequence of the use of any of the contents of this book.

SPECIAL SALES
This book is available at special discounts for bulk purchases for sales promotions or premiums. For more information, e-mail SpecialMarkets@fodors.com.

PRINTED IN CANADA

10 9 8 7 6 5 4 3 2 1

Notes

About Our Writers

Raymond Johnston has worked in media for all of his professional career, hosting a popular radio show in the Midwest in the early 1990s before moving to New York to work for a company that published critical guidebooks on the Internet. In 1996 he moved to Prague, where he has worked as a film critic, a historical and linguistic consultant for TV programs, and a newspaper and magazine journalist and editor. Currently, he works for several websites, including Expats.cz, with news, cultural and historical information about Prague. For this edition he updated the Western Bohemia, Southern Bohemia, Moravia, Experience, and Travel Smart chapters.

Joseph Reaney is an experienced British travel writer and editor based in Prague and specializing in Central and Eastern Europe. As well as writing for international publications like *National Geographic* and *The Guardian*, he also runs his own travel content writing agency, World Words. When he has the time, Joseph also writes and directs comedy productions, from short films to live sketch shows. For this edition, he updated Žižkov and Karlín, Vinohrady and Vršovice, Smíchov and Vyšehrad, and the Prague Castle and Hradčany neighborhood chapters as well as Day Trips from Prague.

Jennifer Rigby is a British journalist and writer who lived in Prague a few years ago and has since missed its beauty, delicious beer, and chilled-out vibe. She now lives and works in the slightly more hectic locations of Yangon, Myanmar, and London, England, writing for a number of leading international publications. But she continues to spend as much time in Prague as she can. In this edition, she wrote and updated the Malá Strana, Staré Město and Josefov, Nové Město, and Letná, Holešovice, and Troja chapters.

Prague Metro